THE PERFECT ENGLISH SPY

THE PERFECT ENGLISH SPY

*Sir Dick White
and the Secret War 1935–90*

TOM BOWER

St. Martin's Press
New York

Library of Congress Cataloging-in-Publication Data

Bower, Tom.
The perfect English spy : the unknown man in charge during the most tumultuous, scandal-ridden era in espionage history / Tom Bower.
p.   cm.
ISBN 0-312-13584-X
1. White, Dick, Sir, 1906–1993. 2. Great Britain. MI5—Officials and employees. 3. Espionage—Great Britain—History—20th century. I. Title.
UB251.G7B68   1995
327.12'092—dc20
[B]   95-31581   CIP

First published in Great Britain by William Heinemann Ltd

First U.S. Edition: November 1995
10 9 8 7 6 5 4 3 2 1

To my parents,
George and Sylvia

Contents

Preface

This is an unusual book about an exceptional man working in a turbulent epoch. Its principal source was Dick White himself, who, while working amid darkness and deceit, believed he was serving an inner truth.

White, a self-effacing, intelligent and honest patriot, dominated the British intelligence services for thirty-five years. Working under nine prime ministers, and serving uniquely as the head of both MI5 and SIS, he was Britain's most respected and experienced intelligence chief, playing a central role in every major crisis of Britain's military and political affairs – from the rise and fall of Hitler, the hunt for British traitors, to the war of shadows and bloodshed across Europe, the Middle East, Africa and behind the Iron Curtain. Even in retirement, White's advice was eagerly sought by new generations in Downing Street and Whitehall.

Like all intelligence officers, White was expected never to discuss his work or even to disclose his employer. The very denial of the intelligence services' existence was deemed to be among their intrinsic strengths. But, unlike most of his fellow officers, White gradually came to dispute the value of that draconian restriction. The increasing number of revelations about the flaws in British intelligence convinced him that both services would suffer more if their embarrassments and failures remained unexplained. So he welcomed, albeit cautiously, a few select journalists, authors and historians seeking a guide to dispel the contradictions and confusion surrounding so many apparent disasters.

My own conversations with White began, on his initiative, in 1980. At the time, I was writing books and producing television documentaries about the Allied treatment of Nazi war criminals and the failure to denazify Germany. I had been the first to use the official British and American records of the immediate postwar era and to discover the evidence of the Allies' collaboration with the Nazis. The effect was quite sensational.

Following White's approach, we met for the tea at the BBC's television studios in Lime Grove and he handed over, in note form, his own recollections of that era. I sensed his fascination with tyrannies and history, and his regret that he had not written his own account of the tumultuous events in which he had participated.

Thereafter, we met occasionally for lunch, either in London or at his home near Arundel. Our meetings became more frequent after 1987. I was exploiting the unprecedented opportunities offered by *glasnost* in the Soviet Union and began to produce a succession of television documentaries about the great Cold War spy sensations. For the first time, it was possible to interview White's hitherto unseen enemies who had operated from the dreaded Lubyanka in Moscow or under its management across the world. Those KGB officers who had controlled Kim Philby, Guy Burgess and George Blake; or who had discovered and interrogated Oleg Penkovsky; or who had inserted the 'illegals' like Gordon Lonsdale into the West; and who had efficiently destroyed SIS's repeated attempts after 1945 to insert agents into communist Europe were suddenly willing to discuss their activities over a bottle of whisky. As I shuttled between London, Washington and Moscow, I frequently consulted White about the credibility of the accounts I was receiving from those Soviet Intelligence officers. Naturally he was fascinated both by their assertions and by their occasional admissions of mistakes.

In the course of our conversations, White invariably digressed to recount memories of other events and the personalities he had encountered during his unique career. As the only officer to be successively chief of MI5 and SIS, White had become not only Keeper of the Flame but also Guardian of the Secrets. Gradually it became apparent that, as a natural listener, he was more than tempted not to allow all the secrets to vanish with his inevitable passing. Increasingly, he dispelled the surface realities and disclosed fascinating secrets about the wars which he had fought.

Eventually I proposed that I write his biography. My suggestion coincided with news of the fatal illness of Andrew Boyle, the
well-known BBC radio editor and biographer. Boyle had known
White since the 1970s. Their relationship had been cemented
after Boyle's historic exposure in 1979 of Anthony Blunt as the
'Fourth Man' in his book *The Climate of Treason*. Boyle's suspicions
had been published only after personal confirmation by White, an
unusual indiscretion.

One of the unpredictable consequences of that book was the
Spycatcher saga and the public exposure of the cancer which had
infected British intelligence for nearly thirty years. White had
been the central figure throughout that shattering 'molehunt'
and throughout so much more of modern British and American
history. Boyle had realised that a biography of White, with his
co-operation, would be unprecedented. For the first time, the outside world would be able to judge the real intelligence war from
its most authentic source rather than from a wave of bestselling
but inaccurate books and films. He began his research in the
1980s.

The Cold War had been fought essentially by intelligence agencies. Through their machinations, politicians were blackmailed
and bribed, wars were started, governments were overthrown
and people were murdered. Whenever the agencies' deeds were
inadvertently exposed, the public's reaction confirmed the practitioners' belief in the need to protect the secrecy of their methods
and operations. They believed themselves to be the guardians of
our freedom and the best judges of the requirements of morality.

Hitherto, the British intelligence services had deliberately
resisted explanations and exposure except on their own terms.
History is not what actually happened but what the surviving
evidence says happened. If the evidence can be hidden and the
secrets kept, then history will record an inaccurate version.[1] As
Boyle began researching the biography, he encountered old and
new restrictions.

Firstly, there was the continuing and traditional refusal of most
retired SIS and MI5 officers to discuss their work; secondly, in the
aftermath of the *Spycatcher* affair in 1987, White partially obeyed
a formal warning from senior government officials not to discuss

intelligence matters with outsiders; and finally Boyle's own illness limited his ability to work. Nevertheless, his relationship
with White resulted in a collection of notes and an incomplete
manuscript which I inherited after Boyle's untimely death in 1991.

Over the following year, White's attitude changed. He welcomed a biography, although he preferred the result to be
approved by the government before publication. Although I
resisted that condition, we continued to discuss his life's work
while, simultaneously, I met an increasing number of retired
MI5 and SIS officers who had served under White. Their
attitude had noticeably changed. The Cold War was over and
they knew that I had secured the co-operation both of American
and Soviet intelligence officers and of Dick White himself. Like
White, more and more retired intelligence officers were attracted
to the notion of bequeathing a more accurate version of their
services to posterity. Accordingly, from 1991, I was benefiting
from long conversations with many dozens of former MI5 and
SIS officers who had not previously discussed their work with
outsiders.

After Dick White's death in February 1993, the existence of
the biography became publicly known. The heads of the two
intelligence services and government ministers were faced by a
dilemma. To allow my continuing relations with former MI5 and
SIS officers would effectively condone breaches of the Official
Secrets Act. To forbid my access could prove embarrassing. The
willingness of some CIA officers to discuss their past activities
was well known, and now KGB officers were available. Could
the British government resist the wave of disclosures without
embarrassment? After all, the purpose of the Act had become
somewhat discredited in the wake of the government's new policy
of openness and accountability. In the event, it soon became
apparent that ministers were willing to ignore some common
assumptions about their new policy.

On 16 July 1993, the same day as Stella Rimington, the
director general of MI5, appeared in an unprecedented photo-
opportunity at MI5's headquarters proclaiming the dawn of a
publicly answerable security service, she authorised the dispatch
of a letter to all former officers warning them that to speak to me

was a breach of the Official Secrets Act. Some recipients feared it was a threat to their pensions. That familiar tone was repeated by John Major, the prime minister. In a written parliamentary answer, he told Rupert Allason MP that retired SIS officers were not authorised to discuss their activities for the purpose of this book.

Fortunately, neither warning was observed by the vast majority of former intelligence officers whom I approached. Instead, in the course of the following year, I obtained insight into and answers to the riddles which have perplexed those of my colleagues and friends who have trod a similar path over many years. It is to those pathfinders that I owe my first thanks. Barrie Penrose, Phillip Knightley, Rupert Allason (alias Nigel West), Richard Norton Taylor, Paul Greengrass and Anthony Cavendish are not loved by most retired intelligence officers. Their exposure of the embarrassments which most of the participants trusted would remain hidden has often proved worse than irritating. All of those authors proved to be exceptionally generous towards me.

Naturally, I am very grateful to those dozens of British, American, Russian, German and East European intelligence officers who individually spent hours and even days revealing secrets and explaining confusions. Suffice it to say that very few of the many I approached refused to help. Although several British officers were initially reluctant, eventually nearly all agreed to answer my questions. Accordingly, I believe that, since very few of the new disclosures are based on the memories of fewer than two people, this biography has got nearer to the truth than I expected at the outset.

Since most of those retired officers requested that their help should not be acknowledged, I will resist mentioning any names, including those of the few who felt no qualms. Similarly, I will resist embarrassing those other government officials who spoke to me. Most co-operated with the intention of contributing to a biography of a man they admired and of helping me to produce as authoritative and as accurate a book about British intelligence as I could manage. To all, I am very grateful.

Thirdly, I am grateful to Eleanor Boyle, who agreed that I might inherit her late husband's papers. Andrew Boyle was the creator of the BBC Radio's *World at One*, setting a new and enduring benchmark for journalism. He was also the author of six fine biographies which remain standard works. I hope that his memory will be enhanced by this book, which he originated.

Robert Fink, my tireless and talented associate in Washington, was as always invaluable. Without his research and enthusiasm this book could not have been written.

Among others who helped were Mark Curthoys, the archivist at Christ Church, Oxford; Kay Walsh and the staff of the National Library, Canberra; and Cleveland Cram, Christopher Gandy, Keith Kyle, Lionel Elvin, the late Lord Bulmer-Thomas, Ted Harrison, Chapman Pincher, David Wise, Lord Dacre of Glanton, Johnny Moorehead, who gave permission for the use of his late father's papers, and Paul Hamann, head of BBC Television's Documentaries Department.

Michael Shaw of Curtis Brown was as always a friend, counsellor and supporter. David Hooper of Biddle & Co. performed his legal task with relish. I am grateful to Tom Weldon and Peter James at Heinemann for their considerable assistance.

Finally, thanks to my wife Veronica and my children for their everlasting and humorous tolerance and their unconditional friendship.

THE PERFECT ENGLISH SPY

CHAPTER ONE

A True Englishman

For a man whose life would pass in the shadows, steeped in secrecy and intrigue, it was fitting that the beginning should be so ordinary. Dick Goldsmith White was born on 20 December 1906, the youngest of three children, in Tonbridge, Kent. The 'Goldsmith' was inexplicable, even to the son, unless his father sought a connection with Sir Julian Goldsmid, the town's member of parliament.

The father, Percy White, an unusually opinionated and independent Kentishman, owned an ironmonger's shop, James White & Son, at 119 High Street in Tonbridge, an inheritance from previous generations. In the late eighteenth century, Percy's great-great-grandfather had sold his farm and livestock and established a workshop, manufacturing agricultural machinery. The double-fronted shop, situated near the railway station, opened during the Napoleonic Wars. From those premises, Percy also sold and hired agricultural machinery, with apparent success.

Dick White's first years were passed in the rooms above the shop overlooking the small town. In the illustrated advertisement which regularly appeared across the front page of Tonbridge's *Free Press*, White & Son offered readers 'their large and varied stock of kitchens, ranges, lamps, fenders, fire-irons, tea trays, brushes etc.'. Dick White remembers his tall, fair-skinned father as a curious mixture: an astute, indefatigable businessman; a romantic; and an outstanding horseman. Among the son's earliest memories was riding in his father's pony-trap to the local point-to-point races. 'He would dress up for the part, wearing his colours and hard hat and always neatly in trim. True or not, people used to say that my father was possibly one of the finest jockeys in Kent. I

like to think that he taught me a good deal, more by example
than anything else.'[1]

Those early memories were cherished. Percy White was still
regarded among locals as energetic and open-minded; although
he was hindered by a tendency to self-indulgent pursuit of
unrealistic and even romantic notions. Gertrude, his wife since
1901, had nothing in common with her husband. Born Gertrude
Farthing in nearby Edenbridge, the daughter of an architect,
she came from a family of careful, unpretentious puritans who
believed that simple, honest behaviour should be the benchmark
of their children's lives. Educated by a governess at home with
her sisters, she learnt to live according to Victorian principles
of decency, supported by aphorisms rather than religion. The
credo passed to the children. Dick White classified himself as a
'puritan' when, six years old, he arrived at the Convent School
in Tonbridge.[2]

Simultaneously his family moved to a bungalow in Lyons Cres-
cent, a quieter area behind Tonbridge's High Street, prompting
neighbours to remark on the Whites' evident prosperity. Servants
cared for the children and the house, there was good food and
sufficient capital to guarantee future comfort. Unlike most neighbouring houses, the new dwelling boasted a bathroom, a flush
lavatory, gas and electricity. The few books in the house did not
suggest a scholarly or learned atmosphere. Percy often restrained
his wife's eagerness to encourage the children to read: 'Why rush
them? They've got the whole of their life ahead of them.'[3]

White's early childhood memories were of a carefree country life
interrupted by one 'frightening' visit with his father to the high-
rise City of London, which resounded with the din of clattering
hooves and the shouts of vendors and draymen. Soon after that
'glorious day', Percy took his family outside the house to see his
new acquisition: 'My father must have been one of the first in
the area to own a car.' The purchase proved to be evidence of
extravagance. Percy, it transpired, was too easily tempted, not
only in buying luxuries but as a gambler and consumer of
alcohol. As his behaviour deteriorated, heated arguments erupted
with his wife and her family about the incompatibility between
his profligacy and her unostentatious lifestyle.

White later spoke of suffering bewildering, miserable solitude during the family's disintegration. As a sensitive and unprecocious seven-year-old who, unlike his elder sister Kathleen, was not yet close enough to his mother to confide his troubles and fears, the only consolation was his mother's declaration that conditions could be even worse: 'You should be grateful for small mercies.' In early 1914, Percy's absences from home lengthened. Ostensibly, he was spending his free time with the local yeomanry, or territorials, but, as his young son learnt from a cruel jibe in the school playground, everyone by then knew about his parents' separation. 'A hollow sense of desolation' was his own description many years later of the shame he felt at a time when divorce was still rare and disapproved of.

On the outbreak of war, as Percy White's visits became briefer and less frequent, the employees in the family shop remained unsupervised and trade deteriorated. In a bid to save the business, Percy's father bought the shop and installed a manager, but the investment proved unsuccessful. Dick White's mother was unused to penury, and watching her suffer only pained the boy further. As he followed the course of the war through the comic *Magnet* and the *Illustrated London News*, with its lavish pictures and stirring accounts of the bloody battles just across the Channel, his consolation was the fantasy that his father was bravely risking his life for King and Country in trenches on the Western Front. Even that illusion was disappointed when he heard by chance that his father was in fact training recruits in England.

The disenchantment and drift was finally halted in 1917. To spare the children further embarrassment, White's parents agreed that while their daughter would remain at home to help in the house and shop, both sons would move after Tudor Hall, a private preparatory school in nearby Hawkhurst, to boarding school. Tonbridge, a well-known local public school, was not considered, from fear of local gossip. Dick White's own desire, fed by his passion for Joseph Conrad, to enter Osborne naval school ended in rejection on the ground that he was 'too skinny'. The inexpensive solution, selected by Gertrude, was a location too far for her estranged husband to visit, but which also epitomised her values.

Bishop's Stortford College in Hertfordshire, socially undistin-
guished and charging fifteen guineas a term, was patronised by
the children of modest, nonconformist families which could not
boast a professional or a public service background. Both Dick
and his brother Alan, homesick and lonely, were received by the
Rev. Samuel Young, the school's firm but fair headmaster who
was deliberately employing conscientious objectors as teachers.
Exceptional morality was matched by puritan propriety.

In what Eric Whelpton, a teacher and future wartime intelligence officer would call 'a cheerless and dismal place'[4] made worse
by food rationing, White gave a confusing impression among his
teachers. Walter Strawn recalls a 'very discreet, intuitive thinker
who never said anything interesting'. The unintentional pose was
successful. 'By obliterating any charisma in his personality, he
engendered trust.'[5] Bobby Sutton, White's housemaster, a soft-
spoken cricketer imbued with a deep commitment towards his
pupils, embraced White and became a father figure for the
remainder of his life. Sutton labelled the boy in his first report
as one of the 'likeliest to succeed'.[6]

Among fellow pupils it was agreed that during those first years
White was a shy, unquestioning and diligent schoolboy in need
of extra coaching and encouragement, instinctively concealing his
grief. Influenced by his mother's simple adage that 'Whenever you
feel like criticising anyone just remember all the people in the
world who haven't had your advantages,' he became intensely
loyal to those whom he befriended, not always a foundation for
sure judgment and objective management, but ideal for breeding
trust.

For a short period, White would be taught by the fiery
Brendan Bracken, later a wartime cabinet minister responsible
for information in Churchill's government who posed ridiculously
as Churchill's illegitimate son. White remembered the future
minister tottering across the school grounds at breakfast time
in full evening dress after dining with friends at the House of
Commons. Having missed the last train from Liverpool Street,
he had spent the night on hard benches in the station waiting
room: 'Everyone watched with astonishment. He was not at his
best but brazened it out, attending prayers in his rumpled finery.'[7]

Among White's younger contemporaries were Denis Green-hill, who would become head of the Foreign Office, Edward Crankshaw, later a historian and Soviet expert, and Peter Wright, who would join MI5. For Greenhill, White was 'a prize pupil, a man after my own heart'. Crankshaw recalled an 'Adonis figure'. Walter Strawn, the teacher, remembered White as 'a shadow', but one with a huge advantage: 'If you run well in England, you're judged to be good at anything.' The 'outstanding sportsman' emerged unpredictably at seventeen. The school journal recorded White as 'captain of cricket, athletics and rugby in his last year. He also set a number of new school athletics records,' running second in the Public Schools' mile. The achievement eroded his shyness, transforming the schoolboy into a hero.

White's athletic glory was not witnessed by his brother. Although only eighteen months older, Alan had suddenly an-nounced his impatience with education and left school. Unknown to his younger brother, he had decided to take a lowly job to support his family. Gertrude became worried about her sons' futures. In search of reassurance, both children were taken to a diviner who claimed an ability to predict talents by feeling and measuring skulls and their bumps. The forecast for both was prophetic. 'Dick would be part of a large organisation because he gets on well with people.' Alan, on the other hand, would spend his life with books. He joined Methuen, a highly reputable publisher, and eventually became well known as its managing director.

Alan's self-sacrifice had been prompted by his father's decline into impoverished and chronic alcoholism. For Dick, the shame of his broken home injected permanent inscrutability and an introverted personality which shunned intimate friendships. By the end of his school career, he had aroused no antipathy but he left behind him, despite his athletic success, scant permanent impression. The *Stortfordian*, the school magazine, contains no mention of White's departure. At the peak of his seniority, he was a prefect, but not head boy or head of his house. But his early wariness and diffidence towards school had been replaced by enthusiasm and self-confidence. From sport, he had learned self-control and the art of pacing himself. That quality, noticed by Young, the headmaster, prompted a generous tribute: 'an outstanding man [with] remarkable gifts of leadership and character [whose] powers and skill as an athlete [will] increase his influence'.[8]

Encouraged by Young, White applied in spring 1925 to Dartmouth, the naval college, but he was rejected because of imminent reductions in the Royal Navy's manpower. Simultaneously, White had applied to Christ Church, Oxford, to read history, an unusual ambition for a Stortfordian. His *curriculum vitae* revealed self-doubt: next to 'Honours History', he had placed a question mark; his prospective career was 'schoolmaster or civil servant'. After completing Christ Church's examination, the interview in the college proved friendly and unhurried. Among the dons was John Masterman, a junior censor and history tutor. Across the room, Masterman saw a tall, lean, athletic-looking young man, blue-eyed, blond and curly haired. In his opinion, the college examinations were 'a façade' but the interviews were serious.[9] White's natural anxiety disappeared. Between the teacher and schoolboy, there was a community of interest.

Masterman had followed his family's naval tradition, but after passing through Osborne and Dartmouth had abandoned that career to study history at Worcester College, Oxford. After receiving a first-class degree and having secured a lectureship at Christ Church, he travelled in 1914 to Heidelberg to improve his German. Unexpectedly, war broke out and he spent the next four years imprisoned, later cursing his misfortune and even disgrace in having, unlike his friends, survived the Flanders carnage in comparative comfort. In peacetime, Masterman would never become acknowledged as an original historian but he was an outstanding teacher, agreeable personality and noted sportsman, passionate about cricket, tennis and hockey. Sport was the first binding link between White and the don.

'I'm pretty certain that I did far better than I ever expected,' White reported hopefully on his return to school. 'Luck and hard work I believe helped.' In the opinion of the other Christ Church history don, E. F. Jacob, White typified the 'very raw and shy' boy who would develop. But, above all, White's entry was secured by the promise of athletic glory for the college, an important inducement in that era.

Oxford in the mid-1920s glowed with excitement, hope and light-hearted self-esteem. The post-war depression and the mourning for a lost generation – over two million Britons had been either killed or disabled – had receded, and the threat of a new war was remote. The Empire seemed secure, a quarter of the globe was coloured red, and the students were filled with uninhibited ebullience. In Masterman's view, Christ Church, rich in its diversity, 'was magnificent yet friendly, regal yet tolerant'.[10] The college did not seek to create a type and yet maintained a quiet cohesion. Among White's contemporaries were Alec Douglas-Home, Quintin Hogg and other future cabinet ministers from Britain's grand families. With limited money, White discreetly distanced himself from those rich Etonians and carefree hedonists: 'It was pretty entirely a college for ambitious, well-to-do young men who were going places, [who would] take their place as members of the ruling class.'[11]

White's social life was limited. Unlike the wealthier students, he was not a habitué of the late train from Paddington, known as the 'Fornicator'. The few women at Oxford led segregated lives and if they visited a male undergraduate's room they were obliged to bring a chaperone. Even Peter Fleming's feature about White in the 'Isis Idol' column of the university magazine elicited no interest from women students. White was no less indifferent. When all the windows of Peckwater Quad in Christ Church were smashed during a riotous party, White was among the innocent few. His abstemious lifestyle, encompassing a disdain of smoking and drinking influenced by his father's fatal decline, had become the pivot of his personal morality.

Abstinence was above all the product of his devotion to sport. Throughout his three years in Oxford, with Tim O'Connor and Ivor Thomas (later Bulmer Thomas), White ran every weekday afternoon except Friday along the Iffley Road, in training for the half-mile. After two hours, White and his friends headed for Vincent's Club, the sportsman's sanctuary on the High Street for tea with anchovy on toast. Running dominated their conversation. In his first year, White won the freshmen's half-mile, mile and three miles. His greatest achievement was to run the Iffley Road mile in 4 minutes 27.4 seconds, for long an unrivalled record that was rewarded with a full blue.

The most important race was against Cambridge. Regularly White won the half-mile. On one occasion, on his return to Oxford on a special university train, he was alarmed by an outburst of hooliganism. Windows were broken, seats slashed and fittings ripped out. 'We'd better get out at the station before Oxford,' he told Ivor Thomas. 'I'm sure there'll be trouble.' The university proctors were indeed awaiting the incoming train. When the two friends met eleven years later for lunch and White revealed that he was an MI5 officer, Thomas, while 'astonished', reflected upon White's anticipation on that train journey.[12]

The climax of rigorous training was White's selection in 1927 to run against Cambridge in the athletics competition at Queen's Club in London. Among the spectators would be Stanley Baldwin, the prime minister, and Lord Birkenhead, the lawyer and Churchill's intimate crony. A formal dinner would be held at the Piccadilly Hotel in the evening. For White, it was the prelude to selection in the 1928 Olympics. 'All we cared was if Dick would win,' recalled Thomas. White's misfortune was to be running two races, the half-mile followed by the one mile. Herbert Elvin, his Cambridge competitor in the first race, realising that White planned to conserve strength, 'spurted in the last twenty yards and beat him by two yards. But Dick was gracious.'[13] Thomas and his friends were 'disappointed'. White was devastated. Tired, he also lost the one mile.

In compensation that summer, he won a record mile along the Iffley Road against Cambridge and against a combined Harvard and Yale team. By common consent, he was credited as secretary of the Athletics Club with having 'created another record by running all his programmes to time'.[14] Masterman recognised that his sporting achievements had helped him 'attain a position of importance among undergraduates . . . He is quite exceptionally respected by and popular among his contemporaries.'[15]

Masterman's generosity of spirit was infectious. Like so many other undergraduates, White had fallen under the spell of the don's warm personality: 'Masterman was shrewd, wise and quick on the uptake. He was really a mine of information and sympathetic understanding. I owed a lot to him from my first term onwards.'[16] Although others criticised Masterman for straining a little too hard to play the part of *éminence grise*, the teacher revelled in his own creation: 'There is no pervading Christ Church type. The glory of Christ Church lies in its diversity.'[17] An uninhibited bond developed between master and pupil, a shared vision and loyalty. White recognised that Oxford's compulsive, timeless enchantment meant that his three years 'had to be inhabited and enjoyed for itself, not as the preparation for anything else'.[18]

Pleasure-seeking coexisted with an agnostic lack of interest in politics and a positive disregard for uprooting anything, for 'putting things right'. His conservatism, influenced by Percy Wyndham-Lewis's critique that Britain was breeding 'revolutionary simpletons' who wanted to tear up the system for its own sake rather than tolerate a quiet life within society, spurred his opposition to the workers during the General Strike in 1926. Led by Masterman, who later admitted that he had failed to consider the issue but had followed the Establishment's condemnation of the trade unions, White travelled with a jocular party of undergraduates to Southampton. There some of them enrolled as special constables, while White and others unloaded food from ships. Down in a hold, White narrowly missed death when a clutch of boxes slipped from a crane. Peering over the railing Masterman 'thought for a moment that the hold was filled with bloody and mutilated bodies. I was mistaken – the contents of the cases had been Heinz's tomatoes and tomato sauce.'[19] After that brief political statement, White returned to Oxford without further interest in the ensuing political turmoil, more concerned to enjoy athletics and consider his future employment. The omens seemed good.

The report or 'collections' for his second year by E.F. Jacob, his modern history tutor, was positive: 'There is no man for whom one could more earnestly desire a first, for his work is always a pleasure to read and he treats it in the right way. He has a really historical mind, but he takes a little time to get going and the question is whether he will do this quickly enough. He is thoughtful rather than powerful; but he has developed late and will go on developing, so there are good hopes.'[20] The report justified the Dean of Christ Church's earlier award to White of a Fell Scholarship worth £40.

White's final year was hectic. Casting aside the temptation to try for a place in the national athletics team which was to compete in Amsterdam, he worked singlemindedly for his final exams. In those last weeks, Jacob summed up White's undergraduate career: 'I have seldom known a more popular man and one who impressed his contemporaries so much through his modesty and intelligence.' The prediction of Keith Feiling, the luminary of the college's history department, was also encouraging: '1st or 2nd. So ends one of the best of the undergraduate careers here of late year.'[21]

The result was narrowly to miss a first, according to White by one mark; a career in academia was therefore not open to him. Since his latest ambition was to become a journalist, the failure did not seem as serious as later transpired. With Masterman's encouragement, White had applied for a Commonwealth Fund Fellowship to study American history at a university in the United States. In his testimonial, Masterman conceded a prejudice: 'I have to write many testimonials in the course of a normal year and I am, I hope, normally cautious in recommending under-graduates – but I find it difficult to avoid using superlatives in the case of White . . . a man of very strong personality though he is by nature unassuming.'[22]

White's preference was to study at an Ivy League college. At the interviews in London in autumn 1927, he met another of the applicants, Eric Linklater, a droll Scot. Linklater, seven years older than White, had survived as a sniper on the Western Front, had then worked as a journalist in India and was ambitious to become a novelist. Before the interview, White was advised to drop his application to an Ivy League college. Without a first, his application was unlikely to be accepted and the board members wanted to steer Oxbridge students towards America's Midwest. When the interviewing board mentioned his preference for studying at Harvard or Yale, White shook his head vigorously: 'No, no, no. I don't want to go to an old institution. I've been to one of those in England. I've plumped for the University of Michigan.'[23]

In the event, White was awarded the fellowship he sought at Michigan. 'It was amazing good luck,' he recalled. Travel to America was still unusual and the award provided sufficient living funds for two years. On 29 August 1928, White boarded the Cunard liner SS *Scythia* at Liverpool for a five-day voyage to New York. Between meals, during which he deliberately sat with Americans, he gave an impression of enthusiasm qualified by uncertainty: all he could say about his future plans was that he hoped to travel around the world.[24]

The Manhattan skyline, basking in glorious morning sunshine, appeared to White to signal the dawn of a new life. During two days of 'orientation sessions', he was overwhelmed by the contrast with Britain. Henry Ford had just launched the first mass-produced motorcar, the Model A; the introduction of tabloids had revolutionised the newspaper industry: 'talking pictures' had transformed Hollywood; and the new Chrysler building dwarfed London's architecture. For a conservative and parochial young Englishman nurtured on the glories of the Empire, the frantic activity, self-confidence and wealth of New Yorkers could provoke either disdain or enthusiasm. As White later acknowledged, 'None of us could dispute the [American dream]. It put us in our places.'[25] Instead of disdaining it, White embraced America and came to admire its virtues.

The train journey to Detroit completed the journey. Warmly welcomed by the president of the Ann Arbor university, he was overwhelmed by his hosts' 'lack of side' and the 'American way' with strangers. The spirit of generosity and equality enthralled the Englishman, who was himself unusually bereft of snobbery. Detroit, he was reminded, was the birthplace of Charles Lindbergh, who two years earlier had completed the first non-stop flight from New York to Paris; it was also the centre of the new automobile industry. Unremarked was the city's cesspit of Prohibition and racketeering.

White's early excitement as he studied America and the Mexican wars soon dissipated into dissatisfaction. His professor was often absent and his fellow students, he concluded, were

immature and unintelligent. In conversation, they voiced undisguised hostility to Britain's imperialism, especially in India,
Palestine and Ireland. Moral rectitude was a posture which White
particularly disliked: 'Just look at the misdeeds of the American
settlers against the indigenous Indians and Mexicans!' Political
differences and a lack of intellectual and cultural stimulation
aggravated his unhappiness that winter. As temperatures fell to
minus twenty degrees centigrade, 'I could not abide, from the first
fall of snow that season, the numbing cold. It seemed to go on and
on.' The only consolation was central heating, a comfort unknown
in Britain.

His written complaint about the boredom to New York
brought a visit from a sympathetic Fellowship administrator.
'I think there was justice in his criticism,' reported the official
who heard that White's ambition was either journalism or the
Diplomatic Service. 'I am satisfied that he is working intelligently
and industriously . . . He is an ambitious fellow and I want to do
everything I can for him . . . I believe he would make a success
if he goes into diplomacy as he is attractive and has an excellent
mind.'[26] It was agreed that he could move to California at the end
of the academic year.

During that first winter, White drove with Linklater from
Philadelphia via Richmond to Charleston in the hot South.
Their recollections confirmed their differences. For Linklater,
'Dick was a young man of hilarious temper . . . whose intellectual
interests in 1929 seemed to be confined to Proust and the more
blue-boltered periods in the history of Mexico.'[27] For his part,
White was made uneasy by Linklater's witty, critical and often
sardonic tone. His companion was a precocious writer already
offering his ambitious first novel to publishers. Their destination
was Hamilton Gilkyson, a wealthy Anglophile whose home
had become a residence for English visitors, giving them an
opportunity to meet politicians, academics and writers. While
Linklater, though nonetheless enjoying the hospitality, was to
express his scorn for the US political system in his successful novel
Juan in America, White admired the country's energetic prosperity
and brash democracy.

By summer, as he travelled by Pullman train from Detroit

to San Francisco and on to Berkeley, White had started a novel and was contemplating life as an author, modelling himself sometimes on Proust, sometimes on nineteenth-century European essayists. But his ambition to emulate Linklater ignored an important truth: that the characteristics which he most deplored in his companion – cynicism, a tendency to criticise and obsessiveness – lay at the root of his success. To Linklater, White's innocence about the deeper influence of Prohibition and the Mob on American politics was evidence that his friend was an *ingénu* rather than an observer.

California was another culture shock. Living on Buena Vista Avenue in Berkeley, enjoying the sun on endless beaches along the Pacific and watching the first hesitant talkie movies in large-screen cinemas, White neglected his studies and before long succumbed to the latest rage – miniature golf. Under Professor Herbert Bolton, he researched the influence of the Spanish Missions on the life of the American Indians, discovering 'great freshness about everything connected with the historical department. For my own purposes, nothing could have been more valuable than the Californian attitude to New World history.' Most days were spent 'reading, running, jumping and sprinting, whatever the weather', and attending an occasional lecture. At the end of the year, White was credited with only six hours' teaching in his history course instead of the normal thirty. Once again, his 'extremely pleasing personality' convinced the Fellowship that their candidate was 'one of the ablest' students who would 'get on very well in whatever he undertakes'.[28]

Unlike his South African room-mate, Vernon Forbes, White did not have a girlfriend. A foursome dinner at the Durant Hotel ended in disarray when 'Dick was ragged and he lost her.'[29] But White's fame was assured in athletics. In a memorable race representing British students, he beat the redoubtable 'Red Haggerty' in the one mile. At Christmas, White and Forbes drove to Santa Barbara: 'It was like a dream.' Even the Crash on Wall Street, 3000 miles away, barely disturbed their idyll. Surrounded by extraordinary wealth, the twenty-three-year-old Englishman was oblivious to the despondency and panic and convinced himself that the American unemployed, unlike those in Britain, were only 'technically' jobless because their mobility meant that 'they cannot be classified by any set institution'.[30] Their plight, he reasoned, was not as 'critical' as that of the European unemployed.

A personal option disappeared with the Crash. Like so many young visitors, White had contemplated remaining in America as a teacher. Instead his future was once more uncertain. 'One never knows exactly what to do, does one?' he regularly asked the more confident Linklater, but received little reassurance. On 26 April 1930, the two students boarded the *Pennsylvania* to sail steerage southwards through the Panama Canal to Cuba. The *Pennsylvania* docked for one day in Havana, the capital of an impoverished economic colony where rich Americans relaxed and other Americans became rich. Smoking Cuban cigars and drinking local wine, White concluded after touring a sugar plantation owned by Hershey, the chocolate-bar manufacturers, and visiting the headquarters of the American-owned railway, that the American-owned investments were 'splendid' and 'wonderful,' while the Cubans were poor administrators. Writing in 1937, already an MI5 officer, White recorded that his 'glimpse' of Cuba had 'increased my respect for American political integrity', especially Washington's policy of 'non-intervention'. On 22 May 1930, when he sailed on the *American Farmer* back to Liverpool, none of his experiences during the previous two years would be more important than the realisation of the inevitability of Britain's decline and of America's predominance, a truism today but blissfully unsuspected in 1930 by the majority of Englishmen.

During his last days in California, White had decided to become a journalist. His talents, he believed, were in 'organising and interpreting current events and in literary criticism'. Alternatively, after two years in America, he offered himself as a specialist in Anglo-American politics and American civilisation. Without contacts, he sought help from the Commonwealth Fellowship for introductions and wrote to several editors asking to be considered as a leader writer, among them his best hope, Evelyn Wrench, the *Spectator*'s owner and editor, and a member of the Fellowship Committee. But Wrench and every other Fleet Street editor dismissed his proposition. His own letters revealed the reason for his disappointment. Two years' study and travel in America to 'obtain an empirical as well as historical knowledge of American civilisation' were not the only qualities required for a journalist. Omitted was any proof that he could write.

His optimism was shortlived. Unemployment in Britain had risen steeply and, without an income, he was compelled to live with his mother in Tonbridge. Ruefully, he compared the status of American Rhodes Scholars returning 'to positions of influence where their opinions carry weight' with the indifference greeting his own reappearance, aggravated by lack of contacts and the 'difficulty of finding the right starting point'. By September 1930, White was desperate. Robert Barrington Ward, then an assistant editor of *The Times* and a Christ Church graduate, offered the prospect of a post in the future but only after an apprenticeship in the provinces. That implied a period with the *Manchester Guardian*. White ruled out living in the north as 'a bit stuffy'.[31] His formal excuse was that his mother, a widow following his father's death during his absence in America, was moving to Blackheath and required him to live in London. His brother joined them, and the three lived together in the house, bought from a friend.

With the prospects of a career in journalism rapidly fading, and given his 'lukewarm' attitude to a secretarial post in a charity because he was 'quite in the dark as to these things', White resigned himself to teaching. 'I have no particular desire to become a schoolmaster if it could be avoided,' he wrote plaintively to Richard Simpson at the Commonwealth Fellowship, who provided a shoulder to cry on. Having presented himself to the Fellowship as someone of great promise, he apologised for becoming 'a nuisance' but accepted Simpson's offer to search for a teaching post. In the meantime, in November, he travelled for five weeks to Florence to learn Italian. Unlike other Englishmen touring Europe, White's visits were 'romantic cultural' rather than political. 'I learned some languages, made friends and got rid of some of my parochialism.'[32]

There was news on his return. Simpson had found a teaching post in Madrid. But White's application arrived too late – an accident he regretted hardly at all. Just before Christmas, as his employment prospects expired, a forlorn White turned to

Masterman for help. His lack of a first precluded a teaching post in Oxford, but his old tutor could arrange his election to a Gladstone Memorial Exhibition at Christ Church which provided a room and sufficient money to survive one year, writing an essay describing Gladstone's attitude towards the American civil war. Quickly disenchanted by Oxford, he abandoned the Gladstone project in the spring and accepted a six-month contract as the advance agent organising the reception of a group of public schoolboys travelling around Australia and New Zealand on a Dominion Office Enterprise designed to interest the wealthy young in settling in those countries. Amid the scenic beauty of the Antipodes and enjoying 'the wholesomeness of its people', White discovered his particular talent: an ability to negotiate with government officials and departments. He was less successful in persuading any of the young men to leave Britain.

Inevitably, the return to Britain and reality was depressing. At twenty-five, once more living with his mother, he recommenced the search for a job. An application to join Reuters using an introduction from a journalist in Sydney was, after an interview, politely rejected. A trawl through the agencies produced no teaching posts. Even Masterman could not help. White's lifebelt was his brother, by then an established publisher at Methuen enjoying the company of a widening circle of authors. Alan offered him the chore of reading unsolicited manuscripts. The work was tedious and aggravated White's lack of self-esteem, already reduced by his failure to write or even to find work as a teacher in a cramming college.

The first break in the gloom in 1931 was engineered by an invitation from Eric Linklater to meet Janet Adam Smith, the assistant literary editor of the *Listener*. During an enjoyable evening, Adam Smith guardedly hinted that perhaps White might some time want to try his hand as a reviewer. Her caution was unnecessary. 'He seemed anxious to accept.'[33] She invited him to the regular Tuesday afternoon editorial conference of a new column in the *Listener* called 'Week by Week', whose anonymous items were a mixture of comment and reflections. Meeting some of London's literary alumni did not compensate for the absence of a regular income, but even entering Broadcasting House, the new headquarters of the BBC's radio service, infused some sense of purpose into an unfulfilling life, however unnotable his journalistic contributions.

In 1932, White's luck finally turned. In the midst of Britain's financial crisis, White was offered a post as assistant master at Whitgift School in Croydon, founded in the sixteenth century by John Whitgift, the Elizabethan Archbishop of Canterbury who had knelt at the dying queen's bedside. Archbishop Whitgift, White laughed, resembled the Vicar of Bray: 'I couldn't believe the offer. I suspected it was a joke in bad taste.' Established for the benefit of the poor, Whitgift had passed through difficult times, including the demolition of its premises in a road-widening scheme, before reincarnation as a direct-grant grammar school in new buildings.

White was hired to teach history, English literature, French and German and to help with sport. The job was a compromise, but there was no alternative. That autumn, having spent the holidays travelling around France and Germany to improve his languages – witnessing in Munich the frenzied adulation of Hitler – he arrived at Whitgift, 'astonished' to find how easily he adapted to his new life. The school, he discovered, set high intellectual standards and the pupils were lively: 'It was a joy to teach those boys – they were brilliant.'[34] Untrained as a teacher, he successfully masked his inexperience from his colleagues behind a faint, cool smile and 'unusual methods of teaching'. 'He was well liked and highly thought of,' recorded the headmaster, 'his abilities as a first-class teacher and an all-round athlete being in constant demand.'[35]

White's patriotism was not popular. His opposition during a debate to the motion that 'in no circumstances will this House participate in a National War' (this echoed the famous Oxford Union debate of February 1933), in which he condemned the spread of pacificist and defeatist sentiments, was unappreciated. Other motions expressing sympathy for Guy Fawkes or even for Hitler exasperated him, but his colleagues appreciated that he was 'never contentious and did his level best to be fair-minded'. Noting that he was clearly above the fray, they were impressed by his demeanour: 'We often felt sure that he was naturally bound to become the next head, though White would seldom join in ordinary shop talk, as so many others did.'[36]

Still reluctant to accept teaching as a permanent vocation, White asked Adam Smith whether he might apply for a job at the BBC, because, he said, 'I'm excited by journalism.' Adam Smith firmly rejected his overture 'as not right for him'. White she dismissed as 'lacking conviction. Political or temperamental'.[37]

After months of crisis and bloody street-fighting, Germany had been hijacked by Hitler and the Nazis, yet White still showed no emotional commitment and only limited interest in politics. The most damning comment he could make about Malcolm Muggeridge's unsuccessful attempt to alert Britain to Stalin's crimes after 1932 was to recall 'the old tag of the Middle Ages that repetition is the mother of study, joined with the saying of modern journalism that a thing has not been said until it has been said seventy times'. Like others, White found Muggeridge's opinions obscure. Muggeridge, in turn, noted White's detached attitude not only to communism but to all the major issues. Only half-jokingly, Muggeridge asked, 'Dick, whom are you trying to impress, or are you just putting on some kind of act?'[38] White's response to such cynicism was laughter.

White had met Muggeridge through Alan, his brother. 'There goes one of nature's earnest pedagogues,' sniped Muggeridge, a remark which upset White, who had contentedly accepted that teaching would be an honourable, unassuming life's profession.[39] Evidently self-contained and never too demanding of others, White showed interest in rather than commitment to ideas and ideals. In the impassioned world of politics, White was a principled outsider, content to remain a servant of Whitgift, immune to the intellectual torment infecting so many of his contemporaries.

Teaching would probably have remained his life's career had he not agreed, in the spring of 1935, to escort fifteen Whitgift boys on the annual Easter trip abroad. Among the other passengers sailing on 16 April from Liverpool to the Mediterranean on board the *Doric* was Lieutenant-Colonel Malcolm Cumming, a thirty-year-old former soldier, educated at Eton and Sandhurst. As the two men enjoyed the sunshine during the crossing from

Gibraltar to Naples, White struck an immediate friendship. Cumming, revealing only that he was employed at the War Office, encouraged the teacher to expound his political views. Unsuspectingly, White exchanged opinions about the world and his background and conceded that when the 'inevitable war' broke out he would 'cheerfully fight if it came to the crunch'.[40] On their return to Liverpool, Cumming merely bade his companion farewell with a platitudinous request that he 'keep in touch'.

CHAPTER TWO

A Reluctant Spy

In July 1935, three months after his return from the Mediterranean, a familiar government buff envelope arrived at Whitgift. Believing that it was a tax demand, White pushed the unopened letter to one side. Only as an afterthought, when he had spotted a War Office address, did he open it. Written by Captain Guy Liddell MC, the courteous and brief note referred to a recommendation by Lieutenant-Colonel Cumming and suggested a meeting 'over lunch'. Puzzled by its friendly tone, White remarked drily to his colleagues in the staff-room, 'What a small world we live in.'

Still unknown to White, Cumming was an MI5 officer who had been sent to join the *Doric* in order to assess whether White was suitable for the service. White's nomination had been provided by Masterman.[1] White would later claim that until the lunch with Liddell, he 'had never heard of MI5'. Although such ignorance would nowadays appear extraordinary, in 1935 the Security Service was never mentioned in newspapers, in Parliament or even in the courts.

On their first encounter during the summer holidays, there was a genuine meeting of minds. Liddell, fourteen years older than White, was a short, bald, pudgy man whose easy, occasionally shy, but unflappable manner deceptively suggested a slight inferiority complex. In fact, married to Calypso Baring, a wealthy socialite, Liddell suffered an unhappy home life which he endured through a perpetual haze of cigarette smoke. Renowned as an outstanding cellist, he had been awarded the Military Cross during the Great War in France and had since earned a reputation within MI5 as one of the more intelligent members of a service which boasted just twenty-nine officers.

Founded in 1909 as MO5 (it changed its name to MI5 in 1916, as the Directorate of Military Intelligence), the service's first director, Captain Vernon Kell, was still in charge at the age of sixty-four. Having joined MO5 in 1907, Kell had established during the First World War a successful counter-espionage organisation which, in the post-war years, was then substantially dismantled, a reflection of the general lack of regard for intelligence. Based in offices at the unfashionable end of Cromwell Road, South Kensington, MI5's task was to identify the enemy, discover his activities and methods and then neutralise him. Essentially, MI5's task, Liddell explained, was defensive – to protect and defend Britain and its Empire against all subversion. The collection of intelligence and counter-intelligence in the rest of the world was the responsibility of MI6 or SIS, the Secret Intelligence Service.

By the mid-1930s, Kell had served five prime ministers and, with the right of direct access to all senior civil servants, had spread an assumption of influence in Whitehall. His stewardship had created a small, independent and loyal service. Having resisted a Whitehall bid to amalgamate MI5 with SIS, he had won a 'turf' battle in 1931 that enabled the service to maintain a separate existence from the War Office – albeit at the cost of being starved of money and first-class minds.[2] Recruits, found through personal recommendation, were expected to supplement their income with private funds. To ensure their reliability, they were drawn from 'military and county' backgrounds.[3] To preserve officers' anonymity, and since the agency was not a legal entity established by statute, their pay was untaxed. The MI5 which White was invited to join, blessed by patriotic professionals, survived on a shoestring.

Kell was proud of his creation. Chauffeured around London in an Invicta that bore a blue pennant decorated with a tortoise and the motto 'Safe but sure', he exploited his authority, his experience and the secrecy of his work to resist suggestions, despite his bad health, for change of for transfer of control to a younger man. Some would accuse him of complacency but others would insist that he was a patriot safeguarding an ignorantly maligned necessity. Every year, Whitehall's senior officials, members of his

Important People's Club, were invited to dinner at the Hyde Park Hotel. At the end, Kell would rise to disclose the service's recent successes, peppering his speech with anecdotes of the year's less serious achievements. This flamboyant splash humoured if not silencing those doubting his organisation's effectiveness.

MI5's limited resources were concentrated on B Division, monitoring extremists among the Irish nationalists, among the communists and marginally among the growing band of British fascists suspected of supplying military information to Nazi Germany.[4] Guy Liddell was the deputy director of MI5's B Division. Recruited after the Great War to Scotland Yard's Special Branch to collect and collate information about extremists, he had led on 16 May 1927 a controversial police raid on Arcos House, the headquarters of the Soviet trade mission in Britain. Alerted by intercepts of telephone conversations and decoded messages between Soviet diplomats in Britain and Moscow, MI5 had expected to discover *prima facie* evidence of espionage and subversion inside the fortified office block. Instead they found, in a locked strongroom, three people completing the incineration of papers. In the aftermath, Anglo-Russian diplomatic relations were ruptured and the Soviets altered their codes, thus preventing further intercepts.

In 1931, Liddell transferred to MI5, there to specialise in monitoring communist activities. Fourteen years after the Bolshevik revolution, capitalist countries had ample reason to believe Moscow's own propaganda, its threats to spread its ideology across the industrialised world. By the time he met White, Liddell had become MI5's expert on subversive Bolshevik activities, not only in trade unions and politics but also inside the armed services, considered to be the major threat to Britain. His approach, in White's opinion, was subtle. The service, said Liddell, needed to prepare for the inevitable war with Germany and White's knowledge of German and French was valuable. White shared the sentiment and 'knew at once that here was a man I took to without any hesitation whatever'.[5]

'You'll have to learn the job from scratch,' Liddell told White, 'and I'm sure it will be interesting. Forget about schoolmastering and freelancing for the BBC. Don't make up your mind today.

Just let me know as soon as you can.' Asked about the salary,
Liddell replied, 'Pretty poor I'm afraid: £350 per year. That's
the bad part, but the good is that it's tax free.' Flattered by the
approach, White was indignant about the terms of employment
and reluctant to accept. At the age of twenty-eight, he was not
seeking a future without security of employment and at less than
half his current remuneration. After a brief period of reflection,
he rejected the invitation. 'They were rather secretive so I wasn't
quite sure what they were trying to say. Everything was by way
of hints. I left it that they would have to say something direct or
leave it.'[6]

Liddell, in the meantime, was excited. 'This fellow White
is impressive. He knows precisely what he intends to do and
how to carry it out.'[7] White, as Liddell recognised, possessed
essential qualities for an intelligence officer. Not only natural
intelligence, resourcefulness, self-motivation, patience, principle
and patriotism, but also the ability to understand that, while
service within MI5 was a team effort, much of the work would be
solitary, depending upon his own judgment and self-confidence.
Liddell improved his offer. Would White be interested, he asked
at a second meeting, in travelling around Germany in an effort to
uncover, albeit an unusual undertaking for an MI5 officer,
Hitler's intentions? Although devoid of strong feelings about
fascism, White had become intrigued by events in Germany.
Faced with the promise of a role in an inevitable war, 'I snapped
at the bait. I could hardly resist. I saw the offer as a sort of
early-up for war service.'[8] Formally, he would be appointed
private secretary to Liddell.

On acceptance, White became MI5's thirtieth officer. During the six months before his notice at Whitgift expired, some
doubts surfaced, especially when a tempting teaching post was
advertised at Wellington College. To seek guidance he consulted
first his mother and brother and then Masterman. 'Not only is
my security as a teacher jeopardised,' White told his former tutor,
'but I'm also uneasy about undertaking a profession which relies
upon secrecy and duplicity.' For patriots such as Masterman, the
'national interest' did on occasion prevail. 'I do not recollect that
I tried to influence him in either direction,' recalled Masterman

ingenuously, 'but his choice of a profession turned out to be of signal benefit to the country.'9

White raised the same concerns with Liddell. The response was a lengthy lecture about the history of espionage. Spies, reminded Liddell, had appeared in the Old Testament; and in the reign of Queen Elizabeth, Robert Cecil and Francis Walsingham had established secret services to counter the treasonable activities of the Jesuits and other Catholics conspiring to promote the Pope's cause. Now, he argued, it was necessary to monitor the activities of the communists and Nazis. Liddell's reason and charm overcame White's indecision. 'It seemed clear to me that fascism was a monumental threat and that something catastrophic was going to take place.' As he later recalled, 'It never crossed my mind to join the British secret service. It was about the last thing I wanted to do. I had aspirations to write and might have gone into publishing. But nothing else.'10 That option had, however, already disappeared: Janet Adam Smith had left the *Listener*, bringing his links with that magazine to an end.

It was White's good fortune that he was entering the Security Service as the youngest and the brightest. He was MI5's first graduate officer. Over the next decade, he would witness both the partial collapse and the rebuilding of British intelligence, enabling him to learn from the mistakes of his superiors and to benefit from the guidance and example of the handful of talented officers. In late autumn 1935, as Liddell embarked upon a succession of indoctrinating conversations in MI5's modest offices, White's dissatisfaction with the 'miserable starting salary' was dispelled. Liddell, he discovered, was endowed with infinite diplomatic skills, a powerful intellect and an engaging personality. An intelligence officer's task, Liddell explained, was to establish first what an enemy said it could do; secondly, what in fact the enemy was capable of doing; and thirdly, what in fact it intended to do. To White, 'Even the obvious needed to be said.'

While engaged in persuading White to accept his underpaid job, Liddell had concealed MI5's precarious existence and inherent weaknesses. White was unaware that within the three armed services and within Whitehall there existed an inherent prejudice against the very idea of intelligence. It was 'a professional backwater, suitable only for officers with a knowledge of foreign languages and for those who were not wanted for command'.[11] Considering the perceived mediocrity of Kell, it was difficult either to change the attitude or, more importantly, to overcome its consequences.

In preparation for his move on 1 January 1936, White had told Whitgift that he would be leaving to 'try his hand at different work'. At the end-of-term ceremony, attended by Dr Cosmo Lang, the Archbishop of Canterbury, the school joined in thanking a popular master. 'Dick White always had a gift of bringing out the best,' testified J.H. Webbe, the school captain. 'He was almost too good for the place.' The visiting prelate added rhetorically but with commendable prescience, 'Is there not some Hercules within this assembly to uplift all our spirits?'

After Christmas, White moved into a 'small cheap flat, just within my marginal means,' in Earls Court. Welcomed by Liddell on 1 January, he was shown a desk and soon adopted an unhurried routine. At the end of the first day, White discovered an ambience resembling Whitgift's staff-room. All officers in the building gathered for a drink by the fire in the common room to discuss the day's business. Mostly they were elderly men, reflecting Kell's preference for social acceptability, a preference which others condemned as unruffled smugness.[12] But, as White would discover, his fellow officers displayed 'a great sense of loyalty to the service'. The only women employees were secretaries or registry clerks looking after the essential files. Visitors often remarked that MI5 was a 'debs' coffee-house' – jolly, long-legged, beautiful girls were recruited for short periods, but any romance with the officers was forbidden. Every Friday afternoon, a female member of the secretariat walked through the offices handing out brown envelopes. In each were white five-pound notes, emphasising the insecurity and secrecy of the organisation. But to White the informality also characterised the nature of 'Kell's extended family'.[13]

In the common room on the first day was Malcolm Cumming, smiling noncommittally: 'So we meet again. I hope they are looking after you?' Also present was Tom 'Tar' Robertson, a solid, careful Sandhurst graduate, introduced to the service in

1933 by Kell's son, who was investigating communist activity in the armed services. His 'great common sense' and directness appealed to White. Among the few to whom he took an instant dislike was Max Knight, alias M, B Division's expert on counter-subversion who, operating from a flat in Dolphin Square, was penetrating both the British Communist Party and the extreme right.

Knight's charm, his Pied Piper nature, attracted many to become agents out of personal loyalty. Through small advertisements he recruited patriots, 'little ships', who could be inserted into factories or offices whenever necessary. Despite his successes in planting an agent posing as a secretary inside the British Communist Party, which would in 1938 expose Soviet espionage at Woolwich Arsenal, and in inserting an agent into a pro-Nazi group, he was at that moment blind to the Soviet Union's own successes in recruiting sympathisers in Britain's universities. Enigmatic personalities grated with White, the purist. Renowned as an eccentric because of his passion for wild animals as pets, Knight's interest in the occult and his suspected bisexuality cast him as 'a bit mad'.[14] The newcomer shared Guy Liddell's instinctive dislike for gung-ho operators.

The bulk of White's other colleagues were retired Indian police officers, unsuccessful applicants to the British army who had settled for an alternative job for life. Then, nearing retirement, burnt out by the sun and the gin, they found it convenient to 'go next door' – the headquarters of the Indian security police was by chance also in the Cromwell Road – and inquire about employment in MI5. Trained to seek out subversives in India, they appealed to Kell as ideal hunters of communists and foreigners in Britain. In that coterie of investigators, White stood out as an intellectual and as an officer who might, with experience, understand the wider problems of intelligence.

At the end of the first week, White accepted Liddell's stricture that he was a 'long-term probationer under training' and was therefore not required to sign the Official Secrets Act 'until further notice'. For Liddell, the use of a raw but potentially gifted beginner in Germany suited his purpose. If necessary, White could be disowned. Training in codes and procedure, although risibly perfunctory, took longer than expected. Internal jealousies aroused by his academic rather than military background were exacerbated by an embarrassing mishap when he came to apply for a German visa. His telephone call to MI5's office from the West End revealed that he had forgotten his passport. Tar Robertson brought it by taxi to the German consulate in Lower Regent Street. White would never deviate from his initial opinion: 'I wasn't really cut out to be an intelligence officer at all. I partly stumbled into it for second-hand patriotic reasons and that suited the needs of my immediate superiors. At the start it was only looked on as an experiment. That was why I went to work for them under cover in Germany. In the end, I had no alternative but to stay.'[15]

Hitler's reoccupation of the Rhineland in March 1936 brought the complaints about White's role to an end. Although Kell had not anticipated a war, his officers acknowledged Liddell's foresight in gathering information about the new regime. Under Liddell's tutelage, White had improved his German and read widely about the country before embarking, in the summer of 1936, on his nine-month tour. Liddell's brief was explicit. White later explained, 'I was specifically warned against running risks by getting too close to defence establishments.' He was not to spy but to immerse himself in the Third Reich. Kell provided some help. Realising that an intelligent Englishman was certain to attract the interest of German dissidents who, once a friendship was established, might hint about the reason for his travels, the director general provided a list of sympathisers: 'Kell was a shrewd old bugger. I had some very good German sources simply handed to me.'[16]

In Berlin, White's first priority were the Olympic Games. In the new stadium, he watched Jesse Owens, the American black athlete, win the 100 metres and three more gold medals. The young spectator observed that Hitler's discomfiture in the face of these triumphs of an 'inferior human being' obliterated the satisfaction he obtained from the roars of his admirers: 'What appalled me most was the way in which decent Germans were falling for Hitler, hook, line and sinker. They had suddenly been brought back from inflation and unemployment. Suddenly everyone had a job. There is no doubt that it was as great a con as any people has ever been subjected to.'[17]

In the capital, journalists became his favoured introduction to the dissidents,[18] among whom was Fritz Hesse, employed by the Deutsche Nachrichten Büro, the official German news agency. Throughout the autumn, White travelled across Germany stunned by 'the extraordinary way in which ordinary Germans had swallowed Hitler's mesmeric and evil influence'. By Christmas, helped by Liddell, he had learnt the self-reliance and patience required by an intelligence officer. Never skimp or rush over small or obvious details; never fail to ask or consult when in doubt; cautiously assume that the enemy is observing you. Hence, as cover in Munich, he even rented a room from notorious 'Jew-baiters'. At the end of the tour, he had earned invaluable experience and credibility among colleagues.

On his return to London, he was formally employed by the Security Service, required to sign the Official Secrets Act and to give an undertaking not to reveal to outsiders either his duties or his employer. To questioners, he would reply that he 'worked for the War Office'. The secrecy cultivated mystery and a sense of omnipotence which concealed MI5's weaknesses. While the secretariat and registry staff had increased to 120, there were still only thirty officers.[19]

With one other officer, White was assigned to fill the void of MI5's ignorance about German intelligence activities in Britain by monitoring the Ausland section of the Nazi Party. Specifically, he investigated whether German nationals or other Europeans living and working in Britain were linked to the Nazis or were acting as agents for German espionage. The assignment was hampered by MI5's lack of knowledge about the identity of those directing the German intelligence organisations.[20] There was even uncertainty about the actual name of Germany's main foreign intelligence service.

White's investigations revealed no German subversion. That finding was dismissed by his supervisors. Inadequate resources, carped senior MI5 officers, were hindering the hunt for the Nazi's agents. In truth, until 1937, Berlin had specifically avoided operations in Britain.[21] But White was being hampered by a fallacy. Kell's officers were lurching towards their great misjudgment, trailing White in their wake. The image of perfectly synchronised Nazi soldiers marching through Berlin, matched by aircraft and tanks of evidently outstanding quality, convinced MI5 that German intelligence was equally magnificent.

The opportunity to correct that self-deception was the recruitment of an agent in the German embassy in London. Jona 'Klop' Ustinov, the press attaché serving Joachim von Ribbentrop, the impassioned Nazi ambassador, was an avowed anti-Nazi who offered his services to Sir Robert Vansittart, the brilliant head of the Foreign Office. Vansittart's forceful warnings about Nazism were being ridiculed and ignored by his political masters and colleagues, so he was eager for Ustinov to be nurtured by MI5.

Born in Czarist Russia and having served with distinction in the German air force in the First World War, Ustinov possessed wit, sagacity and knowledge of Germany, attracting to his flat in Redcliffe Gardens, Earls Court, a succession of British intelligence officers seeking names of those who could be approached in Germany for help. Among the frequent anonymous visitors was one Englishman described by Klop's son, Peter, as distinguished from the others: 'He was a self-possessed, slim and fairly tall man who smiled a lot.'

White's introduction as Ustinov's case officer was significant promotion. In their regular 'gruelling sessions' during 1937, Ustinov identified anti-Nazis in Germany who could be approached: doctors, writers, military officers and teachers. 'Here, without question,' recalled White, 'we had picked a natural winner who wouldn't let us down.' More pertinently, with Liddell deliberately refraining from interfering with a field officer's discretion, White was learning the art of handling an informant. He was later to describe Klop as 'the best and most ingenious operator I had the honour to work with'. During those meetings, an instinctive affection developed between the placid, aesthetic Englishman and the charming German raconteur who, White declared, 'remained my good friend until his death'.[22] Far from presenting a barrier, their contrasting backgrounds cemented their relationship. White, Klop told his son, was 'odd looking, very non-Establishment. A breath of fresh air. We are united by our dislike of certain Englishmen, especially what White calls the SIS types who are "ivory from the neck up".'[23]

SIS's personnel, White discovered, were with notable exceptions, a sharp contrast to his MI5 colleagues. Either they were gentlemen whose education was expensive and insubstantial and who had been recruited at the bars of Boodle's and White's, the elegant clubs in St James's; or they were disparate and otherwise unemployable adventurers. SIS's operations throughout Europe, including Germany, had already sown the seeds of their own destruction. Witnessing at that early stage the imperfections of British intelligence officers was critical to White's reforms in later years.

Since 1919, SIS officers had operated throughout the world in British embassies or legations under the cover of passport control officers. The arrangement was a compromise between the need for intelligence officers to be based abroad and the traditional Foreign Office's dislike for their murky work. Like all compromises, it was unsatisfactory because the cover was obvious; the quality of officers was too often amusingly poor; and the system was breaking down under the pressure of persecuted Jews seeking entry visas to escape Nazism.

Starved of funds and proper technical resources, Admiral Sir Hugh 'Quex' Sinclair, SIS's chief, had agreed to finance a parallel organisation in Europe to be established and supervised by Claude Dansey, a bon vivant who had managed a country club in America before criminal bankruptcy hastened his return to Europe. Under the codename Z Organisation, Dansey had recruited business acquaintances as agents 'for the British Secret Service'. At best it was a second-rate arrangement, but Dansey's agents did identify Germany's intention to wage war – warnings which were ignored not least because Sinclair, who recommended that the Czechs accept Hitler's demands, was an appeaser.[24] Like Kell, Sinclair was preoccupied by the threat of Soviet Russia.

Among those who advised White to distrust a certain type of Englishman – ridiculously self-confident, irritatingly arrogant, seemingly well informed and dismissive of anything that contradicted his prejudices – was Ustinov, who had secretly negotiated British nationality before his resignation from the German

Diplomatic Service. Under Ustinov's tutelage, with so many in Whitehall and Westminster still blinded by the fear of communism, White became the German expert, benefiting too from Vansittart's private network of German informers. Another among that group was Wolfgang zu Putlitz, a titled landowner and anti-Nazi employed as a junior secretary at the German embassy in London. In January 1938, Liddell proposed that White be authorised by both SIS and MI5 to work with Putlitz. Like Ustinov, Putlitz offered invaluable and, at the time, unique insight into the Nazis' intentions and operations, but he soon aroused his handler's concern. Not only was he a dangerous adventurer, he was also an overt homosexual 'married' to his valet. Although Putlitz's background had not been investigated before recruitment, White's fears were allayed by Liddell. Yet, unknown to Liddell, Putlitz was simultaneously working for Soviet intelligence.

White's learning curve was almost vertical. In the months before the outbreak of war, a procession of high-ranking Germans, at great personal risk, passed through his hands to warn British government ministers and senior officials of Hitler's intentions. Their warnings were disregarded as alarmist and exaggerated. The first lesson White absorbed was that, whatever the quality and accuracy of its information, an intelligence service's reports would be ignored if they conflicted with its own prejudices and if the messenger failed to secure the respect and trust of its customers. Vansittart's repeated warnings, based upon reliable sources, that Hitler would sign a pact with Stalin were dismissed by the Foreign Office and SIS because the head of the Foreign Office was himself distrusted. To make any impression, intelligence needed to be authoritatively presented. The second lesson was this: an intelligence service lost credibility if it supplied contradictory reports. During 1939, SIS simultaneously warned that war was likely and that it was avoidable.

'Ever since I joined the Secret Service in 1929,' recalled F.W. Winterbotham, an outstanding SIS officer, 'I realised that among those who trod the carpeted corridors of power in Whitehall, it was fashionable to smile in tolerant disbelief at anything the Secret Service told them. It was frustrating to see the information on German rearmament being quietly ignored.'[25] Among those supplying that rejected intelligence was White: 'It was a question of resolution combined with hope, counterbalancing the Nazi enemies whom we all loathed and detested. I was learning to live in an era of risk from then onwards.'[26]

In early 1939, White returned to Munich posing as an English teacher. Resuming contact with Germans whom he had met on earlier visits, he also called on those listed by Ustinov and Putlitz as anti-Nazis, acutely aware that he was working alone in enemy territory without diplomatic protection.

> Sometimes even the most ordinary, mundane things would disturb me. For instance, I had arranged to meet someone at a dentist's surgery. The receptionist was polite enough to me but showed her true Nazi sympathies when a number of Jews arrived. The woman's attitude appalled me so much that I was almost tempted to say exactly what I thought. For obvious reasons I couldn't, and didn't. The wretched Jews were simply put at the end of the queue.[27]

White was seeking ideologically motivated agents rather than professional pedlars of information. Principally he was recruiting among the anti-Nazis, those who 'looked to Britain as a moral force against fascism' and were willing to report on events in Germany. White was confident that his idealistic approach was a successful basis on which to appeal for help. Among his contracts were Dietrich Bonhoeffer, the pastor, and Adam von Trott, a Rhodes Scholar with good contacts in England. 'I was grooming free minds to join the secret resistance to Nazism,' White believed.[28] 'Our material was decisive about Hitler's intentions, but Chamberlain ignored it.'[29]

White's report to the Foreign Office, based on information from a German contact, that the Italians were preparing to invade Albania, was also dismissed. 'They were sceptical to the last,' recalled White. '"A coup? In Albania? Never," they told me.' But White was vulnerable to similar criticism.

In mid-1937, Walter Krivitsky, a senior Soviet intelligence officer based in the Netherlands, had defected and travelled to the United States. During the autumn he revealed to FBI interrogators the details of Soviet operations in the West. Still innocent about how to treat defectors, the Americans ignored his disclosures. That changed when an American journalist, having published Krivitsky's story in New York's *Saturday Evening Post*, called on the British Embassy to warn that the Russian knew of two NKVD agents in the Foreign Office – a communications officer and a diplomat. (The NKVD was the Soviet secret police.) A third Briton who had been recruited, according to Krivitsky, was an unnamed journalist who had worked for a British newspaper during the Spanish civil war.[30]

By September 1939, the month when Britain at last declared war on Germany, the only lead the British had pursued was to search for the communications officer. An investigation by 'Jasper' Harker, MI5's deputy director general, and Colonel Valentine Vivian of SIS unearthed as the suspect John King, a fifty-five-year-old cipher clerk. Bizarrely, Tar Robertson invited King for a drink in the Bunch of Grapes pub in Jermyn Street. By the end of the evening, King was drunk and Robertson took the keys to his office safe. That night, the MI5 officers found evidence incriminating King and the following day the hapless official confessed, blaming his treachery on blackmail.[31] Immersed in an extramarital affair while posted in Geneva, King had borrowed money without realising that his 'friend' was a Soviet officer, who demanded his co-operation in return for silence.

At the end of 1939, soon after King's unpublicised conviction, Krivitsky came to Britain to be questioned by White and Jane Archer, formerly Sissmore, a trained barrister in B Division and one of MI5's first women officers. The Russian, codenamed the Imperial Consul, identified Soviet diplomats in London who were NKVD officers and expanded on his revelations. The NKVD, he disclosed, had recruited a 'Scotsman of good family, educated at Eton and Oxford, and an idealist who worked for the Russians without payment'.[32]

White, like Archer, was sceptical. He had never previously debriefed or handled a rival intelligence officer, nor had he any experience of Russia and its espionage organisations. Throughout his tour in Germany, he had been barely touched by the Spanish civil war, the raging issue which turned many British liberals into socialists and communists. Nor had he been outraged earlier by the Italian massacres in Abyssinia. While understanding the simplicities of the impending war between democracy and fascism, he was professionally unindoctrinated with knowledge of the profound ideological struggle between fascism and communism and of the NKVD's resulting ability to recruit non-Russian sympathisers as agents.

His prejudice was fed by appearances. The Russians were deemed to be sloppy people. Unlike the Wehrmacht, the Red Army was inefficient and unimpressive, and its recent invasion of Finland proved the communists' incompetence. Britain was by now at war with Germany. White, with Liddell's agreement, discounted the NKVD officer: 'I did not wholly trust Krivitsky. He wasn't using his real name and he wasn't a general. He hadn't mastered enough to give us a proper lead.'[33] Krivitsky's description of the Soviet agents fitted so many Foreign Office officials that MI5 would have needed enormous resources to investigate his claims – and it was an inopportune moment.

White and MI5 were by now fixated on Britain's immediate predicament: 'Our enemy was Germany, not Russia. Our major interest was whether Russia might help the Germans. Krivitsky provided no information about that.'[34] The Russian's information was filed and soon forgotten. MI5 was responsible for the nation's internal security against German subversion, and the service was almost wholly unprepared.

CHAPTER THREE

The Jigsaw

All the elements of Dick White's future glory and humiliation – the unseen pieces of the jigsaw – began to emerge during those intense years of war. The outbreak of hostilities proved disastrous for Vernon Kell but fortuitous for White. Debilitated by asthma and age, Kell vainly struggled to avoid his fate as an early victim of the emergency; while White, blessed with ability, comparative youth and an easy personality which won universal acceptance, watched his star rise beyond his dreams. Unlike other intelligence officers, White was neither fruity nor florid. He did not talk too much or too well. His cold blue eyes promised courage and determination. With an uncluttered head, he looked and sounded a good committee man who could avoid mayhem and pose no threat. In other words, he conformed to the ethic, entrancing Whitehall's sceptics, who watched in disbelief as the Security Service tottered towards disintegration.

Despite the warnings, MI5, like British industry and the nation's military services, was unprepared for the metamorphosis. Overnight, the service's mandate exploded. MI5 officers' previous preoccupation with a handful of extremists and subversives was swamped by responsibilities for vetting thousands of recruits to sensitive government jobs, controlling travel within Britain and monitoring hundreds of new provisions for internal security ordained by Emergency Regulations. Unpreparedness inevitably spawned mistakes.

MI5's suspicions had fallen on Britain's 50,000 enemy aliens as potential fifth columnists, saboteurs and spies. Most were Jewish refugees but others were established residents, Germans and Italians opposed to their dictatorial governments. For Kell those distinctions were irrelevant. Among the foreigners, he warned,

lurked enemy agents. MI5 urged wholesale internment.[1] Despite
his liberal inclinations, White supported his superiors' conclusion:
without mass internment, MI5's controls would collapse. Home
Office officials, noting that Kell's arguments were unsupported
by any evidence, were unimpressed and favoured leniency. MI5,
wrote Norman Birkett, a government adviser, had committed
'gross mistakes and pathological stupidities' in putting its case.[2]
Within Whitehall, respect for MI5 sank.

Kell's status slid further as he initially resisted reorganisation.
The sentiment spread that the MI5 chief, aged sixty-seven, and
his deputies, Sir Eric Holt-Wilson and Jasper Harker, were too
old and too conservative. Although his service had increased to
eighty-three officers and 253 supporting staff,[3] the preparations
for earmarking potential recruits in the event of war had been
limited. Thirty years' service, insisted Kell stubbornly, had taught
him how to protect MI5's internal security. To his credit, German
intelligence had failed to identify more than a handful of MI5's
officers and was still unaware of White's activities in Germany.[4]
But that success was unknown in London. Downing Street's
ordinance was abrupt: Kell's club would abandon its exclusivity.
Reluctantly, during the months of Phoney War, Kell retreated.

Under the supervision of Harker and Liddell, MI5 recruited
another 570 officers and staff.[5] 'The pace things had to be done
was astonishing,' observed White.[6] Overnight, MI5 was revolutionised both in size and in the quality of its officers. Among the
influx of recruits were intellectuals, lawyers, academics, bankers
and some of the best and brightest of the Establishment,
including Victor Rothschild, Hugh Astor, A.P. Herbert and John
Masterman. 'In the national interest,' White later confessed to his
former tutor, 'I think that we appropriated too much talent. The
demand for men of ability in other departments was enormous and
perhaps we were a bit greedy.'[7] The influx, White complained,
produced chaos: 'It wasn't our fault. We had no money.'

MI5 also moved its headquarters. A temporary base in
the Horseferry Road was abandoned in favour of Wormwood
Scrubs, a Victorian prison in west London, and Blenheim Palace,
Oxfordshire. White found the prison secure but farcically inconvenient. The spectacle of well-dressed men and long-legged

secretaries in the insalubrious west London district sparked bus conductors to the routine chant, 'All change for MI5!' Inside the prison, the former cells became cramped offices. Their automatically locking doors without interior handles, small windows and lack of telephones offered a novel interpretation of security. The reality was different. 'Anyone could come into this building,' Liddell told White, 'put up a sign over a cell and say he's starting a new section.'

The atmosphere, however, was congenial. Liddell placed much emphasis on relationships and intellect and little upon formalities. Everyone continued to be addressed by their Christian names and there were no allusions to rank. For the new arrivals, White shone in that firmament. Experienced, intelligent and polite, he appealed to his own generation, unlike the Old Guard, not least because he was laying the foundations for MI5's greatest wartime success, which would mould his own attitude towards traitors, double-agents and deception for the next thirty years.

On his return from Munich in 1939, White had stopped off in Paris to consult officers of the French intelligence agency, the Deuxième Bureau, about the credibility of various anti-Nazi Germans. During those discussions, the French explained their own attempts to persuade captured German agents to feed false information back to Germany. 'The penny suddenly dropped like a blinding glimpse of the obvious,' purred White.[8] After discussions with Kell, himself an organiser of a similar but crude operation during the 1914–18 war, White returned to Paris in October 1939. Here was the birth of MI5's 'double-cross operation'. Direct responsibility was assigned to Section B1(a) under Tar Robertson.

Arthur Owen was White's first double-agent. Codenamed Snow, Owen was a Welshman, who, identified in 1936 as a regular visitor to Hamburg's shipyards, had been recruited by SIS as an informer. During a routine check, SIS discovered that he was also working for the Abwehr, Germany's foreign intelligence service, but he was persuaded that his true loyalty was to Britain. At the outbreak of war, he had collected a German radio transceiver from Victoria Station's left-luggage office and, under Tar Robertson's control, began transmissions to the Abwehr headquarters in Hamburg.

Having convinced the Germans that he was reliable, Owen received the names of other Abwehr contacts in Britain. Two consequences, crucial to MI5's wartime operations, flowed from Snow's success. By intercepting the Abwehr's signals to Owen, the British Radio Security Service (RSS) could monitor future German transmissions, discovering other German agents and so infer that the enemy had not yet developed an espionage network in Britain. Secondly, by controlling Snow, White could monitor the arrival of future German agents.

On 4 April 1940, seven months into the Phoney War, Chamberlain smugly announced that 'Hitler has missed the bus.' Just five days later Germany invaded Denmark and Norway, routing a British expeditionary force. One month later, in the early hours of 10 May, Germany's predicted invasion of Holland and Belgium compelled Chamberlain's resignation and Churchill's appointment as prime minister. Only sixteen days passed before Churchill approved the evacuation of another British expeditionary force from Dunkirk. The responsibility for those disasters was purely military. Warnings of German intentions, gathered by Allied intelligence from many sources, were ignored by politicians and the military chiefs.

Unlike previous prime ministers, Churchill was a passionate believer in the value of intelligence. His experience in the Admiralty during the First World War, as a journalist and as a military historian had revealed a catalogue of opportunities provided by intelligence which, in the absence of proper machinery to co-ordinate and evaluate the disparate sources of information, had been squandered. Under pressure from him, the Joint Intelligence Committee (JIC) was to become more effective in co-ordinating and assessing intelligence.

Churchill went further than this and personally scrutinised his intelligence chiefs. Unlike his predecessors, he was precise about his requirements, and Kell did not match up. On 10 June 1940, a momentous day in the course of the war, Kell was summoned to Downing Street. The Wehrmacht was poised for its final assault on Paris; Italy had declared war against Britain and France;

11,000 British and French troops were being evacuated from Le Havre as the French government contemplated surrender; and the Royal Navy confirmed the loss of an aircraft carrier and two destroyers off Norway. Discussion in the cabinet anticipated Hitler's invasion of Britain, and Churchill was struggling to save the country from toppling into the abyss. Britain's internal security had become a priority.

The prime minister, dissatisfied by the wrangling over internment, did not conceal his intentions towards Kell: 'There were overlaps and underlaps and I felt that this side of the business of national defence needed pulling together.'[9] MI5 had already been erroneously blamed in October 1939 for a security failure, allowing saboteurs to sink HMS *Royal Oak* in Scapa Flow.[10] Although the *Royal Oak*'s destruction was eventually traced to a U-boat, Kell was blamed for a mismanaged operation to search the vacated German embassy in London. MI5's director general, having lost Churchill's and Whitehall's confidence, was dismissed.[11]

Loyally, White criticised Kell's abrupt removal as 'counterproductive' and a 'reshuffling of the pack for its own sake'. Relations with Whitehall, he believed, became unnecessarily complicated. In retrospect, Kell's dismissal provided a cautionary tale for White. The director general's hauteur had alienated too many civil servants, and eventually the politicians' lack of confidence had determined his fate. Even if Whitehall and Westminster did not pry into the details of the Security Service's activities, the mandarins required reassurance that control over that shadowy world was in trustworthy hands. Kell would die a broken man two years later.

On 11 June, as the French government abandoned Paris, Churchill's fears of a fifth column in Britain swept aside Home Office objections and orders were issued for the internment of aliens and British fascists. The lists, compiled by MI5, prompted 27,000 arrests by the end of July. In charge of that operation was Kell's replacement, his deputy Jasper Harker, 'a sort of highly polished barrel which, if tapped, would sound hollow [because it was]'.[12] Harker, on Churchill's orders, was in turn supervised by Lord Swinton, an abrasive but perceptive former secretary of state for air, and chairman of the new Security Executive. In the midst of the crisis, MI5 officers were not trusted to direct their own service.

White was only indirectly involved in the identification of aliens, their arrest and their appearance at tribunals: 'The policy was distasteful and unsuccessful, but I did not oppose it.'[13] Taking any risk at that critical moment was unacceptable. Patriotism in MI5 was paramount. Officers, exemplified by White, were neither vindictive nor xenophobic. They cared for the nation's security. Honest sentiments could nevertheless still cause harm.

The government ordered the deportation of some internees to Canada. The first consignment, 1200 Germans, Austrians and Italians, were dispatched on the *Arandora Star* on 1 July. The following day, the liner was torpedoed and about 600 people drowned. Many of *Arandora*'s dead were active anti-fascists, well-known Germans who had fled Europe after bravely opposing Hitler, or long-established residents in Britain arrested solely because of their foreign birth. It was a symbolic exposé of a harmful and unjust policy. MI5's lists had proved to be utterly indiscriminate. Foreigners had been listed regardless of their activities.

The Security Service was blamed by a Foreign Office official for 'incompetence', for the 'crude, cruel and foolish treatment of every kind of alien'. Churchill blamed the Service for 'witch-finding activities' that highlighted the 'impediment' to its general operations. Although he acknowledged MI5's mistake, White's loyalty was paramount. After all, internment and deportations of innocents continued for a further three years.

Whitehall's dissatisfaction was compounded by disaster. On 24–25 September, German bombs fell on Wormwood Scrubs, destroying part of MI5's registry, including the vital personality index. Amid the charred paper was a recently completed microfilm copy of the index, but it was of poor quality and was imbued with the acrid smell permeating the ruined building. While most of MI5's staff were moved to Blenheim Palace, White and the senior staff were transferred to 58 St James's Street in Mayfair. Two steel-helmeted guards stood at the sand-bagged entrance. Inside, White and the Old Guard seethed with resentment against their new masters, Swinton and his two associates, Sir Joseph Ball, a racist and arch-appeaser, and Sir William Crocker, a solicitor famed for investigating an insurance fraud.[14] Their ire was directed at the triumvirate's demands for radical reforms.

Swinton rightly believed that MI5 lacked professional control and half-correctly argued that it should behave like a police service. Dismissing explanations about the subtlety of long-term penetration and intelligence-gathering, he demanded that the service dispense with reliance upon Special Branch for investigations and use normal policemen, supervised by solicitors, to arrest and interrogate suspects.[15] MI5 types, he barked, don't know how to talk to the working class nor how to interrogate. As a compromise, six Special Branch officers, including William Skardon and Leonard Burt, were attached to MI5. But Swinton's most radical proposal was the complete reorganisation of B Division, MI5's counter-espionage nerve-centre. Those proposals infuriated Liddell and White.

In the wake of Kell's removal, Liddell had been promoted to director of B Division, with White as his deputy. B Division monitored the whole machinery of security controls, supervising visitors entering and departing Britain, vetting those employed in sensitive posts as potential security risks, protecting government and military buildings, managing censorship and the government's relations with newspapers and the BBC, and controlling all operations against communists, fascists, the exiled governments and foreign embassies to prevent espionage, sabotage and subversion.[16] Under White, the division also retained control over the nascent double-cross operations.

Like others in the Old Guard, White was disturbed by Swinton's wilful misunderstanding of the nuances of their work. The politician, it seemed, did not appreciate that counter-intelligence is a methodical, painstakingly intellectual, sedentary chore, composing a picture from multitudinous sources in order to understand the enemy's intentions. MI5 officers fed themselves from files: there was no malice in the soubriquet 'queen' given to the women managing MI5's registry. Paperwork, recording every minute detail of every movement, was the oxygen of successful counter-intelligence. For a politician in a hurry, the spectacle of

seeming inactivity was anathema. 'Swinton's benign and malign,'
accused White. 'He's threatening to destroy the fundamentals.'
Indeed White earned his master's particular dislike, but survived
reprimands thanks to the protection of Liddell.[17]

The combination of ill-preparedness for war, unmanaged recruitment, uncontrollable expansion of responsibilities, a discredited leadership, bomb damage and an internal power struggle
not surprisingly prompted a report in November to Churchill.
MI5, the prime minister was told, was 'on the verge of collapse'.[18]
Harker was judged inadequate and Swinton was blamed for
excessive politicisation. Sir David Petrie, sixty-one, a former
intelligence officer in India and Palestine, was asked to investigate MI5 and recommend changes. Opinions about Petrie were
mixed. Some complained about his lack of intellect. Others like
Masterman believed he epitomised the best: 'He was a rock of
integrity, the type of Scot whose reliability in all conditions was
beyond question, with strong and independent judgment, but
ready and willing to delegate and to trust.'[19] White tended to
neutrality, not least because the alternative was worse. He was
developing the double-cross system and feared Swinton's obstruction. But a row soon blew up.

The cause of their argument was the use of German agents.
White and Liddell were pondering an ideal strategy. 'Fortress
Britain', mused White, 'should admit just as many double-agents
as MI5 wanted and needed.' Twenty-one German agents had
landed in Britain between September and November 1940. All
but one had been easily identified and arrested.[20] Among the
many other agents who followed, several were identified because
their arrival or identification papers had been arranged by Snow.
Turning rather than executing agents appealed to White's
philosophy. But Churchill demanded executions and publicity.
Swinton issued a memorandum forbidding MI5, without his
permission, to negotiate co-operation with any captured agent
in exchange for his life.

White was furious. Five of the captured spies had already
been executed. On the days of execution, the atmosphere in
B Division was muted: 'We'd put the case for the prosecution
together but there was anger about the result.'[21] Since the

Abwehr was aware of their capture, nothing was lost and the public would be impressed with the requirement of vigilance. But the arrest of others was secret and White urged sophistication: 'Intelligence should have precedence over blood-letting.'[22] The surviving eleven agents were held in individual isolation at Latchmere House, codenamed Camp 020, a Victorian mansion surrounded by woods at Ham Common, south of London. Most had been cowed on arrival. Stripped naked, they were stood before a barking, uniformed officer, leaving little to the imagination of those recently in the company of the Gestapo. There was little time for White and Robertson to decide whether the captured agents were suitable as double-agents.

In his many discussions with Robertson, White pondered the complex and twisted motives of their captives. Some were natural adventurers; others were ideologically motivated; others were idealists who postulated that they had 'never existed as agents' except in the furtive minds of their German masters. But all arrived in Britain trusted by the Abwehr. White and his growing team wanted to develop the successful deception of the Abwehr propagated by Snow. Instead of simply protecting the nation from subversion, MI5 would use German agents like Snow to control and manipulate the enemy's intelligence operations. MI5 would thereby not only discover the enemy's plans but deceive the enemy about Britain's capabilities and intentions. If successful, counter-espionage could be both defensive and offensive.

Success would depend upon the quality of MI5's officers, and their organisation, records and ability to manage each individual German agent. In essence, MI5's officers would *become* the double-agent. To win credibility, false information could be digested by the Germans only if mixed with accurate material. To secure that data required the co-operation of Whitehall and the armed services. However, the three military services, lamenting their depleted resources and urgent requirements on the eve of a possible invasion, were dismissive of MI5's unsubstantiated gossip and its claims to control the majority of the Abwehr's agents.[23] To overcome that scepticism, White and Liddell proposed a summit of all intelligence chiefs on 18 November 1940.

At this meeting the two MI5 representatives argued that the double-cross operation was already imperilled by the refusal to supply accurate information for their agents to transmit to the Abwehr. Despite the risks, if a regular stream of consistent and plausible reports were transmitted, there would be considerable advantages. British counter-intelligence would be able to monitor the Abwehr's plans; the double-cross would delude the Abwehr about the success and security of its British network and ciphers and discourage the dispatch of more agents; and, finally, White anticipated that, by enhancing German confidence in their network, the Abwehr would be susceptible to total delusion in one epic moment in the distant future.[24]

No one could disagree with the ambition, but the two MI5 officers were still opposed by critics who resisted revealing accurate reports of German bomb damage and British morale. In the midst of the Blitz, argued the military, the Germans should not be reassured about their successes. The Germans, countered the MI5 representatives, would already be receiving that information, if not from unknown German agents, then certainly from sympathetic Japanese or Spanish diplomats in London.[25]

The summit was White's first Whitehall victory. The Twenty Committee, or Double-Cross Committee, representing the three services, SIS and MI5, was born as an offspring of the Wireless Board, with powers to formulate and approve the information for transmission by German 'agents'. To preserve flexibility and secrecy, the committee's existence was never officially documented or formally approved by the chiefs of staff.[26] Meeting for the first time on 2 January 1941 under the chairmanship of John Masterman, whose wise appearance concealed his reluctance to make decisions, and assisted by John Marriott, a solicitor, White firmly asserted MI5's control over the agents but encouraged co-operation from the services.[27]

Management of the double-cross was carried out in St James's. Regularly at noon, White chaired a meeting of Section B1(a) officers to draw information together and issue guidance. 'He was brilliant,' enthused Patricia McCullum, a secretary. 'Nanny would have said about Dick, "He's a deep one – always there if you wanted him".' White encouraged discussion but took the final decision.[28] When mistakes occurred, remembered Robertson, 'Dick was never aggressive or vindictive.' Steeped in the beauty of duplicity, for a brief but critical period White was manipulating the unseen enemy across the Channel by masterminding a farrago of lies whose exposure might terminate the whole operation.

In January 1941, one agent, codenamed Summer, escaped and, although recaptured, could no longer be trusted. A story was transmitted to the Abwehr that Summer was trying to get back to Europe. Snow's own credibility collapsed after a rendezvous in the North Sea with the Abwehr, approved by Robertson, was aborted. At a meeting with the Abwehr in Lisbon, Snow admitted his double-cross to the Germans. He was imprisoned for the remainder of the war. But by then other agents, variously codenamed Mutt, Jeff, Father, the Snark, Tate and Tricycle, had been recruited, each housed individually with an MI5 officer, and were transmitting a stream of concocted reports to Abwehr headquarters in Hamburg. During 1941, the Abwehr sent twenty-three agents to Britain and all were arrested, their arrival anticipated either through intercepts or because their mission was agreed with an agent already under British control. The mechanics of the tradecraft – secret inks, microdots, radio traffic, channelling money to agents in Britain, couriering documents from Britain to Germany and 'recruitment' of the double-agents – excited White. The experience was to influence the whole of his career.

To confirm the credibility of MI5's ideas, White flew during the summer to Cairo. Increasingly, the three British services in the Middle East were using deception about the disposition of ships, aircraft and troop movements in their war against General Rommel. Dudley Clarke, a remarkable intelligence officer, was, on General Wavell's instructions, constructing a deception operation based on the British army's intended military operations. In other words, deception was part of the offensive. Reassured of the value of MI5's strategy, White returned to London to demolish Swinton's opposition.

In November 1941, White, with Liddell's support, renewed with Swinton, the director of public prosecutions and the attorney general his Whitehall battle against executions: 'I needed some degree of subtlety to win the trust of civil servants who were not thinking in the same way as myself.'[29] Bureaucrats needed persuasion to consider an original proposition: 'how can we use German spies to beat the Germans?'[30] White's style was markedly different to other MI5 officers. 'What was impressive', recalled an insider 'was Dick's alertness and quickness of wit under endless complications.' Eventually, White won the DPP's support for a compromise favourable to MI5's retention of control of double-cross operations. 'I won a reputation in Whitehall and moved into bureaucracy a little too early for my taste.'[31] His patron was the minister of information, Duff Cooper, responsible for the Security Service.

One trait, particularly pleasing to bureaucrats, was White's ability, even when questioning a decision, to adopt a deferential attitude towards superiors. 'Ours not to reason why' appeared to be his cardinal and endearing rule. His admirers thought him altruistic, unrebellious and ultra-loyal, while cynics carped that he lacked the passion to fight openly for principles, quoting his pronouncement, 'It's not our business to rock the boat.'

The critics were heavily outnumbered. Within St James's, White attracted admirers. Although he would reflect many years later, 'There were too many strange faces,' he relished the atmosphere, which encouraged intimate conversations and friendship with some of Britain's most ambitious and successful intellectuals. Just to sit in a room with Arthur Koestler, by then the internationally well-known author of *Darkness at Noon*, Victor Rothschild, an outstanding scientist and millionaire, and Herbert Hart, who would become a world-renowned professor of jurisprudence, excited White: 'It was like Alice in Wonderland.'[32] White was surrounded now not by uneducated former Indian policemen, but by the elite of Britain's intellectuals, a club which he aspired to join. Over croquet he asked Koestler, Rothschild and Hart to produce anti-Nazi propaganda 'to make Goebbels sit up'. After a few weeks, 'the whole thing broke up in terrible disarray and ended in bitter quarrelling', but White's unconditional and trusting friendship with all three typified the atmosphere in St James's. Also passing through White's office were some of the great names of modern British literature, including Evelyn Waugh and Graham Greene.

There was limited time for socialising. White's war was constant hard work. Living in Richmond Court, in Sloane Street, a neighbour of Guy Liddell, he worked not only during the day but at night meeting agents. On his few free weekends, he travelled to Klop Ustinov's Gloucestershire home for advice and friendly comfort. Occasionally, he was accompanied by his secretary, Joan Russell-King. Unlike other officers, White was still unmarried and unburdened by the chore of seeking shelter and rations in London for his family during the Blitz and its aftermath. On his rare free evenings, he joined other MI5 officers at parties, especially enjoying those in Chesterfield Street in Mayfair hosted by Tomas 'Tommy' Harris, regarded as 'the best-equipped operator the double-cross system ever produced'.[33] The charming Anglo-Spaniard brought together a group of recently recruited MI5 and SIS officers – Anthony Blunt, Kim Philby, Guy Burgess, Victor Rothschild, Goronwy Rees and also Guy Liddell – whose names would dominate decades of investigation by British intelligence, not least by White.

Of all those officers, White felt a natural antipathy towards Burgess, the thirty-year-old Etonian and prize-winning historian from Trinity, Cambridge, 'who behaved so badly that no one could have thought for a moment that he was a spy'.[34] Although White would improbably claim, 'I only saw Burgess once as I was going to a party and he was being carried out of a house drunk,'[35] he did not become embroiled like Liddell in long, indiscreet evenings with Blunt and Burgess, at their home in Bentinck Street rented from Rothschild, but kept a firm distance. White claimed not to notice that Burgess and Blunt were homosexuals. Nor did he notice that Blunt was close to Wolfgang zu Putlitz, his own agent, a known homosexual. Some would explain White's blindness or tolerance as innocence, others would argue naivety. Neither is blameworthy in normal life, but both are handicaps for an intelligence officer who suspected nothing while passing through Bentinck Street's den of 'decay and dissolution'. Perhaps regretting his wartime admiration for Rothschild, White did however note the irony of the blue plaque attached to the outside

wall of the millionaire's house announcing that a former occupant
was Edward Gibbon, the historian and author of *Decline and Fall
of the Roman Empire*.[36]

Within that house, the seed was sown of what White would
describe as 'fantastic and beyond belief'[37] – his own unquestioning relationship with Blunt, another piece of the jigsaw.
Anthony Blunt had been introduced to MI5 in August 1940
by Victor Rothschild. To Liddell, Blunt seemed yet another
talented intellectual whom the service was anxious to enlist.
Aged thirty-three, he had been elected a fellow of Trinity,
Cambridge and had written widely about art, especially about
Nicolas Poussin. Blunt's loyal if uninspired service in France
before the evacuation persuaded Liddell to accept Rothschild's
recommendation without further scrutiny. If positive vetting had
existed, the security officer's inquiries would have unearthed the
fact that in October 1939 Blunt had been discharged from an
intelligence course at Minley Manor, Camberley because of his
Marxist beliefs. The information that Blunt was a 'security risk'
had come from MI5.[38]

Less than one year later, unaware that Blunt had been 'returned
to his unit' as a suspected Marxist, White watched as he 'went to
and fro' working in the War Office as assistant to the MI5 liaison
officer. To White, Blunt was just another of that golden elite who
were invading MI5: 'He was a very able man. Liddell could have
stopped his recruitment but there was no particular reason to do
so.' At that time, no MI5 officer considered the possibility of a
Soviet plan to infiltrate the service. 'There was nothing positive
to go on,' lamented White. Vetting would have revealed that
Blunt had never been a member of the Communist Party but
had, while at Cambridge, written extreme left-wing articles. Yet
left-wing opinions among MI5 officers were not uncommon. Even
if White had been minded to check on Blunt's past, 'The feeling
was that anyone who was against the Germans in the war was
on the right side.'[39]

In retrospect, White blamed the refusal to discriminate against
suspected communists upon politicians, especially Max Beaverbrook, Churchill's confidant and a minister, who would have 'profoundly discouraged' any investigations into undergraduate

political activities. 'The climate of opinion was virtually unshockable about the left wing. Beaverbrook specifically directed MI5 that on no account were we to hunt for communists. Everyone against the Germans was on the right side.'[40] But in truth MI5's ex-Indian police officers were oblivious to the disenchantment among Cambridge graduates which had nurtured the climate of treason. Even vetting would not have revealed that, six years earlier, Blunt had been recruited by Burgess, and at the behest of his Soviet controllers had worked assiduously to enter the intelligence service.[41] It was MI5's misfortune that among the many European refugees in London, whose numbers had so alarmed Kell, were officers of the NKVD, not of the Abwehr, and they controlled Blunt.

Although White would claim to have had 'some reservations about Blunt' they concerned his personality rather than his loyalty. Even those reservations, White would concede, dissolved when he witnessed the warmth Liddell showed towards the witty aesthete. Despite Blunt's appalling conceit, White the aspiring writer enjoyed intelligent and civilised conversations about art with him, a man whose career he envied. 'I was interested in art and he always used to sit down next to me in the canteen and chat. He was a very nice and civilised man and I enjoyed talking to him.'[42] Like Liddell, White was simply trusting and therefore vulnerable, especially after Blunt generously offered his advice on various prints White was considering purchasing.

Blunt's ingratiating manner allowed their lunchtime conversations to develop into detailed discussions about MI5's work. On reflection, White realised, Blunt always found the time to talk to those who were preoccupied with sensitive issues connected with the communists and Russia. 'Blunt', he admitted, 'made a general assault on key people to see that they liked him.' The flattery lured Liddell towards a closer friendship, towards increasing indiscretion and finally towards realising Blunt's ambition to be moved from the innocuous D Division, responsible for travel control and munitions security, to the sensitive B Division.

By then, MI5 had established itself as a more solid if unspectacular service under Sir David Petrie, who had been appointed director general in March 1941 on condition that

Swinton be excluded from control. Petrie's reforms benefited Liddell and White, who, as controllers of B Division, effectively managed MI5's most important operations. Under White, Blunt initially supervised MI5's surveillance system, liaising with the security officers of Allied governments-in-exile and 'checking' the contents of the diplomatic bags of neutral countries. Then he moved to section B1(b), the 'steering section' for the whole of B Division, working with Helenus 'Buster' Milmo, a barrister, and Herbert Hart.[43] The mole was inside but his attempt to persuade Liddell to recruit Burgess, so often drunk and obviously degenerate, failed. 'Keep that man out of the office,' warned Liddell, 'and don't leave anything lying about if he does get in.'[44]

In late 1941, criticism of MI5 resumed. Senior officials in the Cabinet Office became anxious about 'the present functioning of MI5'.[45] The police in particular complained about 'amateur' MI5 sleuths investigating subversion. A parallel complaint echoed the sentiment that MI5 officers were ignoring individual's civil rights. A review of the service's operations reported improper use of powers against aliens, especially in camp 020.[46]

Inexplicably, the momentum of the double-cross operation had suddenly declined. Pondering the reasons, White proposed in late 1941 that commandos be dispatched to France to capture an Enigma machine. 'It would', wrote White, 'be of vital assistance to breaking [sic] German codes.' His suggestion was directed to Gordon Welchman, an outstanding mathematician working in Hut 6 at Bletchley Park, a small, ugly estate forty miles north of London which had become Britain's centre for breaking the German codes. Specifically, White wanted Welchman to identify the location of an Enigma machine along the occupied European coastline. Welchman was appalled. Unknown to White – and the Germans – Polish intelligence had delivered an Enigma machine to SIS on the eve of war. After two years, Welchman and a small team were on the verge of breaking its secrets, allowing an expanding group of experts at Bletchley to decipher top-secret messages transmitted among the German military across Europe and North Africa. Their breakthrough on Christmas Day 1941 unleashed 'the most comprehensive and effective system for penetrating the enemy's mind that has ever been evolved'.[47] Its codename was Ultra. White's proposal was firmly vetoed.

White was indoctrinated in the Ultra secret in spring 1942. By then, the dissemination of decoded intercepts was under SIS's control and the daily handover to Churchill of a box containing the latest secrets – 'a ceremony which never lost its uncanny magic' – secured for Stewart Menzies, the new head of SIS, a special status which his service would have been denied had it relied upon human agents. Naturally, MI5 wanted access to the Ultra intercepts. The obstacle was SIS and in particular Felix Cowgill, the head of Section V responsible for counter-intelligence. In 1939, the former Indian police officer, whose staff was increasing from five to twenty-four (twelve in St Albans and twelve overseas)[48] argued that further distribution would endanger security – an ironic claim considering MI5's successes against the Abwehr compared to SIS's dismal failures in occupied Europe.

The disagreement escalated into a major dispute between Petrie and Menzies about responsibility for counter-espionage outside Britain. Petrie's offer to create a joint agency between MI5 and SIS was rejected, but Menzies finally agreed that White could visit Cowgill in St Albans to learn more about the scope of his work.[49] Hugh Trevor-Roper witnessed White's patient negotiations with Cowgill: 'White removed Cowgill's suspicions and the blocks fell. White's strength was his lack of any enemies. He was a conciliator with a purpose.'[50] Cowgill's turf was more extensive than White had anticipated. By reading the Abwehr's decoded messages, SIS was monitoring German operations against British shipping, its military and its diplomats. To White's stupefaction, Ultra intercepts also reported the discussions among senior Abwehr officers about their agents in Britain. There, on paper, was the transcript of Germans expressing their dissatisfaction with their agents' poor performance, hard evidence explaining the double-cross's decline.[51]

White's skill was to persuade Cowgill to move closer to MI5, in a house in Ryder Street, St James's. His problem was well described by another witness to the negotiations, Kim Philby: '[Cowgill's] intellectual endowment was slender. As an intelligence officer he was inhibited by lack of imagination, inattention to detail and sheer ignorance of the world we were fighting in . . . Cowgill revelled in his isolation.'[52] Once the negotiations had succeeded, White and Kim Philby met regularly.[53] Knowing how SIS's personality clashes irritated White, Philby obligingly allowed the MI5 officer to read the relevant Ultra intercepts and the follow-up reports by Section V officers. Naturally, White was grateful, and like so many others was much taken by Philby's unpretentious courtesy, his witty conviviality and his willing complicity in their common quest to outwit Cowgill. Above all, White appreciated that the tweed-jacketed Philby, unlike so many others in the business, was a professional.

Among those who saw the two together was Niall MacDermot, an MI5 officer who worked with White until the end of the war. Introduced to Philby by White, the junior MI5 officer observed maliciously, 'Dick White was thrilled by Philby and thought he was wonderful . . . he told me how brilliant he was and what a pity he wasn't head of section, he was so able.'[54] Philby, a former Cambridge student and *Times* journalist, would claim that he had been nominated to join SIS in 1940 on the initiative of Ester Marsden-Smedley after their evacuation with the army from France.[55] Guy Burgess, however, insisted that he suggested Philby's recruitment in 1939 to Marjorie Maxse, the chief-of-staff of SIS's Section D's training school for propaganda, sabotage and subversion. Burgess had been introduced to Philby in 1932 by Maurice Dobb, a Marxist professor in Cambridge, and they had grown closer ever since Burgess's journey to Moscow in 1934. Burgess's claim seems to be more likely, since Philby was asked to work in SIS's Section D, where he taught propaganda to SOE* agents; on its disbandment he was transferred to the Iberian section.[56]

His passage was smoothed by a succession of introductions initiated by Tomas Harris and Dick Brooman-White, the head of SIS's Iberian section, culminating in a lunch between Harry St John Philby, his father, and Colonel Valentine 'Vee Vee'

* SOE, the Special Operations Executive was established by Churchill to 'set Europe ablaze' by encouraging and supporting local resistance movements throughout occupied Europe.

Vivian, Menzies's deputy. On that occasion, Philby's embracing of communism in Cambridge was mentioned and dismissed by his father as a folly of youth. His son's outstanding qualification was the expertise gained as *The Times* correspondent reporting General Franco's campaign. Philby had even won an award from the general for his sympathetic articles. Unknown to the father, he had proved his loyalty to Moscow by searching the former's belongings for proof of employment by SIS.[57]

The irony was rich. Cowgill and Vivian, both ex-Indian policemen who had waged an unrelenting campaign against communists on the sub-continent, never suspected Philby. To the contrary, Cowgill acknowledged him as diligent and hard working. Equally MI5 offered no opposition, although his name already featured in a registry file.[58] White would deny that he had personally cleared Philby's appointment.[59] Philby, for his part, would observe that White, 'with his usual good sense, was content to delegate a lot of work to his subordinates and to exercise his gifts for chairmanship'. But he added a criticism which was voiced by others, including Masterman, that White's 'most obvious fault was a tendency to agree with the last person he spoke to'.[60] The criticism misunderstood the committee habitué's technique. By avoiding argument and *dirigiste* commands, White sought to build a better atmosphere and obtain co-operation.

With access to the Ultra intercepts, which allowed MI5 to read the communications among Abwehr officers, the fortunes of the double-cross operation began to improve. White and his colleagues proposed the transformation of their defensive operation into an offensive against the Abwehr. In a paper entitled 'MI5 Double-Agents: Their status and the Potential Value of Their Work', White argued that the Double-Cross Committee should plan the deliberate deception of the Germans.[61] The first obstacle was Petrie, who sought to 'restrain White's ardour'.[62] The Double-Cross Committee, the director general argued, was established to catch spies and not to initiate deception. 'It's a defensive and not an aggressive agency, I believe. Deliberate deception is not the role of a counter-espionage agency.'[63] Petrie's conservatism was overruled by others who recognised deception as an important tactic.[64]

The success of deception exerted a profound influence upon White, comprehensively influencing his attitude towards counter-espionage during the Cold War. But the ease of capturing and converting German agents misled him and his subordinates about the parallel contemporary threat in Britain from the communists. The MI5 officer responsible for monitoring communist subversion during that period, under White's supervision, was Roger Hollis.

Born in 1905, Hollis, whose father became the Bishop of Taunton, was a contemporary and acquaintance of White's at Oxford. His easy-going enjoyment of the university's social life proved, in Evelyn Waugh's view, that he was 'a good bottle man', while Sir Harold Acton commented that he was an 'agreeable friend'. Among his circle were two left-wing activists, Claud Cockburn and Maurice Richardson. According to White, Hollis could have become 'a promising scholar of classical bent, but he chose instead an Oxford interlude of wine and roses'. The penalty was Hollis's abrupt rustication from Worcester College, one year before his final examinations.

Employed first by Barclays Bank and later in China by British American Tobacco, Hollis returned home with tuberculosis. In his search for employment, he approached SIS and after rejection was passed in 1938 to MI5, just as Kell was reviewing candidates for a proposed Japanese desk. Impressed by Hollis's Far East experience, Kell asked Jane Archer for an opinion. The aspiring officer was invited to play tennis at the Ealing Club. White was the fourth in a mixed doubles.

During that afternoon, White's impressions of Hollis were mixed: 'He was shy and retiring and physically distinctly frail . . . Nor were his paper qualifications all that impressive.' On the other hand, White and Archer were attracted to 'something gritty and hard headed'. The decisive factor was Meldrum's insistence on Hollis's 'highly honourable and stable family background'. White was persuaded by that testimonial, and Hollis joined MI5. In 1940, he became the section chief responsible for communist activities. 'Roger was hard-working, calm and fair-minded,' concluded White. 'What I liked was his competence and his dry and witty manner.'[65] Others recalled his irksome nasal tone and his predilection for pinching women's bottoms, characteristics redeemed by his fund of 'good, dirty jokes which he told well'.

Hollis's brief was to survey and penetrate communist groups in London and to note their contacts with Soviet diplomats. The task was delicate. The *Daily Worker* had been suppressed in January 1941 on the ground that its anti-war propaganda was proving effective, but MI5 advised against the internment of Communist Party members. There was no suggestion that they would assist the Germans or actually fight against Britain. Monitoring was considered the best defence until, in June 1941, Germany's invasion of the Soviet Union, changed the circumstances of Hollis's work.

In tune with the public's dramatic switch to support their new ally against Hitler, Churchill directed that Russia should be treated by the intelligence services as an ally, and the RSS, the interception agency, was ordered to stop collecting Russian material.[66] Simultaneously, MI5's pressure on communists was to be relaxed. Hollis doubted the Communist Party's overnight conversion to support Britain. Reports from MI5's informers and agents, inserted long before by Max Knight, reconfirmed that the 50,000 party members still loyally supported the Soviet Union, were often willing to aid Soviet subversion and were prepared to embarrass the British government.[67] After consulting White and Liddell, Hollis ignored Churchill's directive and continued MI5's activities against the communists.[68] Regularly, he warned White about individuals who should be excluded from sensitive posts, but others within MI5 argued that it was wrong to discriminate against those who had flirted with communism during the 1930s. A proposal to leak the documented evidence of the party's anti-British stance was firmly rejected by ministers.[69]

White's attitude towards communism at that stage was benign. Conditioned by the public mood, and influenced by Liddell's restraint, he was not noticeably anti-communist. In the twenty years since the Bolshevik revolution, communism had not been perceived as a religion, a malignant conversion of the mind rather than a dispensable political opinion. In the course of his wanderings through Whitehall, he met many communists but evinced no fears. Among those acquaintances was Peter Smolka-Smollett, chief of the Ministry of Information's Russian section. During their conversations, the Austrian-born communist told White that Stalin had no intention of dominating or occupying post-war Europe. White never raised any objection to Smolka-Smollett's continued employment.

Reflecting Liddell's experience, which was based on the inter-cepts of Russian telegrams from Moscow to London up to 1927, White believed that communist subversion directed from Moscow was channelled through the party. As taught by Liddell, there was no distinction between subversion organised by the Communist Party in Britain and that directed by the Soviet Union. Their objective, according to MI5's experts, was to agitate for the over-throw of the Conservative government. Dangerous communists belonged to conspiratorial organisations and were identified by penetrating those groups in Britain. King, the Foreign Office cipher clerk, who was not a communist, was judged to be an aberration.[70]

Under White's supervision, Hollis compiled the evidence (submitted to the Home Office in October 1943), that fifty-seven Communist Party members were employed in secret installations and should be removed. MI5 agents had discovered that the party's leadership had a high-level informant within the government who promised advance warning of any government plan to suppress the party.[71] Other communists were handing over top-secret documents about jet engines, armaments, anti-radar weapons and aircraft production to the party leaders for onward transmission to Moscow. That evidence did not persuade Desmond Morton, a friend of Churchill and Swinton's adviser: 'MI5 tends to see dangerous men too freely and to lack that knowledge of the world and sense of perspective which the Home Secretary rightly sees as essential.'[72] After MI5's first submission for the removal of a communist civil servant in a non-military department was rejected by his minister, the service submitted no further names.

Communist penetration, White agreed, was a side issue. At the end of 1943, his attention was already diverted. In anticipation of the invasion of Europe (for which General

Eisenhower was appointed Supreme Allied Commander), White was commuting between MI5 and the Cabinet Office as chairman of the War Room. Originally, he was appointed deputy chairman under Simon Johnson, but when the chairman was found drunk at White's when he should have been attending the first committee meeting, White was promoted and also became the deputy counter-intelligence adviser to Eisenhower's chief of staff, General Walter Bedell Smith.

The arrival of senior officers of America's recently formed intelligence organisation, the Office of Strategic Services (OSS), was to be another crucial influence upon White's career. Under the London Agreement signed in June 1942 by Sir William Stephenson, the chief of British Security Co-ordination in New York, and Colonel William Donovan, the founder of America's foreign intelligence service, the two countries concluded an unprecedented union between intelligence services. To avoid duplication and to encourage collaboration, the world was divided for the duration of the war between British, American and British–American zones. Liaison officers were appointed in London and Washington to smooth the co-operation, which provided access for American officers to British personnel and facilities. In the long term, nothing would be more important than their joint efforts to intercept and decode German, Japanese and Italian radio signals. A decade later, Donovan would tell Bedell Smith, by then the second director of the OSS's successor organisation, the CIA, 'Bill Stephenson taught us everything we ever knew about foreign intelligence operations.'[73]

The first American trainees and liaison officers arrived from March 1943. Unlike other senior British officers, irritated by the young, inexperienced visitors grotesquely laden with alcohol, tobacco and dollars, White was a natural enthusiast for the new alliance: 'Their definite swiftness off the mark made its own point.'[74] X-2, the OSS's counter-intelligence section in London, was led by James Murphy, an admired Missourian. Their arrival was not auspicious. 'They are confused, untrained and insecure,' White told Liddell, who agreed that co-operation was still too precarious. Tactfully, the two MI5 officers persuaded Murphy that, if the Americans reorganised their headquarters and operations, the British would train American officers and share their files and resources. Among X-2's later arrivals, the most important for White's later career was James 'Jesus' Angleton, a twenty-six-year-old intellectual.

Angleton was an Anglophile, educated at Malvern, an English public school, and at Yale, with a reputation as a poet, fly-fisherman, sportsman and workaholic. Based at 14 Ryder Street, adjacent to MI5's headquarters in St James's, Angleton first met Cowgill and Philby, whose offices were near by, and then White, to be briefed about British counter-intelligence successes. For White, the somewhat emaciated and enigmatic young American resembled 'a famished seer', who worked around the clock, often sleeping in a cot on the premises. White could not recall which of the two first realised that both were Sagittarians, but he admitted enjoying, albeit 'in small doses', his wily conversations with the chain-smoker, whose thick glasses covered a sallow, lizard-like countenance.[75] For Angleton, the Briton, eleven years older, was a revered sparring partner for nit-picking discussions about the intricacies of their work. Like White, Angleton was becoming fascinated by the task of unravelling the mysteries of counter-intelligence.

He was impressed, too, by British successes. Not only did MI5 claim to control all German intelligence operations in Britain, but British intelligence, thanks to Ultra, had compiled an accurate battle order of the Abwehr's headquarters and chain of command, tracing the intense rivalry and suspicions between the Abwehr and the Sicherheitsdienst (SD, the security service of the SS); and pinpointing the Abwehr's failure to foresee the Allied invasion of North Africa. That success, however, was dented by resounding intelligence failures. Four years earlier, on 9 November 1939, the SD had kidnapped two SIS officers at Venlo on the German–Dutch border and it was assumed not only that the service's entire German and Dutch network had been betrayed, but that the Germans knew the identities of many SIS officers. Another salutary failure was the fate of sixty-one agents dispatched from Britain after early 1942 to Holland. Captured on arrival, most had been executed. Unknown to SOE, the Germans had broken SIS's cipher and used the captured British radio officers to transmit messages suggesting that the network was safe. Even the security alerts bravely inserted into the messages were ignored in London.

Discussing those disasters with White, Philby and other British counter-intelligence experts, Angleton became fascinated by the refinements of counter-espionage, where the original penetration was turned back on to the enemy. The game required not merely traditional skills and patience, but dispassionate intellect to identify unnoticed German successes and constant analysis to protect against deception. No intelligence service, conceded White, was invulnerable to the double-cross, including the British. Together they explored the Byzantine possibilities open to the counter-intelligence practitioner for exploiting his vulnerable opponents and sowing discord and confusion. When Angleton departed for Italy in October 1944, eventually to become OSS's counter-intelligence chief in Rome, he had become indoctrinated into the sinister beauty of counter-intelligence. By then White, wearing a brigadier's uniform, though paid a lieutenant-colonel's salary, was overseeing a canvas of counter-intelligence operations stretching across Western Europe.

In the planning for Operation Overlord, the invasion of Europe, responsibility within the Supreme Allied headquarters (SHAEF) was equally divided between nationals of the two allies. Eisenhower's chief of intelligence was Major-General Kenneth Strong, an admired British officer, able to exert decisive leadership to weld all the nationals into a unified team. He would be offered the directorship of the CIA when his patron became president. Serving under Strong were two Americans. Brigadier-General Tom Betts was a professional soldier with limited understanding of intelligence. Compared to the sophisticated Strong, Betts, an assistant to the Chief of Staff, was 'a lumbering oaf'.[76] The head of counter-intelligence was Lieutenant-Colonel Henry Sheen, trained at West Point. A New Yorker from an old military family, he oversaw a section of about thirty officers. His deputy was White, who did not deny the absence of mutual admiration: 'I generally played second fiddle to the relatively untutored Sheen, who had to lean on my abilities to outsmart the rest.'[77]

At the earliest meetings in Norfolk House, Eisenhower's headquarters in St James's Square, or at SHAEF headquarters in Bushey, White noted Strong's lack of interest in non-military intelligence. Although his aloofness was not personal, Strong was not 'a great believer in the value of spies'. In his view, they were 'brave' but failed to provide 'any really valuable information' concerning the German armed forces.[78] To transcend his status as a mere cog in the huge planning machinery and win credibility among the higher ranks through his expertise and personality, White chose to emulate Strong. There was an art, he realised, in the smooth presentation of intelligence which would arouse confidence in British competence. Post-mortems would not be about whether the correct intelligence was supplied but about 'How did you tell them, and in what voice, and did you tell the right person?' The intelligence officer did not inhabit a master–servant relationship, but was the supplier to a customer.

Under White's supervision, a committee had produced quantities of papers and pamphlets, including 'German Secret Services and British Counter Measures' and 'SHAEF Directive No. 7', to forewarn Allied military officers what to expect in occupied Europe and Germany. Other booklets explained German military ranks and the functions of the Abwehr, Gestapo, SS, Nazi Party, the police and other state organisations, or listed the categories of Germans who were, when the Reich was finally occupied, to be dismissed from their jobs or automatically arrested.

White's more serious task, and one which was to be another influence on his subsequent tenure as Britain's intelligence chief, was his contribution towards a counter-intelligence blueprint for the detection and destruction of any German resistance movement in the predicted chaos of Germany's unconditional surrender. Given his experience in pre-war Germany, White's contribution could have been significant. In the event, he was bound by policy to ignore his own eyewitness reports about the credibility of the anti-Nazi Germans.

British government policy, enunciated by Churchill and the Foreign Office, opposed any relationship with anti-Nazi Germans. The German opposition, in Whitehall's opinion, was discredited. The majority voice within the Foreign Office, encouraged by the

British ambassador in Moscow, and that Britain had little to fear from any Soviet threat. Loudly, the Foreign Office preached that the Russians would not interfere in post-war Europe and, in any event, Britain would rather have a strong Russian presence than allow Germany to resume its hegemony.[79] That prejudice was supported by the White House and, not surprisingly, by Stalin himself, anxious about the West's susceptibility to the temptation of ending the war in a separate peace treaty with anti-Nazi Germans.

British suspicion of the anti-Nazis was partially fuelled by the intelligence services. Among their sources were Wolfgang zu Putlitz, the unexposed communist agent, who cautioned White that it would be a mistake to trust the German Social Democrats; and Philby, who concealed perfunctory approaches to Britain by Admiral Canaris, the Abwehr chief, and disseminated reports within SIS which discredited the German opposition.[80] By mid-1944, White had adopted the Allied hard line denying the existence of 'good Germans' and accepting that the war could end only with Hitler's unconditional surrender. The sentiment was understandable in the weeks before the uncertain gamble of landing an army on Normandy's beaches.

On 15 May, Brigadier White was an eyewitness of history. Standing behind King George VI, Churchill and all the American and British chiefs of staff in St Paul's School, he listened to Eisenhower, Montgomery and others deliver the final briefing on the invasion. He left one of the more remarkable gatherings of military commanders 'struck by the brilliance of Montgomery's delivery and the sheer audacity of the military's imagination and organisation'.[81]

Over the following three weeks, White supervised the counter-intelligence operation. If his career had been abruptly terminated at that time, he would still have won a mention in history. Regularly, he was consulting the intelligence chiefs of Europe's exiled governments in London, who were in contact with resistance movements in occupied Europe, for the developing operations against the Germans and the Quislings. He was also monitoring German intelligence plans to establish stay-behind networks if Allied invasion armies advanced through

France. Finally, he contributed to the masterful deployment of the double-cross agents, in Operations Bodyguard and Fortitude, successfully deceiving Hitler into believing that the main Allied landings would be on the Pas de Calais.[82]

The disappointment was to be stranded in London rather than witnessing the kill. SHAEF headquarters did not cross the Channel until two months after the Normandy landings. To his regret, White never heard a bullet fired in battle. Instead, facing only the intermittent danger of the V2 rockets, White shuffled paper and wrote reports. Gradually, his responsibilities expanded to include monitoring the arrest of war criminals and collaborators, the capture of enemy agents, the debriefing of prisoners and the interrogation of escapers. During those weeks he realised that Admiral Canaris had run an idle and corrupt organisation, distrusted by Germany's military chiefs. The Abwehr was an incompetent enemy, easily duped by MI5's double-agents. His analysis in 1939, discounted by his superiors, had proved correct.

By now he understood how easily intelligence services deluded themselves. All the predictions that the assassination of Hitler would be attempted had been discounted by SIS and the JIC.[83] When it occurred on 20 July 1944, it was ignored. In that atmosphere, White's judgment was that of a maverick: 'No event since the outbreak of war has shaken the German administrative machine more profoundly.' He predicted tighter discipline and a hardening of 'the German leaders' determination to resist,' although its capacity 'has been fundamentally weakened'.[84] His report did not encourage any support for anti-Nazi Germans, an omission he would soon regret.

To White's gratification, his contribution to the war effort was being recognised. Walking through darkened corridors, he bumped into Bedell Smith. 'How are things at your end of the business?' White preened himself in the knowledge that Bedell Smith, razor sharp in appreciating detail, had noticed his work. Winning a reputation with the American and the exile governments transformed him into 'a new sort of person for Whitehall'.[85] In his opinion, 'the Americans had the money, the manpower, the weaponry and to some extent the intelligence "know-how" to show themselves and us the way ahead. Mark you, I was often looked on by some of my MI5 colleagues as too pro-American by half.'[86]

At last, at the end of August, White arrived in Paris. SHAEF headquarters had been established in Versailles. Soon after the city's liberation, he established his own headquarters initially in the village of Garches and later in the Rothschild family mansion on avenue de Marigny, off the Champs Élysée, which had been repossessed by his colleague Victor Rothschild. The early days of excitement soon passed. About ten British intelligence officers from MI5 and SIS, including Malcolm Muggeridge, Desmond Bristow and later Kim Philby, shared an unheated building in an atmosphere of developing gloom unrelieved by the full wine cellar. For Bristow, 'It was boring. The war was blowing out. It was all nearly over.'[87]

The contrasting wartime experiences of White and Muggeridge contaminated the atmosphere. Unlike White, the journalist had endured what he believed was a wasted posting in Mozambique and returned hugely sceptical of intelligence and the war. Disillusioned by wartime politics, his task was to round up collaborators. Acting contrary to his orders, he had sought to aid the escape of P.G. Wodehouse, who during the war had broadcast propaganda from Nazi Germany.[88] Irate American officers attempted to deport Muggeridge back to Britain. Countering that order, White lamented that his friend, while an able intelligence officer, was dissolute. In return, Muggeridge condemned White as 'ineffectual'.

Muggeridge's uncertain loyalties were further displayed, to White's puzzlement, in a contretemps over several meals with Rothschild and Philby, a signal for what became explicable only six years later. Shortly after arriving in Paris, Philby and Rothschild had agreed that the Russians should have been given the Ultra intercepts. Muggeridge disagreed. White witnessed a furious argument which culminated in Rothschild grabbing a few Ultra messages, storming from the house and pushing the papers through the Soviet embassy's letter-box. Later that night, Philby and Muggeridge, both drunk, staggered past the Soviet embassy as Philby, 'demented' by the difficulties he had experienced in penetrating the Soviet Union on behalf of SIS, waved his fist at the building.[89] White was baffled. A piece of his jigsaw was missing.

As autumn approached, the deteriorating atmosphere in the small mess was aggravated by the cold. White began to seem adrift, shy and lacking any sense of social importance. His appearance in a brigadier's uniform fuelled his sensitivity about surviving the war without risk. His private life was also a source of chiding. Over dinner with Rothschild, Christopher Harmer, an MI5 double-cross officer, asked his superior why, at thirty-eight, he was still unmarried. White blushed, but there was no explanation.

The personal disillusionment reflected the mood of acrimony sweeping the Palace of Versailles, SHAEF's headquarters, towards the end of September. Ever since 22 August, when Eisenhower, after several arguments with Montgomery, had announced his total control over all the Allied armies, White had sympathised with the American.[90] Eisenhower's differences with Montgomery intensified on 23 September. Six days earlier, Montgomery had dispatched 11,000 British and American airborne troops to capture a succession of canal bridges around Arnhem, Holland. In the days prior to the attack, he had been given intelligence reports showing unexpected German reinforcements in the area, but he had ignored the warnings. On the 23rd, a retreat was ordered. The defeat had cost about 8000 Allied troops and put an end to any civilised relationship between Montgomery and Eisenhower. The atmosphere in Versailles reminded White of 'an overcrowded, sinister whispering gallery in which daily distortions became exaggerated'.

The arguments continued throughout the autumn and into the winter. To solve the dispute, on 12 December Churchill hosted a dinner for Eisenhower and the British chiefs of staff. But when the guests departed nothing had been resolved. Four days later, Montgomery issued a directive in which he declared that the Germans 'cannot stage major offensive operations'.[91] While his directive was still being distributed, the Wehrmacht launched a massive attack through the Ardennes. Again, Montgomery had ignored intelligence warnings. At SHAEF headquarters, White was bombarded with requests for information. As the mayhem diminished towards the end of the month, his reports were soothing. The situation 'was not immediately unstable but needs watching'.

Soon after, paradoxically, White's affection for Eisenhower began to diminish. The cause was the supreme commander's refusal to allow a British assault from Hanover to capture Berlin before the Red Army. Instead, he sanctioned an American push into southern Germany. In a personal message to Stalin on 28 March, he disclosed that the capture of Berlin would be entrusted to the Red Army. For the first time White was visibly outraged by the conduct of his superiors.

American commanders, including Bedell Smith, had become convinced that the Werewolf, the Nazis' putative resistance movement, would wage their final, prolonged resistance from a National Redoubt constructed around Berchtesgaden in Bavaria. An 'unproven fantasy' was White's dismissive view of the American obsession. But it was an obsession reflected in a SHAEF intelligence summary at this time:

> the main trend of German defence policy does seem directed primarily to the safeguarding of the Alpine zone ... Here, defended both by nature and by the most efficient secret weapons yet invented, the powers that have hitherto guided Germany will survive to reorganise insurrection; here armaments will be manufactured in bomb-proof factories, food and equipment will be stored in vast underground caverns and a specially selected corps of young men will be trained in guerrilla warfare, so that a whole underground army can be fitted and directed to liberate Germany from the occupying forces.[92]

'This thing has been blown up out of all proportion,' stormed White to anyone listening in Versailles.[93]

Seven months in Paris had transformed White's benign tolerance of communists. Conversations with French resistance leaders rebuilding the country's security apparatus had awoken him to the danger of trusting Stalin. The reality within the French resistance during the occupation had been sharp antagonism between the right-wing and communist groups. As the end of the war approached, the battle for the control of France seemed inevitable. The French communists, White understood, freed from the constraints of war, would ally themselves to Moscow rather than Washington.

On a recent trip to London, White had noticed a growing conviction among the foreign policy establishment, led by Anthony Eden, that its analysis of Stalin's intentions had been faulty. The foreign secretary had relied upon Sir Archibald Clark Kerr, the British ambassador in Moscow who, according to his staff, was 'a virulent Soviet-hater but obsessed with the need to establish good relations with the Russians if a third war was to be avoided. He always put the best interpretation on their behaviour.'[94] New information proved the opposite. Stalin was refusing the United States and Britain access to liberated Poland. White's colleagues were complaining about the Russian refusal to co-operate. Yet American pressure on Churchill to make every effort to please Stalin was intense. Roosevelt's last cable to Churchill before his death in April 1945 urged the prime minister to 'minimise' the Soviet problem and trust that differences with the Russians were usually 'straighten[ed] out'.[95]

Churchill's misgivings about communists in Britain had been registered one year earlier. On 14 April 1944, in the aftermath of the Teheran summit with Stalin and Roosevelt, he had noted, 'We are purging all our secret establishments of communists because we know they owe no allegiance to us or to our cause and will always betray secrets to the Soviet, even while we are working together . . .'[96] The purge was fictitious, but SIS under Menzies had never stopped fearing communism. 'We've been penetrated by the communists,' Menzies told Angleton in 1944, mindful of MI5 reports, 'and they're on the inside, but we don't know exactly how.'[97] His only sanction was to dissuade MI5 from liaising with Soviet intelligence as 'a waste of effort and an embarrassment'. The Russians, Menzies sniped, are 'more interested in penetrating our intelligence than in helping'.[98]

In the early months of 1945, SIS officers anticipated that the Red Army would prove to be a weapon of deliberate obstruction, while MI5's reports from agents in the British Communist Party indicated the development of a new, brazen loyalty to the revolution. Stalin, it appeared, had laid a smokescreen over his intentions in post-war Europe. Any doubts in White's mind were removed by Klop Ustinov, the Russian-born German whose distrust of the Soviets was more instinctive than his own.

White was bold on his return to Versailles, openly criticising the American policy of handing Berlin to the communists. He was reminded of his student discussions in Michigan, where Americans had expressed their distrust of British imperialism. Eisenhower's staff were blind to communist imperialism. In conferences, White voiced opposition to the Allied demand for Germany's unconditional surrender. The policy had prevented the Allies taking advantage of the July plot: 'It gave the Russians an unnecessary advantage, and the Allies never really produced a credible united front.'[99] Informally, he proposed a scheme to assassinate Hitler 'to shorten the war'. His proposal was rejected by the American planners, who countered that the operation would need the co-operation of a German resistance group. By acknowledging their assistance, the Allies would be compelled to compromise the demand for unconditional surrender. 'The Americans insisted that we couldn't trust any Germans and therefore we ignored their approaches.'[100] White had become disillusioned.

His condemnation of American policy won a personal rebuke from Bedell Smith for bringing counter-intelligence into ridicule: 'You stand in imminent danger of being dismissed. What in God's name are you trying to prove? In my book, what you've been telling people amounts to stabbing your own friends in the back.'[101] Having 'one almighty strip torn off me' was a salutary lesson. The task of the intelligence officer, he now concluded, was never directly to contradict his superiors but to 'assume' that they were arguably right. Watching the Americans making plans to 'surround' the mythical Redoubt, White felt more confused and hurt than humiliated: 'It was a hollow dilemma.'

In retirement, White would criticise himself for 'following the party line' and for 'failing to strike out' and confront his superiors with a different opinion. He reasoned that, had he confided to trusted and important military commanders his opinion that Eisenhower and Bedell Smith were following a bogus trail, he might have prevented 'things sliding and slipping out of my grasp'. The subsequent confession of General Omar Bradley fuelled his irritation: 'It [the Redoubt] grew into so exaggerated a scheme that I am astonished that we could have believed it as innocently as we did.'[102] But Bedell Smith never recanted.

One month after Germany's unconditional surrender, on 10 June, White and other SHAEF staff were called to a ceremony to receive awards. On Eisenhower's personal recommendation, White was awarded the Legion of Merit in the degree of Legionnaire. During the drive to the ceremony, White voiced his embarrassment that he, as a non-combatant, unlike the hundreds of thousands of young men who had died or suffered wounds, should be rewarded. 'Take what's being offered,' said his companion. 'Now and then you have a needless way of eating far too much humble pie.'

In bright sunshine, after Montgomery's own receipt of a medal, White's citation was read: 'It was largely due to the exceptional individual efforts of this officer that the . . . counter-intelligence agencies of the United States, Great Britain and France were joined together in the common production of special intelligence, the excellence of which was a major contribution to the success of Allied counter-intelligence in Europe and the resulting destruction of the German intelligence operations.'[103] White would also be given the Croix de Guerre. Having been awarded an OBE in 1942, he received no additional award in Britain.

At the celebratory party, White expressed fears for the future: 'We're not yet in sight of our immediate targets. Don't forget the disbanding of SHAEF may leave us clinging to the wreckage, unless we have a few lucky breaks in the meantime.'[104] His complaint, echoed by others, was that by dividing the government of Germany into separate zones, the West was weakening itself in the face of the single Soviet zone. To criticise the Russians so forthrightly was still impolitic, but White's suspicions had become hardened by his first personal encounter with senior communists.

The saga had begun on 5 June, just over a month after Admiral Dönitz, having broadcast the news that Hitler was dead, had signed Germany's unconditional surrender. At a meeting in Berlin between Marshal Georgi Zhukov, the Red Army commander, and Eisenhower, Soviet officers revealed that the charred corpses of Hitler and Eva Braun (the mistress he married immediately before their suicide) had been exhumed near the wreckage of the Führer's Chancellery. White received the report the following day. Four days later, everything changed.

At a press conference, Zhukov revealed some dramatic details of Hitler's last days. Then a subordinate officer rose and declared that Hitler's fate was unknown. The Soviets suspected that he was probably still alive. Rumours began circulating. Hitler, it was confidently whispered, had escaped from Berlin and was hiding somewhere in Western Europe, possibly in Spain. The fantasies became 'reality' on 15 June, when newspapers reported Eisenhower's remark that 'Hitler may not be dead.'

It was vital, White was convinced, to establish the truth about Hitler's fate. But an investigation depended upon Soviet co-operation, and access to Berlin required a request by the highest authority. By chance, on his return to Paris from Germany, Eisenhower collided with White at the SHAEF headquarters.

'Have you completed your unfinished task without breaking your neck in the process?' asked the American.

'I believe, sir, we've got a reasonably good chance provided none of us try to cut too many corners.'

'Do you need extra help for sorting out the Nazis?'

After general conversation, White explained the enigma of Hitler's fate: 'Would you authorise an approach to the Russians and allocate resources to investigate Hitler's death? For the sake of posterity,' he added.

'I'll think it over', replied Eisenhower. The supreme commander had recalled an earlier problem. Four months previously, Eisenhower had written to Zhukov, suggesting that White should visit Moscow to negotiate a joint intelligence operation against the Nazis. To Eisenhower's and White's surprise, the offer had been peremptorily rejected. Subsequently, White became convinced that Philby's disclosures to Soviet intelligence had prompted the veto.[105]

Nevertheless, Eisenhower, decided to approve the investigation and White was surprised to hear that the Soviets had agreed his flight to Berlin: 'Their fears had been transformed into curiosity.' Brigadier White was invited to visit the ruins of the Chancellery accompanied by senior Soviet officers. Like so many Allied officers, he did not conceal the extraordinary impact upon him of walking among the ruined masonry, smashed furniture and scattered documents where only weeks earlier Hitler had ruled the Reich. Even forty years later, he recalled those moments vividly.

After a succession of toasts at a preliminary morning vodka session, White brought matters to a head by asking directly: 'Where was Hitler buried. Are there any bones? Have you taken any imprint of the teeth from the corpse?'

A senior Soviet officer drunkenly roared, 'You want to find Hitler's teeth? You can't discount this sort of valuable testimony as proof of his death, can you?' and slammed down on the table a set of dentures. 'Here are Hitler's false teeth,' he laughed.

'The Soviets were laughing up their sleeves,' White realised. Hitler's teeth had never been extracted. 'But they were polite and open.' The Chancellery ruins had been ransacked, but not professionally searched by Soviet intelligence officers. During his own tour, White found a book which turned out to be the diary of Heinz Linge, Hitler's personal servant. Discreetly, he pocketed it.

White returned to Paris persuaded that Hitler was dead. Swiftly, he completed his transfer to Germany. SHAEF had been disbanded on 10 July, and White had been appointed by Montgomery as chief of counter-intelligence in the British zone based at the headquarters in Bad Oeynhausen, a few miles north-west of Herford in Rhine-Westphalia. Their relationship, believed White, had already become 'very close'. He was pleased to be based in Germany rather than England. 'It was a relief to be away from the awful London scene.'[106]

The atmosphere in St James's had become unpleasant. Petrie's uninspired leadership was about to end but the only internal candidate for the succession, Guy Liddell, had, in the wake of his collapsed marriage and his wife's departure with their children for America, become aggrieved and morose. The search for a new director general outside the service confirmed that Whitehall's wave of self-congratulation for wartime successes did not extend to MI5.

Although the service had successfully protected the country from German subversion, and preliminary examination of German intelligence had revealed the success of the double-cross operation, insiders knew that the glory was partly founded on an unpalatable truth: that the Abwehr was a flawed opponent, foolish and incompetent. Not surprisingly, British officers did not seek to minimise their own achievement by publicly diminishing their enemy. After all, the measure of their success depended upon the greatness of their defeated enemy, and it served to emphasise MI5's achievement if they could preserve the myth of German effectiveness.

Well away from that bureaucratic misery, White enjoyed the spoils of victory. Ensconced in a sequestrated castle owned by a baron in the Teutoburg Hills, he lived for the first and only time in his life as a wealthy man. With the services of a butler, a housekeeper and a cook, a succession of friends were invited for good food, the freedom of a wine cellar and long walks in the forest.

The blissful weekends in the castle were some compensation for the disillusion White experienced while working in Montgomery's headquarters. The British military government was operating in darkness: 'We had no policy for post-war Germany.'[107] The absence of political direction was mirrored in the failure of the British army or government to impose an intelligence system in the British zone. Unlike the American zone, where an army of intelligence officers swarmed across the countryside searching for war criminals, scientists and intelligence officers, Montgomery's 21 Army Group boasted a motley collection of officers (whom White blamed for 'shallow thinking') and no counter-intelligence organisation. White was given two months to create one.

Among his responsibilities was the identification and arrest of incriminated Nazis and putting into effect the general policy of denazifying Germany. Within weeks he recognised the hopelessness of his task. The resources available were 'woefully inadequate' and British officers at all ranks opposed the policy. 'I don't know what went wrong that more were not arrested, but the British felt appalled about purging a country. Everyone was weary of the war and wanted to get home and out of the army. Above all, soldiers were prepared to forgive their opposite numbers. There was an irresistible feeling among the British [of the need] to join forces with the Germans.'[108] The avalanche of intelligence and interrogation reports of Nazis, an exciting resource for the Americans, alarmed White. 'To piece all that together, I feared, might go on till Doomsday.'[109]

The British, White concluded, possessed neither the mentality nor the determination to confront and solve the problem. The British Control Commission was staffed mostly by men of low quality, and even those who were neither corrupt nor lazy were adamant that 'We mustn't behave like the Nazis.' Exasperated by the chaos, White was seriously stung by one persistent allegation.

On 12 May, White had received reports that Heinrich Himmler, the SS chief, was in the British zone, probably disguised. The report suggested that Himmler was trying to reach Bavaria. Apart from Adolf Hitler, the self-styled Reichsführer-SS was the most wanted Nazi. White issued a special alert for British intelligence officers. When found, White added, the SS chief was to be handled with special care. On 21 May, Himmler was arrested with two adjutants at a British control point. All three were dressed in uniforms of the Geheime Feldpolizei, a police group which was in the automatic-arrest category. Disguised as a sergeant, Himmler was not recognised. Two days later, he revealed his identity. Contrary to White's orders, Himmler was threatened. Fearfully, he bit on a hollow tooth and swallowed a concealed cyanide capsule.[110]

Himmler's suicide while in British custody aroused American suspicions about Britain's unwillingness to prosecute war criminals. 'There was a lot of misunderstanding,' admitted White, 'and Himmler was treated in the wrong way.' The rumour machine spouted a convincing line. To White's displeasure, the British zone was becoming a safe haven for wanted Nazis, a fact that was soon reported in American newspapers. The flames were fanned in Moscow. Stalin told James Byrne, the American secretary of state, 'Hitler is certainly alive,' and a senior Kremlin official publicly asserted that Hitler and Eva Braun were living, protected by the British, in Germany. Hitler's fate had become inextricably linked to Soviet accusations about British leniency towards Nazi war criminals.

By coincidence, in the midst of that campaign, Hugh Trevor-Roper, a history and classics graduate from Christ Church, was spending the weekend with White in Riehlkirchen. 'I'm fed up with the Russians,' White confided in fury to his fellow intelligence officer. 'They refuse to tell us about Hitler's fate. We've had stories that he was murdered in Berlin replaced by accounts that he's alive on a Baltic island or escaped to South America on a submarine. Now, it's worse.' Convinced by his own investigation in Berlin that Hitler was dead, he asked Roper to fulfil his last intelligence operation and produce the definitive report of Hitler's fate.

Travelling across Germany, Roper found eyewitnesses to Hitler's suicide and three copies of his last will. In November, White presented the conclusive evidence at a formal session of the four Allies in Berlin. Days later, he presented the same report to the JIC in London. He demanded that precedent be broken and the intelligence report be published as a book. Menzies had declared his opposition.

'C just said no but gave no reasons,' White reported to Roper. 'The Royal Navy chap replied, "If you've got no reasons, then it should be published."' White added. 'I'm a member of the JIC and got it through.'[111] *The Last Days of Hitler* became a bestseller, establishing Roper's reputation as a historian.

Bemusement in the face of Soviet distortions was matched by dismay about contradictory policies followed in the American zone. While the US military government hounded Nazis with ferocity, officers in the Counter-Intelligence Corps and OSS were negotiating with German intelligence officers for their services. Emphatically, White refused any relationships with those Germans: 'I would have objected to the use of a Nazi as an agent, and the prospect never arose.' Unknown to him, while he was rejecting outright offers by Abwehr officers to co-operate against the Russians, and while British officers were arresting members of the staff of Reinhard Gehlen, responsible for military intelligence and counter-intelligence against the Red Army, 'The Americans were negotiating with Gehlen and didn't tell us. And that was just for a start'.[112] Equally irritating, American intelligence officers were 'pinching' British agents.[113]

The confusion was complete. Britain's pre-eminence in intelligence was evaporating and among the casualties was the wartime alliance with American intelligence. The American army, five times bigger than the British in Germany, was deploying hundreds more intelligence officers with unlimited resources across Europe. SIS, bereft of successes in Germany, was a poor relation of its erstwhile pupil.

In early 1946, White finally departed Germany. For the first time, he was returning to a marital home, abandoned just one day after his wedding. During the war, he had met Kate Bellamy, a serious, capable divorcee with one daughter, Jenny. Introduced by his brother Alan, who had published two of Kate's novels, marriage at first had seemed impossible. MI5 officers were still expected to resign if they married divorcees or if their own marriages ended in the courts. Petrie had agreed to waive the rule. On 28 November 1945, White was married in a London registry office. He and Kate passed the evening with Alan and his wife at a theatre and restaurant, before spending the night in a freezing flat off Sloane Square. Their first home at 83 Highgate West Hill, in north London, was shared with Kate's daughter. 'Boldness is all, in wedlock and war,' White remarked of his abrupt abandonment of bachelorhood.

But there were two sources of dissatisfaction. His finances were poor. Indeed, in the absence of an inheritance and with only limited savings, White's financial situation would remain unsatisfactory throughout his life. There was also disillusion. Germany's defeat had deflated the prospects in counter-intelligence. There appeared to be no enemy.

The half-completed jigsaw was still invisible.

CHAPTER FOUR

Dangerous Innocence

The aristocracy had deserted MI5. Prominent among the misfits who remained were commuters from the suburbs – men who rarely read books, loved golf and were not listed in *Debrett's*. Tempted to join the post-war exodus of the 'best and brightest', White was reconciled to the fact that at the age of forty his prospects beyond intelligence were meagre. Unlike those shining wartime recruits drawn from the professions and universities who had abandoned government service to return to lucrative and glittering careers, he could not establish an alternative occupation. With minimal savings and no pension, it was, he confessed, 'an awful anticlimax.'[1] Tar Robertson welcomed him back to London with the words, 'It's just ticking over.'

MI5 offered few excitements other than Mary Holland's cooking in the top-floor canteen of Leconfield House, MI5's new headquarters in Curzon Street. Despite food rationing, the chef daily produced outstanding food, 'even whitebait', which helped to relieve the institutional tedium of brown-linoleum corridors, colourless offices and smudged typewritten memos still passing between the gentlemen and the ranks – the intelligence officers from minor public schools against the technicians, the providers of Special Facilities. Divided socially, they remained bound by their patriotism.

Compared to wartime, counter-intelligence in 1946 seemed desultory. There was neither an obvious enemy nor the stimulation of working with an army fighting for national survival. While an operation in wartime might presage historical consequences, in 1946 an operation was likely to involve two watchers and a communist diplomat – the inconsequential result to be filed with thousands of similar report sheets. Intelligence services, to many, seemed justified only during a national emergency. White's dissatisfaction was exacerbated by the appointment of Petrie's successor.

Clement Attlee, Britain's new Labour prime minister, and particularly his more socialist colleagues, influenced by their wartime encounters with MI5 officers, suspected that the service's activities were uncontrolled. MI5, they complained, was a secret conservative group with a historic mission to destabilise the Left. Their fear of surveillance by the secret police required that MI5's new director general should not be hostile to Labour's cause. Recognising the threat Petrie had attempted to prevent MI5's emasculation. On the eve of his retirement in autumn 1945, he had successfully resisted Whitehall's attempts to weaken MI5's powers, to place the service under either direct ministerial or SIS control, and had prevented encroachment on its activities by the police. But he could not persuade the government that his successor should be the internal candidate, Guy Liddell.

To the shock of all MI5 officers, Attlee appointed Percy Sillitoe, a former chief constable of Sheffield and Glasgow as MI5's director general. 'He's an honest policeman,' commented Attlee, provoking White's instant and unforgiving dislike: 'He didn't understand intelligence.'[2] Sillitoe, he complained, possessed the intellect and subtlety one expected of a common policeman: 'One did not need to know Sillitoe well to dislike him.' But unlike other colleagues, who treated Sillitoe like a body rejecting a transplanted organ, White exercised some self-restraint and hid his anger. For he was above all a team player, instinctively loyal and imbued with pride in the service.

Sillitoe was not blind to the antagonism: 'When I joined it I found it so extremely difficult to precisely find out what everyone was doing . . . Some of the blame for my early puzzlement rests, no doubt, with me. I was now among men of a type different from those who had previously worked under me.'[3] Irritated that he could not command 'unquestioning obedience to rules and a scrupulous respect for discipline', he was baffled by his subordinates' failure to volunteer their secrets and wondered 'uneasily what precisely my role was to be'. In particular he would receive only begrudging help from an identified clique which included Liddell, his deputy. All were secretly delighted by the new director general's ignorance of the Ultra secret[4] and even spoke Latin in his presence to emphasise their superiority.[5] Fearing the cabal, Sillitoe ordered a glass partition to be cut in the door of Liddell's office to enable him to identify his deputy's visitors.

There were, however, good reasons for the appointment of an outsider. MI5 could not return to its cosy, pre-war existence. Intelligence required trained, professional officers trusted by the government. Even so, a brash policeman was hardly the appropriate instrument for the reforms White had contemplated in a plan drafted during his last weeks in Germany. Despite their differences, Sillitoe was impressed by White, tall, well built, his sharp blue eyes, easy style, lack of self-importance and wartime experience setting him above and apart from his less well-endowed colleagues.

On his return to Leconfield House, White had been appointed head of B Division, MI5's principal section responsible for counter-espionage. The main target was once again British communists and the Soviet Union – a seemingly more limited prey than in wartime, and a target which White had never previously covered. Britain's defence against Soviet espionage was managed between Liddell and White. Their relationship, said White, remained close. 'We worked quite well together because I was young enough to know all the detail and carry it in my head. He was wise enough to have some of the tricks of the trade.'[6]

The officer directly responsible for communist subversion was still Roger Hollis, whose aloof manner, partly caused by an unhappy marriage, had not endeared him to many colleagues. White remained an admirer. During the war, Hollis had proved himself cynical about the British communists' sudden conversion to the Allied cause and had resisted the suggestion that MI5 might co-operate with Soviet intelligence against the Germans. His briefing to White was reassuring about MI5's continued penetration of the Communist Party but uneasy about the employment of known communists by the British government. The wartime suspicions of Soviet penetration, suspicions nursed especially by Menzies, had not changed but the evidence was non-existent.

The official tolerance of communists was still operative. MI5 was hampered by the Labour government from carrying out overt investigation of communist penetration. Hollis had counted at least eight crypto-communists among Labour members of parliament,[7] whose presence in the Commons reflected the government's refusal to allow a purge of the civil service. 'It's a problem,' agreed White.[8] The government was also restricting MI5's observations of Soviet intelligence in Britain, although MI5's limitations were also, for all White's protestations, self-inflicted.

Monitoring of Soviet activities in London depended upon interception of mail and telephone calls, and MI5's watchers following suspected intelligence officers. Soviet codes were unbreakable and, for political and practical reasons, White had not considered penetrating the embassy. In 1946, neither he nor Liddell had any information about Soviet intelligence activities which did not involve their known sympathisers in the British Communist Party. 'No one had sufficiently thought about the communist threat, and the moment I thought about the Russians,' admitted White, 'I realised it was a completely new and uncharted quantity.'[9] MI5, he realised, 'needed real knowledge on how the Russians were working,' and his best source, he decided, would be case-work to 'build up the picture'.[10]

White was operating in circumstances markedly different from those which had prevailed over the previous decade. There were no captured documents or prisoners of war to interrogate, suspects could no longer be arrested and held indefinitely until they confessed, and the critical ability to read the enemy's communications by decoding their radio signals had disappeared. All the ingredients of MI5's wartime successes were missing, yet the officers' resulting self-esteem had been given a new mystique: a heroic self-image of the Security Service's superiority against the monolithic Russians. MI5 officers, including White, had become 'over-confident'.[11] 'I could put some strength and clarity into the effort,' asserted White, who was starting from scratch. But the first lesson had been ignored by Hollis and Liddell even before his return to Britain.

[1] At Oxford, Dick White excelled as an athlete, setting the record for the mile along the Illfley Road. His great disappointment was to run second in the historic 1927 race against Cambridge.

[2] White's friendships with other athletes would last until he joined MI5 (right and below); White, sailing to the United States to study for two years as a Commonwealth scholar (bottom). His sympathy for America would reinforce the close relationship between the two countries' intelligence services.

[3] Guy Liddell, MI5's deputy director general (above, left), recruited White (below, right) in 1936 and became a close friend; Major General Sir Vernon Kell, the director general of MI5 (above, right) in 1936 employed just thirty officers; Kell's reign was abruptly terminated in 1940 when he was replaced by Sir David Petrie (below, left), a critic of the security service.

[4] During the Second World War, White (top, left and right) supervised the successful 'Double X' operations and then, attached as counter-intelligence supremo to SHAEF, won wide recognition and the rank of brigadier general for his achievements. His diplomacy won over many fellow officers, including Felix Cowgill (right), the suspicious SIS counter-intelligence chief eventually undermined by Kim Philby.

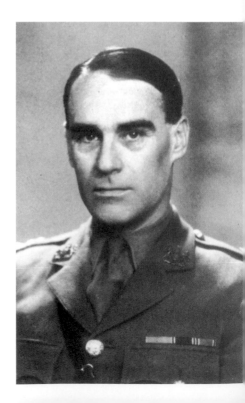

[5] The atomic spies, Klaus Fuchs (above, right) (deported after completing his jail sentence) and Alan Nunn May (left), were White's first serious encounter with communist espionage. Fuchs was persuaded to confess by Henry Arnold (top, right) and the special branch officer William Skardon (top, left). White lost confidence in Skardon for too readily accepting pleas of innocence from suspected agents.

[6] White did not realise until too late that MI5's investigation of Donald Maclean (below, left), the Foreign Office diplomat, as a Soviet spy would explode into a horrendous saga. The first hint was the simultaneous disappearance of Guy Burgess (above, right), another Foreign Office diplomat. Their escape from Britain was masterminded in London by KGB officers Yuri Modin (above, left) and Nikolai Korovin (below, right).

[7] George Carey Foster (left), responsible for Foreign Office security in 1951, was as baffled as Sir Percy Sillitoe (below), MI5's disliked director general, photographed on his departure to Washington in June 1951, about the penetration of the British foreign service by Cambridge educated Marxists.

[8] Kim Philby's (above) public exoneration in 1955 by the British government infuriated White but initially pleased both Sir Stewart Menzies, SIS's retired chief (below, left) and Nicholas Elliott (below, right), the SIS officer who in 1963 finally extracted a confession from the traitor.

On 5 September 1945, Igor Gouzenko, a cipher clerk based in the Soviet embassy in Ottawa, had defected to the Royal Canadian Mounted Police. For two years, he had encoded and decoded messages between Ottawa and the Moscow headquarters of Soviet military intelligence, GRU. In his briefcase, Gouzenko had brought *prima facie* evidence of an enormous Soviet spy ring penetrating the most sensitive activities in Canada, the United States and Britain. His offerings were of monumental importance, not merely to the intelligence services but to the West's relations with the Soviet Union. Overnight, President Truman's impression that he could continue the friendly wartime relationship with Stalin was undermined.

News of Gouzenko's defection was dispatched to London, where it was handed to Kim Philby, by then the head of SIS's Section IX, the Soviet department. Philby had just dealt with another defection which, unlike Gouzenko's, posed a direct threat to his own duplicity. John Reed, the first secretary at the British embassy in Turkey, had sent a message from Istanbul that Konstantin Volkov, an intelligence officer at the Soviet embassy, was offering the names of three British government officials who were Soviet agents: two in the Foreign Office and the third head of a counter-espionage service in London. In return Volkov wanted £27,500 and passage for himself and his wife to Cyprus.[12] After consulting Nikolai Kreschin, alias Max, his Soviet controller in London, Philby, by revealing Volkov's offer to defect and hastening the Russian's arrest, contrived to prevent his own exposure. He then sought out Guy Liddell to discuss Gouzenko's debriefing. They agreed that Roger Hollis should question the defector.

MI5's communist expert flew to Canada to meet Gouzenko on the shores of Lake Ontario. The defector had already exposed more than a dozen GRU agents and sources, but of particular interest to Hollis was the revelation that a British scientist, Allan Nunn May, a participant in the so-called Tube Alloys research team developing the atomic bomb in Chalk River, near Montreal, was a Soviet source and had provided details of the new weapon to Moscow.

Hollis found the whole experience unpleasant. Defectors,

he reasoned, were deserters or, worse, traitors, distastefully different from captured Abwehr agents. Untrained in the art of debriefing, he looked uncomfortably at the squat, ugly stranger whose nervousness was not lessened by his shy questioner. Gouzenko was ready to unburden himself with an unprecedented insight into the sophistication of Soviet espionage.

Ottawa had been the centre of GRU's web across north America, a centre not only for spying but for establishing untraceable 'illegals': using Canadian communists employed inside the civil service, valid documents had been produced to transform Soviet intelligence officers into 'Canadian' nationals, who then moved to the United States. But Hollis was unwilling to hear descriptions of the Soviets' talent. Nor did he want to hear about GRU's insertion of a trusted Canadian citizen, with no connections to the Communist Party, into the prime minister's office. Without Gouzenko's defection, she would have remained undiscovered. Instead of tickling Gouzenko's vanity and absorbing lessons about Soviet intelligence techniques, Hollis abruptly left the defector after just one hour and flew back across the Atlantic to chase Nunn May, now living in London.

The incompetence was compounded. Surveillance of Nunn May had been unrewarding (because, according to Philby, he had tipped off Soviet intelligence),[13] but, when confronted by Leonard Burt, a Special Branch officer, the physicist confessed to spying. There was no more information. The policeman's style froze for ever any chance of identifying the traitor's Soviet contacts. On 1 May 1946, Nunn May was sentenced to ten years' imprisonment.[14]

Nunn May's conviction should have embarrassed MI5. At Cambridge, he had been a vocal communist, protesting against Britain's 'imperialist war' with Germany, yet MI5 had not vetted his recruitment in 1942. But, despite newspaper reports of the scientist's activities, MI5 was not accused of incompetence. Nor was there any internal recrimination. So many left-wing academics had entered government service that the lapse was conveniently deemed excusable. The greater sin was the failure of Hollis, Liddell and later White to initiate a security check of every other scientist involved in the atomic programme. Nunn May was regarded as another aberration.

Inside Leconfield House, the best of the counter-espionage personnel, the meticulous female researchers, identified Hollis as the weak link. 'MI5', Hollis told Anne Glass, 'is a counter-espionage service. We fight subversion. We don't monitor every communist.' His motives were born not of liberalism but of laziness and folly, a state of affairs that was not altered by White's arrival. Individual communists, White agreed, were not to be investigated and Soviet diplomats were not to be approached. The ambivalence was rooted in the government's lingering uncertainty whether Russia was an unfriendly target. White was obeying orders, serving the Whitehall machine: the customer was always right. His duty was to ensure that his fellow countrymen could sleep safely at night. Britain's defence against espionage did not include taking the initiative to discover the enemy's intentions. B Division did not even toy with the notion of recruiting communist diplomats based in London as spies or as 'defectors in place'.[15]

Swinton's complaint six years earlier had not been remedied. MI5 had not become an investigative agency. Assessing Soviet intelligence successes across Europe during the Nazi era, especially the huge Red Orchestra (Röte Kappelle) network – which implied penetrations and operations still unimagined by MI5 – was assigned by Liddell to researchers, Eve Stretfield and John Gwyer, rather than to investigators. Their backroom efforts, regarded as no more than an intellectual chore, were soon forgotten. B Division's only response to Nunn May's conviction was to direct Michael Suppell, one of its more intelligent officers, to write an 'assessment' of Soviet intentions.[16]

On that note, White arranged in October 1946 to revisit Palestine, a British Mandate territory where MI5's control of security was slipping. On his first visit in July 1946, he had survived the Irgun's destruction of the King David Hotel in Jerusalem. The challenge to the British government by terrorists was answered by Attlee's public refusal to consider the establishment of a Jewish state. Faced by the Security Service's demands for drastic reprisals, Attlee officially forbade 'severe action', but his orders were ignored.[17] White had returned to London to seek clarification of government policy. On 27 October, the day after his first son, Adrian 'Johnny', was born, he returned to Palestine no less mystified. His departure did not go unnoticed.

The headline in the *Daily Telegraph* read: 'Troopship mystery man'. The report described an 'important passenger' on the *Duchess of Bedford* troopship:

> He was believed to be travelling incognito, and detectives and army police were in the ship until she left last night. A double berth cabin had been booked in the name of D.G. White. Coded messages awaited his arrival and he was met by an army lieutenant.
>
> The War Office later cleared up the mystery. Colonel D.G. White, of the Intelligence Corps, had been home on leave in the normal way.

He was returning to the Middle East to rejoin his unit, and 'was entitled to travel in civilian clothes when not with his unit'.[18]

As on his later visits to Britain's colonies in the Far East, White was received in Palestine with pleasure by the incumbent senior officers because he could offer dispassionate advice, friendship and support. Brigadier William Magan, the MI5 liaison officer, lamented the declining co-operation from both Arab and Jewish informants as the Zionists, heartened by American support against 'British atrocities', escalated their campaign for a homeland. Finding the terrorists and terminating their activities with the use of considerable violence was not White's choice, but the policy adopted and imposed by the British colonial government. MI5 was operating in a policy vacuum as British authority collapsed. White could offer only comfort, while reflecting that 'An intelligence service is the servant and occasionally the victim of the government it serves.'[19]

White's return to Britain coincided with the arrival in London of Yuri Modin, an English-speaking Soviet diplomat listed as responsible for press relations. In fact, Modin was an officer in Soviet intelligence using the codename Peter. He had been recruited to the NKVD's British Empire section in 1942 aged twenty years. Contrary to MI5's image of a well-managed machine, Modin had discovered that the Soviet intelligence service was chaotic. Stacks of reports from Philby and other British sources remained unread, gathering dust in the archives.

The cause of this neglect was an astonishing assertion by Elena Modrzhinskaya, alias the Blue-eyed Gretchen, an officer in the British section, that the information from the Cambridge Ring was so extraordinary that its authenticity was doubtful. Philby and the others, she believed, were SIS double-agents, deliberately feeding disinformation.[20] Underpinning her analysis was Philby's claim that SIS did not have any agents operating in the Soviet Union.[21] Since that was considered by the NKVD to be ridiculous, Philby was deemed to be lying. British intelligence must, Modrzhinskaya reasoned, have discovered the Cambridge students' left-wing associations before their recruitment and used their background to plant them on the NKVD officers in Britain, all of whom had since been shot by Stalin as suspected spies. It was an extraordinary situation which had been resolved only by Modrzhinskaya's transfer in 1944 and the abandonment of her thesis as the reliability of the information from London served to disprove it.

By then, the pressure of war had reduced staff in the British Empire section to just nine men to cover one-quarter of the globe. Compared to the information supplied from Soviet sources in America and other European countries, the British information, Modin was told, was 'not the most important'. But he soon concluded that 'It was wonderful material.'[22] He had been directed to analyse and grade the material, and then to nominate his agency's five best British sources. The remainder would receive less attention. After fulfilling this administrative chore, Modin worked in the section until his dispatch to Britain to liaise with the network of spies recruited before the war in Cambridge and elsewhere.

Working under the control of Nikolai Rodin, alias Korovin, the tough, professional and unpleasant intelligence chief in London, Modin was successively introduced in a west London public house to John Cairncross and later to Anthony Blunt and Guy Burgess. Cairncross was a former student at Trinity, Cambridge, recruited by James Klugman, a Cambridge student who had worked during the war as private secretary to Lord Hankey, a minister with wide responsibilities including the atomic bomb and the intelligence services and then at Bletchley; after the war he was transferred to the Treasury. In the course of his work, Modin had also met 'a number of Labour MPs, civil servants and journalists'. Some were sources of secret material, others were just 'interesting'.[23]

In theory, operating in London should have been difficult for Modin. MI5's watchers were positioned outside his Bayswater home and were tasked to follow him around the clock. But even in their own city MI5's officers were flummoxed. Inside the embassy, Soviet technicians were monitoring MI5's radio frequencies and providing Modin with his shadows' anticipated movements. If leaving from home, Modin knew precisely at what time the MI5 officers took their regular break for breakfast; and, even if he was followed, thanks to a personal briefing by Blunt about MI5's techniques 'Getting away was easy because they never changed their routine.' Finally, Modin could benefit from MI5's mistakes. The limited numbers of watchers were overstretched because they were following so many Soviet diplomats, wrongly identified as intelligence officers.[24] Having escaped MI5's surveillance, Modin met Burgess and his other sources every two weeks.

By then Burgess, having spent most of the war working as a BBC Radio talks producer, had been appointed the personal assistant to Hector McNeil, minister of state at the Foreign Office. Unlike those who saw Burgess as a repulsive, dishevelled, garlic-chewing, irresponsible pervert, the lazy Labour minister, adopting a minority opinion, became devoted to an exceptionally charming, exceptionally intelligent and engaging conversationalist. From this inner sanctum, Burgess had access to most of the government's foreign policy papers, a cornucopia of sensitive documents at a critical moment, when the four powers were negotiating Europe's future. All those documents were passed to Modin and thence to Vyacheslaw Molotov, Soviet foreign minister, during the actual negotiations.

Burgess's appointment could not be blamed on MI5. Many Labour politicians, like Burgess, had joined the Communist Party briefly in the 1930s and would have rejected any challenge to his appointment. Moreover, the Foreign Office's security was regarded as an internal matter. George Carey Foster, a distinguished wartime officer in Bomber Command, had been appointed the Foreign Office's first full-time chief of security in September 1946. Accommodated in a sumptuous suite in the India Office adjoining the Foreign Office, he was somewhat perplexed: 'At the beginning I sat there not knowing what to do.'[25]

Because Krivitsky's warnings in 1939 had been ignored, security in the Foreign Office was still rudimentary. Vacant offices remained unlocked even if files marked 'Secret' were scattered on the desks, and officials leaving the building were not checked to prevent files being purloined. 'For centuries the Office had operated upon trust,' Carey Foster discovered, 'and in that family atmosphere they couldn't conceive that there was a wrong 'un among them.' He was similarly unaware of the Foreign Office's wartime embarrassments. In Rome, the British ambassador's top-secret papers had been regularly photographed by Italian intelligence, courtesy of a trusted Italian employee in the embassy; the Italians also controlled a valuable source in the Foreign Office in London. Moreover, in the 1930s the Abwehr had read most British ciphers and during the war had bought British secrets from the embassy in Ankara. 'Absolute security,' the Foreign Office appeared convinced, was 'impossible'.[26]

During his introduction to his responsibilities during early 1947, Carey Foster met White. Their conversation about security was a general one and, despite the foreign secretary Ernest Bevin's avowed suspicions of Russia, the two men did not mention the possibility of Soviet infiltration into the Office. But official hostility to the Kremlin's machinations had been declared.[27] One year after Churchill's speech in Fulton, Missouri, when he had described an 'iron curtain' descending across Europe, his host President Truman committed the United States to defeat international communism. On 12 March 1947, Truman's speech to a joint session of Congress promised that the United States would 'assist free peoples to work out their own destinies' and offered help to Greece and Turkey in their struggle against Soviet-inspired subversion. The adoption of this policy, which became known as the Truman Doctrine, was a victory for Ernest Bevin. For nearly two years, he had been urging the American administration to oppose the expansion of Soviet power. During that period, Britain had secretly financed anti-communists in Europe but, paradoxically, MI5's B Division was reacting ineptly to a similar threat in Britain.

In early 1947, Alexander Foote, a Soviet intelligence officer, was posted from Moscow to Washington. *En route* through Berlin, he defected to British intelligence. Foote was a Briton who had been recruited by Soviet intelligence in Spain in 1937 and had spent the war as an NKVD radio operator for the Soviet Lucy ring based in Switzerland. By 1947 he was disillusioned. In the course of his extensive debriefing by Courtney Young, an MI5 officer, Foote provided a richly detailed description of Soviet intelligence.

Among his revelations was the identity of a Soviet intelligence officer codenamed Sonia working in Britain. MI5 identified the woman as Ursula (Ruth) Kuczynski, living in Chipping Norton, near Harwell, the atomic research centre. White ruled out surveillance. The local telephone exchange was too small for the surreptitious installation of a tap; she would be too clever to use the post; and in a village the watchers would not remain unseen for long. White ordered Kuczynski to be questioned immediately.

The task was assigned to Michael Suppell and Jim Skardon, the former Special Branch officer whose affable, pipe-smoking manner did not conceal the absence of the incisive intellect required to destabilise a professional Soviet intelligence officer. Kuczynski admitted that ten years earlier she had been aware of Soviet intelligence when married to a communist in China, but, she insisted, since her divorce, she had had no further contact with politics. In the face of that adamant denial, the policeman bid her farewell. 'She's innocent,' Skardon told White.[28]

Two days after the interview, Kuczynski disappeared. White was 'puzzled' but accepted that, without evidence, Foote's allegations could not be taken further. In fact, Kuczynski had been terrified by MI5's visit and had assumed that further investigation would follow. White's mistake had been not to keep some surveillance after the visit.

The errors were rooted in White's own doubts whether Britain was a major Soviet target. 'The truth', admitted White, 'was [that] Ultra had made British intelligence flabby. We thought we could get by without going back to basics.'[29] MI5's artless tactics towards Soviet intelligence officers in London did not improve his predicament. Following Soviet diplomats through the streets did not fill the gulf of ignorance. Nor did the study of past files in the registry reveal much about the nature of his new enemy. Countless photographs of Soviet diplomats, all of them suspected intelligence officers, taken surreptitiously and marked with speculative comments about their functions, only highlighted MI5's dilemma. Reams of transcripts of intercepted telephone conversations recorded and translated by a team of ageing White Russian and Polish émigrés hoping that the diplomats in Kensington Palace Gardens might momentarily forget that their conversations were tapped had also proved unproductive. The paucity of facts hindered the assessment of Soviet activities in Britain. The darkness was perplexing but the treatment of leads by White's own staff was not helpful. In 1947, for example, R.H. 'Billy' Owen, an SIS officer in Paris, wrote to MI5 observing that the local headquarters of the Soviet trade delegation was in reality an intelligence base. Owen enquired whether that was true of the Soviet trade officers in London. The reply was nonchalant: 'We have not noticed the same.'

MI5 was inherently passive. Recruitment, training and organisation remained unchanged by Sillitoe. B Division under White had still not re-evaluated the activities of Soviet intelligence officers nor issued a guide to their psychological profiles and national characteristics. He did not speak Russian himself but believed he understood the country through its novels, which he 'enjoyed enormously'. White's desk officers likewise did not speak fluent Russian, Polish or any other East European languages. They were discouraged from establishing a relationship with diplomats from the Soviet Union or the new satellite countries. Their task was simply to observe without taking initiatives.

Monitoring left-wing activities in Britain was no less moribund. In 1945, Attlee had forbidden a concerted programme of MI5 infiltration into subversive groups. Ministers and senior officials remained unconvinced about the Security Service. Too many MI5 officers they met were of questionable quality, puzzling specimens whose origins and outbursts suggested fuzzy misunderstanding about the distinction between an aggressive leftist and a subversive. White and a handful of others, the notable exceptions, could not allay the concerns.

Two years later, under pressure from Liddell and White, and more importantly the chiefs of staff, the prime minister agreed to review the evidence. The government's innocence, complained the lobbyists, had become dangerous. Sir Stafford Cripps, the president of the Board of Trade, had agreed to sell twenty Rolls-Royce jet engines, at the time the most advanced in the world, to the Soviet Union. In return, the Soviet Union would supply timber and food. Attlee had agreed that Soviet technicians could be trained in Rolls-Royce's factories to build the engines under licence in Russia. Cripps, opposed to any discrimination against British communists, dispatched Harold Wilson, his junior minister, to Moscow to negotiate further sales of jet aircraft. The negotiations were curtailed by protests from the chiefs of staff and MI5 in London.[30] But neither the chiefs' demand that communists should be blacklisted at establishments carrying out secret work nor White's proposal to increase surveillance of extreme-left agitators operating in factories, the mines and ports was approved.

In March 1948, MI5's reports of increasing subversive activity in Britain coincided with the communist coup in Czechoslovakia, communist-inspired unrest in Italy and France, the breakdown of relations with Russia in Germany, and a plague of war scares in Washington inspired by a telegram on 5 March from General Lucius Clay, the American military governor in Berlin, to the Pentagon that war 'may come with dramatic suddenness'.[31]

On 24 June 1948, Stalin ordered the blockade of Berlin, intended to force the West to abandon the city to the communists. Truman and Attlee were finally persuaded that the Soviet Union was not an ally. The Labour government's overt attitude towards the Soviet Union suddenly changed. MI5 was sent back to war. White was as surprised as the politicians: 'It was only in 1948, at the outbreak of the Cold War, that we were aware that we'd been well and truly let down all the way through the Second World War.'[32] With an enemy in sight, the old war ethic was revived.

Released from political restraints against targeting communists and able to resurrect blacklists of civil servants, White directed the first surveillance of suspected crypto-communists among Labour members of parliament. Their mail was secretly opened, telephone taps were installed and, drawing on the success of Maxwell Knight, White directed increased insertion of agents into subversive movements, including the Communist Party and trade unions. Simultaneously, the surveillance of Soviet and satellite diplomats increased, but the effort was diluted. Although the number of MI5's watchers had been increased, the recruits were less well trained and the number of diplomats from the Soviet's satellite countries had increased. Plodding along pavements and reporting the movement of silent diplomats to deskbound officers in Leconfield House was neither an inspired nor a productive method of discovering traces of Soviet espionage. For the moment, White could not think of a different approach. War had been declared but there was no trace of enemy activity. The first clue was delivered in January 1949.

Sillitoe returned from a trip to Washington that month and summoned White. The director general had been briefed by J. Edgar Hoover, the FBI director, that the Armed Forces Security Agency (AFSA, the predecessor of the National Security Agency) had the previous year, using NKVD codebooks discovered by Finnish intelligence in 1939, decrypted a handful of Soviet messages between America and Moscow. The American operation was codenamed Venona. Decryption of one group of messages dispatched in 1944–5 contained the most secret communications between the British and American governments. In particular, the Soviet informant had disclosed verbatim extracts of telegrams from Churchill to President Truman about the status of the Polish government-in-exile and negotiations between Stalin and Harry Hopkins, the U.S. special envoy. Hoover had already established that over 200 officials, both British and American, had access to those papers. Eliminating the innocent in complete

secrecy was an enormous task. 'I agreed with Hoover', concluded
Sillitoe, 'to total co-operation.'

Hoover, an autocratic but effective director of the FBI, had
never evinced any warmth towards his British colleagues. Unlike
the wartime OSS officers who had created the Central Intelligence Agency in 1947 and continued their close personal
relationships with SIS officers, Hoover had spurned individual
collaboration with British intelligence officers during the war and
did not encourage any change in later years. But his senior officers
adopted a contrasting approach, largely out of necessity to fulfil
the treaty agreement that the FBI and the CIA should co-operate
with British intelligence in the interception and decoding of
radio traffic.

The Anglo-American BRUSA Agreement of 1943 unified the
decrypting efforts of Britain, America, Canada and Australia.
In 1947, a new treaty, the UK–USA Security Agreement, was
signed, dividing the world geographically. Each country was
allocated the collection of SIGINT (signals intelligence, the
interception of radio traffic), and agreed to pool the information.
Canada, Australia and New Zealand eventually became participants.

Under a parallel Anglo-American agreement to exchange
human intelligence and avoid duplication of effort, the four
intelligence and counter-espionage services formally continued
their wartime co-operation. To prove that the partnership was
equal, the British insisted that the centre of liaison should be
in London rather than Washington. The agreement stipulated
that the intelligence agencies of both countries would not operate
in each other's territory without formal permission; that the
Americans would not operate in the British Empire without
permission; and that neither country would recruit a national
of its partner anywhere in the world without consultation and
agreement. In 1947, an American liaison office for the FBI and
CIA had been established in London, while SIS and MI5 posted
liaison officers at the embassy in Washington.

In effect, there was a daily exchange of intelligence information. Every morning, SIS delivered a package to 71 Grosvenor
Street, the CIA's London headquarters, situated above a shop

selling beds and mattresses and rented from MI5. The package contained a summary of reports and analysis collected over the previous twenty-four hours. Simultaneously, the CIA handed over a deciphered message from Washington with similar contents. Through the same exchange, all four agencies also submitted requests for information on targeted personalities and planned operations. For immediate communications, the CIA officers could use the 'scrambler' telephone installed in Grosvenor Street linked to Leconfield House and Broadway Buildings (headquarters of SIS).

Because the Venona investigation was American, the liaison in Washington was conducted initially by Dick Thistlethwaite, MI5's representative, for whom White had considerable respect and affection, and then by his successor, Geoffrey Patterson. Together with Sir Robert Mackenzie, the Foreign Office's security officer in the embassy, the MI5 officers began scrutinising the lists of British officials with access to the telegrams.

MI5's investigation in London was handed by White to Arthur Martin, educated at a grammar school and employed during the war by RSS, the intercept agency. White had been consulting Martin about suspected Soviet intelligence activities in Australia when the Venona material arrived. The investigation would consolidate Martin's position as one of MI5's most outstanding investigative officers.

White next called on Carey Foster. To the surprise of the Foreign Office's security officer, White's demeanour while relating the information was 'very placid'. Whether he was cool or complacent was beyond Carey Foster's immediate judgment. MI5, White explained, expected Soviet espionage and it seemed 'just another case'.[33] Carey Foster's reaction was unambiguous. 'It's inconceivable', he declared, 'that any senior member of the service could be a traitor.' In an era when foreign service officers were a close-knit social group and embassies were more akin to a social gathering than a workplace, it was difficult for Carey Foster or MI5 officers to understand the profile of a British traitor. Everyone, including White, assumed that the traitor was among the lower types – cipher clerks or secretaries.[34]

Carey Foster would work with Martin. The MI5 officer

soon reported that he was hampered by the state of the Foreign
Office registry. The filing system 'had gone to pot during the
war' and was 'still scant'.[35] Martin was also denied the benefit
of the captured Gestapo and Abwehr archives which detailed
the pattern of Soviet espionage throughout Western Europe
before and during the war. The study of the Red Orchestra
network by Eve Stretfield and John Gwyer had grown from
four pages to a completed twenty-seven volumes, but their
work was 'ignored' by MI5 until 1951.[36] Martin's introduction
to Soviet intelligence was methodical but unnecessarily slow. In
Washington, Robert Lamphere, an FBI officer also involved in
the Venona investigation, was 'surprised' when he heard no
reports during the remainder of the year about MI5's work.
But by autumn he was immersed in another dramatic inquiry.

On 23 September 1949, Truman announced that Russia had
exploded an atomic bomb. For White as for every British politician, government official and military officer, it was a stunning
revelation. Since the CIA had predicted that the Russian bomb
would not be completed before 1953 there were good reasons to
suspect treachery. Truman's announcement had been delayed by
two weeks while the intelligence was verified, but the FBI's
Espionage Section was already ferreting to discover whether the
unexpected Russian advance was connected solely to Alan Nunn
May or whether there were other unknown traitors in the
Manhattan Project (codename for the actual construction of the
bomb).[37]

The FBI's search coincided with another monumental breakthrough in Washington by AFSA cryptographers. Two more
Venona messages from Washington to Moscow had been decrypted. One summarised a working document from the Manhattan Project and another identified the author and source
as a British scientist working in New York. The source was
unmistakably identified as Klaus Fuchs, a German-born physicist
who had been recruited to the Manhattan Project from Britain
and in 1949 was working at Harwell. The breakthrough was
passed to White. Reading Fuchs's personal file, White appreciated
MI5's compromised position.

The scientist had been born in 1911, the son of a Lutheran

pastor whose children were all active communists. In July 1933, fearing arrest and imprisonment by the Nazis, Fuchs had fled to Britain on the Communist Party's orders.[38] On arrival, his left-wing opinions were recorded by the immigration officer and passed to MI5. Over the following seven years, Fuchs shone as an outstanding physics researcher at Bristol and Edinburgh universities. That ended in 1940 when, like thousands of other aliens, he was arrested, interned and transported to Canada. By the end of the year, the injustice was recognised and Fuchs returned to Britain.

In the spring of 1941, Dr Rudolf Peierls, a German émigré based at Birmingham University, invited to investigate the feasibility of building an atom bomb, asked Fuchs to join his team. The appointment was delayed. 'There was some difficulty about security clearance,' recalled Peierls, 'and I was told I could not tell him what [the work] was all about . . . But there was no halfway house.'[39]

MI5's file contained two reports identifying Fuchs as a communist. One was written in 1934 by the chief constable of Bristol on the basis of an unofficial message from the German consul in the city. Fuchs was living with a family who were suspected communists and Hitler's representative denounced his countryman as a Soviet spy. In view of the biased source, the information was discounted. The second report was from an infiltrator into the German refugee community who revealed Fuchs's communist activity in Germany which had prompted his flight to avoid arrest by the Gestapo.[40] The file also contained a note recorded by the Enemy Aliens Tribunal. To avoid internment, Fuchs had claimed that he was an opponent of the Nazis, a claim that would later be disputed.[41]

White could see from the file that MI5's vetting of Fuchs was based entirely upon the entries in the file. No officer had conducted interviews or an investigation. 'Between 1941 and 1946 we were busy enough checking subversive organisations,' explained White. 'There was no reason to check Fuchs.'[42] The service, claimed White improbably, had not been told the precise nature of the scientific work which Fuchs would undertake and, in the mood of the moment, after the German invasion of Russia,

MI5 had not categorised Fuchs as a 'danger' to British security.

There was however a convenient caveat. Jane Archer, the MI5 officer directing the communist section, had written: 'Fuchs is more likely to betray secrets to Russians than the enemy.' In White's opinion that could be construed as 'MI5 advised against Fuchs's employment' only for the service to be overruled by a directive from Lord Beaverbrook, minister of State.[43] In the event, Fuchs was given 'a low-security rating' and Archer cautioned, 'Don't let him see more than necessary.'[44]

On 18 June 1942, Fuchs signed the Official Secrets Act. Shortly afterwards he became a British citizen and was fully briefed by Peierls about the atomic project. The following year, Britain agreed to pool its expertise with America and work as a junior partner on the construction of an atomic bomb. Fuchs was transferred with Peierls and a small British team to New York to perfect uranium diffusion. In reply to an American questionnaire about Fuchs's security, MI5 reported that he was politically inactive and unobjectionable.[45]

In 1946, on the basis of Fuchs's outstanding performance in New York and in Los Alamos, New Mexico, he was invited to continue his atomic research at Harwell. The MI5 file, White read, revealed that prior to Fuchs's employment at Harwell, 'inside the holy of holies', there was 'an intensive investigation' by MI5's Russian branch which lasted 'five months,' but 'nothing was discovered'.[46] The 'intensive investigation', White knew, had obviously been limited. Special Branch had been instructed by the government only the year before to target Russia as an enemy and lacked staff and a budget to investigate discreetly Fuchs's background across Europe.[47] Nevertheless, by then MI5 could have discovered from Canadian security officials that Fuchs's principal associate in the internment camp had been Hans Kahle, a well-known German communist organiser and a suspected Soviet intelligence agent. In 1945, Kahle was indeed employed by a Soviet security agency in East Germany.[48]

More embarrassing was the discovery that Michael Suppell, the B Division officer, had reviewed the Fuchs file some months earlier. Two traces of Fuchs had appeared. First, a captured Gestapo document dated 1933 ordered Fuchs's arrest as a communist; and, secondly, a diary seized in Canada following Gouzenko's defection also mentioned Fuchs. Suppell's recommendation that there be an investigation had been ignored.[49]

During his three years' employment at Harwell, Fuchs's work had been highly regarded. He was renowned among the tight community as a shy, unforthcoming bachelor, though he enjoyed a brief affair with a colleague's wife.[50] White's quandary was how to produce independent evidence that Fuchs was a Soviet agent. Espionage, as White would soon tire of repeating, was a crime often devoid of disclosable evidence. Since the Venona decrypts were a closely guarded secret, White and Martin could only brief Henry Arnold, Harwell's security officer, without mentioning the source, that there was 'conclusive information' about Fuchs. Arnold, the MI5 officers hoped, could replace suspicion with evidence to secure a conviction. After July 1949, Fuchs's telephone had been tapped and his mail intercepted. Two months later, Arnold reported that the monitoring had produced no evidence of treachery. But he did suspect that Fuchs was undergoing a crisis and might be entrapped by skilful and gentle questioning.

Since MI5 lacked trained interrogators, White dispatched Jim Skardon to Harwell. The Special Branch officer who, two years earlier, had failed to destabilise Ursula Kuczynski, was also not told by MI5 about the Venona decrypts. Faced once again with a committed ideologue, he was sceptical after his first meeting on 21 September: 'I had no personal confidence when I saw Fuchs that he was guilty.'[51] Skardon's scepticism increased during his conversations: 'You're barking up the wrong tree,' Skardon told White after the second day. 'Fuchs is innocent.'[52] Skardon was on the verge of giving up.

White judged Skardon to be all image and style. He personified the patient and friendly confessor, rather than a ruthless bone-crusher. 'Sincerity', White told Skardon, 'is a wonderful disguise. Go back and continue the questioning.'[53] Skardon was reluctant. Examining the transcripts, neither Martin nor Evelyn McBarnet had found any contradictions in Fuchs's answers.[54] Unaware of Venona, Skardon could find no reason to doubt Fuchs. Eschewing an authoritarian approach, White adopted his instinctive schoolmaster's method: 'I sought to

create understanding rather than obedience. I wanted people
like Skardon to understand and agree what was worth doing.
It taxed my wits to win at the end of the day.'[55] Elliptically,
Martin added his encouragement to Skardon: 'I know he's guilty.'

Just after Christmas, Skardon returned to Harwell and developed a disarming friendship with Fuchs. On 23 January 1950, the
interrogator suggested that the scientist could be still promoted
to direct Harwell if he came clean. After lunch, Fuchs confessed
to his 'new friend'. The extent of Fuchs's treachery astonished
White: 'Nothing less than the full design of the atomic bomb'.
He had become a traitor, the scientist explained, in 1942 after his
recruitment by Peierls: 'I decided to inform Russia.' His contact
was a German-born GRU agent in London. On his transfer to
America, he gave his contact a stream of detailed calculations,
designs and diagrams which enabled Russian scientists to understand how an atomic explosion might be detonated and to build
a facility nearly identical to the American one at Oak Ridge,
Tennessee, where the necessary uranium-235 was manufactured.
On his return to Britain, Fuchs's contact was Ursula Kuczynski,
whom Skardon had interviewed two years earlier. She was to
resurface years later in East Germany.

As Fuchs's debriefing continued, White succumbed to his
contrition and became fascinated by the traitor's profile – a passionate yet intelligently reasoned idealism which was so different
from that of the German double-agents. 'His motives', explained
White, 'were relatively speaking pure. A scientist who got cross
at the Anglo-American ploy in withholding vital information from
an ally fighting a common enemy. They were easily led astray by
the spy rings on the other side of the Atlantic. These consisted
of men carefully selected to prey on such motives.' Endearingly,
White lamented, 'Marx has a peculiar appeal' for scientists.[56]

White's explanation was self-deceptive. Contrary to his notion
of the tormented scientist in the midst of war, Fuchs had been
an active communist since 1932 and had coolly calculated his
espionage. Yet White was even taken in by Fuchs's scathing
condemnation of the 'Russian heavy mob, who had no idea
what he was talking about'.[57] The spycatcher's weakness was his
compassion. Instead of cynical distrust, he squeamishly digested

Fuchs's self-deprecation of his instability. As a child, Fuchs had witnessed his mother's dying gasp – 'Mother, I'm coming' – after she had swallowed hydrochloric acid; both his grandmother and sister had also committed suicide. Human frailty was an easier explanation for MI5's mistakes. Even the truth, Fuchs's own admission that regardless of naturalisation he felt loyalty not to Britain but to the Communist Party, was sentimentalised by White. 'In 1942 there was positive enthusiasm for Russia, who was saving the day against the Nazis.' Security was 'geared to keeping secrets from Japan and Germany'.[58] The corollary, White explained to himself, was someone in Russia giving secrets in 1949 to the United States.

The political ramifications were enormous. A failure by British security had facilitated the Russian atomic bomb programme. The damage report concluded that the Anglo-American alliance was severely embarrassed. There were good reasons to hold MI5 responsible. Not least was White's failure, in the chain of responsibility, to adopt Suppell's suggestion of investigating Fuchs.

Sillitoe's fury, at a meeting with White, Liddell, Robertson and Ronald Read, was breathtaking. 'In future,' roared the director general incoherently, 'you'll do as you're told!' Liddell eventually pacified his superior. Not every recommendation could be checked, he urged, protecting White from further reprimand. After all, Suppell prided himself on suspecting Fuchs, but he had not suspected Ursula Kuczynski, the spy's controller. Counterespionage, Liddell argued, was not like policing. It was agreed that the mistake would be concealed.

Sillitoe and White called on Attlee in Downing Street. The prime minister was briefed that the information available to MI5 after 1933 – that Fuchs was an active communist – had been considered unreliable. White would go further and insist that there had been 'a thorough police investigation' on four occasions which had failed to produce conclusively incriminating evidence.[59] Attlee could only reflect that, if MI5's four investigations had produced no evidence, it was a reflection upon the investigators not the evidence.

On 28 February 1950, Fuchs was sentenced to fourteen years'

imprisonment. Four days later, Attlee defended MI5 in the House of Commons: 'There has been a great deal of loose talk in the press suggesting inefficiency on the part of the security services. I entirely deny that . . . A proper watch was kept at intervals.' That untruth was endorsed by wishful thinking: 'I think we had here quite an extraordinary and exceptional case'.[60] Attlee's misrepresentations, Sillitoe and White knew, were not motivated by sympathy for MI5, but were designed to prevent the collapse of a keystone of the Anglo-American alliance.

In Washington, British officials were negotiating to reverse the recent McMahon Act, which forbade the American Atomic Energy Commission from passing any information to a foreign power.[61] Congress had passed the legislation in 1946, unaware of Britain's wartime participation and of the agreement between Churchill and Roosevelt in 1944 to continue the cooperation after the war. After the McMahon Act, an unofficial relationship had continued, but in 1950 the Attlee government wanted to revive a formal agreement to secure access to America's latest atomic expertise for the building of an independent British bomb. Until Fuchs's arrest and the evidence of MI5's laxity, the negotiations with senators and officials had seemed to be progressing to a successful conclusion.

The Fuchs revelations coincided with a panic sweeping Washington about the communist menace. The new alarm was aroused by China, where one million communist soldiers had swept away the nationalist government. The Marxist takeover unleashed a hunt in Washington for those Americans who had 'lost' China; and in the courts Alger Hiss, a well-known official in the Roosevelt and Truman administrations, was accused of espionage. These feelings of uncertainty fed the fear created by Senator McCarthy's allegation that 200 communists were employed at the State Department. Attlee was told that the Fuchs case terminated any hope of reversing the McMahon Act. For White, it was a salutary lesson of how intelligence directly influenced political negotiations. But it was a lesson lost on Sillitoe.

Sillitoe's behaviour antagonised White. After four years acquaintance, his dislike of his chief was vehement. Sillitoe had even courted publicity at the Old Bailey during Fuchs's trial by giving a press conference. The man apparently refused to understand intelligence, politics or discretion. In early June 1950, their antagonism developed into a crisis. The venue was a meeting in Leconfield House between Bob Lamphere, the FBI agent investigating Fuchs's treachery in the United States, and Sillitoe.

After studying photographs, Fuchs had just formally identified Harry Gold, a member of the American Communist Party, as his contact in Los Alamos and New York. Lamphere had expected that his meeting with Sillitoe would be a informal exchange of gratitude and farewells. Instead, in a stilted policeman manner, Sillitoe complained that MI5 was 'displeased' with Hoover's handling of the case. 'He didn't like Hoover's attempt to get access to Fuchs before the trial,' recalled Lamphere, 'and he didn't like us taking credit for arresting Gold. It was crazy. MI5 would have known nothing about Fuchs without us.' For Lamphere, who believed that 'co-operation with the British was one of the cornerstones on which our own progress in counter-intelligence had been built', it seemed farcical.[62] White thought so too and began to contemplate resigning from MI5.

In America, Lamphere's irritated report to Hoover was temporarily forgotten. Harry Gold's confession had spawned dozens of major investigations across America, revealing an astonishing web of Soviet espionage, embracing Julius and Ethel Rosenberg and a network of American communists controlled from Moscow. Combined with the denunciation of Hiss by *Time* editor Whittaker Chambers and Elizabeth Bentley, both members of the American Communist Party, the FBI was reconstructing an unimagined pattern of Soviet espionage.

The sensational disclosures were effectively ignored by White. He took little interest in the American cases. They were, he asserted, similar to the pre-war Woolwich arsenal case: the straightforward Soviet recruitment of American Communist Party members as spies.[63] A distinction, he declared, should be made between the 'clever, distinguished and well-educated' atomic spies and the inferior types, American citizens who spied in peacetime against their own country.[64] But his understanding of Soviet espionage was flawed. Lessons were ignored because he did not order a painstaking analysis of the Fuchs and American cases in order to discover how the scientist had been managed from Moscow.[65]

The consequence was stark. In the summer of 1950, B Division officers did not anticipate that lapsed members of the British Communist Party might be similarly engaged in espionage. Hoover and his officers were puzzled by MI5's isolation from reality. Moscow's threats appeared as dangerous as the Nazi's. In Washington, Truman was warned that the United States was 'losing the Cold War'. A joint study by the State and Defense Departments circulated in April 1950 as NSC-68 defined the Soviet purpose as 'the complete subversion or forcible destruction of the machinery of government and structure of society in the non-Soviet world, and their replacement by an apparatus and structure subservient to and controlled by the Kremlin'. Truman agreed that, at the next opportunity, Moscow's aggression would be challenged.

On 25 June 1950, 175,000 North Korean soldiers crossed the 38th Parallel and swept towards Seoul. Even to the faint-hearted among the anti-communists, the fears and warnings had proved justified. Attlee's support for war against the communists wavered at the end of November. Alarmed by Truman's readiness to consider using the atomic bomb to stem the communist successes, the prime minister flew to Washington.

The apparent strain in Anglo-American relations over the question of military strategy was of keen interest to Moscow. The Soviets were receiving a steady stream of all the most important exchanges between London and Washington from their source in the Foreign Office, a source which MI5 had still not identified.* Sir Robert Mackenzie, the Old Etonian security officer in the embassy, admitted that the slow pace of investigation was voluntary: 'I fear we put ourselves off.'[66] White put no pressure on the investigators to single out a suspect.[67]

Fuchs's confession had coincided with a new Venona revelation. Arthur Martin reported to White that the leak from Washington

---

* This was denied by Philby (Borovik, *Philby Files*, p. 274), who claimed that Donald Maclean, the Foreign Office traitor, had broken contact with Soviet intelligence in 1949. Yuri Modin contradicts that claim, describing how Maclean passed information through Blunt to the KGB.

of diplomatic secrets was certainly from the British embassy. The Soviet cable had repeated the phrases of a Foreign Office message and, most revealing, included the internal British Foreign Office code on Maclean's telegram. Identifying the Soviet source inside the embassy had narrowed the suspects to thirty-five high-level officials. The source's Soviet codename was known to be Homer. Final identification was a matter of time.

On 21 September, Henry Arnold reported from Harwell a second security alert. Bruno Pontecorvo, an Italian-born experimental physicist, had failed to return from his holiday in Europe. A reconstruction of his background revealed that once again, unknown to MI5, both Pontecorvo and his Swedish wife were communists who had been members of the NKVD's espionage ring in America during the war. By then, Pontecorvo was in Moscow. MI5's investigation by Ronald Read drew 'a complete blank'. Not a single shred of evidence was unearthed even to suggest Pontecorvo's espionage activities. 'We've got no clues,' White was told. Once again, MI5 had embarrassed the government.[68]

To defend himself and MI5 from 'the hammering we're getting in the press', White proposed an unusual palliative. In a personal meeting with Attlee in Downing Street, he suggested that Alan Moorehead, a noted journalist and historian, should write an account of 'the enemy within', defending MI5's record. The initiative, he argued, would reveal the problem of exposing espionage among atomic scientists. Morale, he told the prime minister, was bad. A book would help. Privately, he hoped it would prove his dedication to lifting the shroud over the Security Service.[69] Inadvertently, it would also expose White's mistaken assumptions about Soviet penetration, as MI5 approached its *Götterdämmerung*.

Having signed the Official Secrets Act and accepted an office in the Ministry of Defence, Moorehead was soon repeating White's theme: it was a mistake to believe that 'a man who is once a communist is always a communist'.[70] The three atomic scientists, White persuaded Moorehead, were exceptional cases. Victims of their conscience, their treachery, though criminal, was also understandable. In self-defence, White insisted that discovery of their treachery would have been physically impossible because their contacts with Soviet intelligence officers were rare, brief and unexpected. 'Most men', said White, 'reveal their political beliefs through the work they do, the clubs and associations they join, and the things they say.' Fuchs's life had 'revealed nothing'.[71] Here was the unintended exposure of MI5's desk-bound inactivity. White, the aspiring detective, mirrored the director of the opera house who wanted to sing. And the curtain was about to rise on a consuming tragedy.

By early 1951, by a process of elimination, attention was focused upon six suspects in the British embassy. Arthur Martin's efforts had been aided by a helpful message from Kim Philby, the SIS liaison officer in Washington, whom Martin had known and respected during the war. The SIS officer suggested that MI5 refer to the disclosure by Walter Krivitsky in 1940 that Soviet intelligence had recruited a young Foreign Office official of good family who had been educated at Eton and Oxford. Until Philby's disingenuous message, Martin had not placed much importance on the defector whose description was too wide to be meaningful.

Yet Martin's short list of suspects roughly matched Krivitsky's description. He now turned to the Foreign Office personnel files. Vetting had only recently been introduced and the files proved thin and uninformative. Carey Foster was just as puzzled until he discovered that the Foreign Office held two files on each employee: a personnel file and a private file. White was 'surprised' and then 'annoyed' when told that Sir William Strang, the permanent under secretary, had forbidden MI5 access to the private files. Contemplating a traitor within the Diplomatic Service, Strang exclaimed, was inconceivable.

By the time Strang's veto was removed, Kim Philby was visiting London and called on Carey Foster. As the SIS representative in Washington, Philby was fully briefed on all aspects of the investigation. Carey Foster used the opportunity to invite White to discuss progress. In the course of that brief meeting in Carey Foster's huge room, White told his colleagues, 'You should look for someone who is unstable, living on his nerves. That will be our man.' Carey Foster did not understand. Philby agreed and departed. 'Rather silently, I realise in retrospect,' observed Carey Foster.

On his previous visit to London in summer 1950, Philby had learnt that he was under consideration as a future chief of SIS. Sir Stewart Menzies and John Sinclair, Menzies's designated successor, had agreed that SIS's professional interests required the 'grooming' of a future leader, and both had identified Philby as a candidate. The two had consulted Patrick Reilly, then the Foreign Office liaison officer in SIS, for his opinion. 'I'm not particularly sensitive,' confessed Reilly later, 'but it was the only time in my life when I felt, "There is something wrong with this fellow."' His objection was accepted by Menzies. But Reilly's suggestion that White be transferred to SIS as a future chief was rejected by Menzies and Sinclair. 'It was too much for them,' observed Reilly.[72] Six months later, Philby still trusted that White's investigation would end inconclusively.

Shortly after Philby's return to Washington, Arthur Martin read the private file of Donald Maclean, head of the Foreign Office's American Department. Near the top was a letter from a secretary at a British embassy to Robin Hooper, the head of Foreign Office personnel. Maclean, she disclosed, had confessed to her in a drunken stupor, 'I am the English Alger Hiss.' Hooper had minuted this letter to the Foreign Office's chief clerk, 'It seems that D.M. is up to his old tricks.'

Martin showed the letter to Carey Foster. 'I was astonished,' he told White. 'I never saw the file before.'[73] Carey Foster had forgotten that, less than two years earlier, he had approved psychiatric treatment for Maclean. The doctor's report mentioned Maclean's marital problems and his repressed homosexuality. Carey Foster had taken no action.[74] Security in the Foreign Office was clearly poor. Half-truths, suppositions and guesswork are the ingredients of counter-espionage. For White and Martin, the letter was like treasure trove.

Born in 1913, Maclean was the son of a Calvinist Liberal member of parliament and cabinet minister, who had been educated at Gresham, a minor public school, and Trinity Hall, Cambridge. The tall, handsome, fair-haired man with an elegant, athletic figure had won a first-class degree. Remove the privileged background, White reflected, and he shared some interests with the suspect.

After entering the Diplomatic Service in 1935, Maclean had been posted to Paris in 1938. Two years later, as the German army sped towards the French capital, Maclean married Melinda Marling, a twenty-four-year-old American; they then fled to England. Before their marriage, Maclean told his bride-to-be his secret: that he was betraying his country and working for a communist future. Melinda never betrayed her husband.[75] In 1944, Maclean arrived in Washington. Popular among the other British diplomats, he read nearly all the most sensitive messages between the two wartime allies about their post-war policies and their attitude and negotiating postures towards the Soviet Union, and he enjoyed unescorted twenty-four-hour access to the American Atomic Energy Commission, where he could monitor and report to Moscow the development of the atomic arsenal. The golden life began to disintegrate after Maclean's promotion to head of Chancery at the embassy in Cairo in 1948. The posting ended in a drunken orgy of violence and mental breakdown, probably caused by his double life and the KGB's failure to post an amicable officer in Cairo. But after psychiatric treatment in Britain, he had been promoted in summer 1950 to head the American Department. To White's bewilderment, the Foreign Office seemed more concerned to protect its flock than consider the possible consequences of unstable behaviour.

In March 1951, the Armed Forces Security Agency deciphered another Venona message to Moscow transmitted in 1944, reporting that Homer had visited New York to see his pregnant wife. A quick search by MI5 through the files produced the conclusive evidence that Maclean had undertaken just such a journey. Homer's identity was transmitted to the FBI in Washington. Since MI5 used SIS communication's channels, Philby read the message on its arrival confirming his own suspicions after gleaning confidences from the AFSA specialists whom he had befriended.

In London, Carey Foster rushed to break the news to Strang: 'I told him about our discovery as we were walking through St James's Park. He went white and said, "I don't believe it, George. You will have to go through all the files and evidence again before submitting this to me." '[76] Carey Foster consulted Robert

Mackenzie. 'Everybody believes Maclean to be above suspicion,' Mackenzie agreed. The delay lasted only one day.

A council of war was summoned to meet in Strang's office. In front of the permanent under secretary sat Sillitoe, Liddell, White and Carey Foster. Sillitoe was in overall command, but White was in effective control. To everyone, White epitomised calm professionalism. His cultivated manner reassured them that, as a master of Whitehall's conventions and as one of MI5's most experienced officers, he would appreciate the requirements of the case.

'Similar to Fuchs,' said White. The decrypts proved Maclean's guilt and MI5's task was to procure evidence which could secure a conviction without revealing how the suspicion had first arisen. The most desirable outcome, he continued, would be to observe Maclean in contact with a Soviet intelligence officer. Surveillance was a combined Special Branch and MI5 responsibility. White's liaison with the Branch was James Robertson, a dour Scotsman who had run double agents from Cairo during the war.

In the meantime, White continued, Maclean's office and files should also be examined. He assigned that task to Felix Johnston, a former Royal Navy commander whose conventional manner made him an unlikely intelligence officer. Arrangements should also be made, said White, to withdraw Maclean slowly from the circulation list of top-secret papers. Maclean's telephone at the Foreign Office would be tapped and Sillitoe would obtain the home secretary's approval for a similar intercept at his home in Tatsfield, Kent. However, the technology did not exist to attach a microphone to the instrument to render it live, picking up all conversations in the room even when the telephone was not in use. Arrangements would be made for Maclean's mail to be intercepted. The five, it was agreed, would meet again within one week.

Two issues arose during the following days. On reflection, Sillitoe decided that to forestall any breach with Hoover similar to that which had marred the Fuchs case, the FBI director should be kept informed of all MI5's plans. The messages would be sent through SIS's communications channel. Automatically, they were seen by Philby. Secondly, there was a report from James

Robertson that Special Branch and the MI5 watchers had vetoed surveillance around Maclean's home. 'The watchers', Robertson told Carey Foster, 'say they'll stick out like a sore thumb.' Carey Foster was furious: 'I didn't like Robertson and I didn't think much of his explanation.' The Foreign Office official suspected in retrospect that the plea of insufficient staff suited a pre-disposition towards a relatively leisurely operation.[77]

Throughout the coming weeks, White would remain coldly professional about the Maclean case. Their paths had never crossed and the reports from his officers lent no credibility to the possible seduction of a privileged Englishman by the mysteries of a foreign ideology. Since White had been at university ten years before Maclean and had concentrated upon the rise of Nazism in the 1930s, he was insensitive to the heady atmosphere which had attracted the privileged Cambridge students to communism. More to the point, he was baffled by the mechanics: where, when and how had the Soviets recruited someone in the Foreign Office? It did not occur to him that Maclean was anything other than a loner, unconnected to any network. The reports added nothing to his initial impression. Maclean's files had been secretly perused to check for bias, but his sloping handwriting revealed only a professional diplomat. His telephone calls were unsurprising, his mail was innocuous and his routine rarely changed.

In second week of May, surveillance was increased but was still not carried out beyond London. Robertson reported that the Special Branch officers always followed Maclean to the barrier at Charing Cross Station but insisted that further unobserved surveillance was impossible and beyond their resources. 'I saw Maclean in Pall Mall yesterday,' said Carey Foster. 'The watchers were ridiculously close. Maclean must have seen them.' 'He knows that we're on to him,' agreed White but did not dispute Special Branch's decision. That was Sillitoe's prerogative. 'We need to push him to do something foolish,' said Sillitoe. No one commented or expressed any need for urgency. Nor did anyone mention the surveillance of Soviet intelligence officers in London.

Special Branch reports listed the names of those seen with Maclean. It was a roll call of senior Foreign Office officials and some of London's glitterati. Among the names was Guy

Burgess. White paid no particular attention to it. In 1950, Burgess had been posted as first secretary to the British embassy in Washington. He had returned to London on 7 May and it seemed natural that he should call on the head of the Foreign Office's American Department. Burgess's telephone call to Maclean had been recorded by MI5 and their lunch at the Reform was noted.

White was unaware that Burgess had been ordered by the ambassador to return to London after disgracing himself. Successive driving offences and blatant homosexuality had been reported to the British embassy. Geoffrey Patterson, MI5's representative in Washington, would be blamed for not reporting those circumstances. Unaware that Burgess would shortly be dismissed, White recalled the disreputable character from wartime and inexplicably assumed that the diplomat's meetings with Maclean were 'like a homosexual spree'.[78]

Sex was certainly not mentioned by the two Foreign Office officials over lunch in the Reform. Instead, Burgess revealed to Maclean that he was under investigation. 'I know,' Maclean replied.[79] MI5's watchers had been extraordinarily indiscreet.

Burgess explained that passing on the news by a more conventional method had been impossible. Since the outbreak of the Korean War, Soviet intelligence officers in Washington had been under intense FBI surveillance and had avoided contact with Philby.

Without the knowledge of his Soviet controllers, Burgess had decided to live with Philby in Washington. 'It's madness,' Yuri Modin, his KGB controller had complained when he heard, but it was already too late. In Philby's opinion, Burgess was on the verge of a breakdown and it was safest to care for his fellow conspirator. Together, during the spring of 1951, they had mulled over MI5's pursuit of Maclean and could not conceive of a discreet method of dispatching a warning. Since trans-Atlantic telephone calls were exceptional and were handled individually by operators and since Maclean's mail was monitored, there was no alternative but to engineer Burgess's dismissal from Washington and his return to Britain.

Burgess's first call on his return to London was to Anthony

Blunt, who by coincidence was due to meet Yuri Modin the following day. The Soviet intelligence officer, surprised to hear that Burgess was in Britain, suggested that Burgess and Maclean meet, 'not in an office or unusual place, but in their club'. Burgess was to report back, via Blunt, about Maclean's reaction to his predicament.

By the end of their meal, Burgess knew that Maclean's plight was dire. He had expressed fear of fleeing England and abandoning his wife. 'Even if I run,' Maclean whispered, 'I think I'd get drunk and not make it. I'd never make it past Paris.' But one revelation was the most worrying. 'If questioned,' Maclean told Burgess, 'I'll make a full confession.'[80]

Moscow's reaction to Burgess's report was, in retrospect, judged ill-considered, even disastrous. The original spymasters, whose recruitment of Philby and the others would be hailed as historic achievements, had been replaced by young and inexperienced desk officers, unaware of conditions beyond their frontiers. Unlike the inspiring pre-war and wartime years, which had been dominated by cultured experts, the prevailing approach within the Lubyanka intelligence headquarters was to treat intelligence operations as mechanical affairs rather than deadly games of cunning. Although forewarned about the Venona breakthrough, no one had troubled to anticipate Maclean's eventual exposure. 'Worry about the masses, not individuals' was the unofficial slogan and certainly the principle of the party.[81] In the manner of Soviet intelligence operations, all the details of the escape were decided in Moscow, and the two officers in London were expected to obey their instructions to the letter.

Abandoning any considered subtlety, Moscow approved Nikolai Korovin's recommendation that Maclean, because of his fraught nerves and impulsive manner, should flee Britain as soon as possible. He should cross to France and travel to Switzerland. From there, he would continue to Russia. In the time available, it was declared impossible for Moscow to produce a suitable officer who could, without arousing suspicion, meet Maclean at a French port across the Channel. To pacify Maclean's fears, Burgess was to be ordered to accompany his friend to Paris or Switzerland, where he would be met by Soviet intelligence. From there, Burgess could return to England. 'Moscow did not want to take risks,' Modin realised later. 'They only thought of safety and their own heads. Afterwards it was easy just to blame Burgess. Intelligence services do silly things sometimes.'[82]

While White waited for MI5's watchers to spot a meeting between Maclean and a Russian intelligence officer, Moscow ordered Modin to liaise with Blunt, while Korovin would meet Burgess. At a meeting with Korovin, Burgess rejected the plan. It was too dangerous, he insisted, and contrary to his agreement with Philby. Korovin was adamant: Maclean's escape was the priority. He persuaded Burgess that there would be sufficient time for his unnoticed return. 'You'll get back in time,' lied Korovin, suspecting that his chiefs wanted Burgess secure in Moscow to prevent MI5 discovering Maclean's fate. Burgess was persuaded by Korovin to ignore Philby's wishes and follow the Russian's instructions.[83]

On Monday 21 May, the MI5 group met in Strang's office. White remained silent as Sillitoe argued that, while surveillance had proved unsuccessful, no action could yet be taken because the formal identification of Maclean as the proven suspect had not yet been passed to the FBI. A message would therefore have to be sent. 'We'd fallen out of step with Hoover,' recalled Carey Foster, 'and we wanted him completely in the picture. The message indicated that Maclean would be arrested and interrogated very soon.' There was one small issue arising out of the Venona decrypts of the Soviet wartime messages which also needed clarification. A question should be put to one of the British cipher officers who had served in Washington in 1944. The embassy should be told that an answer was required by 23 May for consideration at a meeting later that week.

On Sillitoe's instructions, the message to the FBI contained a complete account of MI5's intentions. In Carey Foster's words, 'Maclean was to be handed over to MI5 the following Monday. As a responsibility, but not necessarily for questioning.'[84] As usual, the message was sent via SIS and was passed by the cipher clerk to Patterson with a copy for Philby.

Towards the end of the 21 May meeting, Carey Foster mentioned that Burgess's name appeared several times on the list of those seen with Maclean. His dishevelled appearance and permanent odour of whisky had long irritated the security officer, who in 1949 had been exasperated by reports of Burgess's drunken, scandal-ridden tour of British embassies in the Mediterranean. On Burgess's posting to Washington, Carey Foster had written to inform Mackenzie that the 'particularly odious character and drunken homosexual' was getting his last chance.[85] 'Should he be followed?' Carey Foster suggested to Robertson during the meeting. 'No,' replied Robertson. According to Carey Foster, 'He told me something which again left me uneasy, and I suspected it was deliberate. I never trusted him after that.'

That day, Philby wrote to Burgess. The letter concerned the fate of Burgess's second-hand Lincoln, which had been impounded by the ambassador following the traffic offences. 'Urgent measures must be taken on the Lincoln, otherwise it will be too late and the car will be sent to the dump.' Added Philby, 'It is very hot here.'

On Wednesday, 23 May, Mackenzie called on Liddell and White. He was *en route* from Washington to Paris. The procedures, Mackenzie complained, were taking too long. 'From all I hear, Maclean is on the point of cracking up. You ought to pull him in at once and get the truth out of him without all this nonsensical kid-glove treatment.' White sounded unconcerned: 'We have our orders and we must follow them.'[86] Mackenzie was surprised but not annoyed: 'Nearly everyone liked Dick.'[87]

Although there was no sense of urgency among the MI5 officers, White was troubled by the prospect of interrogating Maclean. Jim Skardon would never be able to establish a relationship with a Foreign Office official such as he had with Fuchs. Without any hard evidence, how could MI5 break Maclean's inevitable denials; and, without that evidence, even White could not be absolutely certain of Maclean's guilt. 'Wait and see' seemed an alternative policy.

Across London, in the Soviet embassy, Korovin and Modin were struggling to find an escape route for Maclean. Since Maclean was under surveillance in London, it was agreed that he should leave from home and the best time would be on a Friday. With the weekend intervening, there would be three days before the alarm was raised. The problem was to find a route which did not require passports. That evening, Modin was walking along Oxford Street. In a travel agent's window he spotted an advertisement for day-trips on the *Falaise* to St Malo. The following morning, Blunt passed on the discovery to Burgess. 'Brilliant,' screamed Burgess.[88] They would leave the next day.

In London on Friday, 25 May, White again sat in Strang's office. There was no sense of urgency. Maclean, the watchers reported, was behaving normally, although they had missed him on one evening. Sillitoe pointed out that Melinda would be going into hospital to give birth within two weeks, which would provide a good opportunity to enter the house for a careful search. The questioning should be conducted thereafter.

That afternoon, Carey Foster and Patrick Reilly submitted a written report about the case to Herbert Morrison, the new foreign secretary. Morrison signed his approval for Maclean to be interrogated. In White's recollection, it was understood that the questioning could start after Monday but that, on the Friday, no decision had been taken to start after the weekend. The official note recorded that the interview would not be held until mid-June, when Melinda was certain to be in hospital. There was, White assumed, no urgency.[89]

While those plans were being agreed, Burgess was already cancelling his weekend plans with a boyfriend and scurrying around London to prepare for his departure, telling everyone that he was to tour the north of England.

On Saturday morning, Maclean did not appear for work. The unsuspecting flurry of excitement was stilled by a colleague's confirmation that at the end of the previous day Maclean had announced that he would be collecting his sister off a ship at Tilbury docks. He had taken the day off. 'Carey Foster never told us that Maclean had been given leave,' complained White. 'It would have been crucial.'[90]

The Unthinkable

Stricken with panic, at 10.15 a.m. on Monday, 28 May 1951, George Carey Foster telephoned Dick White. 'Maclean's disappeared,' whispered the Foreign Office official, as if afraid that pedestrians in Whitehall might hear the sensational news.

'How do you know?' asked White.

'I've just had a call from Melinda Maclean. She asked if we might know where Donald is. She says that he walked out of the house last Friday night and hasn't come back. He left with someone called Roger Stiles.'[1]

White was perplexed. Fifteen years in the Security Service had not prepared him for this eventuality. As he sat in Sillitoe's car travelling to the Foreign Office, he agreed with Liddell that their suspect, suffering a breakdown, had probably disappeared for a drunken spree with the unknown Stiles. By the time the three MI5 officers were sitting in Strang's office, an alert had been issued to all Special Branch officers at the ports and airports.

The calm among that group of officials gathered on the first floor of the Foreign Office was surreal. Carey Foster was silently cursing his failure to understand White's advice months earlier to 'look for someone who is unstable, living on his nerves'. White displayed no emotion, although he shared with Sillitoe and Liddell the responsibility for allowing Maclean to disappear. Strang's agitation was undisguised. Everyone agreed that Maclean's unaccountable absence must be kept secret. To avoid revealing that he had been under investigation, no one was to be told, including his colleagues in the Foreign Office. Sillitoe suggested that Maclean's house be searched. Strang vetoed that request: 'We're not sure he's actually disappeared.' White did not contradict the official; but he was already contemplating the possibility that Maclean had crossed the Channel to hide somewhere in Western Europe.

While White returned to Leconfield House, Liddell and Carey Foster briefed Herbert Morrison. After a thirty-minute meeting, noted as 'remarkably cold and unemotional', the two men hurried to Scotland Yard to read Special Branch's regular overnight reports. Among the batch presented was Saturday's report from the Branch officer at Southampton docks. An Austin A40, he reported, had been abandoned by two passengers on the dockyard quay before boarding the *Falaise*. The driver had shouted to a dockside worker, 'We'll be back on Monday!' Liddell suggested that they establish the identity of the car's owner.

At the end of the morning, a Branch officer walked into the room. The Austin, he announced, had been rented by a Mr Guy Burgess. Carey Foster looked at Liddell. 'He was clearly shocked. Amazed,' remembered Carey Foster. The mystery of 'Roger Stiles' had been explained. Carey Foster broke the news personally to White in Leconfield House. The MI5 officer hid his reaction. Remaining calm with a curious smile on his face, he uttered 'no self-reproach and no recrimination'. To the flabbergasted Foreign Office official, White would accept no responsibility for the events.

White's silence reflected bewilderment: 'I couldn't believe it. It really was very challenging to one's sanity to suppose that a man of Burgess's type could be a secret agent of anybody's.'[2] Tensely the two sat in White's office, where they were joined by Liddell, ashen-faced and clearly troubled. Liddell revealed a telephone call he had received the previous night. The caller was David Footman, a long-serving SIS officer, who told a strange story.

Footman had received a telephone call from Goronwy Rees, a Welsh academic and pre-war crony of Burgess, Blunt and others of that circle. Rees reported that Burgess had telephoned on Friday from the Reform Club and told Rees's wife: 'I'm going to do something which will surprise and shock many people. You won't see me for some time.' Rees received the message only on Sunday night after returning home from a weekend with friends. Liddell had taken little notice of the message. It was late on Sunday and it made no sense.[3]

White repeated that it seemed extraordinary that Burgess should be associated with Maclean, and even more inexplicable that Burgess, unsuspected of any complicity, should have travelled with him. But there was scant time for commiserations or post-mortems. White had decided that he would follow Maclean's path across the Channel and seek the assistance of the French police. The gumshoe expedition started badly.

White's passport had expired, an unfortunate echo of his oversight in 1936. After a delay at Heathrow while his passport was replaced, White arrived in Paris to await the results of French police investigations. Over the next days, there was little to be done. Gradually, it was established that two Englishmen had landed in St Malo and, having missed their train, had travelled by taxi to Rennes to board an express for Paris. Thereafter, the trail went cold.

While White fretted in Paris, the two diplomats had travelled via Geneva to Berne. There, Soviet intelligence produced new British passports with distorted photographs. In Zurich, the two boarded an aircraft for Stockholm with a scheduled stop in Prague. There, two passengers unexpectedly did not rejoin the aircraft for their stated destination. Burgess had abandoned his last opportunity to return to London and forestall total exposure. By then, before the end of the week, White had returned to London 'fearing the worst', the futility of the expedition evident to all. 'Like looking for a needle in a haystack', White confessed to a colleague, 'except the needle simply wasn't in it.' Back at Leconfield House, he found the atmosphere despondent. Here was the supreme test of a counter-espionage officer. One entirely unsuspected traitor at the very heart of Britain's political and social life. Another Foreign Office official missing for no apparent reason. 'I didn't believe Burgess was a spy at the beginning,' admitted White.[4]

White's strength was his methodology; start at the fundamentals, challenge every assumption and question every person associated with the two diplomats. Confused and still incredulous, his guidance was priggish: 'We must trust everyone unless there is proof to the contrary.'[5] There was to be no witchhunt. The heart of the investigation would be confined to five officers: Arthur

Martin, Ronald Read, James Robertson, Roger Hollis, Anthony Simkins and Graham Mitchell. 'It was better to have only a few people,' explained Simkins, 'to keep close contact.'

To that small team, White was 'an inspiration'. At their regular meetings, he arrived knowing 'precisely the objective he wanted to attain and how to argue his case to get his way'. The approach was orthodox. Robertson scoured the lists of Soviet diplomats for a possible link to Maclean, while Martin sought similar evidence among satellite diplomats: 'We'd always expected Soviet espionage to be like Fuchs and the Woolwich Arsenal case, so we treated Burgess and Maclean like those.'[6] The comparison bred confusion. Fuchs and Nunn May, White had claimed, 'were not spies at all. They were men with consciences.'[7] Placing Maclean in either category still seemed impossible.

Maclean's disappearance was still secret as the team began their inquiries in the Foreign Office, the small, family-minded service that epitomised Britain's famed old-boy network. The historic *esprit de corps* was jealously preserved. Steadfastly, Strang was resisting Carey Foster's request that Melinda Maclean be interrogated. It seemed clear to Arthur Martin that Melinda could not have been unaware that her husband was a spy. 'She must have known,' he noted perceptively: it would transpire that Maclean had confessed his secret to her in Paris in 1940, before they had even married.[8] 'We must not be harried into bullying tactics. After all she's pregnant,' insisted Strang.

On 30 May, two days after she had telephoned, Melinda Maclean was finally questioned in London by Jim Skardon. Demurely, she explained that she had cooked a ham for Donald's thirty-eighth birthday dinner and just as they began eating someone who called himself Roger Stiles had arrived. After hurried conversations, the two men had gone outside. Then her husband had dashed up the stairs to say good night to his sons and, after packing an overnight suitcase, had promised that he would return very soon. She knew nothing more, she lied to Skardon, concealing her complicity. Yet, once again, the Special Branch officer declared himself satisfied that she was telling the truth.

As the news of Maclean's disappearance seeped out among

Foreign Office officials, irritating whispers were exchanged about Maclean's notoriety in Cambridge as a communist who had speculated that he might teach in Russia, while Burgess had actually visited the country in 1934. 'It was the first I'd heard about that,' Carey Foster told White.[9] But White was only semi-attentive. The Foreign Office was no longer the sole focus of his investigation. His eye was fixed upon his mentor Guy Liddell.

Burgess's disappearance had mortified Liddell. His friendship with the louche rogue was widely known – they had been seen too often at parties, at the opera and in London's clubs. To protect his colleague, White insisted that 'Liddell thought Burgess was a disgraceful figure and ordered that nobody in MI5 was to have any business with him.'[10] But the eyewitness evidence was contradictory. While some confirmed White's recollection that Liddell had urged, 'Keep that man out of the office and don't leave anything lying about if he does get in,'[11] others recalled their open friendship. And White's loyalty could not conceal Liddell's folly the day after Burgess had disappeared.

On the Tuesday morning, Anthony Blunt had telephoned Liddell. Although Blunt had left MI5 in 1945, Liddell trusted his former subordinate, especially since his appointment as surveyor of the king's pictures and director of the Courtauld Institute. Liddell therefore confided that Burgess had disappeared. Blunt feigned surprise. Believing that the Soviet plan was for Burgess to return and understandably anxious to protect himself, he declared reassuringly that there were no grounds for suspicion. Indeed, he lied that he intended to meet his fellow conspirator that evening at the Reform Club for a dinner date.

During that telephone call, Liddell asked Blunt to obtain the keys to Burgess's flat. It would avoid MI5 formally applying for a search warrant, which would be awkward if Burgess did return. Blunt obliged but, without telling Liddell, first searched the flat, taking letters which compromised himself. Ronald Read and a Scotland Yard detective later entered the flat with Blunt. Their search revealed Philby's letter about the Lincoln car but nothing which noticeably incriminated Burgess in espionage. The surprise was inside a guitar case standing in a cupboard. Dozens of letters, exposing Burgess's homosexual relations dating back to his student days in Cambridge, spilled on to the floor. 'Put everything into black bags,' the detective was told. 'We're taking it all back to the office.'

The following day, Blunt telephoned Liddell. Speaking as a concerned friend, he explained that Burgess had not appeared at the Reform, but he surmised, tongue in cheek, that it was an unforeseen delay. Burgess, continued Blunt, posing as a helpful friend, had apparently left a briefcase at the Reform. Its contents might be interesting. That day, Liddell read personal letters to Burgess from a French communist, unusual correspondence for a Foreign office official to carry in his briefcase. On White's return from Paris, Liddell related that Anthony had been 'helpful', as one would expect from an old colleague. There was no reason for White to be suspicious.

At the end of that week, Liddell met Goronwy Rees for lunch. Contradictory versions followed that meeting with one common result: Liddell, the deputy director general of MI5, fell under suspicion as a Soviet agent. Investigating that possibility, a 'torture' for White, further depressed Liddell's subordinates. The source of the controversy was Rees himself, one of the few people whom White would come to dislike intensely, for his dishonesty and opportunism.

Rees, a Welshman born in 1909 whose life during and after Oxford had appeared full of promise, had excelled in pre-war Germany and in wartime Britain as an aspiring writer, intellectual, intelligence officer and university administrator. Well known among Britain's Labour politicians and outstanding academics, Rees was a sociable colleague, drinking a bottle of whisky each day and chain-smoking packets of cigarettes. But White saw another aspect of Rees's character – the unstable bosom friend of Burgess.

In the course of his telephone call to Footman on Sunday night, 27 May, Rees had speculated that Burgess had fled to Russia. Beset by a rush of blood to the head, Rees had given an emotional account of a conversation in 1937 during which Burgess had confided that, despite his public pretence that he was pro-Nazi, in fact he worked for the Comintern, the Soviet front organisation promising international unity for anti-fascists opposed to Hitler, arms merchants and profiteering appeasers. 'I want you to work with me, to help me,' Burgess had urged.[12] Rees insisted that he had refused the invitation but had promised not to reveal Burgess's secret.[13]

Five days later, Rees met Liddell for lunch and repeated his allegations against Burgess. Liddell appeared unimpressed. There was, he urged, no case against his friend.[14] The real culprit was Maclean: 'How could you, or anyone else, be sure whether Guy had accompanied Maclean?' (This was a surprise for Rees because Maclean's escape had not yet been publicised.)

That was the background to White's first meeting with Rees at Leconfield House, on Wednesday, 6 June, eleven days after Burgess's disappearance. The investigators were confused. Allegations were proliferating into unknown territory, naming people involved in activities about which White and his officers were completely ignorant. White's greeting to Rees was cold and strained, reflecting his mistrust: 'I thought he was a four-letter man, an arrogant intellectual, as slippery as an eel.'

'I assumed that MI5 knew about Burgess's background,' Rees told White.

White's anger was aroused: 'You assumed we knew that Burgess was working for the Russians and we did nothing about it? What can you mean?'

White was still furious thirty years later: 'If he had known all these things why hadn't he come forward?'[15] Rees, he would conclude, offered 'a ghastly flavour of corruption and debasedness', whose motives were tainted because he had remained a communist after 1937 and was probably himself linked to Soviet intelligence. Yuri Modin, however, would insist that Rees was never a source.

Among the notes of that conversation was Rees's denunciation of Stuart Hampshire, a philosopher, previously employed by the Foreign Office. Since he was White's friend, his name was ignored. Rees also mentioned Blunt. White disbelieved that allegation too, while Blunt reassuringly agreed with him that Rees could not be trusted. Ever helpful, Blunt also conceded that Burgess must after all have been involved in Maclean's escape.[16]

White remained perplexed. There was no rational explanation why Burgess should have fled with Maclean. Sitting in the Leconfield House canteen, Walter Bell, an MI5 officer, listened to White's lament: 'I can't understand these Russians. How on earth could they employ a man like Burgess as a spy?' Liddell agreed. How could such an indiscreet, dirty man play such a deep game? White had never previously been exposed to such strong nerves. The German agents, his informants among the exile governments in London and the atomic spies had lacked Burgess's audacity. His success, White would later concede, 'was a reflection upon all of us'. Painfully, the focus of suspicion fell upon Liddell, who had been present at Burgess's drunken farewell party before the Foreign Office official had sailed for Washington.

Had Liddell, in the previous few days, uttered an indiscreet remark alerting Burgess to the Maclean investigation; or, even worse, was he party to the conspiracy? On one issue White was emphatic: he did not believe that Liddell had developed a homosexual relationship with Burgess because 'Guy was married to a Baring. He's got a big family to which he's devoted.'[17]

The time for private, reflective bewilderment ended that day. On the evening of 6 June, Sir Robert Mackenzie, now the Foreign Office's regional security officer, called White from Paris. An indiscreet official at the Sûreté (the French Scotland Yard) had revealed the hunt for Maclean to a British journalist. Telephone calls around Fleet Street confirmed that the *Daily Express* would the following morning be running a banner-headline story, 'Yard Hunts Two Britons,' suggesting that two unnamed Foreign Office officials had disappeared and could be travelling to Russia. MI5's cosy security was threatened by the *Daily Express* scoop. Officially, the silence which concealed MI5's existence was justified as protection from the nation's enemies, but conveniently it also prevented exposure of the agency's misfortunes and avoided explanations for the inexcusable. But even White, queasy about the newspaper disclosures, did not anticipate the ensuing earthquake.

The following morning, the *Daily Express* report was transmitted to Washington. For Hoover and Walter Bedell Smith, the wartime general who had effectively become the founding director of the

CIA, it was the first hint of the diplomats' disappearance. In the previous twelve days, since Sillitoe's message that Maclean was to be questioned, nothing further had been reported. The *Daily Express* disclosure, the directors of America's intelligence services agreed, suggested deliberate deception. Their anger was intensified by embarrassment. Dean Acheson, the Anglophile secretary of state, was appearing that day before a senate committee. A hostile senator asked the secretary about the *Daily Express* revelation. Acheson was publicly dumbfounded, thus exposing British duplicity.

In London, eschewing honesty, the Foreign Office released a statement seeking to minimise Maclean's departure to France: 'Mr Maclean had a breakdown a year ago owing to overstrain but was believed to fully have recovered [sic].'[18] But the truth had already been confirmed. The previous night, MI5 reported that two telegrams had arrived from Paris for Melinda Maclean and her mother-in-law, ostensibly from Donald, with assurances that he was well. Questions at the post office counters in Paris revealed that Maclean had not personally handed in the messages. White realised that they had been dispatched by Soviet intelligence.

Five days later, on 11 June, while Morrison made a short and noncommittal statement to the House of Commons, Sillitoe flew to Washington accompanied by Arthur Martin. To White's disgust, MI5's director general allowed himself to be photographed at Heathrow boarding his plane.

The greeting the MI5 officers received in Washington was uncompromising. The Korean war had already cost over 20,000 American lives and nearly 60,000 wounded, and the casualties were increasingly daily. Having dismissed General MacArthur, Truman was desperately anxious for a ceasefire. In that fever of war, and in the grip of the rabid hatred of communism fanned by Senator McCarthy, America's intelligence chiefs spat their antagonism at Sillitoe and British intelligence.

Hoover was famed for his frank discourtesy. Guests might expect meetings lasting three periods: fifteen, twenty and twenty-five minutes. The British visitors were granted a 'middle interview'. Neither spoke while Hoover delivered his bruising invective about MI5's latest disaster. Not only had MI5 allowed Maclean to flee, growled Hoover, but the British had failed to spot the link with Burgess and, multiplying their crime, had concealed the disaster from the FBI. In a parting curse, Hoover repeated his irritation that the British adamantly refused to impose loyalty tests or positive vetting on officials.

Arthur Martin's subsequent conversations with FBI officers, especially Lamphere, were focused upon Burgess. As recollections of the antipathy and outrage they had felt towards the dishevelled diplomat were rekindled, the Americans recalled that his host, Kim Philby, had been remarkably supportive of him. If Maclean had fled alone after weeks of surveillance, no one else would have fallen under immediate suspicion. But disappearing with Burgess unmasked a more complex scenario. Burgess's departure from Washington was so unusual and his recent host was so clearly privy to the investigation that a connection seemed possible. Bedell Smith asked his senior staff to assess the unthinkable: whether the SIS liaison officer could be associated with the treachery.

Soon after Sillitoe's return to London, heavily chastised by Hoover, a long message arrived from Philby in which he offered his thoughts about Burgess. In retrospect, he wrote, there were several indications of Burgess's treachery. After studying Philby's offering, Martin spoke to White: 'There's something odd here. It's not in character. It doesn't ring true.' White agreed. Several references, including a mention of Burgess's photography and some conjecture about his role in the escape plot, sounded odd. The SIS officer had inadvertently placed himself under suspicion and not surprisingly would subsequently avoid reference to his mistake.* As White would later reflect, 'One of the only things to be learnt from spying is that the least likely is the most probable.'[19] White agreed that Philby should be questioned. Obtaining permission, he knew, would require diplomacy.

Considering the rivalry if not mutual dislike between the two services, White's meeting with John Sinclair in Broadway Buildings to discuss the unprecedented MI5 questioning of a senior SIS officer was inevitably fraught. But White's approach

---

* No mention is made of it in his memoir *My Silent War*.

was couched in the most gentle terms. Philby, he explained, had offered assistance and it would be helpful if that could be conducted in London. White did not mention any suspicions about Philby because at that stage they barely existed. Grudgingly, Sinclair agreed to the request.

Philby's SIS career had been faultless. After running the Iberian department in Section V, he had in 1944 contrived to become head of Section IX, the new anti-Soviet division, thus humiliating Felix Cowgill, who had been the expected choice. White still recalled how distasteful he had found Philby's squalid manoeuvre, but that was no cause for suspicion. Thereafter, Philby had sat, and shone, on Menzies's committee to discuss the post-war reorganisation of SIS. On C's recommendation, he had received the Order of the British Empire in recognition of his wartime service. After a two-year posting to Istanbul, he had been posted by Menzies to Washington.

Reflecting that trust, Jack Easton, SIS's third-ranking officer, now sent a handwritten letter to Philby warning him that he would shortly receive a formal cable from Menzies asking him to return to London to help inquiries. Easton's motives were benign: 'I just wanted him to have enough time to put his affairs in order.'[20] Philby would absurdly postulate years later that Easton's letter was part of a conspiracy to offer him the chance of an escape.[21]

Over the next few days, White and Martin diligently compiled a record of Philby's work. There was the discovery that Philby's first wife, Litzi Friedmann, was an Austrian communist. In 1946, White had been asked by SIS to check on Litzi after Philby had applied for permission to divorce his youthful transgression. White had been told by Klop Ustinov that Litzi was a Soviet agent, but that had not been held against Philby.[22] In the post-war climate, Philby's gesture to save an unknown, endangered Jewess was praised rather than questioned.

There was also Philby's handling of the Volkov defection in 1945. Konstantin Volkov's offer to defect had been negotiated with John Reed, a first secretary at the British embassy in Turkey. On Volkov's insistence, Reed's message containing the offer to defect was to be handwritten and sent to London by diplomatic bag. Volkov knew that the British embassy was penetrated by

Soviet intelligence and that some British ciphers could be read by the Russians. After a ten-day journey, the normal duration for post, Reed's letter had been read by Philby, then responsible for SIS's Soviet section. He thereby learnt that Volkov was offering to expose the identity of a Soviet agent in British intelligence. After consulting his superiors it was decided that Philby should negotiate with the defector.

Before Philby's return from Washington, no attempt was made by MI5 to question Reed, but the record showed that back in 1945 Philby had taken an extraordinary ten days in his 'rush' to Turkey. Then the weekend had intervened and when, on the Monday morning, Volkov had been telephoned, the Russian embassy claimed that no one of that name existed. Reed would later lament his misfortune: 'Treachery at that time was not in the air and I fear that I did not suspect it.' Fearing that he had been responsible for Volkov's fate, he had turned on Philby to explain his slow journey to Turkey. Off-handedly, Philby had replied, 'It interfered with my office's leave arrangements.'[23]

White reconsidered Volkov's fate just as Philby flew to London. 'Why', he asked Hollis, 'did you not pursue the case deeper at the time?'

'It didn't seem important,' replied Hollis.

White did not yet suspect the truth: that Philby, savouring the irony of investigating his own case, had deliberately delayed his departure to Istanbul in order to pass a warning to Moscow. During those days, Volkov had been drugged and flown to Russia.

The first meeting between White and Philby would be a conversation between colleagues. Philby had been recalled to London not as a suspect but as a curiosity. By the time Easton greeted him, he was harbouring some suspicions of his own. The returning SIS officer had, on arriving at Heathrow, ignored the waiting chauffeur and used the public bus service. 'The behaviour of a worried man' thought Easton.[24] The two men drove to Leconfield House to meet White. Philby, who had followed the investigation from Washington and knew precisely the limits of the evidence, was later to write:

I could not claim White as a close friend but our personal and official relations had always been excellent, and he had undoubtedly been pleased when I superseded Cowgill. He was bad at dissembling but did his best to put our talk on a friendly footing. He wanted my help, he said, in clearing up this appalling Burgess–Maclean affair.[25]

In White's retrospective opinion, Philby believed that 'he and his friends would always be able to bluff their way out.'[26]

White faced a drunk, an adulterer and a socially assured deceiver whose treachery was concealed beneath polished charm. It was a confrontation between purity and ingrained natural deception, and, some might say, an accomplished deceiver can be destabilised only by another accomplished deceiver. Above all, it was a clash of intellects and White's was inferior. There was also a social gulf between the two men. Philby genuinely assumed himself to be a member of the Establishment, while his interrogator was pure trade.[27] Against those prejudices, White's humanitarian sensitivities precluded the bitterness which should have remorselessly driven an interrogator towards the taste of blood. In Malcolm Muggeridge's words, 'Kim's allergy to nearly all things intellectual and spiritual certainly immunised him against deep worry. He was one of nature's original cavemen.'[28] Unlike White, Muggeridge would long protest Philby's innocence.

At the outset, White suffered the interrogator's most fundamental problem: he did not know the answers to his questions. Indeed, on that first meeting, after reading the background notes about Volkov's failed defection, he was open-minded about Philby, whose only provable transgression was to have tolerated Burgess as a house-guest. On reflection, White admitted that he was working with 'very sketchy evidence'.[29]

In his customary manner, White invited Philby to say what he knew about Maclean. Philby's famous stutter burst forth. In the past, his impediment had emphasised his essentially kindly disposition, encouraging the onlooker to extend protection to the sufferer. The tension rose as Philby denied anything beyond slight acquaintance. White moved on and asked for his assessment of Burgess. Philby answered at length by admitting complete bafflement. 'He tried to convince me', recalled White, 'that it was utterly impossible to imagine any respectable intelligence service employing such an indiscreet, disorganised, drunken, homosexual reprobate.'[30] White was inclined to concur but the evidence pointed the other way.

The two parted on apparently amicable terms. Philby had agreed to complete a written summary of his relationship with Burgess and a résumé of his career, while White hinted that another meeting was probable. White would subsequently regale MI5's recruits with the dictum that espionage is a crime which often leaves no trace or evidence. The investigator relies upon an intuition for coincidences. After considering the circumstances, he might reach the moment of 'epiphany' – all the facts added up to only one conclusion.[31]

Shortly after that encounter, White immersed himself in the research prepared by Arthur Martin and Jane Archer about Philby's past. For the first time, Archer produced a thin MI5 file about Philby compiled in 1939 and then forgotten.[32] A report contrasting Philby's communist sympathies at Cambridge and his sudden espousal of fascism made a deep impression. Alongside was Philby's own résumé. One coincidence was interesting. Philby mentioned his employment by *The Times* covering the Spanish civil war. Krivitsky had claimed that among the Soviet agents he controlled from Barcelona in 1936 was one unnamed English journalist.

The crystallisation of White's mistrust coincided with a letter from Bedell Smith to Menzies, which arrived just after the first conversation with Philby. On 20 June, Bedell Smith had read the reports from his senior officers concerning Philby. Jim Angleton, who had regularly entertained Philby over drunken lunches splattered with indiscretions about the Agency's secrets, had judged the evidence against his wartime friend to be ambivalent. He had even enjoyed an unsuspecting farewell drink with Philby before the Englishman returned home. But Bill Harvey, a former FBI officer whose wife Burgess had grossly insulted in Philby's home, emphatically indicted SIS's liaison officer. Philby, reasoned Harvey, had volunteered to care for Burgess on the ground of their long friendship, and there were other more sinister suspicions, especially concerning the Volkov case.

Renowned for his razor mind, Bedell Smith had returned to Washington from an ambassadorship in Moscow with a deep loathing for 'parlour pinks' and imperfections. 'Every officer', he quipped, 'has the right to one mistake.' Philby had made his, even if there was no hard evidence. In his message to Broadway, Smith advised that Philby was no longer welcome in Washington. For Menzies, who one year earlier had canvassed Philby as a future chief, it was a shocking allegation. Both he and Sinclair voiced their wholehearted commitment to the protection of their protégé and to the reputation of their Service. White's second meeting with Philby was consequently conducted in the aftermath of an unsupportive telephone conversation with Sinclair.

In summoning Philby, White convinced himself that he was sufficiently adept to confound what had become his prey. There was an attraction for MI5's rising star to confront an identical animal in the rival service. Both men had benefited from the exceptional circumstances of wartime and from favourable comparison of their abilities with their less intelligent contemporaries. Philby, White felt, 'had let me down and I was going in for a showdown'.[33] In anticipation, White made one critical decision. The previous year he had been dissatisfied with Skardon's interrogation of Fuchs. The policeman, he felt, lacked determination and intellect, and would be no match for such a skilled SIS officer. Worse still, his appearance would immediately alert Philby to MI5's suspicions. White decided that he would conduct the questioning himself and hope to lead his quarry into self-incrimination. White described his tactics as relying on 'an element of quiet probing and deceptive gentleness'.

But he had a crucial handicap: he had no experience as an interrogator or as a practised debriefer of hostile witnesses. His hope of dramatically tricking Philby into unravelling the tangled web was to ignore the essence of interrogation: endless patience. Instead, experience was blown aside, as it would continue to be over the following two years. In the course of the second interrogation, White initially asked Philby, 'When did you first meet Guy Burgess? Make it as detailed as you like. I'm in no particular hurry.' By the end of his rambling answer White realised Philby was lying. He next asked him to explain how he had financed his initial journey to Spain as *The Times* correspondent, reporting favourably about General Franco. Philby corrected his questioner. Originally, he explained, he had travelled to Spain as a self-financing freelance for the London General Press, a little-known agency, and had obtained *The Times* appointment only in May 1937.[34] 'How did you finance yourself at the beginning?' asked White. Philby replied that he had sold his books, records and other personal possessions. In fact, Soviet intelligence had supplied the money and had replenished their agent's funds by sending Burgess to Europe, but White knew nothing of that.

At that point, White made an error for which he was for ever to blame himself. Rather than patiently itemising each sale with Philby, establishing how much money had been raised and in what conditions, and then calculating the journalist's expenditure in Spain, he doubted the SIS officer's explanation but did not pursue the matter to force his breakdown. White's own character – agreeable, placid and generous – denied the interrogator the instinctive lust for a slow, painful, bloody kill. At the end, White bade a dry farewell, without disguising his suspicions.

Later, on reflection, White commented, 'I got an absolutely significant point out of him and he knew I had got it.' But in reality the opportunity had been missed[35] – as Philby's 1968 memoirs were to confirm. While admitting in a letter written the same year that White 'thought me deeply if not wholly suspect', Philby boasted that his survival had been thanks to the 'ineffective' MI5 officer, who was 'pretty nondescript besides such colleagues as Liddell, Hart, Blunt, Rothschild and Masterman'.[36]

Philby's judgment was, not surprisingly, self-serving. Intellect, the common denominator of those he named, was not the only prerequisite for a successful counter-intelligence officer. Perception and sensitivity were equally important. With the exception of Liddell, none of those MI5 officers mentioned by Philby would have been minded to lead the charge against Philby. Unlike White, they would have been reluctant to contradict the prevailing sentiment that the talented officer was the victim of unsubstantiated conjecture. White was also sensitive to the social division between MI5's hunters and SIS's officers. The

inhabitants of Broadway, especially Philby's friends, displayed
tribal faith in their own kind and arrogantly assumed their rightful
position among Britain's rulers. Their kind was urging Menzies to
resist McCarthyite persecution from Washington and the attack
on their loyalties from Leconfield House. In contrast, White, like
most other MI5 officers whose career activity was to spy on their
own countrymen, concealed neither his relatively humble origins
nor the fact that he lived on his salary. There was pride in his
role as Keeper of the Flame.

Taking a measure of satisfaction in exposing the pretences of a
service which had for too long escaped scrutiny, White submitted
to Menzies a report which concluded that Philby was suspect.
In doing so, he showed great courage, for he was automatically
pitting himself against SIS's rulers: 'I had the whole weight of SIS
against me. That was awful. It was extremely difficult to persuade
people if there was no way of proving my suspicions.'[37] His failure
to do so was excused only by the style of delivery and his
patent honesty. His report coincided with Washington's bullying
insistence that Philby's continued employment endangered the
special relationship, already undermined by Britain's post-war
decline. Reluctantly, Menzies bowed to the pressure. While
telling White that the man could 'not possibly be a traitor', he
asked Philby for his resignation, a bitter pill made sweeter by an
ex-gratia payment of £4,000.

Leaving Leconfield House one evening at this time, White
saw newspaper headlines demanding Sillitoe's resignation. 'The
country's roused,' White commented, perversely relieved by the
newspapers' misconception that Burgess and Maclean were no
more than 'missing diplomats' and that Philby's existence was
unknown. What was more, the signals from Whitehall were
unmistakably to bury everything. Attlee's government was struggling, amid a cabinet crisis, to survive on a slim parliamentary
majority. A new spy scandal was unpalatable, not least because
MI5's investigation threatened to shake the temple.

For weeks, Evelyn McBarnet, an MI5 researcher, had been
reading the hundreds of letters found in Burgess's apartment. The
lengthening index of names extracted from that correspondence
shared several characteristics: many had been left-wing students

in Cambridge during the 1930s – not least Burgess, Maclean and Philby. These revelations were, White acknowledged, 'an admission of MI5's failure. We had failed to monitor what was happening in the universities. We hadn't thought of collecting information about students.'[38]

The investigation changed dramatically. At the outset, White had warned against a witchhunt and had urged, 'We must trust everyone unless there is proof to the contrary.'[39] Now, as the vast tableau of treason unfolded, the purist counter-espionage officer compromised his sense of propriety. What was required was nothing less than an investigation into Britain's ruling class. Nothing, he ordered, was to be taken on trust. Every statement and detail uttered was to be cross-checked, in pursuit of the inconsistencies that separated truth from deception and that might reveal other traitors. 'One must think the unthinkable' become White's refrain.

Extracting information to build up an understanding of Cambridge in the 1930s was complicated by the social gulf between MI5's investigators, educated either at minor public schools or by the state, and the Cambridge graduates, the majority schooled at elite institutions such as Eton, Marlborough and Westminster and by 1951 enjoying real power. 'We had a capital difficulty dealing with the intellectuals,' conceded White.[40] Compounding the social and political gulf were hints of unusual sexual relationships and membership of The Apostles, a self-appointed, secret group of cultural elitists founded at Cambridge a century earlier and at one time counting Alfred Lord Tennyson among its members.

Questions from MI5's officers met silence amounting to obstruction. 'The spirit of the times was against us. Neither the dons nor the graduates would tell us anything, and we didn't even have the power to search the universities' records,' explained White. 'In London, to be anti-MI5 was to be pro-British, unlike America, where to be anti-FBI was anti-American.'[41] Even his own interview with Anthony Eden was unproductive. Restored to the Foreign Office after the 1951 general election, Eden was adamant that, during his many wartime conversations with Burgess, he had never disclosed any 'worthwhile information'. 'It's fanciful,

but everyone is running for cover,' White told Liddell.[42] Yet
gradually he was identifying an emerging pattern.

The story seemed to begin with Clemens Palme Dutt, a
leading communist, who went to Cambridge in 1931 on the
instructions of Maxim Litvinov, the Soviet commissar for foreign
affairs. In 1935, the link had been extended from Dutt to Maurice
Dobb, a Marxist lecturer, and then to James Klugman, another
Cambridge communist and close schoolfriend of Maclean. 'It's
ludicrous and quite impracticable to suggest that a British don
was the recruiter,' exclaimed Liddell. 'Recruiting is a professional's task.'[43]

Ever since his organisation of the Arcos raid in 1927, Liddell
had been respected as an expert on Soviet intelligence. Now he
confessed to White an unmistakable oversight. After Arcos, the
OGPU (the NKVD's predecessor) had gone underground, using
Cambridge's academics as spotters. But the actual recruitment
must have been undertaken by Soviet intelligence officers. Still
undetected and even unsuspected were the Comintern officers,
disguised 'illegals', men like Theodore 'Teddy' Maly, a charming
Hungarian, dispatched to Britain from Moscow as a German
national, to recruit and organise students for later penetration
of the British government. Maclean, Burgess and Philby had
been known among fellow students as communists. Inexplicably,
Burgess had renounced his communism following his visit to
Moscow in 1934 and, like Philby, had joined the Anglo-German
Fellowship, an organisation dedicated to promoting Hitler and
Nazi propaganda in Britain.

In those first weeks, MI5 officers encountered only those who
mixed overtly with the conspirators. Reading their reports, White
barely grasped the tangled emotions, the battle of ideology and
conflicting loyalties which had condemned some former students
to self-diagnosed 'intellectual schizophrenia' and support for the
Bolsheviks. 'There was tension with those who believed that
history belonged to Russia and it was amazing that they didn't
have more success.'[44] The conspiracy of silence greeting the MI5
investigation was replicated in the case of the parallel Foreign
Office inquiry. Sir Norman Brook, secretary of the cabinet, with
Lord Cadogan and Sir Neville Bland, had discovered that many

of Maclean's colleagues were unwilling to betray their friend. 'They're keeping everything very close,' Carey Foster reported to White.[45]

Conventional tactics did produce some insight. Telephone taps were placed on dozens of those identified as having been active before 1939 in the peace movements. One significant lead was a conversation in which Edith Tudor Hart, a pre-war communist, asked her husband to destroy the negatives of a photograph she had taken of Philby. But, when Philby denied all knowledge of the woman, White could take the discovery no further.[46] The professionals were too careful to disclose Tudor Hart's recruitment of Philby for Soviet intelligence.

An impish, perverse sentiment amounting almost to masonry faced White's officers: 'There was the feeling of the British public school, that one ought not to be a sneak. A lot of it seemed to be based on homosexual friendships. I knew next to nothing about such things but it crossed my mind that Blunt was in love with Burgess. It was always evident to me that he was under the influence of Burgess, though I could not understand why that was.'[47]

In an effort to understand Burgess's visit to Moscow in 1934, White summoned Goronwy Rees, the close friend of Burgess in the 1930s. When Rees admitted that he had been invited to travel with Burgess to Moscow, the atmosphere became frosty: 'They treated me as if I were a spy and a traitor with lots to hide.'[48] White asked for the names of others in that circle. Rees replied, 'Why don't you ask Blunt about these things?'[49] White, irritated by Rees's 'violent antipathy to Blunt,' could not bring himself to suspect that his wartime colleague was a traitor. His understanding of Cambridge in the 1930s and the illegal activities of the communists was still too scant, and he rejected Burgess's homosexuality as a source of influence: 'Blunt seemed to be a man of discrimination and civilised tastes. I couldn't believe that he had a relationship with someone so awful as Burgess.' Even a report that Burgess, shortly before his disappearance, had been seen lunching with Blunt at the Reform did not arouse White's suspicions.[50]

Blunt was regarded as an ally, and his help was sought to

explain the relationships, especially with Philby. White, however, sent Courtney Young, an old wartime friend of Blunt's, to question the former MI5 officer. Young, by then an alcoholic, had not properly briefed himself. He had missed the dedication to Burgess in Blunt's first book; he had missed the coincidence that Blunt, after visiting Moscow in 1936, had also forsaken his Marxist beliefs; and he had missed Blunt's presence at Burgess's drunken party before departing to America.[51] Instead, Young reported Blunt's vehement denials, and that suited White. His antipathy towards Rees had increased after hearing from Ronald Read that the Welshman had again denounced Liddell as suspicious.[52]

By October, no evidence had been found against Liddell other than possible carelessness. In contrast, the evidence against Philby had increased, and detecting Soviet penetration of SIS had come to assume paramount importance. Philby's replacement in Washington, John Bruce Lockhart, the architect of SIS's operations in post-war Germany and the nephew of the famed Robert Bruce Lockhart, who had operated against the Bolsheviks in Russia from 1917, had reported that liaison with the CIA was nearly paralysed by the unresolved suspicions. Aggravating the problem, Colonel Valentine Vivian, SIS's security chief, had visited Washington and vouched for Philby. Considering the need for co-operation in Korea and against the communists in Europe, argued Bruce Lockhart, the CIA required immediate reassurance. Since Sillitoe was discredited in Washington and Menzies had rejected the allegations against Philby, there was only one British intelligence officer whom Bedell Smith might trust – namely White, whom he had known during the war.

In the first of several flights to Washington over the following twelve years whenever it became necessary to explain British blunders, White was an ideal ambassador for soothing American sensitivities. Exuding understanding and respect, without patronising anyone, White's strength was his honesty. There was no denying, he told Bedell Smith during their opening encounter in 1951, the damage Philby could have caused. For two years, he had sat at the heart of discussions with the CIA about worldwide strategy and had been privy to some of the most sensitive British and American secret operations in Russia, the Baltic States, the Ukraine, western Europe and Albania. The disaster in Albania, costing many lives, had been particularly painful and could have been caused by treachery. The problem, said White, was the lack of proof. Bedell Smith recognised the obstacle but was critical of MI5's procedures. Philby, he urged, should have 'his guts pulled'. The alternative was a breakdown in the Anglo-American relationship.

White's message on his return was unequivocal. Faced with the threat of a breach with Washington, Sinclair, Menzies's successor, could no longer resist demands for a formal inquiry. In November, Helenus Milmo, the beefy, Irish barrister who had worked in MI5 during the war and had prosecuted the German spies, was briefed by White and Martin to conduct an interrogation in Leconfield House. Philby, White hoped, would be intimidated by the professional.

Before arriving at Leconfield House, Philby had good reason to assume that MI5's investigators had found incriminating evidence. But soon after sitting down at 10 a.m. before an audience of MI5 investigators in the fifth-floor conference room, he realised that Milmo's armoury, a thick brief prepared by Martin, contained only conjecture. Asked to explain why the Soviet radio traffic between London and Moscow and Istanbul had increased after Volkov's offer to defect, Philby pleaded ignorance and repeated that answer to every question and proposition. 'I just had to make sure', Philby subsequently told Yuri Modin, 'that I didn't contradict what I had said previously and volunteer nothing.'[53] Without evidence to challenge the experienced intelligence officer and having failed to provoke Philby into contradictions, Milmo launched into a tirade to terrorise Philby into a confession. White watched aghast. 'It all became a shouting match with Milmo accusing Philby of everything. I was surprised and disappointed that Milmo did not use more legal subtlety.'[54] Others would say that Philby 'was not clever, rather the MI5 officers were not clever enough'.[55]

Just before lunch, it was all over. Instead of lasting days and even weeks, the interrogation was over in less than three hours. 'There's no hope of a confession,' Milmo told White, 'but he's as guilty as hell.' Despite the barrister's bungling, all those present were similarly convinced of Philby's guilt. As the suspect took his leave, White would claim that his parting words to Philby were threatening and prophetic: 'You may think you've had the last laugh, but bear this in mind – we'll haul you back when we're ready, not before. Then the last laugh could be on you.'[56]

Skardon was dispatched on successive but futile visits to Philby's home to extract something, and White consoled himself with the reflection that Milmo, 'a famous legal figure',[57] had agreed to provide a formal report stating that Philby was a security risk. Believing that Milmo's conclusion would be un-equivocally accepted, White presented the paper to Sinclair: 'I insisted that Philby could no longer be employed by SIS.'

But Sinclair rejected Milmo's conclusion. A 'terrible argument' ensued. White discovered that 'trust and loyalty are so much of English nature' that 'Sinclair refused to let one of his chaps down.' Philby, explained Sinclair, was a victim of circumstance. Burgess was simply a nuisance foisted on to him by the Foreign Office. As for White himself, Sinclair added, 'You're in breach of Crow's Law. Do not believe what you want to believe until you know what you ought to know!' The best White could extract was a directive from Bill Steadman, the head of SIS's counter-intelligence, that officers seen socialising with Philby would be warned to 'move away'.[58]

By early 1952, MI5's list of suspects included dozens of notable academics and government officials. But even the successes were marginal. Sifting through the papers found in Burgess's flat, Jane Archer had found official documents written by John Cairncross, a wartime Bletchley officer who had moved to the Treasury and then the Ministry of Defence. In a negative fashion, MI5's surveillance proved productive. As part of an operation masterminded by Anthony Simkins, Cairncross was followed through London. At Ealing Common underground station, the official stood smoking, apparently waiting for someone. His KGB contact Yuri Modin was in fact hovering nearby identifying three MI5 watchers before departing. Cairncross later walked away. 'He's a non-smoker!' exclaimed Simkins on reading the report. 'He was smoking to warn his Soviet contact.' If Simkins and White had acted more adroitly, the history of the Cambridge Ring and the subsequent 'molehunt' would have ended in triumph for the Security Service. Instead, before summoning Cairncross for an interview, the MI5 officers failed to gather the evidence which Bernard Hill, MI5's lawyer, firmly stipulated would be necessary for a prosecution.

Cairncross, a boorish, ill-dressed and even arrogant Scot, admitted a friendship with Burgess and pre-war sympathy for communism but denied any link with espionage. At his second interview with Skardon, he made a limited confession of carelessness with official papers and then resigned from the civil service. But nothing more. 'If he won't confess, there's nothing we can do,' decided Simkins. Absent was any sense that the service was undertaking a protracted investigation. 'There just wasn't time,' Read told a colleague, 'and it wasn't worth it.' The calamity for MI5 lay in the failure of Skardon and Martin to elicit from Cairncross admissions that he had been spotted by Blunt and that Burgess had been the recruiting master for Soviet intelligence. After his resignation he moved to America.

During 1952, the floundering and grappling continued. MI5's net was forever widening, but its efforts were hampered by the orthodox distinction between a Soviet agent and a fellow traveller whose participation was difficult to quantify and whose criminal intent was impossible to prove. 'Since Burgess and Maclean fled,' complained an MI5 officer to Andrew King of SIS, 'we've had innumerable phone calls asking, "Surely you knew that Burgess was a communist?" It seems that everyone knew except us.' King's own interrogation underlined the obstacles to the investigation.

MI5's net had been cast over a number of long-serving SIS officers. Among those recalled to London by White for investigation was King, then the head of station in Vienna. An SIS officer since 1936 and known to White before the war, he had been a Communist Party member at Cambridge. His interrogator, Dick Thistlethwaite, was plainly flustered. King admitted membership of the party but recalled that he had confessed the problem in 1948 to Kenneth Cohen, his director. 'I asked Cohen', King told his interrogator, 'whether any security checks were required. After consulting Menzies, Cohen's response was reassuring: "C says that, since spies are only people of foreign origin, don't bother"'.

Although King could produce no evidence of that exchange, and in 1952 Cohen pleaded bad memory (Menzies was apparently not questioned), MI5 could take the case no further. After the interview, White emerged and shook King's hand. Such a routine had become frustratingly familiar.

Arthur Martin argued that to break the deadlock their investigation should become more aggressive. His plea was ignored and, to avoid further problems, White agreed that Martin, his best analyst, should be dispatched to Malaya to help reorganise General Templer's Special Branch in the struggle with communist insurgents.* 'I'm happy to go,' Martin told a friend. 'The investigation is nearly completed and it will be good for my career.'59

Also sensing the end of the investigation, Modin had no difficulty in driving out of London without MI5 surveillance. He headed for Tatsfield, where he observed Melinda Maclean drive off from her home, likewise without any surveillance. On an open, country road, he swung his car in front of hers. Startled at first, she gave way to fury, before the Soviet intelligence officer produced a token which could only have come from her husband in Moscow. Rapidly, he explained how she should travel to Switzerland and await further instructions for eventual reunion with the fugitive diplomat. With the message passed, Modin returned to London unobserved.

An investigation without a result might not have been to White's credit had the failure been known around Whitehall. But it was MI5's good fortune that neither ministers nor their most senior officials were well informed about the Security Service's activities. The ignorance suited MI5, and any attempt by Whitehall to break the vacuum was politically and practically unrealistic. But one indelible fact had permeated the body politic – namely, MI5 officers' intense dislike of Sillitoe, who was blamed for all the service's misfortunes and the government's multiple

* White had rejected a post as director of intelligence in Malaya. On a personal visit to that country, he told Templer, 'good intelligence is not an end in itself', and advised that the British forces were not well served. Military intelligence officers, on White's recommendation, were inserted into the police, and Jack Morton was appointed as director of intelligence (TB/Hamilton). The success of Templer's slow but sure campaign was credited to the British army's outstanding intelligence operation.

embarrassments. Towards the end of 1952, he was contemplating retirement. Liddell, his prospective successor, had left MI5 earlier that year. Too old at sixty and too discredited by the Burgess connection to become the director general, he was appointed head of security at the Atomic Energy Authority. White had been appointed Sillitoe's deputy.

White was therefore Sillitoe's obvious internal successor. As the disillusionment with the intelligence services spread within Whitehall, his personal behaviour and bearing were noticed by those mandarins who sought solace or scapegoats for past crises. Although the choice ostensibly would be the home secretary's, the prime minister was also to be consulted, an admission that control of the Security Service remained an uneasy alliance between the two ministers ever since MI5 had forcefully broken the relationship with its original parent, the War Office. To overcome that bureaucratic tangle, the new director general needed to be a proven master of tact.

Despite Maclean's escape, White had won the confidence of Frank Newsome, the awesome permanent secretary at the Home Office. 'White had persuaded Whitehall that he was not to blame for the disaster,' Simkins told an inquirer. 'And because the issue was still so secret and delicate, the facts were insufficiently known to disprove his contention.'

The qualities required of an intelligence chief were evident: balance, clarity, judgment, credibility, honesty, cool management in the face of a crisis, and the ability to convey to his political superiors in a relaxed manner the facts which demonstrated the importance of intelligence. Over the previous eighteen years, White had learnt that the intelligence officer cannot force a commander or a politician to accept the truth of intelligence. Everything depended upon his 'voice'. In briefings, he needed the answers and a good memory in order to place the topic within its context but, similarly, he was required to confess if an answer was not available. As Dostoyevsky hinted, 'what matters most is not what people say but how they say it.'

White had displayed those qualities, but he nonetheless despaired of winning the appointment. In 1952, after another reprimand from Sillitoe, his sentiments against his superior hardened:

'I found Sillitoe vapid and shallow and frequently wrong. I was close to leaving to try my hand at something else. I was fortunate that I swallowed my justified anger. For, the next thing I knew, Sillitoe recommended me as head of the Security Service.'[60] The road to the succession had not been as easy as White imagined. Sillitoe had 'bitterly opposed' White's candidature and had urged another chief constable to 'throw his hat in the ring'. The friend had declined to do so and, in turn, Sillitoe lobbied the home secretary to select a former colonial police officer. That failed. White's credentials to become the new director general were too strong to resist. Nevertheless, he expressed 'surprise' when offered the post. Liddell's 'personal disappointment was matched by his warm congratulations' on his former protégé's appointment.[61]

White's revenge on Sillitoe was swift. One year later, the former chief submitted his memoirs, *Cloak Without Dagger*, for vetting. White first opposed their publication and then agreed, but subject to massive deletions. MI5, the new director general insisted, should remain in the shadows. Sillitoe, in revenge, secured Attlee to write the foreword. 'Incredible!' exclaimed White.

In unison, the staff at Leconfield House greeted White's appointment with relief. 'We've got a professional and not a policeman in charge,' smiled Simkins. Malcolm Muggeridge, then the editor of *Punch*, was less complimentary: 'Dear old Dick White, "the schoolmaster". I just can't believe it.'[62]

CHAPTER SIX

Frustrations

As director general of MI5, White was no longer a spy but a diplomat, bureaucrat, turf-fighter, manager and commuter around Whitehall. Soon after his appointment, White visited Sir George Turner, the permanent under secretary at the War Office, the department used by Security Service officers for cover as their 'official' employer. Up to that point, White had contented himself with the thought that his promotion – an internal appointment – confirmed the efficacy of MI5. Unlike Sillitoe, he would be able to give orders and advice drawing on his experience. 'I know the job and I can hand down decisions to my chaps knowing that they will win respect.' Rectifying the mistakes of Sillitoe's leadership would expunge the latest slump in MI5's morale and status.

After pouring a sherry, Turner smiled. 'You think you were made director because you know your job, don't you, Dick?' White nodded. 'Well, in fact you don't know your job. You were appointed because they trust you.' Understandably, White was startled. Turner continued, 'They trust you to spend taxpayers' money carefully and advise ministers wisely. You're the front man to consort with the politicians, speaking to them when necessary and justifying to them what we're doing.'

Forty years later, White was still convinced by that homily. 'It seems a miracle that I got the job, because it doesn't seem my nature was fitted for it.' It was precisely that modesty which favoured White's candidature. Seventeen years of experience had produced a forty-six-year-old intelligence officer, discreet and self-controlled, a survivor thanks to an instinctive avoidance of pitfalls. The blame for MI5's earlier lapses, faulty judgments and humiliations was borne by others, although White's loyalty precluded the casting of any aspersions on his friends. On reflection, his promotion seemed effortless. He shone among his peers, who were generally regarded in Whitehall as a mixture of the mediocre and the obscure.

Unlike Liddell, White displayed stability in his personal life. To his neighbours in Nutborne, near Pulborough in Sussex, he and Kate were a contented civil service couple with two sons, Johnny and Stephen (who was born in 1953). They had moved two years earlier after an insurance company had declared their London hillside house on the verge of collapse – the building remains intact today. Their move to the small Sussex village, however, was dictated by concern for their children. The more perceptive might have noticed that the elder evinced a slight mental handicap, but the parents lovingly brushed aside the impediment to create a normal home. For ten years, neither the 150 villagers nor White's sons had any idea of his employment other than that he was employed by the government. The Whites rarely socialised in the village, preferring to meet friends in London or visit the West End theatre. For their immediate neighbour, an amusing dispute about the method of growing peas was the outstanding anecdote from a decade of close proximity.

In the confined, introspective world of MI5, White's utter reliability was reassuring. He never displayed unease about the purpose of a security service nor did others doubt his allegiance. His reputation as a cautious, cool administrator encouraged trust. 'He knew everything about MI5 to his fingertips,' remarked his colleague Walter Bell. No mention of his appointment appeared in the newspapers nor was anything announced in Parliament. White was not only unknown, he was also invisible. Walking through London in his customary grey suit, he was submerged among the mêlée of office workers. Those encountering this agreeable figure, wholly free of obsessions, would never detect even the hint of a man for whom concealment had become second nature.

He was the anonymous director of an organisation governed by a three-page charter but without any status in law. This absence of legal status was an anomaly, setting MI5 apart from the security services of every other country in the world, whether democracy or dictatorship, but it was justified and even envied as a source of strength. Denied any legal powers, White was nevertheless authorised, in the interests of the nation's security, to pry into the affairs of every individual in the land. The limitations of his authority depended upon his own self-discipline, the animus of his political masters and his taking care to avoid public exposure. 'I could only advise ministers on risks to security. The decision to take action was the politicians.' Under his control were experts in lock-picking, burglary, telephone-tapping, placing bugs, opening sealed letters, organising surveillance, photographing targets in compromising circumstances and blackmailers.

Improperly used, his signature – even his nod of approval – could disturb relationships, careers and lives without any redress for those afflicted. Although in theory his officers required signed authorisation to break into homes, eavesdrop and breach confidentialities, in practice he knew that there was a higher law: thou shall not get caught. Unaccountable to the public, MI5 understood that those in Whitehall whose job was to safeguard the national interest approved of MI5's surreptitious activities. Imbued with liberal values, White was the human face of the secret police, ostensibly avoiding investigations which resembled the McCarthyite purge erupting over America but nevertheless the architect of a counter-attack against Soviet subversion, in pursuit of which he was willing to co-operate with requests from both the CIA and FBI to vet individual British subjects for communist sympathies.

On the fifth floor of Leconfield House, White's office was at the end of a long secretarial enclave, protected by an automatic lock. Approaching his door through the outer offices, the visitor would see a green light above the door. A flash signalled Molly Price-Smith, his secretary, to allow entry. The leather chairs and long conference table gave his room an atmosphere that was both comfortable and efficient. The daily routine varied only in the faces he confronted, among the personal circus of committees and meetings. Internally these enabled him to administer MI5's bureaucracy; externally, they required him to visit the Cabinet Office, the Joint Intelligence Committee, embassies, the directors of foreign intelligence services and occasionally the home secretary's and prime minister's private offices.

Although his domain was considerably expanded compared to the cottage organisation which he had originally joined – in 1953 MI5 employed just over 600 people – he had already formulated the blueprint for complete reorganisation to prevent recurrence of the post-1945 disasters. The omens seemed favourable. Institutions rarely welcome modernisation, but White's promise of change was universally applauded. Unlike his two predecessors he was an insider who understood the need to encourage his colleagues to work together as a team and who trusted those whom he had come to know. Morale and pride in MI5 needed to be restored, professionalism encouraged and a *raison d'être* inculcated within each officer. Few disputed that White was a natural leader, and men of that breed automatically encourage loyalty and affection. It was an outstanding opportunity to launch changes that were long overdue. The blueprint, first written by White in Germany in 1945, had been repeatedly revised with Liddell's help during the grim Sillitoe years. Renaming the divisions 'branches' and reshuffling their responsibilities was a symbol of the reforms. Their substance was the selection of his senior staff.

Observing politicians and military commanders over the years, White had learnt to remain aloof, not too readily available to subordinates. In giving preference to men of loyalty and experience rather than talent, he was fulfilling his desire to delegate: 'I always selected officers whom I could trust completely.'[1] In Lord Fisher's dictum, 'Favouritism is the soul of efficiency', and White's appointments reflected his gratitude to old colleagues. They also reflected MI5's inherent strengths and weaknesses.

Malcolm Cumming, who had probed White's suitability for the Service in 1935, was, despite his intellectual limitations, appointed director of A Branch, responsible for the watchers, the technical resources like microphones and locksmiths, and the registry. 'A good watcher', said White, 'is like a jockey', and in that art MI5's resources had been stretched ever since the 1930s. To cope with the huge and expanding Soviet intelligence presence in London, Cumming was ordered to replenish MI5's old expertise and coherence.[2] Cumming was also ordered to reorganise MI5's registry. Across the ground floor of Leconfield

House were thousands of files, the heart and brains of the organisation. Teams of registry queens, a mixture of harridans and attractive debutantes, methodically cross-referenced every name, sighting and movement for that moment in the future when officers on the floors above might hunt obscure trails and traces. Their methods were still primitive. Unlike the FBI, who made full use of mechanical computers, the queens poked metal rods into holes on the cards to cross-reference inquiries, and transported top-secret documents between headquarters and out-stations in fastened laundry baskets.

The director of the newly created B Branch responsible for personnel was John Marriott, a wartime double-cross officer and solicitor whose efficient rectitude had appealed to White. Others regarded him – the architect of MI5's first personnel office, replacing haphazard patronage with a formal, better-paid career structure – as glacial and unpleasant. Instead of relying upon personal recommendations and the minor public schools, recruits would be drawn from a wider net and would in future be positively vetted – a method favoured by White over lie-detectors. But Marriott would prove unable to orchestrate the radical reforms required. MI5 would be cursed by only four tiers of staff grades, frustrating those whose talent required recognition and promotion, labouring within a service isolated from the outside world.

C Branch under Martin Furnival 'Fruity' Jones, another solicitor, who had worked with White at SHAEF during the war, was responsible for security. Reliable but uninspired was the general judgment of a man without experience of investigations, agent-running or communism.

White's B Division, responsible for counter-espionage, became D Branch under Graham Mitchell, an expert on fascist organisations whose prime target now was the Soviet and communist satellite embassies in London. Born in 1905 and educated at Winchester and Oxford, Mitchell had joined the service in 1939 and, though hindered by polio, had in White's judgment, proved a 'competent' field officer. With Jack Morton, he directed at most thirty officers and secretaries to monitor over 300 Soviet bloc intelligence officers under diplomatic cover. Aware that MI5 was 'swamped', White expounded, 'Let's not just sit here, let's take them on!'[3] But the CIA liaison officers criticised the Branch as 'too desk-bound'. Despite their expansion, 'There were no successes.'[4]

The litmus test was Mitchell's pursuit of the Cambridge Ring. For two years, MI5 had been plagued by the fear of traitors within. Even in the canteen, the sight of a stranger caused whispers, security checks and mutual suspicion. 'The office is in ferment and unsure of itself,' an officer observed. Philby had ended an era of trust. But, freed of Arthur Martin's pressure, Mitchell proposed a gradual deceleration of the investigations. The Philby saga had sharply reduced the FBI's flow of information from the Venona intercepts, and interviews with suspects had become unproductive. White approved in 1954 the termination of inquiries: 'The Soviets had enjoyed good fortune and I doubted that there would be more revelations. Unlike Ultra, where we knew the inside of the German High Command, we never got inside the Russians through Venona.'[5] Philby, he decided, should no longer be investigated. By any measure, White's decision was an admission of failure, a torment not only for himself but for British intelligence services until the end of his life, for the eventual resolution would be an untidy, scandal-ridden débâcle – anathema to an intelligence officer.

E Branch, responsible for security throughout the British Empire, was placed under Bill Magan. Commanding the largest number of officers of any MI5 branch, Magan was trusted by White to oversee the suppression of communism in Malaya and other Far East colonies, and to liaise with the friendly security services of India, the United States, the Dominions, the old Empire and the Commonwealth.

F Branch was White's major innovation. Following Maxwell Knight's pre-war penetration of the British Communist Party, White expanded MI5's operations to infiltrate every leftist organisation in Britain, including the Labour Party, the fringe socialist parties, the trade unions, the peace movements and the student unions. In an era when the West appeared to be on the retreat or at best on the defensive throughout the world, White wanted intelligence about groups posing a threat to Britain, and he planned to use those sources to sneak into the Soviet Union. Even the most sane individuals were convinced, watching the communist-inspired turmoil in France and Italy, of a Soviet plot to undermine British democracy through aggressive, communist trade unionists.

In the late 1940s, White had noticed that a number of British 'peace-loving' organisations had encouraged support for Soviet policies. These organisations, indirectly financed by Moscow, regularly entertained chosen Britons and invited the favoured few to visit the Soviet Union, forbidden territory in those days. Once in Moscow, they were thoroughly screened to establish their credentials as potential Soviet agents, agitators or informants. At a succession of conferences, White agreed with Alexander Kellar, F Branch's new director and a former president of the National Union of Students, that MI5 should recruit British students and trade unionists who, directed to show sympathy towards communism, might thus be invited to Moscow. Like wine, these long-term 'sleepers' would, White hoped, mature and progress up the ranks to work alongside other MI5 sources recruited inside the unions.

On the crazy edge of that effort were F Branch's dirty tricks. In co-operation with the Foreign Office's Information Research Department, MI5's agents were encouraged to disrupt subversive organisations, even impregnating lavatory paper with an itching substance at halls hired by communist organisations. It was often 'good fun' to derail and sabotage the enemy in this way.

More serious were the burglaries of homes and offices occupied by leftists and trade unionists. The most notable, Operation Party Piece, masterminded by Hugh Winterton, was a burglary in 1955 of a flat occupied by a senior Communist Party official. In the haul, MI5 seized and photographed the files detailing the party's entire 55,000 membership.[6] 'It satisfied a belief that the party and the trade unions were being used by Moscow as vehicles for intelligence,' according to a participating MI5 officer. 'We were convinced that agents of influence would be used as agents of intelligence.'

White's final and most controversial decision was to appoint

Roger Hollis as MI5's deputy director general. Since his unremarkable spell monitoring Soviet activities during the war, and
his perfunctory treatment of the two Soviet intelligence officers
Gouzenko and Volkov, he had been director of C Division,
responsible for advising institutions about security. The promotion of Hollis, always dressed in Whitehall's uniform of a
black jacket and pinstripe trousers, betokened White's propensity
to retain weak men and avoid the distress of dismissals. If pressed,
White justified his appointment of this colourless administrator
on the ground that there was no alternative candidate. Others
would criticise White's lack of vision. 'It showed that there
was to be no root-and-branch reorganisation,' Sir John Hunt,
a cabinet secretary, remarked twenty years later. 'And that was
necessary.' White, like his senior staff, remained victims of MI5's
wartime successes. 'I wanted changes,' he claimed, but he lacked
the ruthlessness to put his intention into practice.

Within the government, there was limited interest in White's
reforms. Although MI5 was a guardian of the nation's security,
Churchill, the prime minister since 1951, had not altered his
jaundiced wartime impression of the service. White's relations
with the seventy-eight-year-old premier were not improved when,
in Downing Street on one of their rare meetings, he stepped out
of line during a relaxed conversation in the course of which
Beaverbrook and Bracken were mentioned. Unwittingly and
uncharacteristically, White expressed his profound dislike for
Bracken, whom he had known at school: 'I got a special glare
from the old man. It was not my finest hour I fear. I never
understood how either of those men could be his old friends.'[7]

Direct political control over MI5 was exercised by Sir David
Maxwell-Fyfe, the home secretary, who showed little interest in
the service. At their few meetings, Maxwell-Fyfe told White
to 'wage war on the communists and crypto-communists' and
delegated the details to Frank Newsome, the omnipotent permanent secretary. Neither Maxwell-Fyfe nor Newsome ever
visited Leconfield House. MI5's status as a deliberately isolated,
self-ruling secret army prevented any investigation of its own mistakes. The mandarin, White discovered, did not probe for
explanations to unanswered riddles such as Burgess and Maclean,

nor did he question MI5's obsession with something called 'product', the information classified as 'vital to the nation'.[8] Shielded from supervision and professional management, and sealed off by perpetuation of the 'need to know' rule of confidentiality even at the highest levels within Whitehall, White could assert his total domination.

During his occasional meetings with Newsome, White discussed MI5's requirements, faithfully requesting permission to tap phones and intercept the mail of suspects, including members of parliament who were deemed too close to Moscow. By law, each intercept required the express permission of the home secretary, but Newsome would approve some intercepts without securing the politician's signature. Occasionally, he would take the initiative and suggest that a particular target should be pursued: 'This does seem important and it would be a mark in your favour if . . .' How the name reached Newsome, White was never quite sure, since the civil servant confided to him that Maxwell-Fyfe, 'while respecting MI5, was not interested in its work'.[9] The minister never asked for evidence of MI5's performance.

'Our feeling was that quality control was impossible,' recalled Philip Allen, then the assistant under secretary, who rose to become the Home Office's senior official. 'We were content to let them surface and occasionally provide us with something.' According to Allen, 'Dick seemed occasionally unhappy in his job. He gave the impression of distaste for spying and a wish to become a permanent secretary of a normal department.'[10] That attitude encouraged Newsome not to fear embarrassment. A reluctant spymaster was more likely to be honest. 'Dick didn't hold back on us like others.'

Honesty unintentionally bred defensiveness and even passivity about Soviet intelligence operations in Britain. While complaining about inadequate resources to contain the explosion of such activities, White never commissioned a special study to turn the attack upon the communists. Instead, he tolerated harmless skirmishes. There were attempts to compromise Soviet diplomats in 'honeytraps', including an expensive operation using an attractive girl to travel to Leningrad by boat in an adjoining cabin to a Soviet intelligence officer. The Russian stepped off the boat, never having glanced at the girl. Or White favoured elaborate operations resembling the wartime double-cross techniques to entrap Soviets who had approached émigré communities in London. All proved unsuccessful.[11]

Unlike the FBI, with its teams of specialists trained to approach Soviet and satellite diplomats and seek their defection (albeit with an initial lack of success), White resisted aggressive overtures to recruit Soviet intelligence officers in London. In conversations with Charles Bates, the FBI liaison officer in London, he conceded that MI5 had failed to recruit a single Soviet source: 'He admitted that MI5 didn't understand how the KGB and GRU operated.'[12] White understood his own predicament. MI5 personnel, unlike FBI officers, were not gumshoe investigators, delighted by the theatre of tradecraft on city streets. Their preference was for reading reports and files in Leconfield House, occasionally meeting an agent, but relying on watchers and Special Branch officers to deliver eyewitness information. Little had altered since Swinton had highlighted the problem in 1940.

The pressure for change emanated from Washington. In 1952, Britain had exploded its first atomic bomb, and in 1955, after Congress passed the Atomic Energy Act allowing the British access to American expertise, Bates arrived in London to check security at Britain's atomic installations, then the responsibility of Guy Liddell. Bates reported that security was 'non-existent'. After delivering a protest to the British ambassador in Washington recalling the lapses in the Fuchs and Maclean cases, he found it necessary to return to Britain twice during that year. In conversations with White, he voiced what became a constant complaint about British security. Both the CIA and FBI were regularly using polygraphs, not only on their own officers but also on their sources. Plans were under development to equip mobile polygraph officers to travel abroad to test informants in hotel rooms. Unsuccessfully, Bates urged White to adopt the more scientific approach. 'Positive vetting would be more effective,' replied White. 'There's no evidence of that either' was Bates's retort.

To repair the damage done to its relationship with the FBI, White believed, Britain would have to prove its excellence and indispensability in specialist fields. Among those was the development of scientific aids. Every month, White attended a small, informal committee at the Ministry of Defence chaired by R.V. Jones, the director of scientific intelligence, widely praised for his outstanding wartime contribution to the defeat of Germany's Luftwaffe. With Sir John Sinclair, the chief of SIS, and the director of military intelligence, White discussed MI5's technical problems and queried how they might be solved by scientists. 'It was a legacy of what worked so well during the war,' recalls Jones. 'White appreciated how to use science for intelligence. There was often a smile of appreciation on his face whenever I hit the nail on the head.'

On leaving government service in 1954, Jones recommended that White appoint a permanent scientist. Malcolm Cumming recommended Peter Wright, a radio enthusiast employed at Marconi who had in the previous year helped American technicians understand the revolutionary design of a small transmitter placed by Soviet intelligence in the Great Seal fixed to the wall behind the American ambassador's chair in the Moscow embassy. At their first meeting, according to Wright, White said, 'I'm not sure we need an animal like you in the Security Service.'[13] White denied that exchange, and indeed there was no doubt that the director general welcomed Wright's recruitment. The sentiment was reciprocated. Dick White, wrote Wright, was 'a brilliant, intuitive intelligence officer'.[14]

Wright's reward was to be introduced to an unconventional lifestyle: 'For five years we bugged and burgled our way across London at the State's behest, while pompous bowler-hatted civil servants in Whitehall pretended to look the other way.'[15] His more formal task was to fathom the pattern of Soviet radio signals, and his work directly improved MI5's relations with the American intelligence services. Short of finding defectors, the interception and deciphering of radio signals was the most effective way of discovering the thoughts and intentions of other governments, both friendly and hostile. The excitement of a hot transcript, a conversation between two enemies, was guaranteed to win Whitehall's praise and the customers' approval for extra funds to reproduce the great Ultra success.

Breaking the codes of government messages depended upon the status of the country. Poor Third World countries used codes and machines whose technology was well known and vulnerable to British intelligence. By contrast, the Soviet bloc's was sophisticated, and the sole hope of breaking the codes depended upon access to codebooks.

Operation Halt was designed by MI5 to secure codebooks from foreign embassies.[16] Except for limited successes, including a Czech codebook provided by a defector, most communist traffic remained indecipherable. It was Peter Wright who offered one solution. By inserting a bug in the telephone near the Hagelin cipher machine in the Egyptian embassy, experts at GCHQ (Government Communications Headquarters, where radio signals were intercepted and, if possible, deciphered) could every morning disentangle the precise sound of the wheels being set by the clerks in the code machines. It would allow the British to listen to some Egyptian traffic during the Suez crisis.[17]

Once the insertion of minuscule and undetectable microphone transmitters inside walls became technically possible, MI5 officers, with White's approval, were deployed across the capital to insert them into Soviet and satellite buildings. Those operations had two consequences. Friendly foreign intelligence services requested Wright's radio expertise, a commodity which MI5 readily traded, especially with the CIA. His technology would help White re-establish a closer relationship with American intelligence. Secondly, White's gratitude for Wright's contribution led him eventually to trust the technician more than was judicious. Their convergence towards a closer relationship began just after Wright's recruitment.

On 2 April 1954, Vladimir Petrov, an intelligence officer at the Soviet embassy in Canberra, defected in Australia. Petrov's defection, marked by high drama as his wife was frogmarched on to a plane by two burly Soviet security officers for a return trip to Moscow, was a propaganda coup for the West, with photographs of Evdokia Petrov's abduction reproduced in the world's newspapers. After Mrs Petrov had been rescued at Darwin, with further sensational photographs, a news blackout was imposed on the incident. MI5's close relationship with the

Australian intelligence service ensured that Petrov's disclosures were passed on to White. For Britain, the Soviet's most important revelation was his confirmation that Burgess and Maclean had been recruited by the NKVD in the 1930s and that both were now living in Russia. Although White had already assumed as much, especially after Melinda Maclean with Soviet assistance disappeared from her home in Switzerland in 1953, Petrov's evidence that the two men had been tipped off to flee by an unidentified 'Third Man' was explosive.*

By then White had convinced himself that the flight of Burgess and Maclean was a 'KGB disaster'. He surmised that Burgess, whom he curiously damned as 'disgracefully inept',[18] must have fled because of 'a mistake' born of real stress, or possibly because the Soviets feared that he would not be able to withstand interrogation if left behind. Although his assumption about the Soviet distrust of Burgess was correct, his belief that the Cambridge group was not the product of skilful Soviet recruitment and nurturing, but was 'very largely self-inspired' was an error which was to give rise to damaging complications.[19]

White was convinced that Burgess and Maclean were members of a 'Ring of Five', an OGPU/NKVD cell structure which had been described by a Soviet illegal in an article written in 1933 for the *New Statesman*.[20] The genesis of the Ring of Five, White believed, was a Comintern plan which only later actually had come into 'the hands of the NKVD'. But that belief was mistaken. Philby and the others, it transpired much later, actually had been recruited by Soviet intelligence. The reference to the Comitern, the international movement, had been a ruse to reassure wavering recruits and to mislead MI5. White's confusion derived from his refusal to believe that Burgess could be a ringmaster and from a simple lack of hard evidence about Soviet operations from an insider.

In Moscow, at least forty names had been listed in the pre-war era as sources in the NKVD's British section. A decision to give priority to five was taken for purely administrative reasons. With

---

*Petrov's impeccable source was Filip Kislytsin, a Soviet intelligence officer who had served in London 1945-8.

limited staff and an avalanche of material, Modin had been ordered to select the five most productive sources. Information from the remainder would be read only if time permitted. But thereafter the identities of the five varied as the quality of their information changed. Later in Moscow, Maclean spoke of a 'Ring of Four',[21] and further analysis of the Venona intercepts had already revealed that Boris Krotov, a senior intelligence officer in London, had reported to Moscow on the activities of some eight British spies. White knew by 1955 that MI5's list of suspects included over twenty names, but apparently he did not believe that speculation about a Ring of Five was confusing. Certainly he would have been compromised if the notion of a Ring of Five were to become public. Since only two spies were known, it would suggest that three other traitors were still unaccounted for.

The unresolved riddles would have remained obscured had White not heard, towards the end of 1954, that Petrov would eventually be allowed to sell his story to a newspaper. His revelations, White knew, would increase pressure on the intelligence services to produce a whole series of explanations. The previous year, MI5 had been volubly criticised by newspapers for allowing Melinda Maclean to disappear. 'There was nothing we could do to stop her,' White had lamented. But Petrov was a far more serious threat to MI5. In fact, his disclosures would inaugurate the 'molehunt', the search for a traitor within the service, an all-consuming schizophrenia for White and the next generation of intelligence officers.

With foreboding, White, unusually for the director general of MI5, approached Eden, then waiting impatiently for Churchill's final exit: 'Foreign Secretary, I would like to take the initiative on the Petrov disclosures and publish the material now.'

'Why?'

'It will undermine Philby. It will create uncertainty for Philby. We'll lure him into a new interview and try again to get a confession.'

'The timing's bad,' replied Eden, implying that exposure of the Foreign Office connection might impair his succession to Downing Street.

'It'll look like a cover-up if it comes out in any other way.'

'We'll have to take that risk,' said Eden, who knew that Lord Cadogan, the former permanent under secretary at the Foreign Office, had reviewed the diplomats' cases and recommended improvements in security, but had avoided any recriminations.[22] Dejected, White cursed Eden as a 'very vain man'.

Over the following months, in the course of which he at last became prime minister, Eden continued to resist White's repeated submissions. Initially, the MI5 chief believed that Eden was seeking to avoid unnecessary controversy in the run-up to the general election. But after Eden's victory in May 1955, he discovered his error. Eden had been told by both the Foreign Office and Sinclair that MI5's director general was pursuing a vendetta against Philby which was best ignored. White's proposed initiative, Sinclair insisted, would prove embarrassing because neither MI5's investigations nor Petrov had produced any new information against Philby. For that matter, MI5 had failed to unearth anything new about Burgess and Maclean.[23] Indeed, Graham Mitchell's investigation had effectively ground to a halt.

White was furious, above all with his idiosyncratic and unsubtle opposite number at SIS. Indicative of Sinclair's idiosyncrasies was his daily habit of lunching on a grilled herring and a glass of water. Indicative of his unsubtle mind were his interviews with the permanent under secretary at the Foreign Office: 'He sat there with a clipboard checking off the points.'[24] He represented SIS's uninterrupted military tradition, which precluded mastering the political nuances of intelligence and discounted the possibility of treachery among friends. But White's position was weakened by his own performance. Even Newsome at the Home Office reported that the MI5 director general was 'no longer hunting his prey'.[25]

At precisely that time, demonstrating MI5's fallibility, Yuri Modin, using a French passport, slipped into England and contacted Blunt at the Courtauld Institute. At a later meeting, he gave Blunt an envelope containing £5000 for Philby, whose financial difficulties had been reported to Moscow. MI5 would not become aware of that visit until a decade later.

On 18 September 1955, the *People* newspaper published Petrov's sensational story about Burgess and Maclean, shattering for ever the British government's deception about 'missing diplomats'. The two, wrote Petrov, had been recruited while undergraduates at Cambridge and their escape from Britain had been authorised and arranged by the Russians. For the first time, the government's critics realised that two members of the Establishment had been long-term penetration agents and that there was a third, unnamed agent. Most painfully for White, the draconian laws of secrecy which sheltered the Security Service were shown to have been used to conceal embarrassments rather than to protect the national interest.

London was perplexed, divided and irritated by rumours. The clamour for a government statement stemmed not only from Fleet Street but from Westminster, Whitehall and the clubs of Pall Mall. Macmillan, the new foreign secretary, summoned White: 'We're going to have to say something. There's no alternative.' White speculated about offering a 'general amnesty' to discover the truth but dismissed his own idea as impractical. 'They're all bound up together and have agreed never to reveal their conspiracy.'[26]

Hastily, the government agreed to issue a White Paper setting out the history of Burgess and Maclean. The initial draft, written by Mitchell and White, was handed over for consideration to Patrick Dean, an assistant under secretary of state at the Foreign Office responsible for liaison with SIS, and to Sinclair, before passing through the hands of the Cabinet Office and the most senior Foreign Office officials. What emerged was a serious distortion which White approved and did not condemn in his retirement. 'We thought it was perfectly all right at the time,' he insisted.

Accordingly, the eight-page White Paper foolishly minimised Maclean's position as head of the American Department, suggesting that the section 'does not deal with the major problems of Anglo-American relations'; while Burgess's career on the eve of his visit to Washington was ridiculously described as 'satisfactory and there seemed good reason to hope that he would make a useful career'. In fact, he had been on the verge of dismissal.

The references to MI5's conduct were positively disingenuous, implying that the Security Service had been suspicious of Burgess before he disappeared: 'The . . . question is how Maclean and Burgess made good their escape from this country when the security authorities were on their track.' Clearly, MI5 had been 'on the track' only of Maclean, not of Burgess. The White Paper also claimed that surveillance of Maclean's home had been 'aimed at collecting . . . information and not at preventing an escape'. In truth, none of the senior MI5 officers had even contemplated the possibility of escape. Behind the scenes, White's private assessment of the saga was also faulty, especially about Burgess. The Foreign Office official, he asserted, 'did not do much spying and was not cut out to do much', and his escape 'could not have been part of the Soviet plan'.[27]

Newspapers and politicians found other inconsistencies in the White Paper, not least the absence of any explanation for Maclean's choice of the moment to disappear. As suspicions of a cover-up grew, a wave of criticism fell on the Foreign Office. White's initial relief that MI5 was not mentioned disappeared as the second wave of reaction materialised. Just as he had predicted, Hoover and other FBI officers, annoyed by the British government's dishonesty, were seeking a channel to place Philby's name in the public domain as the Third Man. Simultaneously, a group of pro-Philby SIS officers, with the support of Sir John Sinclair, planned to remove the suspicion from their friend. Both chose Parliament as the place to vent their case. Caught in the middle, White was handicapped by his inability to deliver incriminating evidence against Philby.

Inspired by Hoover, the allegation against Philby was published on 23 October in New York's *Sunday News*. On the following Tuesday, Marcus Lipton, a Labour member of parliament, encouraged indirectly by Hoover, asked, 'Has the prime minister made up his mind to cover up at all costs the dubious third-man activities of Mr Harold Philby . . . and is he determined to stifle all discussion on the very great matters which were evaded in the wretched White Paper, which is an insult to the intelligence of this country?'[28] The Labour attack was countered by Dick Brooman-White, a former SIS officer and Conservative, who ridiculed the notion of Philby's disloyalty. Supported from his own benches, Harold Macmillan (answering for Eden) promised that the whole issue would be debated on 7 November.

Over the following fifteen days, White battled with the pro-Philby faction in SIS, his position weakened by the cabinet's lack of sympathy. Eden had declared his opposition; the home secretary, Gwilym Lloyd George, a political lightweight, bent with the prevailing wind; while Macmillan had developed an instinctive wariness of any pitfalls which might hinder his ambitions.

During their conversations at the Foreign Office, White reflected that Macmillan's wartime experience had fostered a jaundiced opinion of the two non-military intelligence services and that the foreign secretary was sceptical that the Philby saga was handicapping the relationship with the Americans. Macmillan's prejudice, White knew, was shared by senior Foreign Office officials, whose scorn for the failure of SIS to deliver reliable information was capped by their assumption of Philby's innocence. The two men reached an impasse when Macmillan expressed the opinion that the Philby affair was an internecine squabble between MI5 and SIS which should not be referred to him: 'I'm unpersuaded that the Security Service was not at fault.'[29] Macmillan's only concession was to sympathise with the constraints operating upon MI5 in a free society. MI5, he ruled, should not be allowed to reinterrogate Philby. His stubbornness, White complained, had been nurtured by Sinclair.

Convinced that Philby was orchestrating a campaign within SIS against the Security Service, White shuddered at the prospect of a conspiracy among an unrevealed communist ring. Although he had the sympathy and respect of officials in the Cabinet Office, he was unable to turn the tide. Since MI5 was refused permission to renew its questioning of Philby, White asked Jack Easton, SIS's vice-chief and a fellow sceptic, to persuade Sinclair to arrange his own interrogation. Grudgingly Sinclair agreed. 'Produce the evidence,' he told White with evident resentment, 'and there'll be no further dispute.' Invited to a safe house, Philby was questioned by three SIS officers and their conversation was recorded. White was 'livid' when he read the transcript. No attempt had been made to probe the suspect in those areas where MI5 had provided evidence of serious inconsistencies. But the truth was that White had provided no new, irrefutable evidence.

As his date for questioning in the House of Commons loomed, Macmillan rejected White's plea that he resist Foreign Office advice to clear Philby. If Philby could not be convicted, Macmillan insisted, he had to be exonerated: 'We can't stop the man leaving Britain.'[30] Macmillan went on to tell the cabinet, 'It will not be very easy to make a wholly convincing defence of what has happened in the past.' But he was mindful that 'Nothing would be worse than a lot of muckraking and innuendo.' He was therefore willing to approve an inquiry to satisfy the public that 'something is being inquired into', which could be diverted into a harmless debate about 'security in a free society'.[31] Humiliation, White lamented, was the best he could expect. In the event, it was worse than that.

After lunch with King Feisal of Iraq, Macmillan set off for the House of Commons. In the car, he mentioned to Andrew Stark, his assistant private secretary: 'I hope the opposition don't know that Maclean's brother Alan is employed by my family's publishing company.' But he 'was not unduly perturbed,' remembered Stark, 'even if it was a tricky and difficult moment.'[32] Just after 3.30, Macmillan rose in a crowded House and repudiated the notion that there had been a 'tip-off' to the traitors from Washington. 'No evidence has been found that [Philby] was responsible for warning Burgess or Maclean. While in government [sic] he carried out his duties ably and conscientiously. I have no reason to conclude that Mr Philby has at any time betrayed the interests of this country, or to identify him with the so-called "Third Man", if indeed there was one.'

When he heard reports of this statement, White cursed Macmillan as having been 'far too generous. Unnecessarily.'[33] In desperation, he dispatched Hollis to meet Lipton in the House of Commons lobby to seek the source of his information about Philby. Hollis returned empty-handed. The politician was even forced publicly to retract his allegations, thus confirming White's defeat. The final humiliation was the news that Sinclair, who had allowed Philby to be told in advance the substance of Macmillan's statement, had agreed to his suggestion of a press conference the following day.

Standing by the fireplace in a crowded room at his mother's Kensington flat, Philby impressed many as the victim of an injustice whose apparent candour was restrained only by his careful adherence to the Official Secrets Act. 'I have never been a communist,' he said. 'The last time I spoke to a communist, knowing he was one, was in 1934.'[34] Soon afterwards, two SIS colleagues quietly assured Philby that they would seek his re-employment by his old service, alias the Firm. The following year he would move to the Lebanon as a respected journalist and paid SIS agent.

In later years, White would point to that frustrating and unsuccessful battle as 'proof' that Philby's jibe that the MI5 chief's most obvious fault was 'a tendency to agree with the last person he spoke to' was untrue.[35] To mollify him in the wake of the fiasco, White was awarded the KBE, an irony which he did not savour.

In Washington, Philby's exoneration was received with a mixture of fury, bewilderment and resignation. Those who had argued in 1951 for a cessation of intelligence-sharing with the British despite the wartime links had long been overcome by the fund of goodwill towards the two British services. Much of the credit was owed to Kenneth Strong, Eisenhower's wartime intelligence chief, whose judgment had always been appreciated by Bedell Smith, the CIA director. 'We'd be cutting off our nose to spite our face' was the sentiment echoing down the line.[36] In the midst of the Cold War, the CIA was too unsuccessful to deprive itself of help from allied agencies. It was just another of those 'blips and squeezes' which could not be allowed to harm the alliance. The FBI formally closed its case files.

In February 1956, Burgess and Maclean appeared for the first time in Moscow to deliver a public statement. This was followed by publication of a sympathetic biography of Burgess written by Tom Driberg, the Labour politician and informant to both MI5 and the KGB, by a self-defeating autobiography by Goronwy Rees, and by a resumption of correspondence between Burgess and some Establishment friends in London. White was defeated by a web of relationships and a lack of honest patriotism which he found totally alien.

Unexpectedly, Sinclair's nemesis followed shortly afterwards, following events that at last vindicated White's criticisms of SIS. Late on Thursday, 19 April 1956, Malcolm Cumming told White that an SIS operation in Portsmouth harbour had gone terribly wrong. It was the third day of a state visit by Nikita Khrushchev and Marshal Nikolai Bulganin, the Soviet leaders, whose presence in Britain had been hailed by Eden as a reward for his diplomacy and as proof that Britain still counted as one of the Big Three powers. In anticipation of the visit, MI5 and SIS had compiled a list of intelligence operations which were to be undertaken.

The SIS department responsible was the so-called London station, codenamed BIN. Based in Londonderry House, Victoria, and under the command of Nicholas Elliott and his deputy Andrew King, the station operated against foreign diplomats, businessmen and their buildings in Britain. The twenty officers not only monitored the communications of target embassies and personalities, but made the first attempts to recruit foreign diplomats as agents, and to seek help from British visitors to the Soviet Union. Ten days before the visit, John Bruce Lockhart, SIS's controller Western Europe, presented a file containing six proposed operations to Michael Williams, the Foreign Office official responsible for liaison. Bruce Lockhart told Williams, 'I've put the dicey operations at the beginning of the file and the safer ones at the back.'[37]

Among those at the back of the file was a request by the Admiralty that a frogman should examine the propeller and rudder of the *Ordjonikidze*, the cruiser which would transport the Soviet leaders and which would be anchored in Portsmouth harbour. In general terms, it was a routine inspection, carried out by all the naval powers against foreign states. The Admiralty's experts wanted to know the dimensions of the propeller, because the craft was faster than originally estimated by Naval Intelligence and its features were important for setting homing torpedoes.

Williams was distracted by his father's death early that morning. Without comment, he returned the file to Bruce Lockhart, who assumed that the Admiralty's request had been

approved. SIS had followed its normal procedures but Williams
had failed to inform his own superiors of the details of Bruce
Lockhart's shopping list. 'I should have been told,' says Patrick
Dean, 'but I wasn't.'[38] Eden later asserted that he had forbidden
all intelligence operations during the visit.[39] If he gave that order,
it was not received by SIS or MI5. Instead, both intelligence
agencies bugged and monitored the visitors.

The chain of command for the *Ordjonikidze* operation was confused. Elliott had delegated all the operational decisions to Ted
Davies, a junior officer, bypassing King. Davies in turn appointed
Bernard Smith as case officer and thereafter exercised little
supervision. Elliott's reaction when Bruce Lockhart subsequently
criticised the lack of clear command was revelatory: 'We don't
have a chain of command. We work like a club.'[40]

The frogman selected by Elliott for the inspection was Commander Lionel 'Buster' Crabb, a veteran and trusted frogman
who had been used by SIS since the war. 'He begged to be
allowed to do the job for patriotic reasons,' explained Elliott
in self-defence, while admitting that his chosen frogman was 'a
heavy smoker and not in the best of health'.[41]

On 16 April, the day before the cruiser was due to arrive,
Crabb and Bernard Smith arrived in Portsmouth and committed
a catalogue of errors indicative of SIS's incompetence. Instead of
sleeping overnight at the 'Fort', the secure SIS base in nearby
Gosport, Smith, who had just suffered a mild heart attack,
registered with Crabb in a local hotel. Both signed in their real
names. In the column for addresses, Smith scribbled, 'Attached
to the Foreign Office'. That evening, contrary to the fundamental
rules of diving, Crabb drank at least five double whiskys. By
daybreak, the toxicity in his blood remained fatally high.

On the 17th, Crabb commenced his first dive and then surfaced
near the Russian cruiser. After resubmerging, he returned to the
shore for some adjustments and dived again. He did not return.
Smith raised the alarm in London and at that stage White was
alerted. The eyewitness to that moment is Peter Wright, whose
version was broadly confirmed by White: 'We all trooped upstairs.
Dick was sitting at his desk. There was no hint of a welcoming
smile. His charm had all but deserted him, and the years of

schoolmaster training came to the fore.'[42] Having heard SIS's report, 'White looked unconvinced. He smoothed his temples. He shuffled his papers. The clock ticked gently in the corner. Telltale signs of panic oozed from every side of the room. "We must do everything to help you, of course. I will go and see the PM this evening, and see if I can head this thing off."' Cumming was tasked to help SIS mastermind the cover-up.

An MI5 officer and a senior police officer sped to the Portsmouth hotel. They requested the registration book and tore out the page with Crabb's name. The hotel's owner was given a receipt for the page and a warning not to mention the incident. By then, the *Ordjonikidze*'s commander had alerted his superiors that the crew had spotted a frogman surfacing between their ship and an escorting destroyer. No former protest was initially lodged but during a reception the incident was mentioned by the commander to his British hosts. The commander-in-chief Portsmouth, denying knowledge of any frogman, assured the Russian there would be an inquiry and hoped that all discussion had been terminated.

On 29 April, the Admiralty curtly announced that Crabb 'is presumed to be dead as a result of trials with certain underwater equipment'. This bland statement about a well-known character provoked newspaper suspicions and their inquiries were fuelled by a Soviet leak about the subsequent protest to the Admiralty.

Eden was not told of Crabb's disappearance until 3 May. Furious that a grubby shadow had been cast over his international diplomacy and ignoring similar operations by the Soviets against the Royal Navy, Eden told the Commons the next day that Crabb was 'presumed' dead and added an unprecedented rider: 'I think it is necessary, in the special circumstances of this case, to make it clear that what was done was done without the authority or the knowledge of Her Majesty's ministers. Appropriate disciplinary steps are being taken.' Ten days later, in the wake of the subsequent furore, which had exposed the background to the whole operation, Eden insisted in another Commons debate that his explicit instructions had been disobeyed.

On his return to Downing Street, Eden railed to Sir Norman Brook, the cabinet secretary. SIS, he shouted, was 'incompetent and inadequate'. Its future could not be trusted under the present

management. He ordered that Sinclair's retirement should be
rapidly advanced. Who, asked the prime minister, was his
successor? The internal candidate was Jack Easton, second in
command of RAF intelligence during the war, organising special
operations with SOE and SIS, and a member of SIS since 1945.
By informal agreement, an RAF officer was next on the rote to
become chief. But Brook disparaged Easton. Although reliable,
he was judged neither experienced nor inspired enough to reform
SIS. The outstanding candidate, Brook advised, was White. Eden
reacted with resignation rather than rapture.[43]

In any country, to transfer the head of domestic counter-
intelligence to direct the nation's foreign intelligence service
is rare. Not only are the two tasks markedly different, but
mutual antagonism between the services is common. In those
circumstances, White's summons to Downing Street owed everything to Brook, a grammar-school-educated, unrelenting and
accomplished bureaucrat who held White in great esteem.

In their initial conversation, Brook confided that Eden was
neither fit nor the rational strategist he had known during the
war. There were, he said, great difficulties ahead. 'We need
you, Dick,' explained Brook, 'because you know what the British
public will tolerate. You need to bring those qualities to SIS.'[44]
White admitted his reluctance to accept the post. His arguments
were heartfelt. He had barely started his reorganisation of MI5;
he was devoted to the service; and he knew nothing of foreign
intelligence. Unable to sway Brook, he consulted Newsome. The
permanent secretary's advice was conclusive: 'You cannot refuse
a job you're offered.'

White's candidature, signalling a shift of power from the
defence establishment, was strongly opposed by Sinclair. After
their heated arguments about Philby, the retiring chief bore
considerable animosity towards White and insisted that Easton
should succeed. Among White's supporters were Patrick Reilly,
who had proposed him as chief six years earlier, Patrick Dean and
Harold Macmillan, with whom White had become 'very close'.[45]
Sinclair's protests were heard and ignored. The appointment
naturally remained unknown beyond a small circle of Whitehall
officials. Even if newspaper editors came to hear of the change,

they were effectively forbidden to publish news about the up-heaval.

Within MI5, news of White's imminent departure spread gloom. His reforms had only just begun and the contem-poraneous award of a knighthood to Blunt, a suspect among some senior MI5 officers, confirmed how much was left undone. According to Wright, White's transfer 'bolstered' the status of SIS but 'condemned the Service he left to ten years of neglect,' because his successor was Roger Hollis. 'The era of elegance and modernisation had ended,' wrote Wright, and events would prove him partially correct. White justified his deputy's promotion on the ground that he was the best man available, a poor reflection on MI5 and on White himself.

A hasty collection within Leconfield House raised an unusu-ally large sum to buy an old English silver tea-set, which was presented to the outgoing chief in the canteen. In his emotional farewell speech, White recalled his twenty years in MI5. When he joined, thanks to Cumming, there had been just thirty officers, and the war years had proved an era of success. The problems since 1951 were passed off as 'challenges which we will overcome'. In fact, the unresolved Soviet penetration by the Cambridge Ring would dominate the remainder of his life.

On leaving MI5, White could also claim to have improved relations with several countries where MI5 officers were based as representatives, and none had been improved more dramatically than those with Colonel Richard Callanan, the new chief of the Irish Security and Intelligence Service. White had visited Callanan as an afterthought shortly before his abrupt departure. After their formal discussions, Callanan asked whether White had any special requests. 'I'd like to visit Cecil Liddell,' replied White. Liddell, Guy's brother and MI5's liaison officer in Dublin during the Second World War, had retired to an island in Dublin Bay.

Aboard a police launch, White was soon speeding across the choppy sea towards a grey speck. As he approached, he noticed a large white tarpaulin stretched between rocks. Puzzled and straining to see, he took the binoculars from the launch's silent captain. The tarpaulin's message, written in giant letters, was calculated to gratify that small band of pre-war MI5 officers who, like White, had suffered Whitehall's deadly bureaucracy: 'Fuck the War Office'.

CHAPTER SEVEN

The Office

On 14 July 1956 White arrived at 54 Broadway Buildings, alias the 'Firm', the 'Friends' or the 'Office', in the wake of one disaster, the Crabb affair, and amid the makings of another, Suez: 'I was plunged in at the deep end with a lot to learn.' There was no official announcement. Inside Broadway, gossip and a flurry of 'decipher yourself' cables to a number of SIS officers abroad marked his unforeseen arrival. The reluctant spymaster had been catapulted from a department imbued by leaden conservatism into an organisation of buccaneers who espoused the adventurous legacy of SOE's wartime exploits and delighted in international deception.

Newly recruited SIS officers were still dispatched to the Fort in Gosport, a walled encampment originally built by Henry VIII and devoted exclusively to SIS, to receive weapons training, to master clandestine warfare and to practise the art of 'opposed border crossings' – cutting barbed wire to crawl across hostile frontiers and rivers. 'People work for our service,' White was told by Colonel John Munn, the Fort's beloved training officer, 'not for the benefits, but out of a sense of mission. Training at the Fort bestows that sense of purpose.' In his welcoming remarks to White, Jack Easton, his new deputy, confirmed SIS's daredeviltry and quixotry: 'We're still cloak and dagger. Fisticuffs. Too many swashbuckling green thumbs thinking we're about to fight another Second World War.'[1]

White moved into C's official home at 21 Queen Anne's Gate, a pretty and quiet backwater of eighteenth-century townhouses adjacent and to the rear of Broadway Buildings. The polished brass plaque on a nearby doorway read, 'Soldiers', Sailors' and Airmen's Families Association'. But the plaque on number 21 was unrevealing. Most of the house was dedicated to SIS offices, but on the first floor was C's two-room apartment with a large reception room and a pleasant bedroom. An extra room was provided downstairs for White's son Stephen. For the next twelve years, White would live in London during the week and spend his weekends initially in Nutbourne and later in another house at Mertham.

A bridge connected his house with the 'Office'. Every morning, walking through the narrow alley, White felt that he was entering a bunker for another day of waging the Cold War. Broadway was the headquarters of a private army, isolated from the Whitehall machine because officially it did not exist. To cynics, the building represented nothing more than a glamorous Ministry of Works. Others blessed SIS's existence for either saving their personal reputations or securing Britain's interests. To White, there were no thoughts that his officers were wilfully committing crimes, outraging morality and joyfully perpetrating deception. Daily, he entered Broadway oblivious to the criminality enjoined on his subordinates. 'Occasionally supping with the devil' was a professional requirement. 'In Britain, unlike America, I had no need to officially legitimise what had been done.'[2] In the sanitised civil servant's mind, he was serving his country.

Broadway Buildings, less than fifty years old, reeked of dust and decay. Dark corridors, countless nooks and crannies, winding staircases, brown linoleum floors, frosted-glass windows and a clanking iron lift for staff which stopped only on the fourth and seventh floors generated an eerie atmosphere. Those working on other floors used the white-tiled staircase. 'How comes this staircase looks like a public urinal?' asked one officer. 'Because only shits come in here' was the schoolboy reply.

Of course the impression of business as usual among the besuited, starch-collared officers who purposefully glided through the rabbit warren of wooden partitions belied the chaos which had hastened White's appointment. He was there to administer change. His fourth-floor, red-carpeted office was of modest size overlooking St James's underground station. To forestall intrusion by any long-lensed spies based at the headquarters of London Transport opposite, heavy curtains were permanently drawn across the windows, sharply reducing the light within the room. White sat at his large desk with his back to the window. A dowdy fireplace, fronted by a leather fender, remained unused on one side, faced by a glass cabinet filled with out-of-date reference books. Two leather armchairs stood in front of his desk, and a handful of unremarkable photographs of his predecessors hung on the wall. There was neither a safe nor a filing cabinet. Paperwork within Broadway, notorious for its poor registry, was kept to a minimum. Personal files were stored in the secretariat's rooms along the corridor. On White's desk was a bottle of green ink, used for official correspondence on the service's thick, plain and unheaded blue notepaper, and a packet of Senior Service cigarettes, which he regularly smoked.

There were no stacks of cash in the desk drawers to hand to agents, as there had been in Menzies's era, only petty-cash vouchers which White signed for Dora Edwards, his secretary, to buy cigarettes or tea for visitors. Bottles of alcohol were rarely in evidence, for White was no more than a moderate drinker. His room was functional, disguising the occupant's responsibilities and reflecting his meagre personal financial resources. Unlike his predecessors, White literally depended upon his weekly salary.

Also on the desk were four telephones. A white instrument was connected to a direct line to the Foreign Office. A green telephone was a scrambler, which prevented any eavesdropper not connected to the system from understanding the conversation. Later it was replaced by the more sophisticated Pickwick system. The first of two black telephones, which was connected to Broadway's PAX system, was rarely used since White never called his subordinates directly. Instead, such calls were made through the second black telephone connected to his secretary. Dora Edwards, a rich spinster inherited from Sinclair, prided herself on precisely identifying C's mood. Although it was unknown for White to lose his temper or raise his voice, Edwards could spot the state of his nerves and the level of his impatience by the pace of his walk around the office and the flush on his cheeks.

Gently White revised the house rules. His predecessor's 'baize door' regime which denied entry to his office unless the red light disappeared and a green flashed, was discarded. Edwards was ordered to terminate the policy, although that did not imply that White was accessible. On the contrary, throughout his twelve years, White rarely ventured beyond the fourth floor to the remainder of the Broadway offices. He heard only that his officers were crammed into small rooms. But they were not dispirited. The atmosphere was 'cosy. We'd all been through the war and expected another.'[3] White's route within Broadway never varied. Minutes before he left his office, Dora Edwards called Charlie Bourne, the fourth-floor security officer. Bourne summoned the chief's personal lift to descend either to the first floor (for the bridge to Queen Anne's Gate) or to the ground floor.

Throughout Broadway, everyone called White 'C', but among themselves, regardless of rank, only Christian names were used. Some believed that the informality was for security reasons, others traced it back to the intimacy of the pre-war years. But few were troubled that, apart from the most senior officers, no one in the service knew C, who deliberately isolated himself from the majority of his staff. The effect of his invisibility upon morale depended on the individual. Although more accessible than Menzies, it was unknown for White even to attend a Christmas party. His official hospitality for the secretarial staff was restricted to an annual lunch for Edwards and her junior at the Festival Hall's dreary restaurant. 'Secret service organisations don't have reputations, but mystique,' White would explain, 'and the chief needs to adopt a similar pose.'[4] The mystique of intelligence was its officers' rice bowl, its nutrient.

White's relationship with more senior officers was hardly less distant. He never descended to Broadway's basement, where the senior officers, alias the 'robber barons', patronised a small bar from 6 p.m. until dinner. In an inebriated atmosphere, faintly suggestive of a gentleman's club, the loyalties and mutual trust among those colleagues transcended the inevitable professional jealousies. Discussing operations, personalities, mistresses and the fate of their protégés, the old guard pledged unswerving loyalty to one another: 'We're going to keep this the best club in England; we'll never let an agent down.'[5]

Unlike the high priests of the CIA, the Ivy League friends of Allen Dulles, the robber barons were not brilliant, evangelical crusaders drawn from the nation's elite families. Rather, they were the sons of traditional and loyal Britons, educated at public schools but without a first from Oxbridge; in some cases, no other career had been open to them. Basking in the glow of outsiders' blind respect for a secret service about which so little was known, they effortlessly confused the fictitious accounts of the service's glories with unfortunate reality. Preserving the image was important for sustaining self-respect. Some dressed impeccably, others wore suits which bore witness to the stains of sloppy eating and creased old age. If any of those officers appeared in the Office on Saturday mornings, they would be wearing sports jackets with their dogs obediently at heel. As a group, they represented a paradigm of British manners, though their development might be arrested by their secrecy.

Entry into that basement coterie was strictly by invitation only. Over drinks, the barons endlessly retold the colourful legends of past glories and hilarities – of agents in disguise as ornithologists, circus trainers, comedians, athletes, businessmen and grave diggers; of bizarre sexual encounters while acting on His Majesty's Service; and of a garbled telegram which prompted twelve live tortoises to be dispatched from Vienna in a sealed diplomatic pouch. When the lower ranks in SIS spoke of their 'network' of informants, they included the 'old boys' in Broadway's bar, whose trade in stories was broken only to barter for SIS's personnel and resources, regardless of the chief's views. Those colourless, untalented officers not featuring in the auction were flotsam: 'The Firm needs their integrity as ballast,' chortled one baron into his brandy. Here was Broadway's office politics at its most raw.

Among the bar's stalwarts were John Bruce Lockhart, now controller for Africa and the Middle East, who had risen to eminence in post-war Germany when, under cover of the British Control Commission, he had operated with impunity and without fear of embarrassment or arrest; James 'Soapy Sid' Fulton, an ex-master from Eton with a sardonic sense of humour who, on duty tours in the Far East, asked secretaries along for the journey and would even invite White to visit his Mayfair love-nest; Paul Paulson, a Francophile former solicitor, Colonial Service officer and bon viveur; Maurice Oldfield, an admired field officer, another hedonist who drank whisky, told dirty jokes and had won a reputation as a Far East expert; George Young, a brash, popular and outstanding intelligence officer who barked orders, did not suffer fools and was revered as an intellectual because he read books; and John Collins, married to a French heiress, who infamously once quipped, 'I can't understand why people drink water when wine is so much better,' and lunched daily on account at the Écu de France in Jermyn Street.

For those officers and other barons like Nicholas Elliott, the son of the headmaster of Eton, an habitué of White's club in St James's, SIS was at the front line of the Cold War. Through their secret machinations, politicians were bribed, wars were started, governments overthrown and arrangements made for opponents to disappear. Whenever their deeds were exposed, the public reaction confirmed their passion for protecting the secrecy of their methods and operations. They believed themselves to be the guardians of the nation's freedom and the best judges of morality. Above all, they prospered because London's newspaper editors, respecting the government's edict not to pry too deeply into the nation's secret armoury, were still content to cultivate the popular conviction that Britain's spies were efficient, effective and invincible. Of their numbers, none published a more eloquent description of the SIS officer's task than George Young:

> In the press, in Parliament, in the United Nations, from the pulpit there is ceaseless talk about the rule of law, civilised relations between nations, the spread of democratic processes, self-determination and national sovereignty, respect for the rights of man and human dignity.
>
> The reality we all know perfectly well is quite the opposite and consists of an ever-increasing lawlessness, disregard of international contract, cruelty and corruption. The nuclear stalemate is matched by a moral stalemate.
>
> It is the spy who had been called upon to remedy the situation created by the deficiencies of ministers, diplomats, generals and priests.
>
> Men's minds are shaped, of course, by their environment and we spies, although we have our professional mystique, do perhaps live closer to the realities and hard facts of international relations than other practitioners of government. We are relatively free of

the problems of status, of precedence, departmental attitudes and evasions of personal responsibility, which create the official cast of mind . . . And so it is not surprising these days that the spy finds himself the main guardian of intellectual integrity.[6]

For the robber barons, the Crabb affair – a 'non-event caused by bad luck and blown up by the politicians' – was an excuse for SIS's enemies to prove their argument. White, some grumbled, had been appointed to make 'life more comfortable for the Brooks and Reillys'. Their ideal C would have been Kenneth Cohen, the former controller of Europe, 'But he was a Jew just when oil mattered.'[7]

In White's opinion, since the barons had caused the Crabb problem, they were not likely to offer the solution. Their fabulous reputation had been won because their failures were concealed. Puncturing the image by reforms was the price of failures exposed. In White's first months, the patrons of the basement bar, outwardly ebullient and friendly, represented to the chief an alien world who, he suspected, had fed the opposition to his appointment. He neither drank in their bar nor sought their company. It would take several years to persuade him of their loyalty.[8]

Although the gossip in London suggested that the appointment of the director of the rival service offended and even outraged SIS officers, the only serious critics, not 'happy to see Sinclair go',[9] were those responsible for the plight of their service. Of them, White was critical: 'The government had little confidence in SIS. I had to keep the service afloat and regain that confidence. Crabb was typical of an intelligence service which rushed into operations, often encouraged by the Americans, and did them rather badly.'[10]

Inevitably, his critics searched the intelligence community for colourful gossip. To their dismay, there were no anecdotes, no distasteful habits and no scandals. The skeletons had been truly buried. By common consent, White was an accomplished administrator, keeping regular hours, whose desk was cleared at the end of the day. 'He seems to be deliberately colourless,' quipped John Hilton, a future personal assistant. 'He's succeeded in being invisible.' Unlike other Whitehall aristocrats, White, the epitome of a classless society, was rarely seen at state dinners, formal receptions or Buckingham Palace. His financial situation precluded appearances at Ascot or the other social occasions where his predecessors had basked among their peers.

Nor, unlike the social grandees whom he served, was White a member of a prestigious club. The Travellers' in Pall Mall, a brisk ten-minute walk across St James's Park where White had been seen regularly since he had joined during the war, was also favoured by self-made Foreign Office officials. By 1956, he was appalled at the prospect of socialising and dining with Whitehall's habitués. So the following year, at his brother's suggestion, White joined the Garrick, a welcome haven from Whitehall. Surrounded by lawyers, actors and journalists, the aspiring author and poet found the atmosphere convivial and at the same time denied his subordinates a ready source of gossip.

For those SIS officers like John Wyke who operated on the front line, the appointment of a schoolmaster as chief was absurd. Wyke doubted whether a counter-intelligence officer possessed the cool courage to commit himself to offensive operations. 'He'd never run field agents. He'd never run risks. Our operations aren't like MI5's. If something goes wrong in Tripoli you can't telephone the local friendly police chief for help.'[11] There was no suggestion of White's commitment to the Great Game. There was a fear that life would be dull. Wyke voiced a common misunderstanding. Although a schoolmaster, White epitomised the ideal traditions of that profession. Not punishing or forbidding behaviour but rather seeking to understand individual characters and encouraging their best performance. Fortunately for the sceptics, the new chief disguised his disdain for Sinclair and the basement-bar traditionalists by his easy, polite manner, which raised no evident threat to the entrenched. That in turn – his desire to seek compromise rather than confrontation – excited complaints of indecision.

By default, White's first confidant, friend and protégé in Broadway was John Briance, alias the 'Undertaker', a forty-one-year-old former Palestine police officer, normally dressed in black, who supervised the secretariat near the chief's office. They had met in Palestine, where, like White, Briance had survived the explosion at the King David Hotel. Theirs was a partial matching of minds. Briance was a puritan who drank no alcohol, rarely socialised and talked about little else except business. Considering his colonial career, he was unusually critical of MI5, which he openly accused of 'incompetence'.[12] Strangely, that criticism endeared him to White. On Monday mornings, the two travelled together by train to London from Pulborough, a routine which strengthened their relationship. Briance became an intimate with noticeably wide powers to implement White's reforms.

Initially White was unsure of what to do in his new job, other than to remove dead wood – the 'inter-war greats' as Briance dubbed the undesired legacy – and to establish a personnel department to introduce a career structure, training and pensions to attract a higher-calibre staff. In one respect, White resisted any change. Broadway's senior ranks were to remain strictly male. Although secretaries posted abroad were successfully employed in operations, his riposte to John Hilton's complaint that it was unfair to condemn those women unrewarded to the shadows on their return to Britain was unanswerable: 'They're different to us. They've got no balls.' The only permitted exception was the formidable Daphne Park, recently posted to Moscow.

Broadway's formal opening hour was 10 a.m. White normally arrived thirty minutes earlier after a short walk in St James's Park with Kate, part of a fixed routine. Daily, he met one of the five controllers and one of the nine directors of requirements, an organisational structure introduced by Menzies in 1945. The world had been divided into five areas under controllers, answerable to the director of production. The P or production officers in London were the point of contact with the SIS stations around the world tasked with the collection of information requested by SIS's customers. These requests were channelled to the nine directors of requirements: political, air, naval, military, counter-intelligence, economic, financial, GCHQ and scientific.

SIS officers, no longer posing as passport control officers, were usually attached under diplomatic cover to the British embassy. The station chief would be provided by London with a list of priority tasks – to penetrate or support the local government, contact and recruit local personalities, and monitor and recruit Soviet or satellite diplomatic staff. Simultaneously, to avoid diplomatic embarrassments, SIS officers would also target neighbouring countries. Contacting nationals, especially dissidents, was always easier on neutral territory, where the local security service would be less interested if its own jurisdiction were not challenged.

The fruits of all that intelligence activity were available to White at those regular meetings in Broadway. Officers were expected to offer proposals and options rather than await his initiative. 'They were bland meetings,' recalled John Hilton, a personal assistant who took the notes during many of those sessions. 'I can never remember anything exciting being said. The chaps always held their cards close to their chest and would only answer questions. They never volunteered information. Anything important was spoken only in specially arranged meetings.'[13] Except when White required a report from an officer in person, all communications with SIS's staff and the stations abroad were conducted through those fourteen officers.

Besides those regular meetings, specially summoned conferences supervised important operations and dealt with the myriad problems which arose in the management of an espionage service. Unlike his predecessors, White understood case-work. On several occasions, he would emphasise the need to build bonds of loyalty with an agent: keeping his trust yet 'not always being completely honest'.[14]

Honesty was the crux of SIS's relations with Whitehall. The organisational channels of communication, stiff black lines on charts linking the intelligence service with the rest of Whitehall, so beloved of a bureaucracy intent on portraying reliability, obedience and responsibility, had been disturbed by the Crabb imbroglio. White's relationship with the Foreign Office, either mediated through the liaison officer based in Broadway (initially Patrick Reilly, later Denis Greenhill) or conducted in direct discussions on the scrambler telephone with Sir Ivone Kirkpatrick, the permanent under secretary, required repair. White was well aware of the traditional suspicion and even disdain felt for SIS by the Foreign Office's regular diplomats. Not only in London, but in Britain's embassies, 'the other side of the Office' complained that covert collection of intelligence endangered diplomacy. An ambassador was liable to resent the local SIS officer's authority to read his dispatches to the Foreign Office, while the diplomat was barred from sight of those SIS messages marked 'personal communications'.

Even after ten years of spying on his fellow Britons, the transfer to Broadway was a culture shock for White. Foreign intelligence required considerably more duplicity on a grander scale and over a wider canvas than was the case at MI5, and SIS had enjoyed unusual independence despite attendance at the weekly meeting of the Joint Intelligence Committee. Every Thursday morning, White attended the JIC on the third floor of the Ministry of Defence in Storey's Gate, chaired by Patrick Dean, a forty-seven-year-old lawyer who had become a diplomat after serving as the Foreign Office's legal adviser during the war. Dean's cool detachment and classless intellect, marred only by an impression of absent-mindedness, appealed to White.

The JIC's membership, which included representatives from the Foreign Office, GCHQ, MI5, SIS, the armed services and the Cabinet Office, tended to inhibit discussion and encourage passivity. Those gathered in the conference room regularly read SIS's intelligence assessments, while their masters received daily locked boxes from Broadway containing selected original reports and CX Reports, the most sensitive intelligence summaries. Once read, they were returned uncopied to Broadway.

In anticipation of JIC meetings, White would be briefed by a director of requirements, describing how the requests submitted by SIS's customers had been fulfilled and what new material he could offer. Occasionally White would reject a request, invariably from the military, explaining that SIS did not have the capability or the resources or that he considered the effort excessive in relation to the intended result. The fight for turf with the military antagonised him. 'SIS', said White, 'serves national not departmental interests.'[15]

The results of the JIC meetings were transmitted to SIS's stations abroad. Inside each station's 'Red Book' was the detailed shopping list of requirements agreed by the JIC and SIS. Ostensibly, SIS's task was not to set its own agenda but to obey the priorities established by Whitehall. Invariably, the Soviet Union headed the list.

In theory, SIS could not undertake any operation without permission from the Foreign Office. But the guidelines were flexible, depending upon the chance of repercussions if something went awry. Inserting an agent into a foreign country did not need permission or even consultation. Planting a bug in an embassy in London did require White to mention the initiative to his Foreign Office liaison, Patrick Dean, who would discuss the political implications with the Foreign Office's senior official, the permanent under secretary. If of sufficient seriousness, the foreign secretary would be consulted. Subversion could be approved by the permanent under secretary; sabotage or the chance of death would need the prime minister's approval. (Hence Menzies had obtained Attlee's approval for the destruction of Jewish refugee ships sailing from Italy in 1947 and 1948.)[16]

These consultations would usually remain oral, in order to minimise the chances of a security leak. In the robber barons' opinion, voiced by Nicholas Elliott, White never overcame two handicaps. 'The Foreign Office, obsessed with diplomacy, never understood that the Russians saw espionage as a "game of nations". Dick never dismissed their constraints after Crabb,' the reason for his transfer to MI5. Secondly, in the prejudiced opinion of barons like Elliott, 'He was too rarely willing to argue for an operation if Foreign Office officials were opposed. He'd never challenge them, threatening to resign if they refused permission.'[17] Those predilections smoothed relations between White and the Foreign Office, but frustrated his officers.

Occasionally, White would meet the foreign secretary or prime minister, usually at his own request. His professional success owed much to his manner during these encounters, which was unpatronising and pleasant, and most politicians could be seduced by the intimacy and the exclusive revelation of 'an exciting tit-bit'.[18] Since the messenger was credible, the politicians usually accepted his information as true. The foreign secretary from December 1955 was Selwyn Lloyd, a lawyer who had accepted his appointment reluctantly and seemed to share the common view that he was predisposed to ineffectiveness. White was left in no doubt that he was answerable to Eden, the matinee idol of the 1930s.

The prime minister lauded SIS's clandestine activities. Although unimpressed by its wartime record, he had valued SOE's skill in undertaking sabotage and removing obdurate individuals. Ten years later, SIS's ability to launch a clandestine operation in forbidden territory gave an illusion of great-power status which, as Britain's military and economic decline accelerated, appealed to those who yearned for past glories. In recent years, Eden had scored diplomatic triumphs brokering peace in Vietnam and throughout the rest of Indo-China, securing the rearming of West Germany, negotiating a peace agreement with Persia and apparently finalising an agreement with Egypt over the Suez Canal. In parallel, White would discover, there had been SIS successes. But, as Norman Brook had warned, Eden had become emotionally unbalanced and physically weak, requiring daily medication in the wake of unsuccessful operations to remove obstructions in his bile duct.

At their first meeting after his appointment, White was told by the prime minister that Britain's foreign affairs required a 'first-class intelligence service'. White was charged with ensuring that SIS would never again embarrass the government, and that it would efficiently deliver what was required of it. Eden's directive, fluently delivered, was not easy to implement. Although White's understanding of politics and foreign affairs was superior to his predecessor's, it nevertheless remained remarkably limited for a director of foreign intelligence. He successfully resisted most opportunities to travel abroad during his entire stewardship, and had in any case inherited an organisation of vastly contrasting abilities.

Included in White's new estate, located in dozens of offices around Victoria, were the rooms for training officers, bases for out-station operations and a workshop for SIS's Technical Operations. Sited in Artillery Mansions, near Westminster Hall, craftsmen manufactured the accoutrements of espionage: false passports, identity cards and ration books; secret compartments built into suitcases, torches and cigarette lighters; and places for cameras and microphones in boxes and cases which the enemy might never suspect.

On another floor at Artillery Mansions was a Russian intercept operation run by Wilfred 'Biffy' Dunderdale, a fifty-seven-year-old officer whose experience stretched back to the Bolshevik revolution, pre-war Poland and wartime France. Dunderdale had brought the Polish intelligence service's Enigma machine to London in 1939 and had, in the post-war years, skilfully cut an important Russian military telephone landline in East Germany, so forcing the Soviets to revert to uncoded radio communications.[19] Under his command, over 100 White Russian and Polish émigrés were translating those and other conversations, hoping that some indiscretion would reveal a morsel of a secret.

A less useful bequest to White were Sinclair's charts – giant pieces of cardboard marked in three colours by old ladies, indicating the value of each SIS station's product: 'valuable', 'useful' and 'no good'. White heard how John Hilton had once entered Sinclair's office to find the chief on his hands and knees scrutinising the eight-foot chart for the station in Berlin, the epicentre of SIS's Cold War. Countless railway workers across Germany were being paid by SIS to file reports of train movements and sightings of Red Army officers. 'The bread and butter of our work,' Jack Easton asserted. 'It's absolute rubbish,' Hilton told his new chief. 'Like so much else here. Just get rid of it all.' White agreed.

Jack Easton was also marked down for an early departure. In White's opinion, 'Easton was a managerial type. The art of intelligence missed him completely.' Their relations were clouded by White's harsh judgment: 'He couldn't understand foreign countries.'[20] Easton would never reconcile himself to White's rejection: 'I didn't care for the old gang and they got their revenge.'[21] Obligingly, he agreed to remain and care for administrative matters during the transition, complaining that his achievement, the reform of SIS's operations in the Far East, was 'not appreciated'.[22]

Among White's disturbing inheritances were the rackets: cash paid to 'informants' who evaporated when Broadway checked on a report's veracity. The worst offenders were in the Far East. During his time at Leconfield House, White had sought to persuade MI5, SIS and Special Branch to co-ordinate their activities in Singapore, Hong Kong and Malaya, but his efforts had met with failure.[23] SIS's refusal, White knew, had been motivated by self-interest. Living in sumptuous accommodation and surrounded by servants, much as in the days of the Raj, the self-indulgent, expensive lifestyles enjoyed by many SIS and MI5 officers had been reflected in the poor intelligence they delivered. Too many officers could not speak the local languages, were 'unable to place themselves in the shoes of the natives' and were often divorced from direct involvement in operations, lazily relying upon 'informants' through intermediaries and interpreters who, too often, were Britain's enemies.[24]

The outstanding failure, White recognised, was in Hong Kong. John Collins, an SIS station chief, having spent vast sums, claimed to have developed a registry of personality profiles from a network of informers and penetration agents. But, consistently, Collins had failed to produce worthwhile intelligence.[25] His penetration of communist China was wholly unsuccessful; no important source was ever recruited in Peking; and all SIS's agents inserted into the country either disappeared or returned unsuccessful.

Among Collins's many expensive errors was a warning to London that Chinese nuclear submarines had gathered in a port which, inquiries revealed, was silted with sand. Security checks exposed Collins's source as a fabricator loyal to the Kuomintang, the Chinese nationalists. His successor, Edward 'Jimmy' James, would dismiss forty-seven agents on SIS's payroll as 'worthless'.[26] Not only Collins, but James Fulton, the controller for the Far East, was blamed by White. Although praised for his 'acute political sense' by subordinates, Fulton had financed the loser in Singapore's first elections.

Soon after his appointment, White flew to Berlin. With over one hundred officers and staff, Berlin was not only SIS's biggest station, covering the whole of Germany, but also a magnet for every other nation's espionage service. Based in a large granite building at Hitler's Olympic Stadium, the SIS office had been carefully compartmentalised by George Young to assess Soviet political intentions and to discover the capability of the Soviet military and its armaments.

White was received by Peter Lunn, the chief of station and the son of the founder of the British skiing movement. Although small and quietly spoken, Lunn had proved his diligence in Vienna. Faced with the intractable problem of penetrating the Soviet military headquarters there, he had commissioned the revolutionary idea of digging a tunnel under the street from a police post to the main telephone cable running between the Soviet headquarters and their military airfield at Schwechat. British engineers had installed a telephone tap on the cable. Codenamed Operations Lord and Conflict, this success had prompted two more taps – one from a specially established imitation-jewellery shop managed by an Austrian Jew codenamed Mr Prior, and another from a suburban villa in the French sector inhabited by John Wyke and his wife.

Conflict's enormous output had been analysed by the newly created Y Section based at 2 Carlton Gardens in London. Russian and Polish émigrés transcribed the conversations from drums flown in three times weekly by special RAF planes from Vienna. Among the recipients of the 'take' was a grateful CIA, which, while unimpressed with the quality of the information, was starved of alternative intelligence.

As they sat in a car parked in Berlin, Lunn explained to White that the Vienna operation had succeeded only because the Foreign Office had deliberately not been informed. 'I had to tell Harold Caccia, the ambassador, about my plans. Caccia knew the Foreign Office would have forbidden the operation. But Caccia told me, "I couldn't look at myself if there'd been an invasion and I denied the chance of getting the information."'[27] For the same reason, Lunn was forbidden to involve the CIA. Among the most important conversations, continued Lunn, was one between two Russian NCOs discussing which categories of troops had been earmarked for demobilisation. 'That was clear proof that the Soviets had no intention of launching an attack,' said Lunn, pleased by White's evident appreciation.

The fear of a Soviet invasion had been started by a hysterical telegram in March 1948 from General Lucius Clay, the US military commander in Germany, warning Washington that he sensed a change in the Soviet attitude which could signal an imminent outbreak of war. The American Joint Chiefs had ordered the CIA to produce plans for placing an agent at each of the Soviet's military airfields. No fewer than 2000 would have been necessary. The notion was abandoned as ludicrous only after the war scare had proved to be based upon faulty intelligence. The Russian military had neither the ability nor the intention to invade Western Europe.

Lunn's success had been rewarded with promotion to run the Berlin station. There, hampered by the strict edict that SIS officers were not to travel into the Soviet zone but had to recruit Russians venturing into the Western zones of the city, he had in 1953 researched the possibility of tapping the Soviet cables. Having consulted a trusted German telecom engineer, he decided that the most suitable location was at Alt Glienicke, on the border between the Russian and American zones. CIA co-operation was essential for the digging of a 600-yard tunnel and the construction of a telephone-tap chamber under East German territory.

In February 1954, Operation Stopwatch Gold had been inaugurated in London at a joint SIS–CIA conference in Carlton Gardens under the chairmanship of George Young. The American delegation, led by Frank Rowlett, included Bill Harvey, a whisky-drinking, pear-shaped man who tucked a pistol into his waistband and who, three years earlier, had identified Philby as a spy. The minutes were written by George Blake for SIS and Cleveland Cram for the CIA. Under the agreement, the Americans would finance and build the tunnel, while the British would supply the technical tapping equipment. The processing of the tapes, to be flown daily to London, would be divided between London and Washington and the product shared.

On 22 April 1956, shortly before White's appointment, the tunnel had been discovered by Soviet telephone engineers apparently repairing a fault on the cable. Although disappointing for SIS and the CIA, it had, during its eleven months and eleven days of operation, proved successful. Soviet propaganda after its discovery had been quickly terminated as an own-goal.

On his return to London, White spent a morning at the transcription unit in Regent's Park, watching the 300 analysts and translators listen on earphones to the Russians' conversations. The 400,000 hours of conversations among the Soviet military would be analysed for another year under the control of Brigadier Eric Greer, who had fought against the Bolsheviks in 1919, and Squadron Leader Brinley Ryan of the RAF.

Piecemeal, with other British and American specialists, they compiled a mosaic revealing Soviet plans, training and tactics, the Red Army's order of battle, relations between different sections of the Soviet military and intelligence organisations, and the developments and problems of Soviet military equipment. White could not help being impressed. Daily, the analysts heard the problems of a Soviet mechanic who was failing to rectify the continual fracture of a pin on a tank track, thus immobilising the Red Army's armour; and occasionally a badly coded message could be deciphered, twice revealing a KGB network in West Germany.

Every day, other conversations revealed a host of personal details about senior Soviet military officers, discussing the smuggling of fur coats and art treasures. No conversation had been more important than between the wife of General Andrei Greshko, the Red Army commander in Germany, and her daughter. 'Your father', said Madame Greshko speaking excitedly from Moscow, 'met Marshal Bulganin at the Twentieth Party Congress. They had just heard Khrushchev denounce Stalin. It's a great secret but it's true. Amazing.'

'How did Father react?'

'He shat on the floor.'

That intelligence report would, when the full text of Khrushchev's speech was obtained, change the West's perception of Kremlin politics.

In drawing lessons from his three days in Berlin, White committed SIS to collect information rather than to take unnecessary risks; and after reading reports proving the incompetence and poor morale of the Red Army, he judged that there was 'a danger of overestimating the Soviets'. The intercepts proved as much, not least a conversation between two Russian generals revealing that the Red Army had cheated in a football match against the British army by flying in professionals from Moscow's Dynamo team.

The corollary was to appreciate the importance of the American relationship, one of the reasons for Brook's nomination of White to direct SIS. Ever since his two-year Commonwealth Fellowship, White had, unlike so many of his pretentious peers, respected American qualities and achievements. In contrast to others in Britain's intelligence community, he appreciated that, although the relationship with the CIA and FBI was hailed as one between equals, SIS's wartime supremacy would inexorably diminish as President Eisenhower devoted ever greater resources to intelligence. In 1956, the imbalance still seemed unremarkable. British intelligence could summon and deploy impressive resources across the Empire, south-east Asia, Latin America and Europe, boosting the belief among White's senior officers of British supremacy. For the moment, SIS was, in the opinion of Chester Cooper, a CIA liaison officer in London, 'putting on a good front – while pulling back'.[28]

Soon after his appointment, White was invited for drinks by the CIA liaison officers at Cooper's home in Inverness Terrace. Also present was another Anglophile CIA officer, Bronson Tweedy, educated in Britain, who had played rugby against John Bruce Lockhart in a schoolboys' match. Under the intelligence agreements, CIA officers enjoyed access not only to White and Hollis, but to senior British intelligence officers in both services. Their official presence at Leconfield House and Broadway and at JIC meetings was reciprocated by generous hospitality in their homes, where, late into the night, they gleaned insights into British operations and cemented enduring friendships with SIS officers. Their motives were entirely honourable. Both sides desired continued Anglo-American co-operation, but by 1956 both were expressing concern about the effectiveness of British intelligence.

For the two Americans, the Crabb incident reflected the decline of SIS. The frogman, they believed, was 'a slob' and his use was 'bizarre', confirming a disturbing trend in British intelligence. The British withdrawal from Greece in 1948 reflected diminishing resources; the disastrous covert operation in Albania in 1949 suggested incompetence; while the Philby saga threw a complete pall over SIS's security. Over drinks in Cooper's home, White was unexpectedly candid about the task he faced: 'It's much worse than I realised. It's going to be uphill to change the service.'[29]

Unlike SIS, the Americans represented an agency whose intentions were openly proclaimed. The CIA, established under the National Security Act of 1947, was an independent department of American government beyond the control of the State Department and publicly authorised to dispatch covert missions for 'sabotage, subversion and assistance to underground groups'. In Washington, Frank Wisner, a rich Southern intellectual who directed the CIA's Office of Policy Co-ordination, delighted in organising clandestine operations to support anti-communist rioters in East Berlin, finance anti-communist unions and politicians in France and Italy, and overthrow the government of Guatemala.

As its weaknesses became apparent, White believed, the Americans' goodwill was critical to SIS's welfare. Much now depended upon personal relationships. Happily for White, the CIA's director was an Anglophile, Allen Dulles, a pipe-sucking, whisky-drinking, party-hopping socialite who adored the craft of intelligence. Alongside Dulles was James Angleton, another Anglophile, the agency's head of counter-intelligence, who enjoyed a no-knock relationship with the director. There was a mutual admiration between White and these Americans which proved to be SIS's salvation as Britain slipped towards Armageddon in the Middle East.

CHAPTER EIGHT

The Inheritance

White's introduction to SIS was a baptism of fire. At nightfall on 26 July 1956, just twelve days after White's formal appointment as chief, President Gamal Abdel Nasser announced the nationalisation of the Suez Canal. For those Britons still basking in memories of the Allied victory in 1945, and relishing a British Empire spread across the globe, Nasser's edict inflicted a seismic shock. The Egyptian's revolutionary nationalism threatened Britain's strategic lifeline to the Persian Gulf's oil, its pre-eminence across the Middle East, its massive financial investment depended upon the inviolate principle of free passage through the waterway.

In Downing Street that night, Eden's bitterness was not concealed from his guests, King Faisal of Iraq and Nuri es-Said, his prime minister. Neither SIS nor the Foreign Office had provided any warning. After ushering the Arabs into the night, Eden summoned a council of war, which continued until 4 a.m. 'Nasser', the prime minister told his audience emotionally 'must not be allowed to get away with it.'[1] The 'Moslem Mussolini' should be 'destroyed. I want him removed and I don't give a damn if there's anarchy and chaos in Egypt.'[2] Ever since April 1956, when relations with Egypt had first begun to deteriorate seriously, Eden had spoken of wanting Nasser 'murdered', while Macmillan and senior Foreign Office officials openly discussed 'getting rid of Nasser', 'overthrowing him' and 'the death of Nasser'.[3]

Nasser's fate was thus already cast when White became chief: his inheritance included a commitment to Nasser's murder. On arriving at Broadway that morning of 27 July, he was warned by Jack Easton: 'I've had to stop a lot of operations in the Middle East. Too many are suspiciously unsafe.'[4] White ignored Easton and excluded him from further discussion of the Middle East operations.[5] Instead, he chose to be briefed by George Young, a robber baron whom the prime minister ostensibly wanted White to control. 'We'll bump Nasser off,' Young told White, explaining that he had been personally selected to implement Eden's orders. There was no reproach by the new chief during those early days about SIS's participation in a plot to remove Nasser.[6]

White appreciated Young, a forty-seven-year-old Lowland Scotsman, as an energetic, intelligent and resourceful officer, an asset among a mixed group of subordinates. Exceptionally, he could mingle with SIS officers, knowing each individual by name, aware of his problems and understanding where his operations slotted into the overall pattern. White was an eyewitness to the morale boost which Young sparked, consciously ignoring the officer's instinctive grasp for a sledgehammer. Young was an activist, winning plaudits after he had joined SIS in 1946 for his 'Harry Lime' intrigues in Vienna, and for sending Czech and Hungarian refugees back to their homelands to join the Communist Party, to work their way up the hierarchy. Within SIS, he epitomised the prevailing prejudice that, in Britain's interests, robust clandestine operations were justified.

Young and the cabal immersed in the Suez conspiracy, the Special Political Action group, alias the Jolly Fun Tricks Department, quietly mocked White's dilemma. Appointed to prevent further public embarrassment, he was entangled in a maverick venture. But the SPA group, handpicked to fulfil the premier's orders, did not query whether the chief was troubled by moral doubts. After nearly twenty years' service as an intelligence officer – longer than most in SIS – it was assumed that White was untroubled by ethical conflicts. Unlike the CIA's director, he was not a political animal, espousing his favoured foreign policy. Instead, he could be trusted to pursue British interests as ordained by the Foreign Office and the prime minister.

In truth, White was discomfited by the anthithesis of his own gospel. His inheritance was patriotic officers, Establishment cowboys in his opinion, steeped in self-deluding mystery, convinced that SIS operations could influence the course of history. Their ambitions, and White's responsibilities, stretched across the whole world. They dealt, not with a simple threat as in counter-espionage, but with a complex, changing matrix of international ideologies and personalities. Those officers trusted George Young and were in turn trusted by a prime minister who wanted SIS to repeat against Nasser the success of Operation Boot.

Operation Boot had proven Young as a master of intrigue. Under Monty Woodhouse, he had planned the restoration of the Shah of Iran to his throne, a moment of glory for SIS resented by White. In a bloody coup in 1951, the Persian nationalist, Mohammed Mussadeq, had grabbed power, nationalised the Anglo-Iranian Oil Company, Britain's biggest overseas asset and the world's biggest oil-producer, and ordered the ignominious deportation of the British staff. The financial and political damage to Britain was enormous, aggravating fears of other expropriations of British oil-fields in the Gulf. The sole response of Attlee, then still prime minister, had been to admit his sense of outrage. After the Conservatives had won the general election that year, Eden approved a SIS plot to overthrow Mussadeq.

British intelligence could claim historic successes in the Middle East. During the Second World War, SIS operations had influenced the fate of Iran, Palestine, Iraq and Egypt. In the aftermath, SIS officers had resisted Soviet penetration and protected Britain's huge oil investment along the Gulf, albeit that the American oil giants, especially Aramco, posed the worst threat. British companies had been ousted from Saudi Arabia by Aramco with the assistance of Kim Roosevelt, a CIA officer who used his official status to secure commercial advantages. After 1950, Roosevelt began offering bribes to the rulers of the oil-rich Buraimi Oasis on the Saudi border to persuade them to forsake their British tutelage and their contracts with the British-controlled Iraq Petroleum Company and to place themselves under Saudi and Aramco control. SIS officers were organising successful resistance to Roosevelt's ploys, but in late 1952 were compelled to sup with the devil.

In October 1952, SIS's strategy in Iran was destroyed when Mussadeq broke off diplomatic relations with Britain. Expelled with other diplomats from the country, Woodhouse flew to

Washington and, at a conference with Allen Dulles and Roosevelt, handed SIS's network over to the CIA. Roosevelt turned SIS's plan into reality. In August 1953, with Woodhouse's and Young's help, the CIA financed a mob to riot in Teheran. Three hundred died fighting in the capital's streets, and Mussadeq resigned. Away from the limelight, his intimate supporters were murdered. The delight felt by SIS in restoring the Shah overshadowed the seizure of Iran's oil by Aramco, which thus denied Britain the prize.

George Young and other SIS officers drew four lessons from the whole affair. Firstly, despite Philby, the Agency still trusted and respected the British for joint operations; secondly, senior CIA officers appeared more sympathetic to British foreign policy than the State Department; thirdly, SIS's clandestine operations in peacetime were of proven benefit; and fourthly, SIS could promote British interests in the Middle East. White reacted passively to that theology, observing that Eden and Young were obsessed by SIS's desire to reverse Britain's deteriorating status in the world, and in particular in Egypt.

The slide in Egypt had started in July 1952. The Egyptian monarchy had been overthrown by a military coup, weakening Britain's seventy-year hold over the country. Two years later, Eden bowed to nationalist pressure and agreed to withdraw 80,000 British soldiers from the Canal Zone on condition that 4000 technicians would remain to operate the Canal and that, if it were endangered, British soldiers could return to protect the neutral zone along the waterway. Even that agreement outraged the so-called Suez Group in London, which included many in SIS. 'If we cannot hold the Suez Canal, the jugular vein of World and Empire shipping communications,' complained Lord Hankey, 'what can we hold?'[7]

On 20 February 1955, Eden hosted a dinner for Nasser at the British embassy in Cairo. Thereafter he judged the Arab to be Russia's tool for launching the Cold War in the Middle East. Among Eden's sources were SIS reports from Cairo. Freddie Stockwell, the SIS chief in Cairo, and his deputy Ian Critchett confirmed that Nasser was an agent of communist revolution throughout the region, unpopular among Egyptian patriots and nationalists. An important source for their information was a network handled by an 'unofficial assistant', John McGlashan, a British businessman.

McGlashan's network of informants, including James Swinburn, the British manager of the Arab News Agency, and various Egyptian civil servants, was not as comprehensive as one might have imagined after seventy years of British occupation. Indeed, SIS reports were contradicted by the British ambassador. Nasser, insisted Humphrey Trevelyan, was a popular nationalist and opposed to any British military presence without Soviet prompting. White did not attempt to reconcile the contradiction between SIS and Foreign Office assessments, not least because Eden shared SIS's prejudice. Eden's Middle East policy, a diplomatic achievement, was constructed upon a succession of defence pacts, especially the Baghdad Pact, tying nations together against common enemies, above all against Egypt.

The agent of Eden's undoing was John Foster Dulles, the American secretary of state, whom he detested – a sentiment that was reciprocated. The American's aggressive anti-communism was clouded by his intense distrust of British motives and by a personal history of serving Mammon rather than morality. Lengthy negotiations between the two produced confusion and competition rather than an agreed policy. The State Department's antagonism forced Eden to seek other allies in his mission against Nasser and persuaded him to deceive Washington about Britain's intentions.

In early 1956, SIS reported that the Israelis were contemplating a pre-emptive strike across Sinai; and, from a source codenamed Lucky Break in Nasser's cabinet, SIS further disclosed that Nasser was considering signing an agreement with Moscow to finance the construction of a gigantic hydroelectric dam at Aswan, a prestige project of the kind much favoured by emerging Third World countries. Eden urged Eisenhower, whom he had known since the Second World War and who had been president since 1952, to join with Britain to match Moscow in its offer of finance.[8] Simultaneously, he approved SIS preparations for a coup to overthrow Nasser. The operation against Egypt, Eden hoped, would be a joint endeavour with the CIA.

In March, under the chairmanship of Young, six SIS officers met Wilbur Eveland, a CIA Arabist who had flown from Damascus, and Jim Eichelberger, the CIA chief in Cairo, to discuss and co-ordinate policy in the Middle East. Young, proffering SIS reports from its agents in Cairo, declared that Nasser was a communist agent and outlined how, under Operation Straggle, Britain would stage a coup against the Syrian Ba'athist government, followed by the elimination of Nasser. An extension of SIS's plan was to topple the troublesome King Saud of Saudi Arabia in revenge for reneging on British oil interests.[9]

Young's plan reeked of nineteenth-century manipulation: border incidents to provoke unrest among desert tribes, the financing of dissidents and the sowing of confusion through mischievous newspaper reports. SIS's secret weapon, confided Young, were the 'snipcocks', his euphemism for the Israelis. The derogatory name hid Young's enthusiasm for Israel, already involved in murderous encounters with Egyptian army units in the Sinai Desert.[10] Having established links with Mossad, Israel's intelligence service, for joint operations against Egypt and Syria, Young 'thought the Israelis could save the world'.[11]

The CIA's policy towards Nasser was markedly different to SIS's. A strong station had been assembled in Cairo, including Kim Roosevelt and Miles Copeland. In November 1954, as the 80,000 British troops began leaving Egypt, the CIA officers had offered Nasser finance and American weapons if he abandoned Egypt's traditional suppliers, Britain and France. Their offer, demonstrating sympathy towards Arab nationalism, was rejected. One year later, on 19 October 1955, the CIA discovered that Nasser had agreed to buy a huge consignment of weapons from Russia. The prospect of the Red Army occupying the Canal Zone and the oilfields alarmed even the CIA's Nasserites.

George Young was naturally unsurprised. As he stood over Wilbur Eveland, the CIA officer, in the Connaught Hotel on 1 April 1956 dictating key phrases in the dispatch of SIS's proposals to Washington, he presumed that Nasser was a Soviet agent. 'Britain', proclaimed Young, 'is now prepared to fight its last battle. No matter what the cost, we will win.' Young's timescale was precisely one month. 'I'd entered a madhouse,' recalled Eveland some years later. 'We'd heard sheer lunacy.'[12] Other CIA officers were more sympathetic. Over the following weeks, SIS and CIA officers held a succession of conferences to plot the overthrow of the Syrian regime. By the end of April, Foster Dulles declared his opposition to the British plan. His brother Allen Dulles supported it.[13] Young hoped the CIA's support for Straggle would include Nasser's overthrow.

On 19 July, six days after the last British troops had sailed from Egypt, Foster Dulles, against CIA advice, announced America's refusal to fund construction of the Aswan Dam. James Reston, a respected American journalist, condemned Dulles's diplomacy: 'he doesn't stumble into booby traps: he digs them to size, studies them carefully, and then jumps.'[14] Seven days later, Nasser retaliated by nationalising the Canal. In neighbouring Israel, the government began planning a pre-emptive strike against its enemy. News of its intentions reached Young.

'Young arranged collusion with Mossad,' recalls Nigel Clive, an SIS officer, 'and White was told by Young the deployments of SIS staff. He let Young cut him out of all operational activity.' White denied that exclusion from the SPA group. 'The impression arose because I could not take detailed control of SIS's operations against Nasser. But I remained in overall control.'[15]

The SPA was Eden's secret weapon, designed to work in parallel with Britain's armed forces. His objective, as recorded in a cabinet committee minute dated 30 July, was: 'to bring about the downfall of the present Egyptian government'.[16] While the joint chiefs prepared Operation Musketeer, a seaborne invasion of Egypt reminiscent of the Normandy landings, SIS was tasked to negotiate with their chosen successor to Nasser.

In an extensive briefing from Young in August, White was given details about SIS's plans concerning Nasser. No one within SIS recalls White openly voicing his opposition to the discussions about Nasser's murder at that stage. He accepted the credibility of the plot, including the recruitment of Isameddine Mahmoud Khalil, deputy chief of Egypt's air force intelligence, to organise a group of officers to mount the coup against Nasser. Khalil had been promised by John Farmer, an SIS officer based in Beirut, money as a reward, and intelligence about Israel to provide justification for his travels.

On meeting Patrick Reilly at the Foreign Office, White confided, 'We've got a group of dissident military officers who will go against Nasser.' He further explained that SIS plan was for that group to murder Nasser. When Reilly voiced his suspicions about the Egyptians' reliability, White appeared unperturbed.[17]

Young's attitude towards Arabs should have forewarned White about his officer's judgment. The Arab's 'chief characteristic', Young would subsequently tell an audience, 'is a simple joy in destruction which has to be experienced to be believed . . . There is no gladder sound to the Arab ear than the crunch of glass, and his favourite spectacle is that of human suffering . . . While the European has been building, the Arab has looted and torn down.'[18] For Chester Cooper, the CIA liaison officer in London, George Young epitomised SIS unpredictability. At a stag dinner hosted by Patrick Dean, with White also present, Young declaimed a 'worrying attitude about SIS's work': 'Intelligence is a game like rugby. We're not doing anything serious.'[19] White's silent smile was forced. He had no sense of the Game. Young, Cooper knew, was determined to remove and even murder Nasser and was supported by some CIA officers.[20] To these officers White did not appear minded to disobey Eden.

Among the methods under discussion was the assembly of an electric razor containing explosives, which would be handed to Nasser. Another was to recruit a hit team. A third, considered by SIS's Technical Service officers, was the insertion of poison gas into the ventilation system of Nasser's headquarters.[21] As SIS officers began disappearing into Whitehall's underground bunkers to plan their contribution towards the invasion of Egypt,[22] none of the service's projects had yet been approved.

On 1 August, as the undisguised preparations for invasion unfolded and Eden was bombarded by a chorus of ferocious and conflicting demands for consultations, international conferences and agreements, he confided to Foster Dulles that he intended to destroy Nasser. Privately, Dulles appeared to encourage him.[23] But in public, with the presidential elections due on 6 November, President Eisenhower uttered scant support. Washington's mixed signals alarmed Eden. SIS seemed a discreet channel for discovering the truth. The venue for this probe was the Mayfair flat of Geoffrey McDermott, chairman of the Joint Intelligence Staff. Invited for a drink, Chester Cooper met George Young. 'Just between two old boys,' Young said to Cooper, 'what is Washington up to? Every proposal for either bashing the Gyppos or appealing to the UN gets knocked down in Foggy Bottom. Chums in Downing Street tell me our old boy is feeling queer and is all nerves. Your friends at home had better come up with something constructive pretty soon.'[24] Cooper failed. Eden pressed on alone.

On 27 August, as Julian Amery, a Conservative member of parliament with close links to SIS, flew with two SIS officers to Paris to meet representatives of the anti-Nasser movement,[25] cabinet ministers met and agreed that, if Nasser were not quickly removed, Britain would be 'finished'.[26] But, on the same day, SIS's contribution towards Britain's plot disintegrated. Egyptian security police raided Swinburn's home in Cairo, seized a hoard of incriminating paperwork and identified over twenty of his informants. Within days, SIS's network had been crushed. Some agents were subsequently executed and SIS's 'diplomats' were expelled. Swinburn's evident lack of security, rashly tolerated by Stockwell, was, White perceived, an appalling indictment of SIS.

SIS's status in the Joint Intelligence Committee meetings declined in parallel with White's disenchantment. In that uninspiring forum, White's discomfort with SIS's involvement in Eden's subterfuge became apparent to Patrick Dean, the chairman of the committee: 'He appeared reserved, mindful of the Foreign Office's disdain for the intelligence profession and its practitioners.'[27] In a bid to assert SIS's independence from the Foreign Office and Eden, White told Dean, 'My service is concerned with national, not departmental, requirements.' But his gesture was futile. His service's credibility was low.

'All the secrecy, the special handling and the refusal to disclose the sources gave SIS's material a spurious value,' observed John Hunt, the Cabinet Office representative.[28] The

CIA representatives, attending segments of the JIC meetings, were less jaundiced. White's 'modest manner' impressed Bronson Tweedy: 'An untypical civil servant, beguilingly dilettante, who uttered his views with conviction and without fear. A man whose edges were round, not square.'[29] The CIA's personal affection for White would prove critical for SIS.

Despite SIS's setback in Cairo, the discussions about Nasser's overthrow continued and appeared to have won American support. On 21 September, Foster Dulles first suggested a joint US–British group to destabilise Nasser's regime, and four days later he told Macmillan (now Chancellor of the Exchequer) that America wanted to remove Nasser by covert action.[30] Soon after, Dulles was admitted to hospital with cancer. In his absence, on 6 October, the CIA presented a plan for Nasser's demise. At first, Eisenhower did not exclude the idea, but soon after he ruled out both assassination and Nasser's overthrow.[31]

This was the critical moment. Eden and, in his own capacity, White understood the perils if British and American policies were to diverge. Officially, the Eisenhower administration, including CIA officers, was no longer trusted with the secrets of Britain's intentions. Washington knew of an Anglo–French plan to invade Egypt but not of the conspiracy to contrive a war.

On 21 October, at a meeting of unusual secrecy in Sèvres, outside Paris, the prime ministers of France and Israel, and Patrick Dean, representing Britain, signed an agreement which would serve as the pretext for an Anglo–French invasion of Egypt. First, Israel would attack Egypt; then Britain and France would call upon the belligerents to withdraw from the Canal. Once Nasser had refused, as he inevitably would, an Anglo–French force would land in Egypt to enforce peace, protect the Canal and overthrow the president. In London, only fourteen people – cabinet ministers, chiefs of staff and senior officials – were briefed about the conspiracy by Eden. Other ministers, civil servants and military officers knew only about Operation Musketeer, the intention to invade, but not about the Sèvres agreement.

White was apprised of the conspiracy by Norman Brook. At an extraordinary meeting in Downing Street, the cabinet secretary asked White to pledge not to reveal to anyone what he was about to be told. White was 'very surprised. After all, I had signed the Official Secrets Act and knew more secrets than most, so it was unusual to say the least.' Having uttered an appropriate oath, White heard the details of Eden's secret agreement. 'Nothing will deter Eden from his policy,' Brook said. The cabinet secretary, who White realised 'was working closely with Eden', had conjoined the SIS chief as an accomplice to an unprecedented deception in modern British history.

For the conspirators, White's inclusion had become a necessity. Since Foreign Office officials, on the initiative of Sir Ivone Kirkpatrick, the permanent under secretary, were unaware of the conspiracy with Israel, Eden needed to use SIS's radio link and ciphers to communicate with David Ben-Gurion (the Israeli prime minister) and Israeli military intelligence. This was a wise precaution, because the British ambassador in Tel Aviv had earlier reported to London, 'we must treat the Israelis as sick people'.[32] The diplomat's antagonism towards Israel precluded his use as an emissary. White was 'not totally surprised by the conspiracy'. George Young's relationship with the Israelis had 'suggested something was up between us SIS and Mossad'.[33]

White then crossed the narrow road to meet Selwyn Lloyd at the Foreign Office. Lloyd, some said, had ordered the removal of a file from his office concerning Nasser's murder. Sitting next to the foreign secretary in his imposing room was Anthony Nutting. The minister of state searched White's face to detect his reaction as Lloyd outlined the agreement with France and Israel. The chief remained expressionless: 'I was determined not to reveal my feelings. I couldn't say that I disagreed with cabinet policy. Everything had been decided before I arrived.'[34] Only a handful of officials in Whitehall would summon the courage to confront Eden about his secret policy.

As White returned to Broadway, he was greeted by Peter Lunn. Silently he passed his colleague until he turned, his face anguished. Unspoken was his opinion of duplicity, intrigue and blackmail which had marked the briefings in Downing Street. For White, the alliance with Washington was pivotal to Britain's existence, yet he had just learnt that Eden was both contemptuous and fearful of US hegemony.

The following day, White met Field Marshal Templer, chief of the Imperial General Staff, whose strategy against the communists in Malaya was proving successful. White complained that his service was not being asked the pertinent questions through the JIC about the state of the Egyptian air force and whether the Egyptian military would actually fight. Templer merely sighed: 'Eden's barely consulting us.'[35] White was effectively isolated from the Whitehall machine but simultaneously expected to obey Eden's instructions.

Even in retrospect, White did not think that he could have voiced opposition to Eden. But he was to claim that at his next meeting with the prime minister he expressly told Eden that he would not sanction SIS's further involvement in Nasser's assassination.[36] By then, since SIS no longer had any officers in Cairo, it had been decided that the hit-team would be sent by the Special Political Action group from London. But White later insisted that the service's involvement in any assassination plot was thereafter excluded, permanently and for ever. Others involved smile at the suggestion that he defied the prime minister.

In other respects, White approved SIS's involvement in Eden's conspiracy. Nicholas Elliott had been dispatched to Tel Aviv to act as liaison officer with the Israeli government, denying the British ambassador information about the conspiracy. The exclusion even covered SIS. Baffled senior officers in Broadway complained of not receiving telegrams. No explanation was offered. 'It left a bad taste,' White conceded.[37]

As the countdown to the invasion proceeded, Allen Dulles arrived in London for dinner with Selwyn Lloyd and used the opportunity, with Richard Helms, an instinctive, astute intelligence officer, to meet the new chief. The CIA director had welcomed White's appointment as a break from precedent. Menzies had spoken a lot but said nothing, while Sinclair had said nothing at all. By contrast, White was 'honest, without the bullshit of parrying questions by mentioning "forbidden ground"'. The CIA director spoke of a 'sensation that White was businesslike and candid'.[38]

Over dinner with White and George Young, the two Americans discussed their interest in the 'imminent' coup in Syria and listened sympathetically to Britain's anti-Nasserism. Both sensed that 'the air was blue with Israelis', although Young, while admitting that 'something would happen in Egypt', was unwilling to explain the circumstances.[39] Neither Dulles nor his officers would be told in advance about the Sèvres conspiracy. By the end of the evening, nothing had been resolved about joint SIS and CIA operations in the Middle East other than confirmation that the two intelligence services were inextricably bound by history, purpose, sentiment and personal relations – regardless of politicians' whims. In the circumstances, for White, that was a considerable achievement.

On 29 October, the Israeli army crossed into the Sinai Desert and attacked Egyptian units. The following day, as agreed, the British and French governments issued an ultimatum to both Israel and Egypt to cease fighting. Failure to comply, the ultimatum warned, would provoke the dispatch of an Anglo–French force to secure the Canal's safety. A Royal Navy taskforce, assembled in the eastern Mediterranean, was alerted to take aboard troops in Malta and Cyprus. SIS was unable to advise the joint chiefs of staff about the state of Egypt's armed forces. On 31 October, as Israeli paratroops dug in close to the Canal, and after Nasser had refused to withdraw from the Canal Zone, French and RAF bombers struck Egyptian airfields around Cairo, destroying 260 planes. The uproar in the House of Commons, echoing similar fury across the world, drowned protests that Red Army units were moving into Budapest to crush the Hungarian uprising against communism and a less effective revolt in Poland. The die had been cast, and the first casualty was the British government's relations with Washington.[40]

Eisenhower, opposed to Britain's colonial pretensions, incredulous about the appalling military planning and outraged by the suspected Anglo–French conspiracy, demanded that Eden desist from invading Egypt. The 'special relationship' between American and British diplomats and military staff splintered. To White's credit, the only remaining contact was between SIS and the CIA.

After Swinburn's arrest, the focus of Britain's intelligence efforts had shifted to Cyprus, where 28,000 British soldiers were unprofitably engaged in fighting Eoka terrorists. Sensing the hopelessness of the venture, White ordered John Bruce Lockhart to 'stop playing soldiers' and, instead of crossing the Egyptian desert in a jeep for subversive operations, to stay in Europe and monitor the uprising in Hungary. In his place, Paul Paulson, dressed as a brigadier, was dispatched to the island to mastermind the landing of SIS's team with the first wave of troops on the beaches. One unit would install the puppet government in Cairo once Nasser was toppled. Another unit would seize and interrogate captured Egyptian officials about potential resistance, capture Soviet advisers, sabotage a small number of installations and collect general intelligence.

In anticipation, Paulson seized formal control of the Near East Broadcasting Station, owned and successfully managed by SIS, broadcasting a mixture of music and chat. Ralph Poston, the station's director, knew that among his staff were two SIS officers, but until the 'brigadier' produced a briefcase of propaganda scripts to counter Cairo's potent Voice of the Arabs, he had been unaware of his station's use for 'psychological warfare'.

After hearing SIS's inept broadcasts of virulent anti-Nasserism on the renamed Voice of Britain, urging Egyptians to overthrow Nasser and surrender, Poston and a number of Arab employees resigned in protest. Paulson, reflecting SIS's general status, was marooned in Cyprus broadcasting risible propaganda and providing no intelligence.

As 100,000 troops and a huge air force assembled around Cyprus, the prime source of intelligence about Egypt was intercepts obtained by GCHQ in Cyprus, limited intercepts of land-line conversations in Egypt and intercepts in Egyptian embassies, especially those obtained in London by MI5.[41] To understand those heated extracts, the actual conversations of the enemy, required cool heads and rational minds. But the specialists in SIS, the JIC and military intelligence could not grasp the subtext from the snatches. In unison, they wildly overestimated Egypt's ability to resist the landings.

On 31 October, as the Allied task force, harassed by the US Sixth Fleet, sailed towards Egypt, Cooper and Tweedy, the

CIA officers in London, were ordered to break off relations with SIS on Middle East matters and leave the British 'to boil in their own oil'.[42] CIA intelligence assessments compiled in Washington were withheld and the British defence staff were denied the air reconnaissance photographs from America's new and secret U2 aircraft, flying at 80,00 feet and capturing an image of 120 miles of land on one photograph.

Chester Cooper in particular felt vulnerable. In the days before the emergency, he had reported his unexpected exclusion from JIC discussions, but he had never predicted war.[43] To senior CIA officers, the Suez venture, coinciding with fighting on the streets of Budapest and the agency's publication of the text of Khrushchev's speech to the Twentieth Party Congress condemning Stalin, was the equivalent of 'pissing into a waterfall'.[44]

On 3 November, Robert Amory, the CIA's deputy director, telephoned Cooper: 'Tell your friends to comply with the goddamn ceasefire or go ahead with the goddamn invasion. Either way, we'll back 'em up if they do it fast. What we can't stand is their goddamn hesitation waltz while Hungary is burning.'[45] Cooper, as critical as any CIA officer of British policies, felt constrained by personal considerations: 'White was courteous, affectionate and intelligent so one could be very fond of him, and that coloured one's judgment of SIS.' Using his gentle diplomacy, White summoned the CIA officer and sought to repair SIS's relationship with the agency. The first result was the unofficial supply of U2 photographs of the Egyptian coastline and Cairo's airports. Then came the intelligence assessments and, in particular, the CIA's response to an urgent request from White on 5 November.

In the early hours of that day, the first British and French paratroops had landed near Port Said. The reaction from Moscow was unexpected. The Soviet leaders, having crushed the Hungarian revolt, threatened military intervention in the Suez Canal Zone. The Kremlin's warning statement also hinted that atomic bombs might be launched against Britain and France if they failed to withdraw from Egypt. As Eden's position unravelled, he frantically asked White whether the Soviets possessed that capability.

Over the previous years, SIS had provided countless 'assessments', 'appreciations' and 'advices', but the service, without informants in Moscow and lacking any credible agents inside the Soviet military, could not judge the reality of the threat. White appealed to Cooper for the CIA's assessment. 'I called Washington and threatened to return home the following day if there was no telegram with the information in the morning,' Cooper told White afterwards. In later years, CIA officers would speak with pride about their special relationship with SIS during those dark days.

The telegram from Washington arrived on 6 November, election day in America, and was presented to the JIC by Cooper on the same day. Russia's rocket threat, it concluded, was a bluff. At the end of the meeting, White's embarrassing display of affection towards Cooper reflected his general disillusion.

On Eisenhower's orders, nothing was done to forestall the collapse of Britain's financial reserves and its oil supplies were cut. The president, ignoring Eden's last, begging message – 'I have no doubt that the Bear is using Nasser' – insisted on a British withdrawal.[46] A majority of Eden's cabinet, excluded from the conspiracy, opposed the war. As British troops waded ashore in Egypt, therefore, Eden on 6 November announced his acceptance of a UN ceasefire resolution. 'We've now achieved the impossible,' signalled his commander from Cyprus. 'We're going both ways at once.'[47] 'I might not have started it,' observed Churchill, 'but I certainly would not have stopped it.' Nasser had survived and the Suez Canal was blocked on his orders by scuttled ships.

On 23 November, Eden, stricken by illness and exhaustion, flew to Jamaica to recuperate. While his cabinet and the Conservative Party fretted and feuded about their survival and the succession, their prime minister's surrender provoked vociferous complaints around Broadway from George Young: 'We should have gone on and taken Nasser's scalp.' White remained silent. His anonymity was protection from retribution.

White did not commission a post-mortem on SIS's clumsy performance, even after the discovery that Isameddine Khalil, SIS's sponsored organiser for the anti-Nasser coup, the recipient of £165,000, had been exposed as a double-agent.[48] Although it could be seen as a sign of weakness that White refrained from discussion, he would explain that an unsettling investigation would have hampered his plan for gradual change. An intelligence service can only reflect the government's policy, and the blame for the disaster lay elsewhere. To have dissected SIS's activities would, he believed, have irretrievably damaged the Service. Instead, White emerged with credit.

He had proved himself willing to accept and implement Whitehall's requirements even if he personally disagreed with the purpose. These were the very qualities which made his candidature so attractive. 'He is so good at getting on with people,' remarked Dean. 'Very honest, straightforward and never conceited.' His taciturn nature and social reserve comforted those who might otherwise have feared that he would abuse his knowledge of personal iniquities. Always available when required, White was certainly 'not a gossip'. His most compelling asset was 'imagination in the right sense'. Foreign Office officials explaining their requirements and problems 'came away feeling encouraged',[49] even if SIS failed to satisfy their requirements.

The aftermath of Suez nevertheless exercised a considerable impact upon White's career. Britain, humiliated and diminished as one of the Big Three, was in strategic retreat. Eden's disparagement by Eisenhower, re-elected to the presidency, extended to a complete freeze on Anglo–American personal relations in Washington. In response, a wave of anti-Americanism erupted in Britain, where petrol rationing had been imposed.

The freeze did not affect the intelligence community. In gratitude, White and Dean entertained Cooper for lunch at Brooks's club. 'You should receive an honour for your services,' enthused White. Not far from St James's, queues of Britons were patiently waiting to apply for emigration permits to Australia, New Zealand and Canada. Over that lunch, it was apparent that the popular disenchantment embraced White. He mentioned that he had seen John Osborne's controversial new play, *Look Back in Anger*, and it was evident that he felt a glow of sympathy towards the so-called 'angry young men'. He had been particularly struck by Anthony Eden's denial on 20 December to the House of Commons that there had been any collusion between Britain, France and Israel. Over Christmas, White reflected upon his inheritance. Contrary to his initial forebodings, the work promised to be 'more interesting than in MI5', but SIS, still dominated by Menzies's legacy, required rehabilitation.[50]

Like Suez, the Hungarian uprising had reflected SIS's weaknesses. In the absence of any sources in Moscow or in any communist government, SIS predictions had been manifestly wrong. The only voice forecasting the Kremlin's invasion, that of the ambassador in Budapest, Leslie 'Bunny' Fry, had been derided. 'He's such an extraordinary, hopeless man,' commented Denis Greenhill in the Foreign Office, 'we can't take this seriously.' Instead of perfecting the collection of pure intelligence, SIS had for too long prospered as an agent for agitation, coups and wars, the bedrock of its activities in the decade since the Nazi defeat. 'The emphasis was on gung-ho operations,' complained White, 'a hangover from SOE and World War Two. It was all dangerous.'[51]

Too many Whitehall powerbrokers – politicians and military chiefs – had urged SIS to wage an aggressive underground war against the Soviet Union. But unlike Allen Dulles and Frank Wisner, thrilled by the crusade of dispatching hundreds of agents to rouse the subjugated East Europeans against the Red Army, White had no confidence in a clandestine crusade against communism. SIS's attempt to overthrow Enver Hoxha, the Stalinist dictator in Albania in 1949, had been disastrous. Dozens of brave patriots had been betrayed and, after public trials, executed. The East Europeans had shown in Berlin in 1953 and recently in Budapest and Warsaw limited appetite for bloodshed.

White's attitude was summarised by a famous exchange in 1953. The CIA station chief in Berlin demanded weapons for the German insurgents: 'Blood of martyrs fertilises the tree of liberty.' To which John Bross, the CIA's director for Europe, replied, 'Crap. No bloodbath.'[52] Extricating the robber barons from the 'freedom business' in Eastern Europe, a deep-rooted sentiment that White recognised, required delicacy.

SIS had resumed clandestine operations against Russia in 1944 after Churchill's three-year moratorium. 'Menzies had ordered the resumption of operations without Churchill's knowledge because he knew that the Soviets would be the major problem'.[53] After Germany's defeat, SIS officers stationed in a great circle – from Sweden to Turkey and then across Asia to Japan – had waged an undeclared war against Russia. Some had been SIS officers since the Bolshevik revolution; others had been trained during the war against Hitler.

In newly liberated Europe, under the direction of Kenneth Cohen, the able SIS controller, agents had been recruited from the thousands of destitute young men – Ukrainians, Georgians, Poles, Czechs, Hungarians, Byelorussians, Latvians, Estonians and Lithuanians – surviving in cramped refugee camps scattered around Germany. In those deprived surroundings, it was not difficult for SIS-sponsored 'charities' – the Organisation for Assistance to Foreign Displaced Persons in Germany, the Latvian Liberation Committee and the Estonian National Council – to spot young idealists prepared for the ultimate sacrifice. Drawn to appeals of nationalism and anti-communism, they were trained by SIS officers in the use of weapons, radios, codes, spy tradecraft, sabotage and survival and returned as agents to their Soviet-occupied homelands.

Others had been recruited from political groups in Eastern Europe which had fought with Hitler against Stalin and, according to their leaders' assurances to SIS, were still fighting for freedom against the Soviet occupation. SIS officers were persuaded that those resistance movements, if supported by the West, would continue their struggle and provide intelligence. In an atmosphere of hysterical fear, aroused by a belief that 'The Russians are coming,' any avowed anti-communist became an ally. In forging alliances with those nationalists, SIS ignored their wartime sympathies and the murderous deeds committed under the Nazi banner. More pertinently, SIS was persuaded by the partisans' own accounts of their continuing struggle against the Red Army in the Slovak mountains, in the Baltic and Polish forests and in the Ukrainian hills.

Millions of pounds had been spent creating 'democratic' political organisations; on radio stations; on balloons launched across Eastern Europe to release thousands of leaflets inviting dissidents to defect; on paramilitary battalions; and on flying unmarked Dakotas or Hastings at tree-top height across the Iron Curtain, to parachute agents into the countryside to join partisan groups and to report on the impenetrable and unknown. During his first weeks in Broadway, White had encountered the directors of those operations, still recounting the excitement of their 'Joe', after months of complicated planning and hours of tense countdown, disappearing into the darkness.

If their Joe's radio signal appeared, and if their messages were received, there was jubilation. Just getting a Joe into communist territory was counted a success, even if the agent's resulting information was questionable. In those pre-satellite days, an agent near a Soviet military airfield at the outbreak of war could add precious minutes of warning to a surprise first strike. It was primitive but matched the fears of invasion. Reviewing the files of those past operations, White echoed a CIA sceptic: 'The only thing these drops achieved is to confirm the laws of gravity.' There is a view, White cautioned, that 'if you puff enough hot air, the Russians will blow away.' There was a false notion abroad that 'when they can't do what needs to be done, they do what they can do, and all too often that has no bearing on what needs to be done.' The cost of SIS enthusiasm was being counted when White arrived. The review, awaking memories of MI5's wartime double-cross operation and reflecting his own investigation of Soviet espionage ever since, profoundly influenced his attitude towards the KGB.

No one in SIS had been burnt worse than Harry Carr, the secretive controller for Northern Department, responsible for Russia. Recruited to SIS in 1920, Carr had between 1944 and 1954 dispatched over one hundred Balt agents by E-boat to their homelands. Based at the Special Liaison Centre in Ryder Street, St James's, Carr had boasted that SIS controlled a network of agents which stretched from the Baltic States as far as the Urals. Local Balt partisans in the Soviet Union, recruited by Carr's agents, had even been exfiltrated by sea and brought to London for training, before being returned to Russia. During discussions in London in the early 1950s, CIA officers, anxious to learn about the problems of infiltrating agents into Russia, were persuaded by Carr's supercilious recounting of SIS successes.[54] 'We had a good time together swapping lies,' commented one CIA officer when in late 1954 SIS began to suspect an awful truth.[55]

For ten years, all Carr's operations had been controlled from Moscow. All the intelligence proudly supplied to the Foreign Office and cabinet by SIS had been invented by the KGB and its predecessor organisations. Even the 'local partisans' brought to Britain were KGB officers. The seeds of the Soviet success had been sown in 1944 when Carr's first agents, dispatched from Sweden, had been captured and turned, luring all future SIS agents into the Soviet web. The KGB's double-cross, so perfectly mirroring White's own wartime success against the Abwehr, had humiliated Carr. But SIS had concealed from Whitehall the terrible blow to its credibility. By the time White arrived in Broadway, Carr had been transferred to Copenhagen pending retirement.

A more explicit SIS failure, reviewed in those early days by White, was the service's involvement in supporting the Ukrainian nationalists – the NTS (People's Labour Union) and OUN (Organisation of Ukrainian Nationalists). SIS had invested heavily in the Ukrainian nationalist movement for twenty-five years. In 1934, it had dispatched Georgi Okolovich and Stefan Bandera, both Ukrainians, into Russia as key agents whose subsequent reports were judged by Broadway as reliable. SIS officers were less enchanted after the Nazi invasion of Russia in June 1941 by Okolovich's readiness to collaborate with German intelligence. Following the Nazi defeat, the Ukrainians were not immediately re-embraced by SIS despite their repeated advances. Over the ensuing two years, well-armed Ukrainian groups none-theless fought the Soviet communists. But by 1949 nearly all of the NTS partisans were dead.

Their demise was unknown to SIS when Operation Shrapnel was approved by Whitehall. Harold Shergold, John Bruce Lockhart and other SIS officers in Germany were urged from London to recruit Ukrainian agents for operations with the partisan armies. In an expensive exercise, 'front' organisations – the New Union for Turko-Tatar Independence 'Idel-Urala', the Congress for Freedom in Culture, the Northern Caucasian

National Committee – directed those selected for training to a camp in Bad Homburg. Between 1949 and 1954, SIS and the CIA trained and dispatched from Germany, Italy and Austria into the Ukraine over 150 men.

During those years, Mike Lykowski, alias Mike Peters, an SIS officer working with the CIA at the Joint Centre in Frankfurt, paid tens of thousands of dollars to Ukrainian agents who often reappeared wearing new clothes, boasting the ownership of new cars and hosting champagne parties in nightclubs. Occasionally, they disappeared from Frankfurt for ever. As the flow of 'intelligence' radioed to West Germany increased, SIS confidently assured customers in Whitehall that it was running a reliable network supplemented by agents in Poland and Czechoslovakia. Occasionally, a cautious CIA officer queried SIS whether those Ukrainian agents inside Russia were free or under control, and whether the exercise was worth the risk. The answer was always reassuring. Others in the CIA like Richard Helms were cynical: 'They're just sending people in to put their feet in the water.' 'They're dreamers with their feet planted firmly in the air,' carped Al Ulmer. 'There's no strategy.'[56]

The cynics remained in a minority until 1955 when, in the wake of Harry Carr's humiliation, Bruce Lockhart became suspicious. Bromide tests confirmed that the whole operation had been under the control of Soviet intelligence since the first group had been captured after landing by parachute in 1950. The Soviets had enticed and then penetrated all the other missions from the West. SIS agents had been arrested and usually executed. Others agreed to participate in the double-cross. Some Western observers suspected that the KGB had even infiltrated the Centre in Frankfurt. It was tempting to blame Kim Philby's treachery. The truth was more prosaic. SIS had once again succumbed to an apparently superior intelligence service, which in 1925 had successfully established The Trust, a 'resistance' group created by Soviet intelligence to lure Sidney Reilly, the SIS agent, into Russia and to his death.

The first steps towards dismantlement of SIS's expensive commitment to those foreign missions were taken before White's arrival. On 28 February 1956, SIS and CIA representatives met in London for a two-day conference. SIS's consequent message to the NTS leaders was unequivocal:

> The British feel that seven years are quite sufficient to properly assess each factor of British/NTS collaboration. They have concluded that the collaboration has been most unproductive. The results obtained scarcely compensate for the time and resources invested.
>
> British intelligence has therefore decided to completely terminate such collaboration.

Control over NTS had been handed over to the CIA by the time of White's arrival, but among the continuing SIS operations for infiltrating agents into the Soviet Union was Michael Whittall's, based on Prince's Island, in the Marmara Sea, Turkey. Caucasian anti-communists, recruited in Istanbul by the North Caucasian Emigration Society, another front organisation, were being parachuted into the Soviet Union. Since most had disappeared, White assumed that they too had been captured. The operation, he ordered, should end. In surveying the infiltration operations with George Young, John Bruce Lockhart, Arthur Crouchley, the Northern Area controller, and Paul Paulson, his successor, White castigated those who believed that just getting an agent into the Soviet Union would produce information: 'It's important to remove the Iron Curtain sentiment of sending someone over the wall for the sake of it.'

But SIS was not totally to blame. There was pressure to co-operate from the CIA, which had also suffered losses in Poland. Millions of dollars in gold had been spent dispatching agents to fight alongside WIN, a resistance movement. In 1952, the Agency had realised that the 'resistance' were all Polish intelligence officers, actors in a huge double-cross. Allen Dulles had consoled himself: 'At least we're getting the kind of experience we need for the next war.'[57]

White derided Dulles's romanticism and Wisner's recklessness. Their costly operations had caused many deaths and delivered no intelligence. 'I decided', recalled White, 'to resist American pressure to become involved in further clandestine warfare.' Both SIS and the CIA had underestimated the KGB's abilities. The KGB had proved as adept as MI5 in deception. During their discussions, George Young persuaded White that he had warned about KGB penetration and the risk of double-cross. His warnings, insisted Young, had been ignored due to 'enormous pressure' from the chiefs of staff, who, desperate for information, had provided so many facilities. Young's claim that he had expressed his foreboding was misleading. The alarm had been raised by Kenneth Cohen, the controller of Europe, who had retired in 1954. But Young's accurate description of the military's pressure influenced White.

The monthly meetings between White and the chiefs of staff to discuss clandestine operations demonstrated how difficult it was to resist the military's demands: 'They still had not mastered the transition from war to peace. Their values and their ethos remained those of wartime. They inadequately appreciated the difficulties. Those clandestine operations using émigrés had assumed their own momentum.' The military, said White, 'were too dangerous to deal with. I wanted to end our relationship.'[58] White blamed his predecessors: 'Sinclair and Easton were weak and effectively no good. Despite being staff officers of the best tradition, they bowed to the chiefs and allowed the Dunderdales and Carrs to become laws unto themselves.'[59]

For years, at the end of the day, Wilfred 'Biffy' Dunderdale, an SIS officer since 1921, had just walked into Menzies's office for a chat: 'C, these operations are too secret to be put on paper.' The customary informality between White's predecessors and their officers had obscured a clear chain of command. Dunderdale's pride was SIS's confused structure. 'The Russians could never understand our service because of the muddle of command. Much better than military organisation.'[60] So much had been agreed orally with non-existent controls that no one within SIS had realised that Dunderdale's White Russian émigré groups in Paris and London included Soviet intelligence officers. Dunderdale assumed that the relationship would continue with White. 'Biffy is cagey and won't talk to others involved in his anti-Russian operations,' Easton told White. 'He thinks it's all a competition.'[61]

There was a similar problem with Harold Gibson, a veteran SIS officer who had conducted operations against the Bolsheviks since the 1920s. 'He plays his cards too close to his chest,' Easton complained to White. 'He stood for hours outside Menzies's office for a meeting and then all you'd get was a mouth of cottonwool. No meat.'

Not only were the cowboy operations to end, dictated White, but the cowboys were to be removed: 'We need professionals, not people running their own rackets.'[62] Loyalty and readiness to work in obscurity were not substitutes for quality. Slush funds had proliferated, but there was insufficient product. The most recent disaster, regaled with smirks in Broadway's basement bar, was about the Hungarian recruited by SIS in Vienna to ensnare Soviet agents. His encouraging reports had been rewarded by thousands of pounds of SIS's money. 'Last heard of in South America,' laughed a baron, adding that all his reports were 'duds, of course'.[63]

The driving force for change was John Briance, White's personal assistant. 'The problems', Briance admitted, 'are enormous. All those bureaucratic obstacles and dead wood after years of service!'[64] The list of dismissals was compiled in the evenings in White's office. Briance and occasionally Peter Lunn sat reading through personal files drawn from SIS's disorganised registry. Dunderdale, Carr, Gibson, Crouchley and others were given golden handshakes. Even in that ambiance, White was the perfect chairman. Voices were rarely raised, and there were no flamboyant displays.

Although 'embarrassed by having to fire so many people' – in fact some would criticise his indecisiveness, his retention of too many incompetents to avoid a backlash – White deliberately protected Stanislas Mayer, a pre-war director of Polish intelligence who had masterminded the initial stages of breaking the Enigma code machine. He was to be retained for life. One file missing from the registry was Menzies's. The wartime chief had deliberately avoided any records to preserve the fiction that he was the illegitimate son of Edward VII. 'I paid ten shillings,' laughed White, 'and got the name of his real father from Somerset House.'[65]

Menzies's more permanent legacy, the robber barons, could not be moved. Their influence and traditions were, White acknowledged, SIS's undisturbable skeleton. Among the most powerful was John Bruce Lockhart, recruited by Menzies in 1945 in Germany and soon afterwards appointed the chief of SIS's biggest station, Bad Salzuflen. The bluff sportsman's pedigree was impeccable. His uncle, Robert Bruce Lockhart, had been dispatched to Moscow by SIS's first chief in 1918 to destroy the Bolshevik revolution. The plot's audacity had bequeathed an awed respect for SIS among Soviet intelligence officers which still held sway in 1945.

Germany was the front line of the Cold War and the ideal training ground for young SIS officers. Bruce Lockhart's genial influence was pervasive among a generation of SIS personnel operating in an occupied country, oblivious to any rules. But their results reflected White's criticisms. In some respects, Bruce Lockhart's regime won plaudits. His black propaganda was hailed as outstanding. Forged statements of Swiss bank accounts were dispatched from Zurich to senior government officials in East Berlin in anticipation that communist censors would open and query the contents. Embarrassing documents about East German officials 'surfaced' for use as blackmail. Other forgeries were sent to West German communists to stimulate distrust among party members. At the time it was considered a great success. 'We've got more money,' admitted Lawrence Deneufville of the CIA about Bruce Lockhart, 'but he's got more brains.'[66]

Bruce Lockhart had always been close to the CIA. During the Korean War, he had organised the 'stay-behind' networks in Europe, competing with Bill Colby of the CIA. Both services were 'stumbling over each other' and facing complaints from European intelligence agencies about incompatible equipment and training manuals. With Bill Stewart of the CIA, Bruce Lockhart had negotiated a co-operation agreement. He had then agreed co-operation with the CIA on targeting non-Soviet targets in Western Europe. 'The British', Rolfe Kingsley reported to Washington, 'don't trust the French, whom they think are beastly; or the intentions of the Germans.' In fact, SIS suspicions went deeper. French politicians and left-wing organisations were distrusted as Russian stooges; and the ambitions of some Germans for rearmament, atomic power and national revival aroused alarm. It was Bruce Lockhart who, when CIA and SIS officers were seeking to recruit the same personalities as agents, agreed with Stewart to consult and avoid competition.

It was also Bruce Lockhart who, after refusing to touch Reinhard Gehlen's new American-sponsored Bundesnachrichten-dienst, the foreign intelligence service based near Munich, succumbed in 1953 when Jim Critchfield, the CIA officer attached to Gehlen's headquarters, arranged an introductory lunch at Bad Godesberg. Critchfield had smiled as Bruce Lockhart agreed that Bill Steadman, a quiet-spoken SIS counter-intelligence specialist, educated at Vienna University, should be attached to the BND. To cement the agreement, Bruce Lockhart would, in 1955, teach Gehlen golf on the south coast: 'He looked like a Camberley general. Trustworthy but he knew nothing about spying.'[67]

But, despite Bruce Lockhart's diplomacy, some complained the results were poor. In those post-war years, SIS did not recruit one high-level communist official prepared to stay in Eastern Europe and supply information. 'The failure to attract defectors was heartbreaking,' observed John Taylor, then a young SIS officer serving under Bruce Lockhart. Only cooks, mechanics and low-ranking soldiers defected. Their sole value was as 'talent spotters' – identifying those Russians and others whose defection would be valuable. During Bruce Lockhart's reign, SIS officers had even approached former Gestapo officers, including Klaus Barbie, the 'Butcher of Lyons',[68] to penetrate the communist parties in Germany and Eastern Europe. Generous sums were paid but the information was judged valueless because there was no 'collateral' – that is, confirmation from aerial reconnaissance, Sigint or prisoner-of-war interrogations.

The disappointments were Menzies's legacy. During the Second World War defectors were called 'deserters', and after 1945, when Menzies eschewed any post-mortem, there was no talk of a 'defector in place'. In 1948, Menzies had appointed a Defectors Committee of three SIS officers – Robin Brooke, James Fulton and Jack Easton – to compile every three months a summary of reports on attempts to recruit Soviet defectors.[69] 'Our results were not impressive,' admitted Easton.[70] The truth was even worse.

One 'defector', Colonel J. Tasoev, had declared on his arrival in Britain his wish to return home. In the ensuing discussions, Harold Perkins had advised Menzies that Tasoev should be drugged and dropped into the North Sea. Instead, he had been returned to Berlin, judged as a successful Soviet 'dangle'.[71] Infiltrations from Germany had also caused embarrassments. In 1953, John Howe, an SIS officer, had dispatched a Czech agent into his homeland with a radio. A message from the agent asked for a spare part. When an SIS officer, accredited as a British diplomat, arrived in a Prague graveyard, he was arrested by Czech security police. The British ambassador was then expelled.

Other recruitments had proved expensive and unproductive. In October 1953, Vladimir Krutikov, an economist, had been arrested in Paris on phoney charges of drunkenness. In jail, Kenneth Cohen, the SIS officer, posing as a representative of 'Luke & Co.', had offered to save the Russian if he became a British source. Krutikov agreed. Over the following year, Cohen handed over 500,000 French francs for information and documents from the Soviet Ministry of Trade. One year later, Krutikov was 'arrested' and 'sentenced' to twenty-five years. SIS had never realised, according to the KGB, that the Russian was not a genuine defector.

By then, Bruce Lockhart was SIS's controller for Western Europe, and in that area White's inheritance was the bedrock of SIS's best achievements. Spying on allies was the most sensitive of the service's operations, while using allies to spy on Britain's enemies was considered astute. The crux of SIS's success lay in the personal relations between the robber barons and the chiefs of intelligence services across Scandinavia, the Benelux countries and France, relationships cultivated during the Second World War. The leaders of the resistance, and especially their intelligence chiefs based in London, had returned home to rebuild their services, grateful for the hospitality during their exile and espousing mutual interests with British intelligence officers.

In the post-war years, SIS officers, targeting a communist official in those countries, especially Denmark, Norway and Holland, could rely on their friends in the local intelligence service for assistance. Leslie Mitchell, posted to Copenhagen, could exploit the relationships he developed during the war running the 'Shetland Bus' – the fast boat returning Danish and Norwegian resistance fighters across the North Sea. 'A Russian diplomat posted in Denmark', recalled Mitchell, 'could not be protected as in Moscow. He was living in our surroundings and vulnerable to our approaches. We could see the weaknesses and, if lucky, exploit them.'[72]

Other SIS officers relied upon relations with exiled officials and politicians who, after returning home in 1944, opposed their government's policy. Providing money through front organisations, SIS could influence elections and buy information about its allies, often more important than espionage against the Soviets. SIS stations in Western Europe also recruited local politicians, businessmen, journalists and students to penetrate communist countries on Britain's behalf. These so-called access agents, especially Scandinavians, travelled with fewer restrictions than British subjects. Often, they were recruited by SIS officers posing under a 'false flag', as officials of other countries. The pattern had been established in Sweden soon after the war. The Soviets, it became known, needed telecommunications equipment, so the SIS station in Stockholm recruited a Swedish expert to offer his services to the Russians.

That sophistication, disguising SIS's involvement, was the option which the robber barons offered White in response to his disparagement of the past clandestine warfare and his request for 'well-placed informants'. Their offer satisfied White's priorities for collecting raw intelligence, the penetration of hostile intelligence services and the establishment of close relationships with friendly intelligence agencies. Recruits would include members of Western communist parties who regularly visited the Soviet Union.

Under the supervision of the newly established Russian Orbit Group, more SIS officers were to be sent into the Soviet bloc under diplomatic cover rather than as unprotected foreigners. 'The great outdoor tradition has ended,' sighed a robber baron. 'SIS officers will become diplomat-minded and behave accordingly.' Under White's regime, officers were to be assessed less on displays of bravado and more on their care and judgment. But the new methods were shrewd. To supplement the limited numbers of

SIS officers, the recently reorganised London station under Peter Lunn was to enlist British journalists, academics, students, industrialists, businessmen and others travelling to communist countries and the Middle East to collect intelligence or act as postmen. The organisations particularly favoured as recruiting grounds were the BBC, the British Council, the National Union of Students, the Anglo-Russian Translation Agency, national newspapers, publishing companies and Christian missionaries.

SIS's new methods were noticed by the KGB. In a training manual, KGB officers were reminded that:

> SIS operations are based upon comprehensive long-term planning, displaying flexibility, drive and astute camouflage of their activities. They use trade and other business connections as cover; their working methods are sophisticated and cunning [operating under other nationalities]; they engage in extensive disinformation; they resort to crude means or outright force [terror, bribery, blackmail, provocation, intimidation, riots and insurrection]; they maintain tight security, caution and tremendous patience; and they strive, using important members of their own ruling class, to acquire agents among high-placed government officials.[73]

Although the KGB's appreciation was flattering, White's arrival at Broadway coincided with a dramatic change in the tradecraft of espionage. Technology had altered the purpose of agents. The U2 'spy' plane reduced the fear of an unexpected Soviet invasion and provided irrefutable evidence of missiles and military manoeuvres. The demand made of the intelligence services had altered from 'What have they got?' to 'What are their intentions?' That question required more sophisticated understanding about the Soviet Union and Kremlin politics. Despite his personal interest, White knew both his own and SIS's limitations: 'The experts in Broadway were just insufficiently scholarly.'[74]

To rectify SIS's artlessness, George Young had already retained Hugh Seton-Watson, Malcolm Mackintosh and Professor Leonard Schapiro, the son of Lithuanians and a passionate anti-Bolshevik, to provide studies of Soviet political and military personalities. Foreign Office officials would be provided for the first time with seemingly authoratitive profiles and studies of their antagonists rather than random, uncollated stereotypical reports exaggerating Russian invincibility. But those were still early days. By the time White arrived, SIS had not mastered the intrigues and personality battles within the Kremlin, and his own impromptu comments lacked perception.[75] His quiet manner suggested passivity – the cautious, patient collector of information – and that irked men committed to action. But, in the wake of Suez, White faced more important questions than pleasing the barons. First, whether SIS would be thrust into the heart of foreign policy formulation or continue merely replying to requests for information; and whether he could repair the fractured relationship with the CIA. The answer to the first was no. Arranging an affirmative answer to the second was White's achievement.

Soon after Eden's resignation on 9 January 1957, the CIA director Allen Dulles invited White to Washington 'to mend fences'. As with so many former OSS officers, the sixty-three-year-old Dulles's affection for his British wartime colleagues was automatic but in White's case the relationship was more like that of father and son. Unlike Menzies, who had spent so much time in his clubs or at the races, White was a new breed who was expected to shape a professional organisation. Renowned for his outstanding operations in Berne during World War Two, Dulles prided himself on understanding the profession of intelligence. In White he appreciated a similar spirit. Both chiefs expressed their delight that Philby and Suez had not interrupted the UK–USA agreement to share signals and exchange intelligence. Unspoken was the knowledge that the balance between the two services had irretrievably shifted in the agency's favour.

White was entertained to lunch at the Alibi Club, Dulles's favoured haunt. Over an endless supply of alcohol, the American embarked on an amusing *tour d'horizon* about their mutual pact to defeat communism for the benefit of his guests who included John Briance, Cleveland Cram, a CIA British specialist, and Richard Helms, the CIA's chief of operations. Sukarno of Indonesia should be removed; Lee Kuan Yew in Singapore should be supported; operations into China from Hong Kong should be maintained and even increased; and there should be more co-operation in the Middle East. Painfully for the British, Eisenhower had announced a new doctrine on 5 January, threatening to challenge and defeat Soviet domination of the Middle East. Mindful of Britain's identical purpose over the Suez Canal, White assured Dulles that SIS remained committed to fight communism and seek opportunities for Nasser's removal.

Back in Dulles's private office near the State Department, his four guests watched the director demonstrate his adjustable leather chair, specially constructed to alleviate persistent back pains. Dulles invited White to test the invention. The SIS chief obliged and suddenly found himself lying horizontal and shaking. Dulles had released a lever and started the vibrator. Everyone laughed. White was thrilled. He knew that Dulles would never have pulled the same prank on the head of any other foreign service: the alliance was recemented. The CIA was vital to SIS's well-being, he regularly attested, although he no less often complained that American intelligence officers were 'clumsy' practitioners.[76]

CHAPTER NINE

Empire Wars

In March 1958, White made what he later described as 'my worst decision'. Jack Easton, his deputy, had agreed to resign. White's choice of vice-chief could be either George Young or John Bruce Lockhart. Despite the Suez débâcle, White preferred Young. 'I felt', he told Peter Lunn, 'I had to choose the man with the best headpiece.' Others believed White's decision was political, to appease the other robber barons.

For Bruce Lockhart, the moment was bitter-sweet. He had known Young at St Andrew's University, where he had inherited his elder's lecture notes. That act of friendship, helping him to pass his final examinations, Bruce Lockhart repaid by introducing Young to the Firm in 1946.

According to Broadway folklore, on hearing the news Bruce Lockhart left his office and walked around London for several hours. He would deny that version and suggest that he had not expected the post: 'I'm not very good with Whitehall and that's important now.' To close friends he sighed, 'Dick's afraid of George.' White certainly respected Young. His journalism and literary interests were a magnet for White's frustrated ambitions, and his record in Vienna, Iran and even recently in Broadway displayed intuition and political acceptability. On the eve of 'spy wars', when the destruction of a U2 spy plane shot down in May 1960 over Sverdlovsk would wreck the superpower summit in Paris intended to save the world from a nuclear holocaust, SIS's status depended upon satisfying Whitehall of its competence to defeat the KGB's *Blitzkrieg*. Young was suited, White reasoned, for that diplomacy.

Not long after the announcement, White appreciated his error. Young's acumen was outweighed by his eccentricities. His Vice, he discovered, occasionally lurched into uncontrollable indiscretions. Under the influence of his wife, a Dutch colonialist, Young was transforming from a socialist into an aggressive racist. 'I didn't realise that he was so right-wing,' White would admit.[1] Young's wife had also converted her husband into an aggressive vegetarian. While staying in Tangiers with Teddy Dunlop, an SIS officer, Young exploded in fury after his host had bought two chickens at the local market: 'I refuse to travel in your car with meat!'[2] In Broadway, Elliott also noticed troublesome quirks: 'He was always doing something mad in the office. He would tell visiting ambassadors whose opinions he disliked, "You should be in jail."'[3] Judgment of character was not White's strong quality. He was too trusting, too fair, at times squeamishly reluctant to twist the jugular of the mavericks.

Those traits were disregarded in Whitehall. White's image was untypical, that of a slightly unconventional civil servant but one 'comfortable with the nobs'. Unlike his colleagues, he enjoyed the company of academics and writers, regularly entertaining his senior officers for lunch at the Garrick, an uncommon venue for discussing the secrets of the state. Usually dressed in a blue suit, soft collar and Christ Church tie, he visibly enjoyed the interludes in those surroundings. Here was the window to the real world. To the few stiff SIS officers invited to White's comfortable apartment in Queen Anne's Gate, he and Kate appeared to have imported the Garrick's Bohemian atmosphere. His visitors remarked on the relaxed and casually dressed chief's lenient treatment of his two sons, while the conversation ranged across literature, theatre, exhibitions and modern philosophy. Unknown to his visitors, White relaxed by composing poems.

Unlike most other intelligence officers, British and American, White's perceptions were not narrow and professional but reflective. He wanted to watch, listen and leave in peace the events his service was monitoring, rather than engage in warfare. The passivity was reflected in his lifestyle. The family's country house had moved to the White House in Nutbourne near Pulborough in West Sussex, close to his mother. His brother Alan also bought a house in the village and his sister Kathleen, a secretary to a headmistress, was encouraged to spend the weekends with her brothers. 'My family life', White admitted, 'kept me sane.' His professional life was never discussed. His second knighthood, the KCMG, conferred in 1960 by the Queen, was taken with modesty, provoking a friend's telegram: 'Twice a night at your age. Congratulations'. On the rare occasions when he returned from abroad, his only comment was to curse his exhaustion and lament the journey. He would need 24 hours to recover from a trans-Atlantic flight.

Before the eve of his retirement from SIS, White never travelled to Africa, the Far East or the Middle East (except Israel), whether to scrutinise the activities of SIS stations or to meet directors of other intelligence agencies. Although Britain's military alliances and commercial interests in the Empire and Third World were critical to the country's financial security, and although those regions had become bitter and bloody battlegrounds of Cold War rivalry, White preferred to rely upon the barons in Broadway. His imperfect knowledge and indifference to the shifts and eddies of internal affairs in the Third World were a recipe for avoiding mistakes rather than initiating successes. His was the passivity of a counter-intelligence officer, a spycatcher, rather than a patriotic adventurer fighting communist infiltration into Britain's Empire and the Third World. George Young and the other barons disturbed and challenged his purist style.

Ever since Suez, White had regretted his passivity towards Young's plot to assassinate Nasser. In the months afterwards, the edicts dispensed through SIS's echelons suggested his distaste for uncontrollable adventures and an instinctive reserve towards operations in Africa, Asia and the Middle East. From the outset, the barons sought to sidestep his fiats, while Harold Macmillan, the new prime minister, overruled him. Of the six prime ministers whom White directly served, his relationship with Macmillan was 'the most close'.[4] Despite the premier's scepticism towards SIS, White was seduced by the raconteur's patrician charm and literary erudition. Macmillan kindled another father–son relationship, undermining White's inclination to steer SIS away from gung-ho operations and even assassination.

White's excuse for excluding SIS from involvement in the Empire wars was the Attlee Doctrine, an administrative decree issued in 1946, which reiterated the ban on SIS operating within Britain's colonies, which were classed as domestic territories and therefore the exclusive responsibility of MI5. Even in the Dominions of Canada, Australia and New Zealand, SIS was excluded. MI5 officers established a declared liaison relationship with the local security service and avoided covert and hostile operations. That arrangement had not been challenged on India's independence in 1947, and, a decade later in Africa, Britain's colonial administrators, confident that their preparations for democratic self-government would prove successful, assumed that Britain would not spy on former colonies.

After leaving Leconfield House, White's reluctance to engage in turf wars with MI5 was resented by certain officers in Broadway, led by Young and supported outside by the Suez Group of ministers in Macmillan's government, eager to destroy Soviet-supported nationalists of the Nasser stamp thought to be mushrooming throughout the Third World. To those politicians, including Julian Amery and Duncan Sandys, SIS was the ideal instrument for waging war against international communism.*

The Doctrine's first casualty were Britain's interests in Africa. When White became chief, Britain's eleven colonies south of the Sahara were destined to become independent. On his own initiative, George Young had in 1956 sent Frank Steele, a former government official in Uganda, around Africa, to Britain's colonies and those controlled by Belgium, France and Portugal, to identify the ideal location of future SIS stations. Steele's reception by British ambassadors and officials was frosty. 'They fear the tail wagging the dog,' Steele reported, complaining that too many British diplomats were blind to the impending anti-colonial revolution. In the Belgian Congo, the ambassador launched a tirade against Steele for questioning the diplomat's prediction that the colonial regime would last 'at least another fifteen years'. In other capitals, Steele was abruptly warned that any SIS presence would be 'over my dead body'.

That consensus still prevailed in 1957, when Kwame Nkrumah,

---

* Exceptionally, SIS did retain stations on White's insistence in Malaya and Singapore after their independence.

the self-styled Redeemer, celebrated the transformation of the Gold Coast into Ghana, Britain's first African colony to become independent. Unexpectedly he at once dissociated himself from Britain, attacked white neo-colonialism and permitted the Soviet embassy to become the KGB's headquarters for the whole continent. The local MI5 officer, isolated from the Ghanaian security service, could offer no intelligence to London about Soviet activities. White appeared undisturbed by those events. In Broadway, the continent did not even boast a director. Responsibility was assigned to the controller of the Middle East who, because there was no demand in the Joint Intelligence Committee for intelligence from Africa, devoted few resources to Africa.

In late 1959, John Bruce Lockhart, the controller for Middle East and Africa since Suez, flew for the first time to Africa. The continent, he realised, was an ideal laboratory in which to manipulate Lenin's preconditions for revolution: poverty, colonialism and exploitation. His report to White in spring 1960 coincided with an approach by Bronson Tweedy, appointed the CIA's first director for Africa. On Allen Dulles's orders, Tweedy was seeking permission for the Agency to establish a station in Nigeria, which was also about to become independent. Under the post-war agreement with Britain, the CIA was also bound by the Attlee Doctrine and so banned from operating in Nigeria, a 'domestic' territory, without Britain's concurrence.

What Dulles feared, explained Tweedy, was Moscow's seductive influence over the so-called non-aligned Third World. Africa, he continued, could be 'lost' to the communists, who were succouring, financing and arming African independence movements. 'No one in London seems to know what's happening,' Tweedy told White. The former director general of MI5 was courteous but cool. Loyal to his old service, knowing that Hollis would resent any CIA presence with its inevitably aggressive activities, White suggested that Tweedy approach MI5, but he did not wish the American 'good luck'. Sentimentally, he sympathised with the traditional division of the world which kept the CIA out of the Empire.

Tweedy's approach to Hollis was flatly rejected. 'Each concession', Tweedy would report, 'will be like extracting a tooth.'

But Hollis's obduracy became vulnerable in summer 1960. On 30 June, the Congo, a huge, mineral-rich country, was formally declared independent by its Belgian colonisers. Unprepared for self-government, within days the country was tottering towards civil war. As predicted by Frank Steele, tribal disputes fuelled by fierce ideological differences had pitted the Congo's political leaders against each other. But even Steele had not foreseen that the battle for control would pitch the KGB against the CIA, SIS, Mossad and the Belgian intelligence service.

The previous year, on Bruce Lockhart's initiative, Daphne Park had arrived in Leopoldville, the Congo's capital, as the SIS officer. By independence day, Park, a formidable woman both intellectually and physically, who had trained OSS officers for the wartime Jedburgh missions behind German lines, had ingratiated herself over early-evening whiskies with the president-elect, several pro-Western ministers and the local security chief. Her reports in June 1960 anticipated that after independence Patrice Lumumba, the prime minister, and Antoine Gizenga, his deputy, would be aligned with Moscow against the West.

Seven days after the Belgian monarch had tactlessly announced the end of the colonial era, Larry Devlin, a CIA officer, slipped into Leopoldville on Dulles's urgent orders. The Congolese army had mutinied and the European community was fleeing the country to escape rape, torture and murder. By the end of July, Devlin reported to Washington that 'at least 1000 Soviets' had arrived in the country to airlift weapons in 'Red Cross boxes' to army units loyal to Gizenga. A substantial KGB contingent, including a Frenchman posing as a journalist, was aggressively encouraging military units to stage a coup. Amid the chaos, a CIA emissary from Washington handed an envelope to Devlin containing instructions to murder Lumumba. The order, apparently from Eisenhower, was ignored, but it reflected Washington's terror that Moscow intended to transform the Congo into a base for the subversion of Africa.

'Civil war in Africa', Macmillan wrote in his diary on 4 August, 'might be the prelude to war in the world . . . I have felt uneasy about the summer of 1960. It has a terrible similarity to 1914. Now Congo may play the role of Serbia . . .'[5] At the end of August, Macmillan directed SIS to co-operate with the CIA to overthrow Lumumba. White transmitted the order to Park without relish. By 7 September, Devlin, Park and the Mossad representative had persuaded Colonel Joseph Mobutu, the army chief of staff, to stage a coup. As a preliminary, Devlin arranged for the visas of key KGB officers to be cancelled and 'advised on which ministers should be removed and who should be promoted'.[6]

Mobutu's victory, deposing Lumumba on 14 September, was hailed as a triumph for the West and, as Soviet diplomats flew home, a defeat of Soviet subversion. White never claimed any credit. Broadway's accolades were handed to Bruce Lockhart and Young, proxies of Macmillan's penchant for gung-ho, clandestine operations. Now that the Cold War had been firmly launched in Africa, Bruce Lockhart assumed the authority to challenge MI5 for total access to the continent.

In the monthly meetings of the Africa Committee, attended by representatives of MI5, SIS, the Colonial Office, the Foreign office and the Commonwealth Relations Office ostensibly to agree policy and intelligence requirements, Bruce Lockhart found his colleagues 'a difficult bunch', who chose to interpret Macmillan's 'winds of change' speech differently to SIS. (In February 1960 the prime minister had told the South African parliament that 'The wind of change is blowing through this continent.')[7] The Colonial Office officials were honourably pursuing their thankless chore of preparing colonies for independence. The Foreign Office officials were cynically concerned with Britain's interests. In between were staff of the new Commonwealth Relations Office, drawn from the Ministry of Pensions and Transport, and blessed with rosy-tinted ambitions for a community of independent nations. Instead of agreeing decisions, the committee was consistently embroiled in demarcation disputes. As the KGB's organisation in Ghana ballooned to twenty-six officers, Bruce Lockhart returned to his office 'choleric with fury', complaining that Whitehall was forbidding any SIS presence or activity.

Bruce Lockhart's anger was directed particularly at Cyril Costley-White and Morris James, the Commonwealth Relations Office officials responsible for intelligence. Seated in a wheelchair,

Costley-White unswervingly forbade any SIS operation in the Commonwealth. Citing the Attlee Doctrine, the official spoke, as if it were a tenet of Catholic faith, of the purity of Britain's relationship with its former colonies. 'A crippled mind in a crippled body!' screamed Young on hearing Bruce Lockhart's complaints. 'They don't understand communist manipulation and they don't realise they're handicapping British interests.' White remained aloof, disinclined to engage in a Whitehall battle. Idealism had no place in his motives. Rather, he was the tolerant pragmatist who sought to stem the torrent of complaints and laments about the sunshine past.

Costley-White's resistance, White understood, illustrated Whitehall's traditional fear that SIS's clandestine operations risked discovery and would rupture not only diplomacy but the historic trust among members of the family. There was, said the chief, a long-term mission to persuade Whitehall officials of a halfway house: namely, that SIS officers, unburdened by stilted diplomatic formalities, could collect intelligence informally by cultivating private relationships, a technique which ambassadors still found unusual in Africa. Educating Whitehall depended upon winning trust for SIS, and that required time. In the meantime, White would not agitate for change – an indulgence in procrastination which would soon cause embarrassment.

The CIA's success in the Congo galvanised Richard Bissell, a brilliant CIA deputy director of plans, to visit White in the autumn of 1960. Renowned as a gung-ho operator, who would plan the invasion of Cuba in the Bay of Pigs, Bissell was keen to develop closer relations with SIS. Naturally receptive, White hosted a dinner at Brown's Hotel and later accepted a return invitation at the home of Carlton Swift, the deputy CIA liaison officer in London.

Bissell had affection and respect for White. Two years earlier, he had appealed to him to help overcome Eisenhower's restrictions on U2 flights. On the president's instructions, each mission required his personal, signed approval. To bypass White House control, Bissell suggested during the meeting in Broadway that some flights should become a joint SIS–CIA operation. U2 planes would be based at Lakenheath in Suffolk and their operations would be approved by the British prime minister. Liaison would be through RAF officers based in Washington. White's enthusiastic lobbying in Whitehall secured agreement. SIS would receive invaluable intelligence at neither cost nor risk.[8]

Even if US investment in the U2 flights over Russia, in rocket-launched satellites and in computers to decode intercepted messages, not to mention America's sheer manpower, had diminished Britain's contribution to the partnership, SIS's position remained significant. The residual influence the British enjoyed in their shrinking Empire still provided essential information and real estate for military bases. The U2s used the British bases in Cyprus and Lakenheath; the National Security Agency was tied by treaty to pool its resources and information with Britain's GCHQ, benefiting from British intercept facilities, particularly in Cyprus, Hong Kong and Cheltenham; and, above all, CIA officers had good personal relations with SIS officers. 'The CIA was inclined to see a mystique in us,' White reasoned. 'SIS is an important channel to digest material from the CIA,'[9] a disseminator of CIA information around Whitehall.

That trust was the basis of a conference Bissell called in London in autumn 1960 of all CIA European and Middle East station chiefs to discuss clandestine operations against the communists similar to that carried out in the Congo. White was disturbed by Bissell and by the mood in Washington. Within the new CIA headquarters at Langley, Virginia, the talk, reflecting conversations with the new president John Kennedy and his brother Robert, appointed attorney general, was about 'getting rid' of presidents. Fidel Castro of Cuba, Rafael Trujillo of the Dominican Republic, Patrice Lumumba in the Congo and Achmad Sukarno of Indonesia were all at one time targeted for assassination.

SIS, White insisted, would no longer consider those affairs: 'We are gathering intelligence. We are not freelance angels of justice.' The symbol of change was White's decision to stop training SIS officers in the use of weapons and parachutes. But the robber barons, Macmillan and CIA officers continued to put pressure on him to embark on more 'wet jobs' to defeat communist subversion. It was a period of profound realignment for Britain and consequently for SIS. The change was apparent after the murder on 17 January 1961 of Lumumba apparently by a rival tribe. The removal of one enemy encouraged the CIA to pressurise SIS into co-operating in south-east Asia.

Historically, SIS's expertise in south-east Asia was superior to the CIA's. From Bangkok, SIS had financed pro-Western candidates in the Laos elections in 1954, effectively forestalling communist victory, and was attempting similar tactics with the Buddhists in Vietnam. In 1954, Maurice Oldfield, based in Singapore, had flown to Washington with Sir John Sinclair and Fergie Dempster, the SIS officer in Saigon, to discuss combined operations in the Far East with Allen Dulles.

Oldfield shone as an operator. Born in Derbyshire in 1915, he was a medieval historian who had travelled widely in Europe before 1939 to become fluent in German and French. Posted in 1941 to Egypt, he had served in Security Intelligence Middle East (SIME) as a counter-intelligence officer and had then joined SIS. Unlike the traditional SIS clansmen, Oldfield acknowledged that the service's future depended upon its relations with the CIA; this gave him a reputation among the Americans as an indispensable ally in the Far East who 'showed CIA officers how to cope with the locals, giving us background on local personalities and access to his files'.[10]

The gathering in Washington was summoned to combat communist subversion in Vietnam and Indonesia. Dulles had urged SIS to join the Agency in a robust rearguard action, modelled on what had been done in Iran. In the course of meetings over two weeks, the SIS team negotiated with Dulles and Frank Wisner the Four-Square Agreement. Responsibility for the Far East was divided. The CIA would retain control over the Philippines, while SIS remained sovereign in Burma, Singapore and Malaya. The two agencies would co-operate in Vietnam, Cambodia, Laos, Thailand and Indonesia. To save time, the two ambassadors and two intelligence officers in any country in the region could undertake operations without reference to Washington or London. For Oldfield and Dempster, scornful of local British ambassadors for 'standing under fans drinking

G & T', the Agreement was a licence to wage war against communist agitation. Their enthusiasm ensnared Sam Halpern, the CIA officer in Singapore: 'Fergie taught me that there was intelligence and hard intelligence, while Oldfield never made a statement without supporting facts.'[11] But their zest was not translated into success.

On his return to Saigon, both Dempster and the CIA officers, hampered by their inability to speak Vietnamese, achieved nothing more than liaison with the local security agency. 'We were led down the garden path,' admitted Halpern. 'The Saigon police were penetrated.' In the north, the combined SIS–CIA efforts were equally unsuccessful. In 1955, Dempster attempted, after recruiting the author Graham Greene, to cultivate a row within the Hanoi politburo which would lead to the assassination of Ho Chi-Minh. The plan disintegrated: 'We fell flat on our faces.' There would be no repeated attempt. On his arrival at Broadway in 1956, White had stipulated: 'robust operations' were to be curtailed.

In Bangkok, Michael Wrigley, the SIS station chief and a friend of Oldfield since their days at SIME, would be advised that his proposals to combat and finance the murder of local communists agitating against the pro-Western monarchy, in particular a senior officer of the Pathet Lao, the communist army, were too aggressive. 'Forget it,' advised Oldfield, referring to a proposed £10,000 payment plus a British passport for an assassin. 'We don't do that sort of thing any more.' 'They've got no balls,' Wrigley told a friend. 'I blame the Foreign Office. They do nothing except write history.' Under White, Wrigley believed, SIS was becoming wet and would become wetter. It was a sentiment echoed by many SIS officers in the Far East irritated by White's caution. In 1957, Sam Halpern, by then the CIA's desk officer for Indonesia, criticised the same pattern.

Reliable reports that the Soviet Union was building a new airport on Great Natuna Basar island in the South China Sea suggested that Moscow was developing a military alliance with President Sukarno of Indonesia. An SIS agent in Djakarta reported that the Soviets had even provided the president with a blonde air hostess as a permanent companion, although that would be dismissed as CIA propaganda. In Washington, Allen Dulles fumed about the tendency of Third World leaders to flirt with communism, spending vast sums on prestige projects for self-glorification. Frank Wisner exclaimed, 'It's time we held Sukarno's feet to the fire,'[12] and in 1958 Dulles gave him $10 million to fulfil his ambition.[13]

In Oldfield's office in Phoenix Park, Singapore, Foster Collins, the CIA's station chief, revealed the Agency's plan to finance and arm Permasta, a group of rebel officers in Sumatra who would 'cause Sukarno some trouble'. The Briton's response was enthusiastic. Oldfield had recruited Dr Sumitro Djojohodi-koesoemo, the Indonesian trade minister, and two other senior politicians, as British agents. Their reports confirmed growing Russian influence. Foster Collins's proposal to pay and arm the Sumatran colonels ($30,000 for each colonel and $100,000 to their political party) was sent by Oldfield to London for approval. The plan was rejected by White. Halfheartedly backing a handful of disgruntled colonels, he reasoned, was a recipe for repeating Suez-type disasters. Even George Young sent a warning: Dulles was failing to appreciate that anti-Western sentiment in south-east Asia was inspired by nationalism, not communism. With Foreign Office endorsement, Oldfield was ordered to limit himself to 'neutral' support. 'He prefers us to do the covert stuff,' Collins said in commiseration, not concealing his frustration.

Macmillan intervened soon afterwards. The prime minister, visiting Washington, was asked by Eisenhower for assistance in Indonesia. Unknown to SIS, a CIA team was already operating in Sumatra and had provoked a revolt. SIS's help was required to supply the rebels. Macmillan agreed. The SIS station in Singapore received new orders prefaced with the phrase, 'The prime minister has agreed ...' The station was to provide 'full facilities' to the CIA. Under Oldfield's direction, American transport planes, crewed by Poles and flying from the Philippines, were to be discreetly refuelled at the RAF base at Changi airport. Their American insignia were removed before flying over Sumatra to drop weapons to the rebels.

Within five months, the CIA's operation ignominiously collapsed. 'Just about everything went wrong,' lamented Halpern.

White appeared vindicated and his opinion was endorsed by Andrew Gilchrist, chairman of the JIC in the Far East. Arguing against involvement in operations, Gilchrist ruled that SIS was committed to intelligence-gathering and should not be distracted into any war.[14]

But Allen Dulles's pressure on SIS persisted. The CIA's activities were a sideshow to the director's obsessive belief that Moscow planned to turn the Red Sea into a communist-controlled zone. Anti-Russian sentiment had become akin to a fever.[15] Just after Thanksgiving, November 1962, James Critchfield, the director of the CIA's Middle East division, sat in White's office warning: 'The Russians are waging war across Arabia. We've got to stop them.' The chief, bemused by an American's one-dimensional view of the world, did not conceal his sarcasm: 'Jim, you're my Cold War warrior.' Like all CIA officers, especially those whose relationship with SIS stretched back to wartime and post-war Germany, Critchfield showed undisguised respect for White, but he was disappointed by the laconic response.

Reports to CIA officers from agents infiltrated into several Arab governments, and the analysis from thousands of daily intercepts of Arab messages recorded by eavesdroppers, pinpointed hundreds of Soviet military advisers and front-line officers across the Middle East. Since Suez, the small contingent dispatched to Egypt had grown. 'Their influence is everywhere,' Critchfield declared, 'and it's spreading down to the Gulf. The KGB are at the cutting edge to grab control of the oil.' Critchfield was *en route* to Beirut to meet all the CIA station chiefs based in Arab countries. The officers had been summoned for a two-day conference to summarise Russia's strength and intentions, and to plot the Agency's defeat of Nasser. In the vacuum since the British humiliation in 1956, Critchfield, an enthusiastic student of the Arab world, was eager to assume SIS's mantle and oversee Nasser's destruction.

Just two months earlier, a real war had erupted in the Yemen. With Soviet support, Nasser was pouring troops into the desolate country. Critchfield speculated that the Egyptian leader wanted to foment revolution against Saudi Arabia, the oil sheikhdoms and particularly Aden, a British colony. 'Moscow wants to control the Gulf,' concluded Critchfield. 'We cannot afford to lose.' The CIA officer's hopes for a meeting of minds with White were disappointed.

Arabs have always attracted a certain type of Englishman who admires their character and attitude towards life. White, however, had little affection for Arabs and his limited understanding of Arab politics prevented any evident sympathy with their turbulent nationalist movements. Even warnings that the sheikhdoms would become battlegrounds of Cold War rivalry did not move him.

Before Suez, a network of military bases and alliances in Egypt, Iraq, Jordan, Sudan, Kenya, Cyprus, Malta and Aden and stretching along the Gulf reinforced British pre-eminence in the region. SIS and MI5 officers, sometimes working with a resident officer appointed by the Foreign Office, had influenced and manipulated Arab politicians and rulers. Many Arab leaders preferred dealing with sympathetic SIS officers rather than with traditional Foreign Office diplomats. The 'back channel' permitted conversations to be discreet and honest, and SIS could destabilise mutual enemies.

Suez had disrupted SIS's intimate relationships. Erstwhile friendly Arabs were aghast that their information might have been passed by the British government to their bitter enemies, the Israelis. Although the crisis had not eradicated the popular belief in SIS omnipotence, the service's capabilities remorselessly deteriorated in the two years after Suez. In 1958, SIS had reached its nadir.

In Egypt, there were no SIS officers or sources of information; in Jordan, King Hussein, fearing assassination, had appealed to the CIA for help and, after temporary rejection, accepted British paratroops; in Syria, the regime's hostility to Britain barred any SIS presence; while in Iraq, Nuri es-Said, the British protégé, was murdered in July by General Abdul Kerim Kassem, an anti-British nationalist whose existence had passed unnoticed by SIS. With Nuri es-Said's disappearance, the Baghdad Pact, the bastion of Britain's military and political influence in the Middle East, disintegrated.

The passing of the old order, fanned by Moscow's rabid

anti-colonialism and anti-British sentiment, sparked jittery reports of communist and Nasserite conspiracies. In Washington and London, politicians advocated a counter-offensive by the intelligence services. In a bygone era, White's predecessors would have dispatched agents like Sidney Reilly, Paul Dukes or Robert Bruce Lockhart to influence the course of history. White, however, had declared his opposition to cowboys undertaking 'wet jobs' or 'robust operations'. 'I did not believe', said White, 'that SIS could any more set its own agenda.'[16]

But among White's 'customers' was an imperial caucus, alias the Suez Group, surrounding the prime minister. The tone was particularly set by Duncan Sandys, Churchill's former son-in-law, the secretary of state for Commonwealth relations and the colonial secretary, and by Julian Amery, Macmillan's son-in-law, the minister of aviation. White understood the potential influence of Amery upon SIS. During the war, Amery had served bravely with SOE in the Balkans and had subsequently been involved in SIS's joint operation with the CIA to overthrow the communist regime in Albania. Unrepentant about that disaster, Amery still advocated clandestine operations to protect Britain's political relationships and financial investments. After all, despite White's prejudices, Amery had, with Macmillan's support, galvanised Young and Bruce Lockhart in 1958 into joining the fight against Eoka in Cyprus. Although George Grivas, the Eoka leader, had escaped death, his terrorists had suffered some 'nasties' and Archbishop Makarios, the Greek Cypriot prelate, had been blackmailed, with SIS information about his homosexuality, into conceding Britain two military bases in the independence agreements.

Now Amery wanted SIS to combat Soviet and Egyptian subversion, remove Nasser and prevent control of the Middle East's oil supplies shifting to American multinationals. 'We were not objective about Nasser,' smiled Amery.[17] Amery's ally within SIS was George Young, the only SIS baron who could claim any knowledge of the Middle East, although he was not an Arabist. In his lectures to SIS officers, Young explained that an Arab with a Kalashnikov and Mercedes would be even more aggressive than one with a musket and camel. 'When the British Council premises go up in flames,' he said grimly, 'the odour of roasting pansy is incense in the nostrils of Allah.'[18]

White listened silently to Young's outright criticism of the Arabs, his contemptuous dismissal of the developing world and his castigation of bogus economic aid which encouraged the recipients' 'greater sense of their own inadequacy'. Although he opposed Young's support for British military intervention, he did not initially hinder those who embraced his deputy's opinions. The hatred of Nasser which permeated Whitehall and Westminster was contained only by the desire for revenge. White, regardless of his personal opinion, could only serve that desire.

Responsibility for the Middle East had been assigned by White to Bruce Lockhart, the first of several European experts called upon to tighten up SIS's strategy for the region. 'John's a wily operator,' observed John Christie, one of SIS's few Arabists, 'but he knows nothing about Arabs.' It was White's misfortune that no one in Broadway was any better informed. With Bruce Lockhart, Young influenced the more adventurous SIS officers based in the Middle East into pursuing an interventionist agenda contrary to White's conservative edicts.

The new regional centre of SIS operations against Egypt, Syria and Moscow's conspiracies was located in Beirut. The Lebanon had become the crossroads for Arab agitators and exiles involved in the upsurge of plots, assassinations, terrorism, coups, counter-coups and wars, and was itself perceived by both the Foreign Office and the State Department as a major target of subversion by the Soviet Union and Nasser. In 1958, Eisenhower had farcically landed American marines on the beaches to 'save' Lebanon from communism. The country suited SIS's favoured tactic of operating under a 'false flag', from the safety of one country across frontiers into neighbouring 'enemy' states.

The new station chief in Beirut was Paul Paulson, the former solicitor who, though spirited, honourable and universally popular, was also not an Arabist. He had been nominated by Broadway's personnel officer on the ground that he was entitled to a senior foreign posting and by others urging that his fluent French and jovial personality would aid the administration of an embassy which boasted more intelligence officers than diplomats.

White bowed to the sentiment and at a short meeting in early 1958 wished him well.

Paulson arrived in Beirut briefed to support any Lebanese who opposed communism and Nasser, and to collect intelligence about those governments actively destabilising Britain's allies. To young officers then based in Beirut, like Denis Rowley and Frank Steele, that implied 'political action' – actively influencing the internal affairs of sovereign countries. Their overwhelming obstacle was widespread emotional enthusiasm for Nasser and a condemnation of 'British intelligence', which paradoxically was credited by Arab politicians with countless deeds of manipulation and destruction way beyond its competence.

As in most 'friendly' countries, SIS's essential ally in Beirut was the local security service. In return for cash, the chief of police and his officers supplied information about Britain's enemies operating in the capital and identified candidates for British recruitment. Beirut's hectic social life provided an ideal environment in which SIS officers could reassure themselves that those identified as possible recruits were suitable for crossing into neighbouring states to collect intelligence, foment unrest and plot revolts.

The recruitment technique which Paulson and his officers used was flawed. Under SIS doctrine as taught in the New Entry courses, SIS's eight officers in Beirut were discouraged from engaging in personal recruitment and even from meeting their sources. Instead, to protect their security, SIS officers were bound to use 'cut-outs' – non-SIS officers – as intermediaries. Alternatively, they were encouraged more than in other areas to use 'unofficial assistants', either local Englishmen or other nationalities casually recruited to act as middlemen. That orthodoxy, introduced decades earlier by John Teague, would prove disastrous. Since the SIS officers rarely met agents, they could not judge their veracity. Nor, since few of the SIS officers, including Paulson, spoke Arabic, could they assess their intermediaries' reliability.

One foundation of Paulson's operation was Maroun Arab, a Lebanese who had been promoted within the embassy to become oriental counsellor and a local SIS informant. Arab would collect gossip and information in Beirut's bars, newspaper offices and ministries. In turn, Paulson would dispatch Arab's unverified reports, presenting opinion as fact, in CX dispatches to London.

Paulson's second stratagem was to deploy Denis Rowley to enjoy an expensive lifestyle in Beirut's restaurants and nightclubs. Mingling with Lebanon's playboys, Paulson reasoned, would eventually be rewarded by invaluable contacts. Among Rowley's sources, through an intermediary, was an agent described as 'a member of the Lebanese Communist Party'. The agent's regular reports were valued in London by Harold Shergold and others as worthy of the monthly £500 payments. A subsequent investigation by SIS's Security Directorate revealed that the agent was a fabricating machine. Tens of thousands of pounds had been wasted on invented rubbish, and it was not an isolated case. Rackets were endemic to espionage. SIS often discovered that sources it was paying were bogus. After Rowley's resignation, he could argue that SIS's weak control encouraged the abuses.

Paulson's third gambit was widespread recruitment, including attempts to recruit two senior *Observer* journalists. One, under the codename Jester, was asked to 'collect intelligence' in Jordan. A second was requested to provide political intelligence from Iraq and Syria. Both attempts were failures.

SIS's money was also spent on pro-Western politicians. Among Paulson's first beneficiaries was Kamil Chamoun, the leader of the Maronite Christians, who, in the weeks before Lebanon's presidential election, received suitcases of cash from Harry Hale, another SIS officer. More SIS money was given to returning officers to rig the ballot and ensure the election of a pro-Western government. The result was victory for just such a government, although the CIA and other Western intelligence agencies would justifiably, claim some credit.

More money and weapons were channelled by Paulson's officers through intermediaries – Lebanese and other European nationals – to various Syrian groups ambitious to overthrow the successive governments in Damascus. The Syrian conspirators, used as sources of information rather than as British candidates for government, were often arrested, tortured and executed. Paulson would never discover from the intermediaries how much of SIS's thousands of pounds actually reached the Syrians and how much was siphoned off, or even whether the Syrians were betrayed before they left Lebanon.

How much White knew of the real and imagined operations was uncertain. His officers in Beirut were convinced that the chief was 'unaware' of their activities. That impression was conveyed by the barons in Broadway, religiously protecting their interests from supervision. White, they agreed over drinks in the basement bar, 'would be horrified if he knew what we were doing. Anyway, he doesn't seem interested.' The impression was confirmed by Paulson. On his occasional return to London, he would be welcomed by White in a brief and routine encounter: 'How's it going? How do you see things in your area?' Despite the detachment, White responded to Whitehall's fear of Nasser's subversion and, even if SIS's challenge along the southern Mediterranean was disappointing, the service was successfully defending Britain's allies in the Gulf.

In Oman, an oil-rich sheikhdom controlled by Shell, a revolt against the sultan was supported by an unusual alliance of King Saud of Saudi Arabia, Aramco, the American oil giant, and Nasser. Britain's oil interests depended upon the sultan's survival. A British military contingent aided by SIS was organising his defence; after a degree of bloodshed, there was stalemate. With SIS's further assistance, the revolt would eventually be defeated by the deployment of an SAS squadron to take the impregnable Akhdar or Green Mountain, where the rebels had hitherto withstood every assault.

Kuwait, the source of 40 per cent of Britain's oil, was also threatened by Nasser's nationalism. British Petroleum executives urged John Bruce Lockhart to defend their interests, not least from their American rivals. John Christie, the SIS officer in Bahrain, was dispatched to open an SIS station and to convince the Kuwaiti ruling family, the Al Sabahs, that their nation's security and their personal wealth depended upon SIS creating a counter-intelligence service to infiltrate Kuwaiti society. It was patient, methodical work of a class appreciated by White, unlike a proposal from Christie to kidnap a known terrorist responsible for bomb outrages, a proposal which was rejected. Christie was, Broadway signalled, to confine himself to pure intelligence, such as escorting British army officers to the Mutla Ridge on the Iraqi border to prepare maps for use if Iraq invaded.

Across the border in Iraq, SIS was also well established. Under Henry Coombe-Tenant, the SIS chief in Baghdad, the service was exploiting Britain's historic influence despite the antagonism of the Kassem regime. Police and army officers, recruited by SIS twenty years earlier, had become senior officers in the military and security services. Businessmen, both British and other European nationals, were regularly debriefed after their conversations with government ministers, allowing SIS to penetrate government agencies. Baghdad was one of the few locations where SIS could insert a locally born British national into the government.

Those human sources, combined with signals intelligence gathered in Baghdad and Cyprus and information obtained from Israel's Mossad and Iran's Savak, provided one of Bruce Lockhart's few gems. Iraq, the CIA would subsequently judge, proved SIS's adeptness in exercising a unique talent to identify and exploit human weaknesses. SIS's reports predicted that Kassem was minded to invade Kuwait.

Britain's aggressive response to the Arab threat was the theme of a three-day SIS conference in the summer of 1960. All SIS station chiefs in the Middle East were summoned to the Fort in Gosport. Present were Alexis Forte from Teheran, Paul Paulson from Beirut, Henry Coombe-Tenant from Baghdad, Norman Derbyshire from Bahrain, John Christie from Kuwait and Ryder Latham from Turkey. White was not present. The issue, said Bruce Lockhart, was how to penetrate the Nasserite movement.

The tone was set by Forte, who, while chief in Baghdad in 1958, had failed to anticipate the overthrow of Britain's protégé and was renowned for sending agents across the border into Russia on missions from which they never returned. His reputation had recovered in Teheran, where, every week, he spent thirty minutes in a private audience with the shah. 'We could defeat Kassem', explained Forte to his SIS colleagues, 'by sending Wilfred Thesiger to the southern tribes of Iraq. He should distribute Mepacrine anti-malarial tablets to the tribesmen. They'd be in hock to us for ever more.' In the undignified row that took place at the bar that night, the philistinism evident in some officers confirmed that SIS's transition into White's ideal intelligence service was not yet a glimmer on the horizon. On the contrary, the turbulence in the Middle East over the next two years nearly compelled White to abandon his principles.

The turmoil started after 19 June 1961, when Kuwait was declared by Britain to be a sovereign nation. Six days later, Kassem announced Kuwait's annexation by Iraq. The SIS station in Baghdad reported that the announcement must be propaganda, since neither the Iraqi air force nor the spearhead tank brigade had been mobilised, although rail flatcars were standing ready. Nevertheless, forty-five British warships and 6500 British troops were dispatched to Kuwait as a signal that, despite Suez, Britain would protect its interests. As British troops dug trenches in the sandy wilderness along the border, succumbing to heatstroke and discovering the inadequacies of their equipment, the Iraqi threat dissipated. SIS reports had proved accurate. But, for White, the aftermath was unexpected. By the end of the following year, chafed by an internecine Whitehall battle, he was ensnared in an alliance with the CIA against President Kennedy's administration.

The Kuwaiti operation had prompted a protest to White from Carlton Swift, the CIA's deputy liaison officer in London. 'What you're doing', complained Swift, 'is not in America's interests. The State Department is unhappy with the Foreign Office. Will you let us see the raw intelligence on which you're basing the policy?'

'I think we can help you,' replied White. He thereupon provided evidence that a coalition of Arab nationalists and the Soviet Union had endangered British interests.

The intelligence did not impress the White House. President Kennedy, advocating 'more progressive policies' towards Nasser and other Third World leaders, was offended by the notion that Britain's presence in the Gulf benefited the region's stability. On his directive, London's overtures for discussions on joint planning of the region's defence after Britain's withdrawal from the Gulf were rejected.[19] Only the CIA sympathised with anti-Nasserites in Britain. Allen Dulles and Jim Critchfield, the CIA's Middle East director, hoped that the Agency could ally itself with SIS against Nasser, despite President Kennedy. But White House attention was focused on the crisis in Cuba and Berlin. To begin with, SIS seemed to be an uncertain ally.

Isolated and buffeted by antagonism from Washington, Moscow and Cairo, the British government, sensitive to the nation's perilous finances, had begun revising its policy towards Nasser. The tone was set by Norman Brook, the cabinet secretary. In a memorandum to Macmillan after the Kuwait operation, he observed; 'We are fighting a losing battle propping up these reactionary regimes. Our policy takes no account of the rising tide of nationalism in these countries. We are bound to find ourselves in the end on the losing side.' He added, 'We cannot win the propaganda battle against nationalism and it is idle to spend money in trying to shout down Cairo Radio.'[20] The Foreign Office and Macmillan supported that opinion, especially Brook's prediction that 'Forces of liberalism will eventually come to the top and when they do, we shall certainly be unable to keep the Ruler in his place by military means.' Macmillan even sympathised with Brook's cynical honesty: 'Our policy is a pretty short-run affair. What we are doing is to get the oil out of these territories for as long as the inhabitants remain fairly primitive ... We ought not to be looking at Kuwait as a long-term commitment.'

White agreed, endorsing the policy of Britain's gradual withdrawal from military alliances and intervention. After all, even after Britain had deterred the Iraqi invasion, the Kuwaiti government, fearing nationalist riots, had insisted that British troops departed. But within SIS the retreat was opposed by George Young. The vice-chief was outraged that Archie Roosevelt should still be strangely allied with Aramco in Saudi Arabia in support of King Saud's ambitions to absorb British oil interests in Kuwait, Abu Dhabi and Oman. The Vice also railed about Britain's 'infection by a moralising bug'. Citing Israel, he urged a return to ruthlessness and a cessation of cowardice and surrender masquerading as morality. On several occasions, White's choice

[9] The discovery of
Commander Lionel
Crabb's (above, right)
headless corpse in
Portsmouth waters in
1956 prompted White's
transfer from MI5, where
he had served for three
years as director
general, to become chief
of SIS. Peter Lunn
(left), then SIS station
chief in Berlin, briefed
White about his new
task. John Bruce
Lockhart (above, left),
one of SIS's famous
'robber barons' became
SIS's deputy chief in
1961.

[10] Among White's major successes as SIS chief was to secure the continuing close relationship with the CIA. Allen Dulles and John McCone (above) were his favourites. Throughout his twelve years as chief, he relied upon Richard Helms (right), a wartime OSS officer and controversial CIA director, whose personal trust of White was vital in the wake of Britain's spy scandals.

[11] The exposure of William Vassall (below, left), a British Admiralty clerk, and George Blake, an SIS officer, as Soviet spies fuelled fears that Soviet intelligence enjoyed a firm grip on Britain's most secret institutions. Blake, pictured in Hamburg in 1945 as a serving SIS officer (below, right) and in 1990 in Moscow with Vassilli Dozhdalov (above), one of his KGB controllers, escaped from Wormwood Scrubs in 1966, intensifying the conviction of Soviet penetration of Britain's institutions.

[12] White's management between 1961 and 1962 of Colonel Oleg Penkovsky, (below, left) an officer in Soviet military intelligence, radically improved SIS's status. But Joe Bulik (below, right) of the CIA was critical of SIS's handling of the Soviet spy. The CIA/SIS team photographed in London (above, from left to right): Michael Stokes, Harry 'Shergie' Shergold, Joe Bulik and George Kiesvalter.

[13] Greville Wynne (right) the tempestuous British businessman was SIS's and the CIA's link to Penkovsky. After their public trial in May 1963 (above), Penkovsky (top) was shot and Wynne imprisoned despite British government protestations of his innocence.

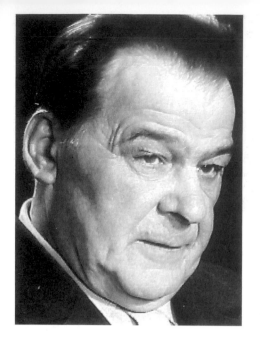

[14] White denied CIA criticisms of SIS for Penkovsky's exposure by Lt Gen Nikolai Chystiakov (above, left) and Lt Gen Oleg Gribanov (below, left) of the KGB. Vladimir Semichastney (above, right), the KGB chairman, insisted that Penkovsky had been spotted talking to a British intelligence officer. Joe Bulik (below, right) is still angry that neither the CIA nor SIS sought to save Penkovsky's life.

[15] Konon Molody, alias Gordon Lonsdale, (top, fifth from right) and Rudolph Abel, alias William Fisher, (top, sixth from right) were two KGB 'illegals' whose success in establishing themselves in London and New York raised new fears of Soviet success. Gordon Lonsdale, the 'Canadian citizen' posing at the Statue of Liberty in New York (left). The KGB view of Lonsdale's exchange in 1964 in Berlin for Greville Wynne (above).

[16] Of the prime ministers whom White directly served, he had limited respect for Sir Anthony Eden, photographed in a broadcast during the Suez crisis (above, left); he became disillusioned with Harold Wilson (below, left) and positively fearful of George Brown (below, right) the Labour foreign secretary who appointed a dud as White's successor in SIS; and, while acknowledging Harold Macmillan's wry disdain for the intelligence services, White became an admiring confidant of the patrician Tory (above, right).

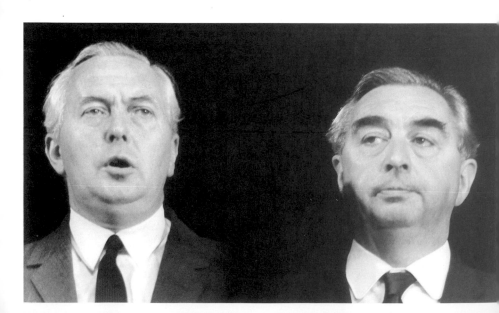

of officers had prompted an abrasive challenge from Young: 'What do you want, secret intelligence or jobs for the boys?' Bruce Lockhart repeated his observation of three years earlier, 'George frightens him.'

There had been ample opportunities for White to seize the excuse and openly admit that Young's appointment was 'my worst mistake' and dismiss him, not least when his deputy approved a 'wet job' in Iran contrary to his orders. But White has procrastinated. Both in intellect and in experience, Young was too competent to ignore. 'Dick wanted to avoid the hiatus [sic]. He wanted a quiet life,' recalled Nicholas Elliott. But, after Young's outburst in favour of aggressive operations in the Middle East, he was encouraged by White to retire. Young explained that he was leaving SIS because he was too impatient to wait for the succession on White's retirement. White provided corroboration for that excuse: 'Young thought I would go very quickly and he would take over. I helped him out into the business world.'[21] In 1961, Young moved to Kleinwort Benson, the merchant bankers, where several former SIS officers were later employed.

To avoid further insubordination and gradually to reduce the unassailable power of the remaining barons, White did not appoint a new vice-chief. Instead, Bruce Lockhart was made deputy, nominated to act as White's representative in his absence but without the historic authority of his predecessors. White's unannounced reason for Young's removal was his anxiety to consolidate SIS's relations with Mossad, Israel's foreign intelligence service. Young's new anti-Semitism had not only been embarrassing but attracted those in SIS and the Foreign Office harbouring pro-Arab sentiments.

Relations between the countries were still fraught. Not just because the Suez conspiracy had been comprehensively betrayed but because there remained the residue of antagonism aroused during Britain's mandate in Palestine. Attempts since 1951 by David Ben-Gurion, the Israeli prime minister, to establish proper relations with SIS had been resisted, not least by Sir John Sinclair, whose prejudices born during the brutality of the Palestinian era were unassailable.

In the wake of Suez, on Macmillan's personal instructions,

White had been quietly building relations with Israel. To avoid the Arabist Foreign Office, Macmillan wanted to continue using SIS's channels to communicate with Ben-Gurion. In 1958, Nicholas Elliott negotiated the visit to Britain of Isser Harel, the director of Mossad. Superficially, there seemed little in common between White and the Israeli. Barely the size of a midget, Harel had been born in Russia in 1912 and had travelled to Palestine in 1929. During the war he had fought with the Haganah, the Jewish underground army, against the Germans and the British, and after independence became effectively the founder of Mossad.

Harel's visit to meet White had been opposed by the CIA, in particular by Dulles and Angleton. The two Americans urged Harel to preserve the exclusivity of their relationship, but he resisted. 'We must overcome our past prejudices,' the Israeli told White on his arrival. 'If we can work together, then so can our governments.'[22] 'The problem', White replied, 'is the Foreign Office's prejudices.'

During that visit, Harel persuaded White of the extraordinary service Mossad could offer. Not only had the agency penetrated many parts of the Middle East, but, more importantly, Harel's officers could supply unique material about the Soviet Union and KGB operations. 'We understood the Russians and especially the Bolsheviks,' smiled Harel, 'because so many of us come from there. Through our people, we have contacts throughout Eastern Europe.' Moreover, Israeli intelligence was successfully monitoring KGB operations in Israel itself. Many Jewish immigrants from Russia had been recruited by the KGB before their departure in the hope that they would later travel to the West, infiltrate important institutions and report back to Moscow. But on arrival in Israel, they either admitted that relationship or carelessly revealed their secret allegiance. In the event, Mossad was accumulating unique information about KGB methods – their subversion and provocations – which Harel now offered White.

Two years later, in 1960, White undertook a rare foreign visit. At the end of April, he flew to Tel Aviv to be received by Harel. The Israeli made great efforts to impress his visitor. Accommodated in Mossad's own luxurious guesthouse, White was given a 'special tour' – to demonstrate to the Englishman that the young Israeli state was a permanent reality, too important to ignore and worthy of serious partnership. At the end of four days, the two intelligence chiefs concluded that while both countries had special and possibly conflicting interests, they could forge a partnership in other areas. Enthusiastically, White agreed that SIS should post a liaison officer to Israel. Unlike other countries, said Harel, 'we'd welcome a woman.' White was grateful for that bonus. Posting female SIS officers abroad was often difficult. 'We gave them a good time,' recalled Harel, suggesting that all the women's requirements – professional and personal – were met.

'He's wonderful man,' Harel told his colleagues after mentioning that he intended to invite White for dinner to his own home. The occasion was 28 April, White's last evening in Israel. During their conversation, White recounted an anecdote. Anyone wanting to change a $100 bill in South America, he said laughingly, in the course of his story, required special identification papers. Harel became agitated, made an excuse and left the room. White was unaware of what followed.

Unknown to the SIS officers, Harel was to fly the following morning to Argentina to mastermind the kidnap of Adolf Eichmann, the Nazi war criminal. Fearing that his aide had prepared $100 bills for his travel expenses, he quietly telephoned. His fears were confirmed. During that night, bank managers were roused to provide smaller denominations.

At the airport the following morning, Harel bid White farewell. 'I felt great warmth towards him,' recalled the Israeli. 'We would give the British much more than we ever got back and it was a lot due to White.' As the chief boarded the plane, Harel dashed for another aircraft to accomplish his epic operation.[23] Back in England, White introduced Paul Paulson, controller Middle East, and a weak ambassador in Whitehall about his new alliance just as SIS, contrary to White's wishes, was sucked into a new clandestine war.

On 26 September 1962, Egyptian-backed Yemeni insurgents attacked the Imam's palace in San'a and declared that Mohammed al-Badr, the ruler, was dead. In fact he had escaped. Encouraged by Radio Cairo's broadcasts, radicals in the colony of Aden demanded independence from Britain and union with Yemen – attracting Third World support, especially in the United Nations. Overnight, Britain's last secure base in the Gulf was imperilled, inflaming the imperial caucus in Macmillan's cabinet, especially Sandys and Amery.

Yemen and South Arabia were cruel, hot, isolated territories wracked by bloody and treacherous tribal disputes. In the years after the British had established a coaling station in Aden in 1839, successive government representatives came to understand that the tribal chiefs in the peninsula with whom they negotiated did not always represent their clans, nor could they tolerate each other. 'Anybody who claims to understand South Arabian politics has been sadly misinformed,' wrote Brigadier James Lunt many years before Arab nationalism threatened the Crown colony.[24] Lunt's dictum had been accepted. Settling a government in the hinterland's parched mountains and desert was beyond British competence and not in its interest.

But in 1957, the Suez Group in Macmillan's cabinet, shaken by the retreat from Egypt and Iraq, and uncertain about the security of the military bases in Cyprus and Kenya, transformed the insignificant base in Aden into the region's bastion of British military power. After BP's construction of a refinery in 1954, Aden had been transformed from a humid and impoverished port built on an extinct volcano into the fourth largest fuelling station in the world, supplying an endless procession of passenger and cargo ships. From that Middle East crossroads, the Royal Navy commanded the approaches to the Red Sea and the Suez Canal and could claim a strategic presence in the Indian Ocean. The RAF built an enormous runway and declared the base 'strategic', although its use was severely restricted.

To secure Aden's future, the Macmillan government organised in February 1959 the Federation of South Arabia, combining the tribal chiefs of the areas bordering on the colony. Beyond the new Federation was the Yemen, populated by unusually fearless and violent tribesmen whose ruler, the Imam's father, had until recently enjoyed, as a family pastime, public executions every Friday in the capital's main square.

The coup in September 1962 terminated the Imam's rule.

As Egyptian troops poured into Ta'izz, the Yemeni capital, Radio Cairo's sermons, urging nationalism and revolution in Aden, switched their target and began to call down vengeance upon the South Arabian tribal chiefs. Fearful, the chiefs sought British protection against Nasser's threats to sweep across the peninsula and impose his revolution not only in the Yemen but in the Federation. In Whitehall, White's customers demanded information and inquired about his proposals for operations. His response was meagre.

Terence O'Bryan Tear, the SIS officer in Aden, knew little about the Yemen. Because there had been neither demand for intelligence from London nor any incentive to take the uncomfortable risk of travelling in the hinterland, he had rarely ventured beyond Aden. O'Bryan Tear could not even offer much information about Nasser's activities in Aden itself. Under the Attlee Doctrine, that was the responsibility of the Aden Intelligence Centre run by MI5, an amateur and inadequate organisation whose poor performance was marginally surpassed by the local Special Branch. After more than a century's occupation, Britain's intelligence services could still not even provide a reliable guide to Yemen's tribes.[25]

SIS's alternative source of information might have been Cairo. But since 1956 SIS had no formal representative in Egypt and had failed to recruit any Egyptian officials and politicians as agents anywhere in Europe or the Middle East. No SIS officer was stationed in Riyadh, but the ambassador reported that the Saudis, veteran opponents of British interests, intended to support a royalist counter-offensive against Nasser.

Accordingly, White could offer his customers no eyewitness account of Nasser's intentions nor could he assess the status of the revolt which threatened Aden. P17, the SIS section responsible for Aden, could only repeat Colonial Office reports that along the colony's borders Egyptian intelligence officers were recruiting Yemeni tribesmen, providing rifles and money, and urging patience until called upon to revolt. To the SIS officer in Broadway charged with the daily responsibility for monitoring and combating the aggression, White's response to the Aden crisis was equivocal: 'He was frightened by the huge Egyptian commitment and didn't want to get sucked in.'²⁶ White believed that his sentiments were prudent, given that Whitehall's reaction to the revolt was divided and confused.

Selwyn Lloyd's successor as foreign secretary, Sir Alec Douglas-Home, supported by Sir Stewart Crawford, the under secretary, and officials in the Foreign Office's Arabian Department, especially Robert Walmsley and later Frank Brenchley, advocated recognition of Yemen's revolutionary government. It would be a mistake, they argued, to antagonise Nasser. Instead, Britain should reconcile itself to the proposition that Nasser's policies were consistent with Macmillan's 'winds of change'.

Against recognition was Peter Thorneycroft, the irredeemably smooth minister of defence, who demanded protection for the base in Aden; Duncan Sandys, who demanded continuation of the Federation; and Julian Amery, an advocate of using Aden as a base for British operations against Nasser. 'The loss of Aden', warned Amery, 'would signal the end of the British Empire.'

Amery had for some time detected White's lack of interest in Arab affairs and the Islamic world. Only months earlier, in May 1962, when John Bruce Lockhart had arranged for the shah of Iran to be discreetly helicoptered to the Fort in Portsmouth to spend the day with SIS, White had passed up the opportunity to meet the monarch. Amery had later tackled White about his 'dislike of operations' or 'bashes'. Among a coterie of officers, a tale was circulating that White, on the occasion of a colleague's recent retirement, had read the man's own account of his career skulduggery and had scribbled, 'if he had followed all this to its conclusion, then our moral confusion would be complete.'

There could be no meeting of minds between Amery and the chief of SIS, but as a realist about the service's place in Whitehall's hierarchy White sensed that his personal position was on a tightrope when his 'political masters were at odds'. But he did not anticipate how once again he would be spectacularly trounced.

Shortly after Nasser's coup in autumn 1962, King Hussein of Jordan had arrived unannounced in London. Inviting Amery to Claridge's, the monarch urged, 'Don't let your government recognise the Republicans. Nasser just wants to grab Saudi

Arabia's oil but the Royalists are tough.'[27] Hussein and Amery agreed that N.L.D. 'Billy' McLean, the Conservative member of parliament for Inverness, should tour the area to deliver an informed report to Macmillan. The choice of McLean was pertinent to the pressures upon White in the ensuing months. Amery and McLean had served together as SOE officers in 1944, leading guerrillas against the Germans in Albania. Both had suffered hardship, enjoyed adventure and displayed considerable courage in combat. Both had also been involved in SIS's Albanian operation. Consequently, their approach to the Yemen crisis was very different from that of traditional Conservative politicians. Both had first-hand experience of guerrilla warfare and of the treatment of intelligence, and both were passionate anti-communists who were politically committed to the destruction of Nasser. The Suez Group had renamed itself the Aden Group.

In early December, McLean cabled Amery from Saudi Arabia that the Imam and the Royalist forces controlled at least half of the Yemen and that therefore the Republican regime, although backed by 15,000 Egyptian soldiers, should not be recognised. McLean concluded that, if properly supported, the Royalists could defeat the Egyptian army. To Amery's irritation, that report was rejected by Douglas-Home. 'The Royalists have no hope,' said the foreign secretary. Recognition of the Republicans would 'reduce the venom of Nasser's attack on our position in Aden'. Resistance was pointless since 'the Republicans are in control and subjected to minor Royalist skirmishing'.[28]

'He's an appeaser,' declared Amery to friends who tasted an opportunity to bloody Nasser. 'Recognition would be humiliating and a devastating blow to our prestige and authority.' He supported his argument by producing Saudi intelligence reports showing that Royalist tribes opposed to Nasser were, with Saudi support, harassing the Egyptians. 'The Royalists need our help,' Amery told Macmillan 'and they will win the war.' Instinctively the prime minister was cautious, but he was suspicious of SIS: 'One was never sure which side SIS was on because they had so much contact with the Americans.'[29]

Macmillan sought White's opinion. Although opposed to Nasser, White agreed with Norman Brook and Douglas-Home that Britain's future as a world policeman was limited and declining. Although it was true that, without Aden, Britain's influence would recede further, he was disinclined to accept Amery's information about the strength of the Royalists or to succumb to his suggestion of aggressive operations against the Egyptians.

Macmillan's rejoinder was wounding. The information which Amery and Sandys had provided from the Saudi Arabian intelligence service, said the prime minister, exposed SIS's weakness. White could provide no eyewitness intelligence about the situation. For that, the cabinet was relying upon information picked up from a German television journalist, from American diplomats and from Foreign Office officials, especially Christopher Gandy, the British minister confined to Ta'izz, the republican capital, who campaigned for recognition and dismissed the threat of any alleged Royalist army. On the other side, and more valuable were the GCHQ intercepts of messages between Egyptian army commanders in the Yemen, struggling in the wild terrain against the Royalists, vindicated Amery's warnings. The Egyptians were suffering logistical problems and harassment from Royalists. White's caution aroused Macmillan's suspicion.

The intelligence chief's nightmare was compounded by the personal vitriol among those participating in the Whitehall battle. Gandy's advocacy of 'appeasement' brought him into conflict with Kennedy Trevaskis, the aggressive governor of the West Aden Protectorate. The two had been antagonists since their schooldays at Marlborough, where Trevaskis had beaten the younger Gandy for refusing to play team sports. For his part, Gandy claimed that the 'tail was wagging the dog' in the Great Game. The imperial caucus in London, he believed, were ignorant of Yemen's realities and 'moved by nostalgia for lost causes'.[30]

Overshadowing all the personality battles and conflicting intelligence reports was John Kennedy's pressure upon Macmillan to recognise the Egyptian regime. Intent upon building bridges with Nasser, Kennedy cabled Downing Street that the Egyptian president 'could not afford to pull out' of the Yemen and to allow the war to continue 'will increase violence and endanger Saudi Arabia'.[31] Kennedy had not reckoned on the Aden Group. 'The American thesis is that the one way of getting Nasser out of the

Yemen is to give him his victory,' cabled Sir Charles Johnston, the governor general of Aden, to Macmillan.[32] 'American policy is a menace . . . The State Department wishes to save Nasser from the consequences of his adventure.'[33]

On 19 December, McLean visited Macmillan in Downing Street to deliver his report. 'It was', in Amery's opinion, 'one of the few turning points in history which I have witnessed.'[34] The prime minister was persuaded by his old friend that the Americans misunderstood and exaggerated the threat of Egyptian tanks against Royalist tribesmen. Nasser's subversion could be halted.[35]

Indelicately, White and SIS had been marginalised. At a cabinet meeting on 1 January 1963, ministers were presented with 'an intelligence report' concluding that the Royalists, if supported could win the war.[36] The report was written not by SIS but by McLean. Britain's independent identity, the cabinet was told, would be 'swallowed up in the Pax Americana' if Egypt's control of the Yemen was recognised.[37] Ministers agreed that recognition should be refused. Macmillan added that, to avoid annoying Nasser and Kennedy, Britain would give no direct assistance to the Royalists.

With Amery's assistance and Saudi finance, McLean established an office in London under David Stirling, the creator of SAS, to recruit former SAS officers as mercenaries to assist the Royalists against Nasser. Among those recruited was David Smiley, another of Amery's former SOE colleagues from the Albanian adventure, a professional soldier in the Blues who had recently returned from suppressing the revolt in Oman. For Smiley, like the politicians, this was an opportunity to revenge Britain's retreat at Suez and defeat Moscow's subversion.

The stakes rose on 23 February. British positions in the Federation were attacked by Yemeni tribesmen. Overnight, Macmillan found himself buffeted by conflicting demands. Sandys and Amery urged retaliation, while an emissary from Washington complained that British policy endangered the stability of Saudi Arabia.[38] Having looked in vain to SIS for information, Macmillan read McLean's latest eyewitness accounts that Egypt's army had increased to 30,000. According to Gandy, in London for consultations, 'Macmillan said he was reminded of the Bonny Prince Charlie conflict in the Scotland of 1745: the Highlanders were more attractive, but one knew that the Lowlanders would win in the end.'[39] The prime minister bowed to Amery's pressure and allowed retaliation. The Yemeni tribesmen withdrew.

Two weeks later, Macmillan read in the *Guardian* an eyewitness account from inside the Yemen by Clare Hollingsworth, which suggested an imminent battle between Republicans and Royalists. Macmillan noted, 'Has our intelligence anything to say? It seems to me that Miss Hollingsworth's article is better than anything we have got out of our people so far because it is a coherent account by someone who has obviously been there which we never get.'[40]

Macmillan's dissatisfaction with SIS was applauded by Amery. British Arabists, furious about the Foreign Office's policy of appeasement, were pressing for action. 'Everyone is freebooting,' White was told by the desk officer. 'Even the ADC to the governor general in Aden.'[41] In conversation with Amery, White was under pressure to take a position. 'You should be undertaking active operations,' urged the minister, reflecting on the era when SIS set off bombs and overthrew governments.

'The world has changed,' replied White, resisting an invitation to 'knock the stuffing out of Nasser'. There was to be no repeat of 1956. 'That's not our job any more. We seek and supply information.'

'By giving Nasser a bloody nose, we get the Russians,' countered Amery.

Unmoved, White did not want SIS to bear responsibility for any deaths. McLean, he condemned as 'a colourful romantic'.

Suspecting that White did not want to offend the CIA, Amery, yearning for the old SIS led by a George Young type who delighted in subterfuge and manipulation to overthrow the Nassers of the world, engaged in a plot to involve the British government in a secret war in the Yemen. One critical meeting was on the playing fields of the Dragon school at Oxford. The minister met Kennedy Trevaskis and agreed that the Royalists should be supported against Nasser. 'It's the last fling of the Arab idealists,' White was told.[42]

In a secret decision, Macmillan appointed Amery as 'minister for Yemen', to mastermind British support of the Royalists. Faced with a divided cabinet obstructing any chance of an agreed government policy, and anxious to be personally distant from any involvement, the prime minister allowed Amery to supervise a 'private war' against Nasser. There was no public announcement nor any mention in the official cabinet minutes. 'It was a private war, totally obscured from public view and remarkably successful,' declares Amery.[43]

Working from his office at the Ministry of Aviation, aided only by his Private Office staff, Amery 'gave advice' to McLean and the mercenaries across the whole spectrum of waging a guerrilla war, including the deployment of SAS officers to assist in sabotage and the strategy of any offensive. As a token of British support, a consignment of 50,000 Enfield rifles was shipped to the Royalist tribesmen through Aden. 'I batted on my own,' Amery recalled, 'without SIS. White was reluctant to get involved.'

That was not quite accurate. On Macmillan's orders, SIS was placed at Amery's disposal. All relevant SIS reports were to be sent to the minister's Private Office at the Ministry of Aviation. Paulson was told to help him; and a taskforce, managed by O'Bryan Tear on his return to London, with the help of Dennis Womersley and Desmond Harney of P17, was created in Broadway to co-ordinate the supply of weapons and personnel to the Royalists.

To strengthen the liaison with King Faisal of Saudi Arabia, John Christie was ordered to open a new SIS station in Jeddah. Every Thursday afternoon, Christie rather than the ambassador met the monarch to provide a 'back channel' report to Amery. Regularly, he also met Kamal Adham, the Saudi chief of intelligence, who provided the best account of what was going on in the Yemen. Despite SIS's efforts, Amery still complained that the information gathered by McLean and the Saudis was better than anything contributed by British intelligence.

For White, Amery was a dangerous pirate. Giving Nasser a bloody nose would embroil Britain in unsustainable commitments to the Royalists and risked confrontation with the Soviet Union. Unlike Amery, White was unexcited by warfare and death in battle. He would derive no pleasure from the report that McLean and Mark Lennox-Boyd, operating with the Royalists, had successfully shot down a Russian MiG fighter, killing the pilot.

During those days of tension, Jim Critchfield, the CIA's director for the Mideast, called on White. Like so many CIA officers, Critchfield enjoyed his access to Broadway and would usually route his travels through London to compare notes with his British colleagues, although he dismissed Paulson as 'a fuddy-duddy'. The West, he had convinced Helms, could not afford to allow Nasser to win the Yemen war. 'It's a strategic move, a two-pronged effort by Moscow to make the Red Sea into a Russian lake,' he warned, aware that Mossad was reporting the same. The CIA, he suggested to Helms, should fight Nasser regardless of President Kennedy's policies. Critchfield arrived in Broadway to suggest closer liaison between the CIA and SIS, bypassing the State Department and Foreign Office.

White welcomed the opportunity to hear the American's opinion. He had long understood that, unlike SIS, the agency was becoming a centre for an alternative foreign policy to the State Department's. Increasingly, the CIA mirrored Amery's pugnacity as opposed to the Foreign Office's deliberation. Yet to Critchfield White appeared 'perplexed'.

'It's not simple,' observed White.

'You don't believe fighting the KGB is the issue?' Critchfield responded. He insisted that the intercepts proved Soviet involvement.

Arab states, unaware of the Second World War's Ultra operation – still a well-protected secret – were encoding their messages using either the old German Enigma machine or with new encoders purchased from a British manufacturer, not realising that the secrets of their machinery were passed on to SIS. The intercepts proved, explained Critchfield, that Russian pilots were flying Tu16s from Cairo to Yemen. CIA agents in Cairo had watched as the planes, originating from Moscow, had their Soviet markings replaced during the night by Egyptian insignia.

Despite the evidence, White politely spurned Critchfield's warnings of doom. As a sympathiser with Kennedy's New Frontier, he rejected the thesis of a Soviet threat. Yet, on Macmillan's orders, there was no alternative but to engage in the undeclared war, and the CIA had, unlike SIS, penetrated the heart of Egypt's war machine.

Soon after America's recognition of the Republican government in the Yemen, James Fees, a CIA officer, had arrived in Ta'izz under cover as a consular official. Energetic, intelligent and aggressively anti-Soviet, Fees spoke Russian and would become a knowledgeable Arabist. Equipped with his own light aircraft masquerading as US humanitarian aid transport, he established a network of agents in the capital and around the country. With three other CIA officers – two Lebanese-born Americans who posed as Arab businessmen and a Syrian-born American – he had charmed and bribed his way into the citadels of the Republican and Egyptian military headquarters. In exchange for gold coins, he soon obtained and dispatched to Washington a copy of the enemy's war-room map displaying the dispositions of all the military units, its order of battle, targets, the after-battle reports and intended political initiatives.

Fees was also delivering intelligence which exposed flaws in SIS's operation and which Amery, benefiting from the regular SIS–CIA exchange of information, used to enhance his own stewardship of the war. In that material was a report that Royalist tribesmen were being harassed by Egyptian bombs containing poison gas.

That news placed White in the middle, between Colonial Office demands for retaliation and Foreign Office officials who stoutly denied the physical evidence. Spurned by a desire to embarrass the doubters, SIS delivered the evidence – a bomb casing – to London. Obligingly, the *Daily Telegraph* published 'evidence' of an Egyptian poison-gas bomb. The newspaper report was delivered to the United Nations, an organisation proving to be hysterically anti-British. The ruse backfired badly. The bomb had contained tear gas. 'We are all agreed that it would be best to let the matter die a natural death,' wrote a British diplomat at the United Nations chuckling over SIS's embarrassment.[44] The sympathisers were within the CIA.

In early November 1963, Richard Helms, the CIA deputy

director for plans, visited White in London. Invariably their conversations lapsed into mutual commiseration about constraints on their respective budgets, but Helms, although preoccupied by the Vietnam war and China, also listened to White's lament about Yemen. Despite his reluctant involvement and his position between feuding Whitehall departments, White loyally sought CIA help to improve Britain's position. American companies were building roads for Nasser's 30,000-strong army in south Yemen. The White House's directive not to support the Royalists and to allow the rebel take-over of Aden was damaging SIS. 'We've been ordered to save Aden and the Federation,' said White, 'but it's impossible without American help.' Helms agreed to approach Dean Rusk, the secretary of state, urging that his department cease opposing British policy. The CIA, despite the State Department's opposition, was SIS's ally in the evolving war.

On 10 December 1963, a grenade was thrown at Sir Kennedy Trevaskis, newly appointed governor general of Aden, inside the colony's airport terminal. Trevaskis survived and ordered a state of emergency; the war escalated.

SIS's commitment was organised by John da Silva, the new station chief formerly involved in the Oman war, whose sentiments about Nasser and Aden's future reflected Amery's. In a personal report to White in London, da Silva urged that SIS had 'a legitimate interest' in undertaking operations against Nasser both because of Soviet involvement and because of Egyptian subversion undermining Britain's position. His report coincided with a CIA 'National Estimate' proclaiming the existence of 'a Soviet threat' in the area.[45]

White, under pressure from Macmillan and Amery to pursue a subversive war, finally succumbed. Any irritation was silenced by the knowledge that past successes in Cyprus had proved him to be wrong. Where the combined *diktat* of politicians and military demanded SIS's involvement in gung-ho activities, he had no alternative but to obey. He would claim to have been finally persuaded that the war in the Yemen endangered Britain and was an opportunity to reverse the Suez humiliation. 'I want an aggressive policy against Nasser,' White told colleagues.[46]

But, unlike his predecessors, he would not embark on any operation without Whitehall's approval. The complication was the politicians' own feud.

In October 1963 Macmillan resigned and was succeeded by Alec Douglas-Home. Richard 'Rab' Butler, the new foreign secretary, an appeaser of Hitler even in 1940, opposed any activity which might irritate Nasser. The deadlock continued until summer 1964, when da Silva reported from Aden that Britain's position was 'in danger of collapse'. White's response was encouraging: 'Spell out your proposals in a report and we'll go ahead.'

Under similar pressure from Sandys and Thorneycroft to confront Nasser, White was invited by Douglas-Home to submit the case for the prime minister's arbitration. In two thirty-minute meetings in the Cabinet Room, White argued for clandestine intervention. His style combined 'deference and a desire to serve British interests' with an assurance of professionalism which his colleagues would later describe as 'a brilliant performance'. Douglas-Home, with a general election imminent, agreed to a compromise. Both the Royalists and the mercenaries were to be secretly supported.

SIS officers in the region – Christie, da Silva and Jeff Douglas in Bahrain – were allowed to provide the mercenaries with information and to put all SIS's facilities at their disposal. Officially the assistance was to be 'indirect'. Smiley would discover that several British mercenaries were in fact serving SAS officers 'on official leave'.[47] Amery even telephoned Christie directly. 'Would it be plausible', asked Amery, 'if the RAF dropped rifles to the Royalists pretending that they came from Jordan rather than Cyprus?' Christie, surprised by the personal telephone call, agreed that there was no problem. Thousands of rifles would be parachuted into the wilderness from unmarked or Saudi planes to be used as currency rather than for warfare.

Indirect support to the Royalists from Aden was orchestrated by da Silva on the grounds that the unpopular Egyptians were a 'legitimate defensive target'. SIS emphasised that its involvement was directed against the Egyptians rather than in support of the Royalists. Money was channelled by means of the Colonial Development and Welfare Acts to the South Arabian Federal

Treasury, another 50,000 rifles were delivered and intelligence from GCHQ intercepts pinpointed the enemy's location and weak points. SIS co-ordinated the tribesmen to cross the border into the Yemen from the Federation to attack Egyptian officers. Bombs, planted under the direction of SIS, destroyed Egyptian military and intelligence headquarters along the frontier. Garrison towns were shot up and political personalities were murdered. 'The tribesmen didn't need to be told how to wage war. That came naturally. So did the bloodshed. SIS just manipulated them,' according to one SIS officer.

In London, White took 'a lively interest in the war. After all, we were spending lots of money.'[48] The results flowed quickly. By autumn, it was claimed that RAF bombing of Harib in retaliation for an Egyptian attack on a camel train carrying weapons to British and French mercenaries had forced the first of several Egyptian retreats, dividing and isolating the army and forcing it to rely upon supplies by air. It was the preliminary to a complete withdrawal.

James Fees, the CIA officer in Ta'izz, was less convinced about SIS's success. 'I never noticed that the Egyptians were worried by SIS. Their army was fighting far away from the British and they were terrified of the Yemenis. In any case, the Egyptians were infiltrating into Aden and turning the town into a barbed-wire fortress.'[49] For a brief moment in autumn 1964, however, it did seem that despite White's reservations SIS was stemming Nasser's subversion and defeating Moscow's grand strategy. The possibility for political negotiations had been created by SIS.

If, contrary to White's intentions, SIS was adopting a more robust policy around the world, it appeared to be more successful than he envisaged. But, by then, White's greater pride was the real damage SIS was inflicting upon the KGB on their own turf, in Russia and Soviet-occupied Eastern Europe.

CHAPTER TEN

Traitors, Heroes and Noddy

Every successful general needs luck and it was White's fortune that eight years earlier, soon after becoming chief, he had been handed the ammunition which would revive SIS's status in Whitehall and mitigate a disaster.

In 1958, an envelope marked 'Secret – Deliver to British Ambassador' had been pushed under the door of a junior British diplomat's apartment in Warsaw. Inside, written in capital letters in English, were three pages describing the structure of the Polish intelligence service, the Urzad Bezpieczeństwa, in London, a list and description of Polish intelligence officers based in Britain and details of the relationship between the UB and the KGB. On the third page, the writer stated that he would supply more information in return for a large payment in Polish currency and a promise of asylum, should that prove necessary. Finally, he stated that he would return to the apartment in exactly one month for the reply.

The ambassador handed the letter to John Quine, the embassy's SIS officer. Quine was a forty-six-year-old wartime naval officer who, after recruitment to SIS in 1945, had been stationed in Tokyo for six years before arriving in Warsaw in 1957. His excited response to the letter was tinged with suspicion that the exercise was a trick organised by Polish intelligence.

The letter was forwarded to Robert Dawson, the director of DP4, responsible for eastern Europe. Broadway's initial caution was natural. Mindful of the CIA's entrapment by the WIN deception and of the disasters in the Baltic and Ukraine, every detail was checked. The conclusive evidence was his revelation of Poles in Britain, unknown to MI5, who after surveillance were proved to be intelligence officers. White, 'a shrewd judge if a defector was genuine',[1] declared the informant reliable. The source was identified as a senior UB intelligence officer, motivated to betrayal by financial greed and hostility towards the Russians since the revolt in 1956. He was SIS's first major source of information behind the Iron Curtain since 1945.

'If you decide to betray one superpower, you're not going to trust the other. That's why he's come to us,' reasoned one of Broadway's sages. 'The Poles hate the French because of Napoleon; they can't forgive the Germans after Hitler. That leaves us. All we did was let them down in 1939 and let them die in the RAF during the war.' The Polish intelligence officer was codenamed Noddy.

Quine was told to move into the British diplomat's apartment and wait. When, on the expected day, the dark-haired forty-year-old Polish colonel arrived, he knew that Quine was the embassy's SIS officer. The terms of payment, about £500 per month in zloty banknotes, and methods for future meetings were agreed. Always at Noddy's initiative, Quine would be told at which restaurant, museum or unmarked cars he could collect an envelope. In restaurants, he was to eat with his wife and friends and watch the Pole go to the lavatory. After seeing him emerge, he would go to the identified cubicle and find an envelope stuffed behind the cistern. In museums, there would be brush contacts. Noddy relied on the SIS officer to lose the regular UB surveillance.

An exchange of questions and answers developed between Broadway's specialists and the Pole. Noddy's access to senior KGB officers and his regular journeys to Moscow for briefings provided unprecedented information and gossip about both Soviet intelligence and politics.

Six months later, another UB officer approached an embassy secretary and offered his services. Through Quine, that Pole supplied information about operations against French and American citizens living in Warsaw, especially a blackmail operation against an American diplomat. By 1960, Quine's successor, Colin Figures, was continuing to receive information from three UB officers. The third had access to military and political personalities in Moscow. Eventually, he would be posted to Washington, where he remained in contact with SIS.

From the outset, White enthusiastically directed that the Polish material should be passed to the CIA. For the chief of the CIA's east European desk, a sceptic about British intelligence since Philby and the discovery that a Czech network financed by SIS since the late 1940s had been totally compromised by the KGB, the information was 'the best we'd ever had'.[2]

At the same time White received a second godsend. This was Operation Rafter, a discovery by Peter Wright, MI5's scientific officer. In 1956, Wright had begun scrutinising counter-intelligence operations directed against MI5 by KGB officers based in the Soviet embassy. After monitoring the radio signals received inside the embassy, Wright spotted that the KGB was listening to messages between MI5's watchers. The Security Service's operations, especially its surveillance of a suspected employee in a British missile development laboratory, were compromised.

Wright's revelation sparked a revolution in ideas and radio equipment within SIS. In a lecture, he introduced his ideas to the CIA and was applauded: 'SIS gave us an idea how to beat the KGB on their own turf. It was a very important aspect of our relationship.'[3] Equipment was developed in Britain and the United States enabling intelligence officers based in communist countries to monitor local counter-intelligence officers, while other micro-radios were designed to communicate with agents in coded bursts across Moscow or Warsaw, avoiding surreptitious personal meetings which could be seen by the KGB. By 1965, SIS's technique of operating in communist countries had been fundamentally changed to the communists' disadvantage.

A third stroke of good fortune for White was delivered from Moscow. In a chance encounter, an SIS officer met a member of Khrushchev's family. In a hurried exchange, the Russian admitted to being a former CIA source now eager to resume contact with the West. White was visibly excited by the chance to provide a service to the Agency.

SIS's accumulated credit in Washington was therefore substantial when, in 1959, Howard Roman, a CIA officer, arrived in London with disturbing news. Roman, a Harvard scholar of German literature, met Martin Furnival Jones and Arthur Martin in Leconfield House. His message was deemed so important that it required personal delivery. A Polish intelligence officer had told the CIA that two Soviet agents were operating in Britain. One worked in a Royal Naval research establishment and the other was employed by SIS. The CIA source, later identified as Michael Goleniewski, was the vice-chairman of Polish military intelligence. Every Polish intelligence officer travelling abroad, requiring passports and forged documents, was channelled through Goleniewski's office. His offerings were, CIA officers would say grimly, 'a horrendous take'. The origin of Goleniewski's information about the British spies was a succession of 'top-secret' SIS documents passed to Warsaw from the KGB in Moscow.

The two unidentified spies in Britain were codenamed Lambda 1 and 2. By 1961, MI5 had identified Lambda 1 as Harry Houghton, employed at the Underwater Weapons Establishment in Portland. Surveillance of Houghton had led to Gordon Lonsdale, a KGB illegal living in London whose real name was Konon Molodi. Further MI5 surveillance of Lonsdale led to the Ruislip home of Peter and Helen Kroger, ostensibly New Zealand nationals running an antiquarian book business. In fact, the Krogers were Morris and Lona Cohen, American communists working for the KGB. Both had fled from New York in August 1950 after the exposure of the Rosenberg atomic spy ring.

In a skilful operation, on 7 January 1961 Charles Elwell of MI5 orchestrated the arrest in London of Lonsdale and Houghton while in the act of exchanging secret documents and money. Hollis's delight that there was cast-iron evidence to allow a criminal trial was tempered by Harold Macmillan's displeasure. In the prime minister's opinion, the exposure of successful Soviet espionage in Britain would confirm the incompetence of MI5 and arouse damaging speculation of more communist penetration of the British government. To stem the political embarrassment, Macmillan commissioned two reports into Britain's whole security system. The second, by Lord Radcliffe, highlighted communist penetration of the civil service and trade unions and the continuing failure of 'positive vetting', which White had introduced.

Macmillan's displeasure preyed on White as Terence Lecky, the quiet and wealthy head of SIS's counter-intelligence, and his deputy Geoffrey Hinton sought the identity of Lambda 2. The result of that investigation, White gradually realised, would prove another turning point in SIS's history. Suggestions of a security breach had been investigated by Lecky in the year before Roman's visit. The first clue had been an inexplicable disappearance of agents. One of the Polish UB sources had mentioned rumours and provided names of people who had disappeared, but Lecky made no progress.

The second pointer had been the strange demeanour of some agents when meeting their SIS controlling officer: 'Sometimes the agents failed to turn up at meetings and were later unconvincing about their reasons. Then the content of their reports deteriorated or was reduced.'[4] A Czech source suggested that the KGB had mounted an operation to control British agents. But Lecky, initially suspecting a leak in Berlin, decided that the information was too imprecise.

A third hint was a defector's report that a British agent had been executed. His death was blamed by Lecky on an unresolved burglary of a safe in the British embassy in Brussels.[5] Lecky had stopped his inquiries in early 1959. He had not considered the possibility of a traitor.

During 1960, White became dissatisfied with Lecky's renewed investigation and appointed Harold Shergold, SIS's best Soviet specialist, to join the hunt. Shergold, an alumnus of both Oxford and Cambridge and a former teacher, had become attached to SIS in Bad Salzuflen in 1945 after serving as a military intelligence officer in North Africa and Italy. By 1960, his reputation epitomised SIS's best qualities. In White's opinion, 'Shergold became the lynchpin of the investigation.'[6]

At the beginning of 1961, after studying those with access to the SIS document seen by Goleniewski, Shergold identified the best suspect. It was George Blake, a middle-ranking officer who was currently studying Arabic at the Foreign Office school in the hills outside Beirut.

Reading Blake's file, White became 'alarmed and perhaps surprised' that, despite the exposure of Philby a decade earlier, SIS's internal security procedures had barely improved. Blake's itinerant background and the absence of any positive vetting, he realised, represented a glaring risk which he had not spotted in the previous five years. In 1956, White had circulated a memorandum expressing his 'dissatisfaction' with internal security. A lorry-load of top-secret SIS files had been found abandoned in Cyprus and an expensive racket involving SIS investment in a Rolls-Royce dealership had been exposed in Rome. White was unsure whether security had improved since. Blake's career suggested the worst. If guilty, Blake's exposure jeopardised White's own reputation as a counter-intelligence expert.

Blake was born George Behar in Rotterdam in 1922. His father was a Constantinople Jew who became, by dint of service in the British army during the First World War, a British subject and passed British citizenship to his son without either of them ever visiting Britain. Brought up with his Dutch mother, Blake was in Holland at the outbreak of the Second World War. Courageously, he smuggled himself through occupied France to Spain and, after an unpleasant period of internment, arrived in Britain to volunteer to fight. After training in the navy, he was seconded in 1943 to the Dutch section of SIS, escorting agents before their parachute drops into enemy-occupied Holland.

By 1947, when Blake was working in Hamburg to build an intelligence network in the Soviet zone, he had proved himself to be sufficiently effective and diligent to be offered a permanent post in SIS by Andrew King and Kenneth Cohen. 'We were attracted by his foreign languages and cosmopolitan background,' King told White. 'So few Britons spoke foreign languages.' The perfunctory security checks assumed Blake's allegiances. 'They didn't realise that, throughout the war, my loyalty was to the anti-Nazi cause, not to Britain,' Blake would say.[7]

After a course in Russian at Cambridge, Blake was posted in 1948 as vice-consul to Seoul, South Korea. As the undercover SIS officer, his task was to establish intelligence sources around Vladivostok, the Soviet naval base 450 miles away. Since there were no communications between Korea and that area, Blake's task was impossible. His attempts to establish a network in Korea were likewise futile. Blake's failure earned a reprimand from Maurice Firth, head of the Singapore station. Just weeks before the war, Firth, a snob who disliked foreigners, had visited Blake and, after voicing his dissatisfaction to his face, told colleagues, 'He doesn't belong in the service.'[8]

Soon after the North Korean invasion on 24 June 1950, Blake was arrested at the British Legation by communist soldiers. Over the following three years in captivity, he endured great suffering and, after reading *Das Kapital*, became converted to communism. One night, he surreptitiously offered his services as an agent to the KGB: 'I'd come to the conclusion that I was no longer fighting on the right side.'[9] White's interpretation would be less prosaic: 'Blake felt abandoned, unimportant and wanted to prove himself.'[10] In 1953, Blake returned to Britain 'as a hero' among his fellow SIS officers.[11] John Wyke, SIS's technician responsible for the Vienna and Berlin taps, was one of many who harboured 'admiration for the man who had survived real horrors., His reputation was high.'

In Blake's file, White saw that he had been questioned on his return by two SIS officers. Since SIS was still blessed by an atmosphere of trust, his assurances and denials were accepted not least because his account was supported by his fellow prisoners. The file did not reveal that the critical examination which cleared him of suspicion had lasted just two hours. Jack Easton signed Blake's clearance: 'We regarded North Korea as a bit primitive and we didn't suspect them of turning him. We were not thinking of their Russian masters.'[12]

Six weeks later, Blake met Nikolai Rodin, alias Korovin, still the KGB's resident in London, who would remain his contact for the next two years.

After Coronation Day, 2 June 1953, when Blake's safe return had been toasted with champagne, he was appointed the deputy to Colonel Tom Gimson of Y Section, processing the recordings of telephone intercepts of Russian diplomats and Red Army officers in Vienna and elsewhere in Europe. He also took the formal notes at the meeting agreeing the construction of the Berlin tunnel. A copy was passed to Korovin less than one week later.

In January 1955, Blake was posted to Berlin. Working in the political section under Rex Bosley, his task was to recruit Soviet and especially KGB officers. Under a separate directive,

Operation Lyeautey, organised by Nigel Clive's Special Political Action group in London, he was to collect incriminating material about all Soviet officials based in Berlin which could be used for blackmail.

Blake betrayed at least 400 people. His method was simple. Peter Lunn, the station chief, had introduced a card index of all SIS's agents throughout Germany. In the event of an agent's alert or arrest, the duty officer would pull the card and see which of fifty SIS officers should be summoned to cope with the emergency. Occasionally Blake was the night-duty officer. Alone in the hub of SIS's network, he copied the names of all the service's agents and, at regular meetings in East Berlin, passed the contents of SIS's whole structure to his KGB controller.

In 1959, Blake was posted to DP4, an outpost of the London station based in Artillery Mansions. Among sixty staff managed by Dickie Franks, Blake's task was to recruit British businessmen, students and tourists travelling in Russia; to recruit Soviet and communist diplomats stationed in Britain; to plant interpreters employed by SIS in otherwise normal negotiations and on visits behind the Iron Curtain; and to place microphones and telephone taps in Soviet and satellite embassies and buildings.

White recalled a sensation akin to a cold shiver as he rightly assumed that Blake had betrayed to the KGB all of those activities and the SIS personnel involved. 'Much worse than Philby,' he concluded. Fifteen years of work in Germany could have been destroyed; there would certainly have been considerable harm to the London operations; and how the CIA would react to news of the betrayal of the Berlin tunnel before it was even built required little imagination.

In February 1961, when Blake was identified as the suspect, he was studying Arabic at the Foreign Office college in Shemlan, in the Lebanon with his pregnant wife, surrounded by friends. White spent some time pondering his strategy. No SIS officer had ever been prosecuted for espionage; the pursuit of Philby had failed for lack of evidence; and the Blake case was similarly impaired. Even as chief of SIS, White's instincts – 'my second nature', he would say – were those of a counter-intelligence officer.[13] Knowledge of the investigation had been confined so far to four officers and four researchers. He gathered the senior officers for a conference.

The fourth officer was John Quine, the former Tokyo station chief who had become Blake's friend before the Korean war. While based in Warsaw, Quine had noticed the intense surveillance upon his movements but only now realised that the probable cause was betrayal by his friend. On Blake's return from Korea, the two men had enjoyed an evening in a pub in Victoria Street. 'He mentioned', Quine told White, 'that our security checks had been "superficial". But I hadn't noticed anything odd.'

'Trust is more easily produced than suspicion,' remarked White as he led the discussion. 'Too much vetting relied upon the old-boy network, but we can't tolerate Gestapo-style coverage.' The evidence appeared overwhelming, but before challenging Blake, White wanted one element confirmed. The SIS researchers had noticed an old and otherwise innocuous report from an SIS officer in Berlin. The officer had recounted that he had developed a relationship with a Soviet trade official. After many drinks, the Russian had inadvertently revealed that a KGB officer had warned him not to trust a particular German on the ground that he was an SIS agent. Critically, the trade official insisted to his British drinking companion, 'The KGB told me this.'

White wanted to pinpoint precisely the time when the Russian heard that information. Was Blake in Berlin at that time and therefore the KGB's source? Was the KGB's information old or new? Twice, John Quine was sent to a Moscow conference on East–West trade where the Russian trade official was present. Posing under an assumed name as a member of the British delegation, Quine approached the Russian and, in conversation, referred to that drunken revelation. On the second occasion, the Russian gave the precise date when he heard about the KGB's British source. 'I'm ninety per cent certain that Blake's our man,' said Shergold on hearing the news. 'The moment of epiphany,' sighed White. 'Everything has fallen into place.' There was still, however, no evidence for a prosecution. 'We need a confession,' said White, 'and an assessment of the damage he's caused.'

It was two weeks before Easter. White feared that to delay

Blake's return would risk an internal leak that would provoke his escape. To question him in Beirut was insecure. Blake, he decided, should be brought back to Britain as soon as possible. Two letters were sent to Nicholas Elliott, the station chief in Beirut. The first revealed that Blake was a suspected KGB agent. Without arousing suspicion, he should be asked to return to Britain for consultations about his future posting. The second letter was for Elliott to hand to Blake. By 'accident', Elliott met Blake in a theatre and casually passed on the message. According to Blake, 'I knew there was something wrong.' Having rejected his immediate thought of driving to Damascus and flying straight to Moscow, Blake contacted Nedosekin, the KGB's head of station in Beirut, and, on a deserted beach, asked for checks in Moscow. The quick response from the Centre approved Blake's return to London as 'safe'.

On 6 April 1961, Blake was welcomed at Broadway Buildings by Shergold and Ian Critchett. 'There's a few things we'd like to discuss with you,' said Shergold disarmingly. The venue would be a large, elegant room in Carlton Gardens. White's experience with Fuchs and Philby suggested that a confession could be obtained only by skilful interrogation based on irrefutable evidence. All the awful lessons of the 1951 investigations had been learnt. Everything depended upon the interrogator and the atmosphere. Having excluded both a confrontation similar to Philby's 'trial' and the use of a Special Branch officer like Skardon, White opted for the 'gamble' of an SIS tribunal led by Shergold. Although Shergold was naturally shy, White reasoned that the Soviet specialist's cool persistence might just spark Blake's confession to someone he knew and respected.

Alongside Shergold were Lecky and Ben Johnson, a former police officer used to interrogating defectors. On the table were fourteen flagged files, the SIS documents which the Polish intelligence officer had allegedly seen. On each document were Blake's initials, proving that he had read and returned the copy. Only one document, an economic report, had such limited circulation that Blake was the only possible source. Hidden microphones recorded that the gentle introduction had, by the end of the first day, culminated in an accusation that Blake had spied for Russia. 'Absolutely untrue!' exploded Blake.

During the second day, Blake maintained his denials. Silently, Blake was cursing Korovin, his KGB handler, for refusing to discuss the technique for resisting an interrogation. But so far he had avoided any damaging contradictions. During the breaks, realising there would be surveillance, he would make no attempt to contact the Soviet embassy. 'What was the point?' he would later say. 'They could not have helped me.' That evening, White was beginning to doubt his earlier hunch that Blake could not cope with the stress of accusations. 'If he doesn't confess,' White told a colleague, 'we'll invite him to fly to Moscow. Be patient.' As before, Blake spent the night in his mother's home. 'Patience,' White reminded himself.

At the end of the third day, Shergold was fretting. There were few questions remaining. 'After another half hour,' Shergold would later say, 'Blake might have been free.'[14] But the pressure of eight years' deceit was weakening his resistance. White had correctly guessed that Blake, an emotional rather than a professional traitor, would not realise that SIS was powerless without a confession.

Shergold's question, just before the session concluded, bore a hint of desperation: 'We know that you were working for the Soviets, but we understand why. While you were their prisoner in Korea, you were tortured and made to confess that you were a British intelligence officer. From then on you were blackmailed and had no choice but to collaborate with them.'[15] Blake was indignant. 'No, nobody tortured me! No, nobody blackmailed me!' he spluttered, losing his self-control. 'I approached the Soviets and offered my services to them of my own accord.'[16] He wanted everyone to know, he recalls, 'that I acted out of conviction, out of a belief in communism, and not under duress or for financial gain.'

Unrestrained, Blake launched into an uninterrupted monologue confessing his treachery. 'They listened to me in amazed silence,' recalled Blake.[17] At one stage, the traitor stopped. 'Am I boring you?'

'Not at all,' replied the polite interrogator.

'Perhaps you should give me a revolver and leave me alone

in the room?' suggested Blake.

'Oh no,' exclaimed a voice. 'It's not as serious as that!'

While Blake's confession continued, Johnson slipped out and crossed St James's Park to Broadway. White, obviously relieved by his successful tactics, now faced a new problem. In his office, SIS's lawyer was warning that Blake's confession was unusable in a trial: 'He hasn't been cautioned. He can renege on it and the judge could throw the case out.' White gritted his teeth: 'We need to do it by the book. We'll have to play him along. Ring Shergold and tell him to offer Blake a drink and tell him to go home for the night. It's most important that he doesn't realise we're going to prosecute.'

Blake should have been charged that night, but White wanted to discover the extent of the damage inflicted by Blake's treachery. Telephoning Sir Reginald Manningham-Buller, the attorney general, he secured the politician's agreement that SIS officers 'could have Blake over the weekend'.

'Just make sure you bring him back alive,' laughed the law officer.

Shaken and under stress, Blake returned to his mother's house for the night. The following day, he travelled with Shergold and Quine to spend the weekend in Shergold's Hampshire cottage. Both Shergold's wife and mother were present in order to create a 'relaxed atmosphere'. Blake made pancakes while Special Branch officers guarded the house. In that surreal atmosphere, he unleashed a torrent of confessions. 'I photographed every document which crossed my desk and more,' he told his colleagues. 'It was quite mechanical. It was as if I had ceased to exist.'

The news was passed to White. 'He's like a sponge,' remarked the chief disdainfully about a disgruntled cheat whose deeds had caused dozens of deaths. 'No backbone and unstable. Having taken a high-minded line, he's just crumpled up. He's a Walter Mitty character. He even believes that he deserves punishment.'[18] To White, Blake was not a master spy or an ideological convert like Philby. Firth was right. He didn't belong in the service. At Shergold's cottage he was simply 'satisfying a need for self-importance and placating his anger with some SIS personalities'.

An unusual burst of activity spread along the fourth floor in Broadway. One secretary, visiting a sick relation, was telephoned by White: 'We've caught the herring. There's a lot to do. Could you return?' She arrived to discover that others similarly summoned were shattered and even tearful at finding they had been betrayed by a friend. 'I'm having difficulty persuading some of the staff that he's a spy,' White confessed.[19]

Over that weekend, a faction of senior MI6 officers urged White that the public trial would damage the Service. Their opposition was supported by the prime minister, who envisaged only embarrassment. 'The government could fall on this,' Macmillan told White apocalyptically, suggesting an offer of immunity. White resisted the pressure. 'The cost of doing nothing would be enormous,' he replied, 'both within the service and with the Americans.' But he would agree to a deal. In return for a prosecution, he bowed to Macmillan's insistence that the attorney general would make arrangements to render Blake liable to imprisonment for more than the maximum fourteen years.

Soon after that conversation, White met Edward Heath, the Foreign Office minister delegated to supervise the case. 'Poor Dick,' sighed Heath. 'You're in the soup. You'll have to fire everyone and start again.'

'Why, Minister?'

'The Russians can now identify every MI6 officer.'

White ridiculed Heath's conviction that the service was compromised. SIS was so compartmentalised that Blake would only know a fraction of its activities. 'They might know my officers' identities,' replied White, 'but they don't know what they're doing.'[20] Politicians, White realised, 'just don't understand that we work on thin ice'.

White's message to his team in Shergold's cottage that Blake would be prosecuted caused a flutter. Shergold was in favour, while Quine was less enthusiastic. SIS, he believed, was to blame for recruiting someone of Blake's unstable background and then retaining him after his return from a communist prison. White was unmoved. His major fear was that, once charged, Blake would change his mind. 'We can't go through the agony of our operations being presented in court,' he told his officers. 'If he isn't prepared to plead guilty, we'll just put him on a plane to Moscow.' But, reassured by Quine and Shergold that Blake was prepared to sign a formal confession, White contacted Special Branch to make the arrangements.

'I was taking great risks,' reflected White. 'I could not afford any embarrassments. My MI5 experience was important, even to the point that I selected the Special Branch officers to be involved.' As a final precaution SIS also arranged that Blake would be offered Edward Cox as a 'good and helpful solicitor'. Cox, employed previously by SIS, could be relied upon to ignore his client's interests and persuade Blake to sign the confession and plead guilty.

On Sunday night, White dispatched two coded telegrams to Peter Lunn, then the station chief in Bonn. The first revealed that a traitor had been unearthed in SIS and that West German intelligence would need to be informed. 'The subject of this telegram is revealed in the following cable.' As Lunn decrypted the numbers to reveal five letters in the second telegram, an earthquake was erupting throughout SIS. In Broadway, in the dozens of SIS technical and training offices throughout Victoria and even at the Fort in Gosport, the turmoil of emotions paralysed activity. The unthinkable had occurred. A member of the Firm was rotten.

White attended the short hearing at the Old Bailey on 3 May 1961. In the dock, Blake assumed that he would receive the maximum fourteen years' imprisonment. With remission, he could expect an earlier release. Sir Reginald Manningham-Buller, the attorney general, had proposed to Macmillan that Blake should be charged on five counts, separating five periods of his service. White understood that the politician, who would personally prosecute, wanted to hit Blake 'with the biggest hammer possible'.

In previous weeks, SIS officers had contacted agents and sources throughout the satellite countries and had concluded that Blake's treachery had cost at least forty lives, among them a Red Army technical expert whom Blake had personally known. That information was discreetly passed by Manningham-Buller to Lord Parker, the lord chief justice, who presided at the secret trial. No mention of the deaths would be made in the courtroom. To public astonishment, Parker passed five fourteen-year sentences, three to run consecutively, making a total of forty-two years' imprisonment, the longest prison sentence ever imposed by a British court. Blake was stunned. In the aftermath, the government fiercely denied any suggestion of an understanding or even a link between the unproven deaths and the sentence. Since no member of the public had heard the prosecutor's speech, the denials were accepted. Thereafter, White would express 'shock' at the severity of the sentence.[21]

Some weeks later, White personally delivered the 'damage report' to John McCone, the new CIA director. The four-page letter on his thick blue paper, topped with 'Dear John' and signed 'Dick' in green ink, was an embarrassing catalogue which Quine had compiled and completed with Blake's assistance in Wormwood Scrubs prison. White's audience for the ninety-minute session in Washington included James Angleton, the chief of the Agency's counter-intelligence section, and John Maury, chief of the Soviet Division. They were unusually sympathetic. 'It can happen to anyone,' said Angleton consolingly. In the CIA's opinion, White had displayed consummate investigative skill and apparent honesty, a contrast to Menzies during the Philby saga. Shergold, they read in John Caswell's report from the CIA liaison office in London, had instilled confidence in the investigation. 'The waters aren't disturbed by this one,' declared Cleveland Cram, the CIA's British desk officer, mindful that MI5 was 'smelling of roses' after its arrest of Lonsdale and the Krogers.[22] Other CIA officers were not as generous. Bill Harvey, who had identified Philby as a spy and had 'sweated blood' building the Berlin tunnel, was unforgiving: 'Here we go again. We should never trust the Brits.'[23]

Only later was White's damage report dubbed 'a catalogue of horrors'. CIA officers noticed several omissions, including Blake's disclosure to the Russians that the Allies were developing a transmission responder similar to the KGB's transmitter found in the American ambassador's office in Moscow. 'We didn't like that surprise,' Cram told a friend.

But McCone, a quiet, dignified and astute Roman Catholic, bore White no ill-feeling. His forbearance was born of his instant rapport with White. The new director's awareness of White's enthusiasm for America since his student days in California prompted an invitation for lunch with Robert Kennedy, the attorney general. 'America took a lot of trouble over me,' White told his hosts, heartened that he was 'speaking to Americans in a way they understood'.[24] Despite the Blake disaster, he prided himself that no harm had been done to the special relationship. Whatever SIS's failings, he knew that the CIA had also exposed itself as a blundering organisation. McCone's appointment had followed the dismissal of Allen Dulles after the disastrous invasion of Cuba in April 1961.

The following day, White was invited to McCone's home. Over dinner, the two agreed that the landings in the Bay of Pigs had offended every cardinal rule for intelligence operations. No accurate assessment of the actual conditions in Cuba had been produced, leading to a gross overestimate of anti-Castro sentiment; the effectiveness of Cuban counter-intelligence had been underestimated; and the exiles recruited by the CIA to stage the invasion had been inadequate. 'As bad as Suez,' said White wryly. 'Half-hearted and hesitant.' Allen Dulles had paid the ultimate price for his love of clandestine war.

Towards the end of the meal, their conversation turned to John le Carré's recently published novel, *The Spy Who Came in from the Cold*. With unusual indignation, White groaned that the author was a former MI5 and MI6 officer. 'He hasn't done us any good. He makes all intelligence officers look like philanderers and drunks. He's presenting a service without trust or loyalty, where agents are sacrificed and deceived without compunction.' Le Carré's portrayal of cynicism, betrayal, defeatism and lack of conviction, he added, suggested that the sacrifice for the good fight was not worth while. Expanding on his irritation, he added, 'He's getting his revenge on the old-school ties in British intelligence. He wants to show them who's on top.'[25] Whether White could not see or wilfully ignored the exaggerated importance le Carré had bestowed upon SIS was unclear, but it certainly was not unwelcome.

The following day, Angleton invited White to his office. the counter-intelligence director proposed that the two services pool their resources. 'We had a War Room together during the war,' enthused Angleton, referring to the joint offices in Ryder Street, 'and we should reincarnate this structure.' Even the thought alarmed White but, ever the diplomat and anxious to protect the special relationship, he answered with a smile, 'I'll certainly think about it, Jim. It's an interesting proposition.'

The rumour mill in London was uninterested in SIS's relationship with the CIA. Instead, it was reflecting that the reaction to the Blake affair was just the tip of Whitehall's dissatisfaction with the Service. SIS's relationship with bureaucrats, it was murmured, had become unhealthy. The evidence was the directive that SIS abandon Broadway Buildings and move across the River Thames to Century House, a drab, twenty-storey speculative office block at 100 Westminster Bridge Road. Excessively hot in summer and too cold in winter, the concrete tower's interior furnishing was as colourless and forlorn as the exterior. Intended to house the service's staff of 2000, the 'Bastard Modern' headquarters was spontaneously condemned as too small and too inconvenient for access to Whitehall and the clubs in Pall Mall. 'A ratty mess without an aura of history' was the apt description by one inhabitant when the move was announced for 1964. To cynics, SIS's enforced remoteness suggested that the service had been condemned as an outcast as continuing punishment for the 1956 disasters and so much more.

No one, however, seems to have thought that the relocation reflected upon White personally, despite the blandness of his tenth-floor office. But, having failed to win the Whitehall battle, he chose to interpret the move as symbolic, not least as an opportunity to cease using green ink. 'My God,' he told Helms, 'I had to get rid of that colour.'[26] Green showed up badly, he complained, on MI6's thick blue stationery. 'It's all so outdated.' The symbolism, he reflected, would begin a new era in SIS.

An operation was under way, masterminded by himself, which had muted the CIA's criticisms and would, he hoped, convert SIS's Whitehall critics. The climax for White himself had been on the very day of Blake's conviction. That same night, as Blake was taken to Wormwood Scrubs, he had met 'The Spy of the Century'.

Colonel Oleg Penkovsky, an officer serving in GRU, Soviet military intelligence, was spending sixteen days in London betraying secrets that were arguably more important than Blake's offerings. White was glowing with pride that the Soviet myth about how the West could not attract high-ranking ideological spies was being dispelled.[27] In a late-night meeting at a London hotel on that day, White personally encouraged Penkovsky to continue his treachery. In White's world, one nation's hero was another's traitor. As he would occasionally say, 'Normal people aren't traitors.'

Born in 1919, the son of a lieutenant in the czar's army and well connected at the highest levels of the Soviet military, Colonel Penkovsky had tried unsuccessfully three times from August 1960 to contact the CIA. His arrival in London, courtesy of SIS, proved in White's opinion the unsurpassed competence of the British service. The contact had been made in December 1960 by Greville Wynne, the organiser of a delegation of British machine manufacturers in Moscow seeking Soviet orders. Penkovsky, the intelligence officer attached to the businessman, asked that a message be passed on to the CIA. For fear of a KGB provocation, his request was ostensibly ignored but, on his return to London, Wynne reported the encounter to Dickie Franks, head of SIS's London station.

Eyewitnesses noticed that White's face, on hearing the news, underwent a noticeable change. Excitement radiated from the normally taciturn chief as he contemplated how the previous twenty-five years had prepared him to exploit this opportunity. Handling a Soviet defector overrode all the subtleties of foreign affairs, for it would give to Western intelligence the inside knowledge of the enemy's 'intentions'. Here, moreover, was an opportunity to redress the unbalanced relationship with the CIA – although there was need for great care. During those exciting weeks, Bill Steadman, the SIS officer in Geneva, would inexplicably reject an offer of collaboration by a Soviet intelligence officer wanting to defect, in a manner reminiscent of the loss of a Soviet defector in Tokyo by the SIS station chief, Maclachlan Silverwood-Cope a decade earlier. Defectors required gentle treatment – 'enormous care' – just like traitors. Breaking with customary practice, White decided that with so much at stake he would supervise Penkovsky's treatment himself.

On 25 January 1961, six weeks after the Russian's approach to the British businessman, Shergold flew to Washington to meet Joe Bulik, responsible for CIA operations inside the Soviet Union. 'The CIA didn't have anyone in Moscow,' grumbled Bulik, chafing at the Agency's failure to respond to Penkovsky's overtures. Shergold offered to run Penkovsky as a joint operation. Bulik, Russian-born, bore considerable respect for Shergold, but not for SIS. His opposition to co-operation was overruled by Richard Helms, the chief of operations for the director of plans. Despite the evidence of SIS's insecurity, said Helms, the CIA had no alternative because Penkovsky was in contact with the British and only SIS possessed officers in Moscow.

Before returning to Moscow in early April 1961, Wynne was briefed by Dickie Franks on how to handle the Russian. Aged forty-one, Wynne appeared ideal for the task of go-between. Patriotic and intelligent, he could travel to Moscow under perfect cover. Confident about his agent, Franks promised to pay for his efforts. Wynne returned from Moscow flush with success. Penkovsky had handed over a package of documents and revealed that he would lead a purchasing delegation to Britain on 20 April.

It was a historic moment. Blake had just been convicted; Fidel Castro had proclaimed victory over the CIA at the Bay of Pigs; and Yuri Gagarin had become the first man to orbit the earth. The dominant fear in the West was of a 'missile gap' in the Soviet's favour allowing Khrushchev to blackmail Kennedy into submission. Politicians, officials and the chiefs of staff in Washington and London were scrambling for any information about Soviet intentions and capabilities. White believed that he was in the unique position of having the answers. Penkovsky confirmed White's dictum that 'Good intelligence is always a matter of good opportunity and opportunism.'[28]

In preparation for his arrival, it was agreed that the Russian's debriefing would be handled by two CIA and two SIS officers. Bulik arrived in London with George Kisevalter. Both were fluent in Russian and both felt a natural rapport with Russians.

Kisevalter had won admiration for his outstanding relationship with Lieutenant-Colonel Pyotr Popov, a GRU officer in Berlin who, before his arrest, had been an important source. Shergold would be joined by Michael Stokes, derided by both CIA officers as a 'fill-in' and 'hopeless'.[29]

Their meetings with Penkovsky, initially codenamed Hero, took place at the Mount Royal Hotel near Marble Arch. Since Penkovsky had originally contacted the CIA, the Americans took the lead. At 9.45 p.m. on 20 April, after saying good night to the others of the Soviet delegation, Penkovsky silently left his own room and went by the back stairs to room 360. The door was opened by Bulik. 'Initially it was like meeting a girlfriend for the first date. There was a little tension in the air. But it didn't take long to break down. Here was a man who had held a secret in his heart for many months and was obviously waiting to unload. And he did unload.'[30]

During the first sessions, taped by a recorder in Shergold's briefcase, Penkovsky revealed a cornucopia of information about Soviet missile developments, nuclear plans, tactics and strategy, the locations of military headquarters and the identities of KGB and GRU officers. For the first time, the West would realise that Khrushchev's boasts about missile superiority were bogus and, more importantly, that the missiles and other Russian weaponry were produced and maintained in such appalling conditions that they were mostly unusable.

Over bottles of wine, Penkovsky also provided the first anecdotal evidence of the life, personalities and foibles of Russia's military chiefs. In an era when the private lives of Russia's leaders were completely unknown – even the Kremlin's secret telephone directory produced by Penkovsky was an invaluable guide to the Soviet power structure – political gossip about the enemy lent an unanticipated insight into the minds of those who were directly threatening the West.

When he read the report of the debriefing, White was tingling with excitement. He knew that distribution of that material around SIS's customers would bring glory upon SIS. But after twenty-five years in the business he felt no gratitude towards his benefactor. Shergold's reports revealed an unstable individual lusting for fortune and fame as 'the best spy in history'. Penkovsky's 'huge vanity', White surmised, proved his credibility, but like all defectors 'he was deranged by his experience'. The chief assumed that he understood Russians: 'I was passionate about their literature and knew them through all the wonderful novels I'd read.'[31] He concluded that Penkovsky, like so many fictional characters, was 'neurotic, highly risky and crazy'. The proof was his insistence that American agents 'immediately' plant small nuclear devices in Moscow's military headquarters. 'He wants revenge,' concluded White without affection.

White's attitude, reflected by Shergold, grated with Bulik and Kisevalter. Both Americans felt compassion towards Penkovsky and an affinity with his Russian temperament. When Penkovsky requested $1000 immediately for presents and Shergold offered $50, Bulik grunted at the embarrassment: 'You're tightfisted.' The American was also irritated by Stokes: 'At the first meeting he laid back on the bed as if bored. I could have kicked his ass.'[32] The Americans criticised the SIS officers for insensitivity. 'They've got no feel,' complained Bulik. 'The Americans glad-hand their agents more than the British,' admitted White, and it was true that Shergold was a 'puritanical technician' who, unlike Bulik, could not have arranged the young prostitutes whom Penkovsky demanded. Shergold also needed cajoling to pander to Penkovsky's inordinate desire for reward and recognition.

After a formal ceremony for which the Russian wore the respective uniforms of colonels in the American and British armies and swore allegiance to the United States and Britain, Penkovsky demanded an audience with the Queen. 'After all,' he exclaimed, 'Yuri Gagarin met her. Look what I'm doing for you! What's Gagarin done?' Shergold 'sweated' during that discussion.[33] White was not surprised by Penkovsky's request. 'Build up Penkovsky's fantasy,' he ordered. Like Fuchs, Penkovsky displayed 'alarming vanity that he and he alone could change the world'.[34] Since it was impossible for Penkovsky to have an audience with the Queen, White decided, to avoid endangering security, that he would meet Penkovsky personally. He was the first and only high-ranking Soviet intelligence officer whom White would meet during his period of service.

At 9.30 p.m., on 3 May, the evening of George Blake's trial, Shergold interrupted an explanation to the Russian about handling a Minnox camera. 'Now listen attentively. In ten or fifteen minutes a high-ranking representative of the Ministry of Defence of Great Britain will come here. He is personally speaking for Lord Mountbatten.' In a rehearsal of the theatre which would follow, Shergold encouraged Penkovsky to use the opportunity to pledge his loyalty to the West. 'The man who is coming', continued Shergold, 'is called Sir Dick White.' The name meant nothing to Penkovsky. Soviet intelligence had consistently failed to pierce White's anonymity.[35]

Shortly afterwards White knocked on the door and entered. The room was hot, stuffy and smoke-filled. There was no bed, just chairs and a table strewn with paper. The windows were closed to prevent anyone overhearing their conversation. To the Russian, White personified a well-dressed English gentleman. 'Colonel, the message I have to deliver to you is from Lord Mountbatten, the chief of the Defence Department of England. First, Lord Mountbatten regrets very much that he cannot see you personally. He asked me to relay this message to you. "I have been shown the oath of allegiance which you have made for the governments of Great Britain and the United States. I am filled with admiration for the great stand you have taken, and we are mindful of the great risks that you are running. I have also had reported to me the information which you have passed on to us. I can only tell you that it would be of the highest value and importance to the Free World."'

When Kisevalter had completed the translation, Penkovsky stood solemnly and made a speech filled with emotion, hyperbole and unswerving commitment to die for the cause and 'to swear my fealty to my Queen, Elizabeth II, and to the president of the United States, whom I am serving as their soldier.' Penkovsky concluded by hoping that in the future he would 'be blessed . . . personally by the Queen'.[36]

Having listened impassively to the emotional outburst, White came to the two important issues. 'I beg', he said waiting for the translation, 'that he proceed with caution in view of the great risk.' He then assured the spy that once he had fled Russia and come to the West, the intelligence services' obligations 'will be firmly and clearly fulfilled'. Penkovsky stared blankly. White's words of caution had been ignored: 'I realised it was not what he wanted to hear. He wanted to be praised personally by the Queen for his monumental contribution and to have a medal pinned on his breast. There was no possibility of this.'[37]

Penkovsky launched into a speech asking White to 'convey my gratitude to Lord Mountbatten' and to inform the Queen 'that her forces have been increased by one member – this colonel who is located in Moscow'. White smiled: 'To meet you has been delightful.' Bulik had opened a bottle of white wine and White proposed the toast: 'You have had many hours together to make this possible. Well now, we shall all drink to the colonel's health.' The glasses were emptied and White sought to break the tension by asking Penskovsky whether he spoke any English. 'Now that you're a colonel in the United States army, I think this will be necessary.'

'You'll also have to learn American,' added Shergold.

Five minutes later White departed: 'If you'll excuse me, I think I will leave you to your work. The very best luck to you in the accomplishment of your mission.'

As White left, Penkovsky sought reassurance from Kisevalter: 'Did I say everything properly?'

'Very well,' replied Kisevalter. 'I feel sure that Lord Mountbatten will tell Her Majesty about you.' Bulik noticed that Penkovsky was 'unimpressed'.[38]

For different reasons, White shared the sentiment: 'Penkovsky was the classic example of the pathology that affects the mind of the really important spy. Just like Fuchs, Penkovsky thought: "single-handed I can alter the balance of power".'[39]

As Penkovsky's material was processed, White's attendance at the weekly JIC meetings took on a new character. This was an agent, he reasoned, who would elevate SIS's reputation with his Whitehall customers. The military even established a unit in SIS's headquarters to analyse Penkovsky's material. With discernible self-assurance, White told JIC meetings, 'We have important information from a source.' Cynics in the Cabinet Office, however, unaware of the provenance, wondered aloud 'if this is all true'. In the wake of the spy scandals and general suspicion that the staff of the intelligence services were incompetent, SIS's information was judged by that minority to be 'rubbish, given credibility because it was believed by the intelligence services themselves'.[40]

It was much the same in Washington. Suggestions that Khrushchev's boasts of Soviet missile superiority were untrue were ignored. Experts were unwilling to abandon their fear of the missile gap. It was, White realised, the classic conundrum of intelligence: unless it confirmed preconceptions, it was classified as unreliable. Only trust in the messenger could reverse that prejudice.

Penkovsky returned to Moscow on 6 May with a Minnox camera, film for 1000 shots and a shopping list of requirements – 'Only the top-secret stuff, Oleg, forget the plain secret material,' instructed Bulik – and established that Wynne would continue as intermediary. During an emotional farewell, Shergold told Penkovsky, 'Sir Dick White asked me to give his special regards to you.'

Over fourteen months, Penkovsky's passing of exposed film of 5000 secret papers aroused no suspicion in Moscow. Twice he returned to the West, to London and Paris, where he met the same four SIS and CIA officers; he met Wynne in Moscow; and he was then placed in contact with Janet Chisholm, the wife of Roderick 'Rauri' Chisholm, the SIS officer in the Moscow embassy.

Using the Chisholms was a risk. Both had known George Blake while posted in Berlin and their files were accordingly marked, 'Sovbloc Red', alerting officers to the danger of using them. 'I thought long and hard before agreeing to Janet's use,' explained White. 'I didn't like the risk, but all the alternatives like safe houses and dead drops were too dangerous. The Russians could always deduce the SIS officer because they knew British practice. After all, they had our complete order of battle.'[41] The primitive alternatives of signals passed through telephone calls or messages thrown over the wall of America House in Moscow were discussed and abandoned. The best solution was White's instinct that the KGB would not follow a diplomat's wife, especially walking with her children.

SIS's handling of the exchanges was perfect. Among the small circle in Century House who were indoctrinated, there was mutual congratulation. The CIA was appreciative too, although there were doubters among the widening circle aware of the Soviet source who questioned Penkovsky's credibility and urged a polygraph test. White vetoed the idea: 'It would have destroyed his trust in us. I didn't have any faith in the technique.'[42] White's 'negative' to Washington emphasised that Penkovsky, whom he had met, was unique and could be antagonised. Helms and Maury, although irritated by SIS's superior attitude, were powerless to overrule White, especially since the operation was based in London. The proof of Penkovsky's credibility was the use of his material in the Oval Office.

At their summit in Vienna in June 1961, Khrushchev had threatened President Kennedy that he intended to sign a separate peace treaty with East Germany and to isolate West Berlin – what he called 'the testicles of the West'. If the West interfered, warned Khrushchev, 'You want war, that is your problem.' Kennedy, chastened by the Bay of Pigs fiasco but prepared for a Soviet challenge to the West, replied, 'It's going to be a cold winter of war.'[43]

Back in Washington, Kennedy read Penkovsky's reports about Khrushchev's intention to cut off Berlin, wage a war of nerves and prepare for a limited war within Germany. The president was confronted with the classic dilemma posed by intelligence. Was Penkovsky's information accurate and, if so, what policy could America pursue? The problem was compounded in early August when Penkovsky discovered that Khrushchev had ordered that a wall be built across Berlin, isolating the Western sectors. To Penkovsky's frustration, he had no means of contacting SIS in an emergency.

President Kennedy was resting at Hyannis Port on 13 August when East German builders began at midnight to build the Wall. For eighteen hours he would be unaware of the unfolding drama. The CIA, like MI6, had no advance knowledge of the Soviet operation. Their combined sources in East Berlin had not noticed the gathering of trucks containing the concrete and barbed wire which were installed that night. It was an unmitigated blunder by all Western intelligence services, casting serious doubt on their value. But Penkovsky's information provided the real picture.

Kennedy's reaction to the Berlin crisis was muted. His officials advised that the sensitive issue was Khrushchev's overall intention. Two weeks later, on 1 September, the evidence suggested that the Soviet leader was pushing the world into war. The Soviets, contrary to their promises, exploded in the atmosphere an atomic bomb in central Asia. Many urged Kennedy to retaliate.[44] Instead, the president listened to those who, reading Penkovsky's reports, suspected that Khrushchev's claims of Soviet atomic superiority were a bluff.

Penkovsky had revealed that, compared to America's 1004 delivery systems, the Soviets had between ten and fifty intercontinental missiles, cumbersome and even obsolete. Khrushchev, according to Penkovsky, was bluffing to protect his vulnerable personal power base in Moscow. The missile gap was thus to the US and not the Soviet advantage, a view supported by U2 photographs. Fear of the Soviet threat receded, and the Kremlin was told that the White House no longer believed in Soviet superiority – a dramatic turning point in the Cold War.[45]

In May 1962, White travelled with Macmillan to Washington. The prime minister, a natural sceptic about intelligence, was, White noticed, impressed with the way the Penkovsky material had, over a period of months, decisively altered the US administration's attitude towards the Soviet Union. Kennedy recognised that he had been wrong to believe that the missile gap was in Russia's favour. 'You see, Prime Minister,' White said to Macmillan, 'the Americans accept that the Russians are going down, not up.'[46]

Four months later, the tension was heightened. On 5 August, the Russians, having rejected a ban on nuclear tests, exploded a forty-megaton bomb in the Arctic and were suspected of secretly shipping missiles to Cuba. In Washington, the Soviet ambassador and a senior KGB officer assured the Kennedys that there were no missiles in Cuba. Publicly, the president reassured Americans that rumours of a Soviet deception were unfounded. Only John McCone, the director of the CIA, warned Kennedy that Khrushchev was lying. His source was the U2 photographs supported by Penkovsky's information. Although it would take several days before the president was convinced, the critical assessment about how long it would take before the missiles might be ready for firing was based on Penkovsky's information. 'It was uniquely important,' attests Helms.[47]

Yet, at that moment of triumph, Penkovsky's fate had been sealed. Nikolai Chistyakov, chief of the KGB's investigation department, had just opened an inquiry into his possible treachery. Penkovsky had told Wynne a month earlier about his unease, but that news had not been properly digested by either SIS or the CIA. Instead, the two services were bickering about their use of Penkovsky. The disagreements had surfaced on 31 October 1961. White had met the CIA director in London to agree procedures if Penkovsky dispatched an alert of a Soviet intention to attack the West. White was sceptical about the spy's political reports. Made cautious by his counter-intelligence background, he was beginning to have fears about the Russian. That autumn, Penkovsky requested details of an escape plan. While Shergold had ruled out all options, including Penkovsky's flight to the British embassy ('because they can't get him out of the country'), Bulik insisted that a route had to be found, even if it was a submarine rescue through the Black Sea.[48] Secondly, problems had arisen with Wynne, who was complaining that his business was suffering, that he was not being paid (although Shergold claimed that he had received £15,000) and that he was not getting the recognition he deserved.

For the moment, the use of Wynne was not an issue because Penkovsky was meeting Janet Chisholm in Moscow. Their twelve weekly meetings, mostly inside apartment blocks, had not been observed by the KGB. Nevertheless, Bulik complained, 'The pace set by the British was a little too hard and fast.' The CIA suggested that, for his own protection, Penkovsky be told to stop work for some months. The backlog of material to be analysed, Maury suggested, was enormous. Penkovsky's security was endangered by his exposure. The British disagreed, ignoring the KGB practice with Blake and Philby of arranging meetings only rarely, thus protecting their agents' security for years on end.

Shergold, after consulting White, warned Maury that it would be a 'tactical and psychological mistake' to mothball Penkovsky. The proposal, he explained, 'presupposes . . . that agents are ideal and logical persons. It is our view that such agents rarely, if ever, exist. HERO does not at any time consider that he is an agent . . . HERO revels in what he is doing [and] is determined to be the best of his kind ever.'[49]

Shergold and White therefore rejected outright the CIA's wish for a moratorium. Even a visit to London by Quentin Johnson, the chief of operations in the CIA's Soviet Division, to persuade Shergold to cut off Penkovsky was fruitless. 'It would destroy Penkovsky,' said Shergold. 'He would feel we are rejecting him.' Bulik also urged Shergold to slacken the pace: 'Shergold said that there was no danger. We were getting too much information and he wanted to carry on. I didn't have the evidence to disagree with him.'[50] Shergold's orders came from White, although his explanation for his method of management struck the CIA as self-interested: 'We had very little control over Penkovsky and did our utmost to avoid mistakes which would endanger him.'[51] Nevertheless a letter was prepared for Janet Chisholm to deliver on 2 February 1962, urging Penkovsky to be exceptionally careful. Penkovsky did not arrive for the meeting and later warned that Chisholm was under surveillance.

On 5 April, White flew to Washington to consult Helms and Maury. By then, he was suspicious that Penkovsky might have been arrested and turned, and so have become as KGB double-agent. He wanted the Russian's future reports treated with circumspection. Although a sensible precaution, its significance highlighted White's preoccupation with a KGB double-cross, founded on his past experience. The Americans were sceptical of his warnings. In turn, White concluded uncharitably that Helms was 'not properly equipped for the job', though he was relieved that Dulles had been replaced by McCone, a calmer, more professional intelligence officer in White's opinion.[52] Helms, with so many crises in Vietnam, the Middle East, India and China passing across his desk, was unaware of White's reservations. Maury and Bulik, however, were sensitive to SIS's attitude.

On 2 July, Wynne arrived in Moscow, though Bulik had believed that Wynne was no longer involved in the operation.

'It was the Brits asserting their control,' lamented Bulik, mindful that even Penkovsky had by then voiced his dislike of the British businessman. 'Unfortunately we trusted MI6's judgment about the man.' Three days later, Wynne had arranged to meet Penkovsky at the Pekin restaurant in central Moscow. When the two met, Wynne appeared to be under surveillance. This had been prompted by the businessman's own behaviour. At SIS's behest, he had visited Moscow three times on the pretext of bringing more delegations to Russia, but, unprepared, he had provided no details to the Soviet authorities, a failure which aroused suspicion.

Wynne's aborted meeting at the Pekin intensified the KGB's interest in him, but not immediately in Penkovsky. The KGB's investigator, Chistyakov, had not made any connection between the two men. The conversations between Wynne and Penkovsky in the Englishman's room at the National Hotel were never recorded by the KGB.[53] Bulik would complain that the CIA was not told about Wynne's visit to Moscow and that 'The Brits kept us in the dark about Wynne and his problems.' The problems, it later transpired, were Wynne's inability to remain silent or to control his alcohol intake and his boasts of success with women. 'We were being opportunistic with Wynne,' conceded White, 'but Shergold met him and approved his use.'[54] Bulik had formed a prejudice against joint operations. 'They don't work,' he said.[55] 'It's silly rivalry. We're taking the risk of operational control,' countered White. 'The Americans are just taking the benefits. The Americans don't spare anyone. They wanted everything their own way and blame everyone else.'[56]

Two new factors now entered into the operation. Firstly, about 150 people in Washington had become aware, regardless of attempts to disguise the identity, of a unique source in Moscow. The danger of a leak to the Russians by an unidentified American agent was a real one. During that period, the KGB had at least two sources within Washington's intelligence community: Lieutenant-Colonel William Whalen, an intelligence adviser to the joint chiefs of staff, and Jack Dunlap, at the National Security Agency. It is reasonable to assume that there was another, undetected.

Secondly, in February 1962 an encounter between Penkovsky and a British diplomat was spotted by a KGB surveillance officer in GUM, the Moscow store.[57] According to White, Rauri Chisholm did meet Penkovsky 'to keep an eye on him' after his wife had stopped seeing him at the apartment block.[58] Those meetings were confirmed by another officer in the British embassy.

To relieve the pressure on SIS and in an effort to win more control over Penkovsky, during the summer the CIA established a station in their Moscow embassy. Three officers, under various covers, were beginning to sense their potential in the heavily policed city. One, Rodney Carlson, was tasked to contact Penkovsky. A second, Richard Jacob, was briefed merely to acclimatise himself and undertake no operations.

While that was under way, in August, after Wynne's visit, Penkovsky fell under suspicion. That month, General Oleg Gribanov, the head of the KGB's counter-intelligence, conferred with Chistyakov. The evidence, admitted Gribanov, was poor. 'It's just a suspicion. He has so many meetings with foreigners.' On 20 October, on Chistyakov's suggestion, the KGB surreptitiously entered Penkovsky's apartment and discovered the Minnox camera.[59] Two days later, at 13.55 on 22 October, Penkovsky was arrested outside GRU headquarters and taken to the Lubyanka. Accused of treachery, he proclaimed his innocence.

Four hours after his arrest, the Minnox was produced and Penkovsky was taken to Vladimir Semichastney's office. Visibly dejected, Penkovsky confessed and offered to become a double-agent: 'I'm a colonel in the British army, they'll believe what I say.' Semichastney refused: 'He was too disreputable to trust.'[60] Chistyakov was more scathing: 'I've never seen a brave man after his arrest.' Penkovsky, Chistyakov agreed with White, was motivated not by ideology but by greed, vanity and anger that he had been denied promotion.

In his confession, Penkovsky explained that he was controlled only by SIS through Wynne. It was only then that Chistyakov realised that there was a connection. Through KGB officers in London, Chistyakov discovered that Wynne was expected at a trade fair in Budapest.

The trap was set on 2 November. In Moscow, Richard Jacob, a CIA officer, was told that a prearranged signal indicated that a message had been left in a dead drop by Penkovsky. Instead of a message, Jacob found the KGB and was arrested. That same day in Budapest, Wynne was entertaining Hungarian officials. Since Penkovsky's arrest was unknown to SIS, Wynne had received no warning against travelling to a communist country. At the end of the day, he was arrested and flown to Moscow.

To begin with, Wynne stoutly denied all knowledge of espionage. 'I'm a businessman,' he told Chistyakov. 'I know nothing about spying.' The KGB investigator's only evidence against Wynne was Penkovsky's own confession, so he arranged for Wynne and Penkovsky to pass each other under escort in a corridor. Wynne began confessing soon after. 'He only admitted what was obvious,' said Chistyakov. 'He tried to find out what we had against him before he spoke.'[61]

Wynne's disappearance sent a frisson through White. Helms shared the dismay: 'You feel an enormous sadness and frustration, but that comes with the turf in the espionage business.'[62] For days, the British embassy's demands to be informed of Wynne's fate were ignored. Only a threat of diplomatic reprisals produced an admission that he had been arrested. On a Sunday morning, Shergold summoned Cleveland Cram, the CIA liaison officer, to a safe house in St James's and passed on the news. The SIS officer's restrained tone reflected White's acceptance of Penkovsky's fate. Together with Norman Mott, another SIS officer, Cram would 'clean up' the aftermath.

The mood in Washington was, by contrast, one of anger. Bulik sent a message to White proposing that the Russians be offered Gordon Lonsdale in exchange for Penkovsky and Wynne. White refused. 'The British always deny involvement in espionage,' he replied. 'There was no reason for the Russians to release Penkovsky, a Russian national, just as we would not release Blake.' Moreover, in the House of Commons, a junior Foreign Office minister had said of Wynne, 'So far as I know, he had no connection with British intelligence.'[63] White also rejected Maury's proposal that, to save Penkovsky, the CIA should threaten to publicise the information he had supplied. Negotiations for any release would have to await the end of the inevitable trial, allowing both sides to deny that their nationals were spies.

Upset that the CIA was prepared to let Penkovsky die and scathing about SIS's disregard for the Russian's life, Bulik produced another plan to save Penkovsky. The Soviets, he suggested, should be blackmailed: if they did not spare Penkovsky's life, the CIA would publish evidence of their own espionage activities. After Helms had vetoed that proposal, Jim Angleton passed the message to London, where it was also rejected. 'There was no gratitude,' complained Bulik. 'He was expendable. An abandoned hero. Nobody had the courage to take the risk to gain the life of a man.' SIS's attitude towards Penkovsky was spotted by Chistyakov: 'MI6 wanted him to work as long as possible. They didn't want to bring him out. Their pressure on Penkovsky for more information gave us the evidence.'[64]

At the public trial, Wynne was sentenced to eight years' imprisonment and Penkovsky to death. Penkovsky was shot at 4.30 p.m. on 16 May 1963. 'We never found out everything,' laments Chistyakov, 'especially about the sessions in London and Paris. Our investigation was poor.'[65] Throughout the military and GRU there was a purge of all those who had been in contact with Penkovsky. The chief of GRU, General Ivan Serov, Penkovsky's mentor, was demoted and then dismissed.

White was content. Universally, there were plaudits for SIS's success. The remaining issue was critical: a post-mortem to discover how Penkovsky had been exposed. It proved fruitless. Both SIS and the CIA ruled out the possibility that Penkovsky's meetings with Janet Chisholm had been seen by the KGB,[66] and no leaks could be traced in either London or Washington. Most pertinently, at his last meetings in Moscow with a CIA and an SIS officer, Penkovsky himself had never suggested that he was under suspicion. Shergold concluded, 'We have no knowledge of the cause of Penkovsky's arrest.' Photographs later released by the KGB and supposedly showing Penkovsky and Janet Chisholm separately entering the apartment block in Moscow were in fact reconstructions for the training of intelligence officers. 'Our officers never saw those meetings,' confirmed Chistyakov.[67]*

In the aftermath, White supported the suggestion of exploiting Penkovsky's life for propaganda. But after the first draft chapter of a book written in London was rejected by the CIA as lacking credibility, White lost interest until shortly after Wynne returned to Britain in April 1964. The businessman had been exchanged for Gordon Lonsdale, the KGB illegal.

Gaunt and distressed, Wynne stoutly maintained in public that he was an innocent businessman tyrannised and tortured by the KGB. In private, he was dissatisfied by SIS's treatment. Probably his vanity was impossible to satisfy, but few efforts were made. When he discovered that the CIA had ghosted a book, *The Penkovsky Papers*, for publication after his release, he insisted on writing a short foreword publicly admitting his connection with Penkovsky.

White was furious. Wynne had become an embarrassment, brazenly complaining that his business was ruined and that SIS was equivocating about compensation. White was flummoxed. SIS did not have the legal power, he said ingeniously, to grant Wynne the amount he required. Not surprisingly, Wynne was incredulous. 'Dickie Franks tried to reason with him,' according to White, 'but Wynne wouldn't see reason.' The $213,700 resettlement expenses he was paid by the CIA were, Wynne claimed, insufficient.

Dissatisfied, Wynne wrote *The Man from Moscow*, a colourfully embroidered and substantially fictitious account of his life which became a bestseller. Given the solemn ministerial denials in parliament that Wynne was a spy, White was embarrassed. 'It was a pity that Wynne was used,' he admitted.[68] But at Penkovsky's endgame there was another agenda which influenced White's attitude.

---

* The photograph of Penkovsky shows him wearing a fur hat, but it was clearly established by the CIA investigation that Penkovsky never wore hats even in the coldest weather [TB/Peyton]. That the photographs were reconstructions was confirmed to the author by General Nikolai Chistyakov, the head of the KGB's special investigations department, and by General Oleg Gribanov.

The SIS success with Penkovsky was offset by White's suspicions that the Russian might have been, towards the end, a double-agent. That misgiving had been expunged, but White had become convinced that another undiscovered tumour existed within the intelligence service. Until that possibility was resolved, White knew, his relationships with Whitehall and more importantly with Washington would be troubled.

CHAPTER ELEVEN

Scandal

Among the handful of White's colleagues who could discern his normally well-concealed moments of passion was Arthur Martin, the ambitious and diligent MI5 officer who had patiently sifted the evidence in 1951 to identify Donald Maclean as a Soviet spy. In the dismal decade since that fiasco, Martin had not discussed with White the threads of their inconclusive investigations, which had been terminated in 1954.

The MI5 officer knew that the former director general's professional success owed much to a pragmatic acceptance that his masters were disinclined to disturb Britons' confidence in their rulers' patriotism. The qualities which made White attractive to Whitehall, as a conciliator and not a fighter, precluded emotional quests for 'Karla' or 'Bill Hayden' – the KGB chief and SIS's arch-traitor immortalised by John le Carré. Whenever the temptation arose to reopen the Philby file, White's political instincts resisted his professional and moral ambitions.

White's masters had no appetite for reopening old wounds, for investigating youthful transgressions of more than twenty years earlier. Simply filling in the gaps for history was worse than pointless, it was damaging. Pragmatism warned that, even if the evidence against Philby and the others were sufficient for a criminal prosecution and conviction, White should drop the case. Not surprisingly, the government became agitated in 1959 on hearing that Guy Burgess was considering returning to Britain. Since there was no evidence to secure his criminal conviction, MI5 was understandably nervous. To forestall embarrassment, rumours were circulated that the police had been directed to apply for an arrest warrant, but the government's charade was not tested thanks to the KGB's refusal to allow Burgess to depart.

Accordingly, Martin would hesitate even to refer to those cases lest it evoke White's impatience of past failures. But that altered in autumn 1962 when in conversation with his former chief Martin unexpectedly noticed excitement in his eyes. Summoned to Broadway, Martin was joined in a task which White considered pivotal to the lifeblood of Britain's intelligence service: namely, an answer to one question – was Philby a traitor?

Although it is hard to understand forty years later, the British public in that era was still unaware of the turmoil generated among a handful of Whitehall officials by the disappearance of Burgess and Maclean, and it was no less unaware of the allegations against Philby. Rebuffed by the impenetrable secrecy of SIS's affairs, even those who regarded themselves as well informed remained oblivious to Philby's seniority in the service and of the scale of treason committed by their respected and influential fellow countrymen. After the White Paper in 1955, there had been neither a reason nor an opportunity to reopen the case. On the contrary, White's political masters were inclined to seal the question for ever. Unforeseen circumstances forced their hand.

On 22 December 1961, Anatoli Golitsin, a KGB officer serving in the First Directorate involved in operations against Britain and America, had defected to the CIA in Helsinki, an event of considerable importance not least because it predated Penkovsky's appearance. Over the following weeks, Golitsin revealed the identities of several KGB informants employed by Western intelligence agencies.

In the spring of 1962, Arthur Martin and Terence Lecky, the head of R5, SIS's counter-intelligence section, were allowed to meet Golitsin. In his conversation with the two Britons, Golitsin spoke vaguely of a 'Ring of Five' spies having operated in Britain, but notably he did *not* mention Philby or the codename Stanley, nor did he show more than passing awareness of the 1951 saga.* Nevertheless, it was a decisive breakthrough for White. For the

---

* Several CIA, MI5 and SIS officers who have read the case notes insist that Golitsin supplied no confirmation about Philby – the suggestion that he did so is an invention by Peter Wright.

first time, after ten years, his suspicions about a Ring of Five were confirmed from a Russian source. Although many years later White would modestly describe Golitsin's information as 'important', at the time he was mesmerised. Indeed, the Russian's news caused a prolonged earthquake within British intelligence for the next sixteen years. At the centre of that turbulence stood White, wrestling to control the consequences of his initial quest to extract a confession from the traitor.

In 1962, Philby was living in Beirut. Ever since Macmillan had publicly exonerated the SIS officer seven years earlier, a faithful group of former colleagues had offered their friendship and financial assistance. Leading that band were Dick Brooman-White and Nicholas Elliott, who would explain that his involvement sprang from his deep affection for Aileen, Philby's wife, and from Macmillan's unequivocal statement. Brooman-White, a former SIS officer who was a member of parliament, had been a contemporary of Philby's at Cambridge but apparently had not noticed his friend's communist activities. In August 1956, the two SIS officers had prevailed upon the editors of the *Observer* and the *Economist* to retain Philby as a journalist in Beirut and had secured Sinclair's agreement that he would be paid a small retainer by SIS for reports about the region.

Aged forty-four, Philby had initially lived with his father in a small village twenty miles from Beirut. Adopting a relatively quiet routine, he travelled to Beirut to collect mail, to cable stories to newspapers in London, and to drink at the bar of either the famous St George's Hotel or the cheaper Normandy. In that small Anglo-American community, he had resumed a friendship with Sam Pope Brewer, the American correspondent of the *New York Times*, and in particular with his wife Eleanor. Philby's intimate charm ensnared the trusting Eleanor, who in 1959 became his third wife. They lived on the rue Kantari.

On becoming SIS chief in 1956, White had shown no emotion about Philby's resumed relationship with the agency. His retainer continued to be paid although Paul Paulson, the Beirut station chief, who barely met him. That changed in March 1960 when Paulson was replaced by Nicholas Elliott as the senior SIS representative. Elliott owed his survival as an intelligence officer to a mixture of Establishment background, charm, experience and some successes. Known to White since 1940, he was recognised as one of SIS's robber barons, serving SIS since 1938 in Cairo, Istanbul, Berne, Vienna and London.

White was irritated that Elliott should number himself among Philby's staunchest supporters. In 1951, believing his friend to be innocent and made despondent by Philby's apparent resignation in the face of MI5's accusations, Elliott had exclaimed during an intimate dinner: 'You must fight like hell. If it was me, I'd get my father to personally protest my innocence to the prime minister.'[1] Philby, Elliott would recount nonplussed, just smiled wanly. White's instruction to Elliott just before his departure to Beirut was to 'keep an eye on Philby,' but Elliott was not ordered 'to check whether Philby was in contact with the KGB'.[2] There was no 'plot' to feed Philby false information and follow its passage to Moscow. He was under no pressure other than to respond to Elliott's overt and innocent friendship.[3]

On his first day in Beirut, Elliott had taken his wife Elizabeth to taste the famed French and Lebanese cuisine at the Hotel Lucullus. To his surprise, at a nearby table sat Philby with his father and new wife. 'He came across and gave me a hug,' recalled Elliott. 'It was a most agreeable reunion.'[4] On his own admission, Elliott was ignorant of Arab politics and sought Philby's tuition. In return, under Elliott's tutelage, Philby began travelling widely throughout the Middle East, writing articles for his London newspapers and also submitting reports to SIS about political developments in most Arab states. 'Philby was useful as a source on Arab politics,' Elliott would tell colleagues.

Not all in Broadway were impressed with Philby. John Christie, an Arabist, reading Philby's reports in the Middle East Requirements section condemned the information as worthless. 'You could have read it all in *The Economist* last week,' he told George Young, alluding to Philby's employment with the journal. 'He's got a lot of it wrong as well. It's invented. He's taking us to the cleaners.' Young was unmoved: 'I'm Vice. Circulate it.'

White seemed unmoved by reports that Elliott was socialising more and more with Philby, meeting him regularly at parties for British diplomats and journalists. The SIS officer even hosted a lunch to introduce Humphrey Trevelyan, the British diplomat, to St John Philby, Kim's father. On 29 September 1960, the two Philbys, father and son, sat until 5 p.m. drinking and reminiscing about Arabia with the SIS chief of station and the Foreign Office's senior Arab specialist. The following afternoon, St John died of a heart attack.

Unsuspected by Elliott, Philby was in contact with Petrukov, a low-ranking KGB officer in Beirut. During their occasional meetings, Philby passed on information which had inevitably leaked during his social banter with Elliott and Miles Copeland, a CIA officer, about their attitudes and activities in the region.[5] 'Philby was friendly with all the Yanks in Beirut,' recalled George Young. 'A lot of them babbled. He was pretty good at getting them to talk.'[6] In October 1962, Elliott returned to London as temporary director for Africa. He could not recall White asking about Philby throughout that period, even in the aftermath of George Blake's entrapment.

Elliott's replacement was Peter Lunn. It was in the nature of relationships among some SIS officers in those days that Lunn's father had introduced Elliott's father to his future wife in the Pyrenees, and that Elliott's own wife was a cousin of Lunn's wife. Before leaving London, Lunn had consulted Terence Lecky, the head of R5. Lecky had assured Lunn: 'Philby is not a spy.' Lunn had also consulted White. 'Of course, he's a traitor,' said White. 'Just keep a eye on him. Let's wait and see what happens.' Lunn departed convinced that White did not harbour any strategy towards Philby. The circumstances altered just after he arrived in Beirut.

Flora Solomon, a one-time friend of Philby's, had just complained to Victor Rothschild that the *Observer* was using a known communist as their reporter. Ever since his wartime service with MI5, the brilliant scientist and member of the banking family had maintained an unusual interest in Britain's intelligence affairs, not least because of his friendship with White. Through Rothschild, Solomon met Arthur Martin and recounted to him how, in 1937, Philby had urged her to join him and 'work for peace'. She had understood that, while Philby was pretending in public to be pro-Nazi, he was employed as an active communist agent. 'I wish I'd come earlier,' Solomon told Martin.

White was fired by Solomon's disclosure: 'Why didn't she tell us ten years ago?' In strictly legal terms, as evidence in a criminal prosecution, Solomon's information was worthless, but from the SIS file which would subsequently be read by a succession of counter-intelligence officers and by SIS's liaison officers in Washington, it is clear that Solomon's information stimulated Roger Hollis, Martin and White into agreeing that there was new hope of confronting Philby. But where, when and how? Any initiative by SIS needed the prime minister's approval. Macmillan, White realised, was more than ever anxious to avoid further espionage scandals. The politicians were losing their balance over the issue. Recently Hollis had unexpectedly suffered the prime minister's fury when he had proudly reported the arrest of William John Vassall, an executive officer in the Admiralty, identified as a spy by Golitsin.

While posted to Moscow, Vassall, a homosexual, had been compromised in an operation masterminded by General Oleg Gribanov, who specialised in sexual honeytraps on Western diplomats. Vassall's arrest in September 1962, after eight years' successful espionage, was particularly embarrassing to the government. His pronounced homosexuality and ostentatious standard of living proved that positive vetting had failed and that security was still lax. His arrest had been reported in sensational headlines. 'I'm not at all pleased,' Macmillan said, glaring at Hollis. 'When my gamekeeper shoots a fox, he doesn't go and hang it up outside the Master of the Foxhounds' drawing room; he buries it out of sight. But you just can't shoot a spy as you did in the war. You have to try him . . . Better to discover him, and then control him, but never catch him . . .'[7]

Vassall's conviction had provoked renewed derision against the government. Satirists in BBC Television's *That Was The Week That Was* and in the Cambridge Footlights' *Beyond the Fringe* were exploiting the espionage scandals as fodder for hilarious indictments of Supermac's regime. Sensitive about the Conservatives' unpopularity, Macmillan increasingly emphasised to White during their regular conversations, 'Keep a lid on things.'[8] If he were to approach him about Philby, White knew that the politician would not tolerate any publicity. There was 'no possibility of sending Philby to prison. Getting a confession was the only course rather than punishing the man.'[9]

In considering how to create an opportunity to question Philby, White contemplated awaiting his return to Britain for one of his occasional discussions with his two newspapers. To accelerate matters, he could arrange for one of the papers to cable Philby to return for consultations. Fearing the repercussions of failure in London, White ruled out that idea. Philby, he reasoned, would feel more threatened in London and hence less likely to confess. In any case, the security services lacked an adequate interrogator and Philby would, in the aftermath, reveal to friends the services' latest humiliation.

White also ruled out any suggestion of arresting and abducting Philby to London. First, SIS did not have the resources in Lebanon to mount such an operation; secondly, the Lebanese government would be offended, endangering the Foreign Office's and SIS's only secure base in the Middle East; and, thirdly, even if Philby were brought to London, the insufficient evidence would preclude a trial and magnify the embarrassment. Assassination was never seriously considered. Having decided upon a confrontation in Beirut, White presented his plan to Macmillan, afraid that any delay risked a leak of his intentions reaching Philby.

'We cannot ignore the new information,' White told the prime minister. 'We would be criticised by the Americans if we took no action. We need to discover what damage he caused.' White confirmed that the evidence against Philby was insufficient for a prosecution but the concealment of his past could be proven. 'You've got to look at the time,' continued White. 'Although it happened over ten years ago, there is an intelligence interest to tie up all the loose ends. A full damage report with all the details of how the Russians had operated and who else was working with Philby is of great importance.'[10] White suggested that Philby should be treated as a gentleman and be offered immunity in return for a full confession and total co-operation. By the end of their conversation, Macmillan warmed to that hitherto untested notion. The plan was approved by Sir Reginald Manningham-Buller, the attorney general, and by Sir Harold Caccia, the Foreign Office's permanent under secretary. White agreed with Hollis that Arthur Martin should fly to Beirut as soon as possible. News of that decision reached Elliott.

For Philby's friend, this new proof of treachery came as a shock. He approached White and suggested that there was more chance that Philby could be persuaded to confess by an outraged sympathiser than by a stiff, lower-middle-class MI5 officer. White saw considerable merit in the proposal. Sending Elliott to denounce Philby would be more convincing than sending anyone else. After all, Elliott had been 'Philby's greatest supporter in 1951 and his anger would suggest we had more proof than he realised'.

'I can't force you, but I'd be very grateful if you went,' said White. That decision would be criticised in Broadway's corridors and in the basement bar as a sign of White's weakness. Even Elliott fuelled that reproach: 'Dick wanted a quiet life. He wasn't a buccaneer, out to expose Philby. By then he had given up the hunt for Philby. There was no long-term pursuit. He was more interested in protesting his reputation than bringing the house down.'[11] White contradicted that criticism: 'We had no other card to play.'[12]

One trick was played upon Elliott. In his briefing, White told the Old Etonian that there was a KGB source who had also betrayed Philby. Elliott would always believe that 'we'd fully penetrated the KGB, so we had confirmation'. That was untrue, as all SIS and MI5 officers who have seen the Philby file have confirmed. There was no KGB source, but the suggestion enhanced Elliott's conviction of his friend's treachery.

The arrangements in Beirut were delegated to Lunn. Since their first meeting in Lunn's flat in October, the SIS officer had barely seen Philby. He could recall only that on that occasion Philby's hand had shaken as he grasped the proffered drink. At the end of their inconsequential chat, Philby had stressed that when they met later that night at Miles Copeland's house they should pretend not to know each other. Lunn was puzzled by this pretence of security.

On instructions from White, Lunn telephoned Philby and in a casual voice suggested they should meet at an apartment owned by an embassy secretary in the Christian quarter near the beach. Lunn gave no hint that their meeting would be other than a conversation about future plans which was best conducted in private. A local SIS technician installed a microphone in the flat near where Philby would sit. The hidden cable ran to a neighbouring room where the conversation would be recorded. 'The technology was very dicey in those days,' Lunn would complain. Elliott flew to Beirut on 11 January 1963. The meeting would take place the following day.

Some SIS officers would see a piquancy in the scenario. Peter Lunn, a pious Catholic, and Nicholas Elliott, a lapsed Anglican, both waiting to extract a confession from a non-believer in a Christian–Moslem sanctuary.

At 4 p.m. Philby arrived at the flat. Elliott opened the door. Philby's first, innocuous comment would fuel the ferocious molehunt within MI5 for the next decade: 'I rather thought it would be you.' In later years Philby's absence of surprise at seeing Elliott rather than Lunn would be construed as suggesting that he had been alerted to the interrogation by a KGB mole inside MI5. Philby himself would deny, twenty-five years later in Moscow, that there was a tip-off. 'There was no need for one. The truth is that I had been preparing for twelve years for this . . . I knew exactly how to handle it.'[13] The truth, not surprisingly, was different. Philby's behaviour proved the success of White's tactics.

That first exchange between Philby and Elliott, overheard on headphones by Lunn, was strained, as might be expected when a relationship between old friends becomes a confrontation. Elliott's first question concerned the bandages around Philby's head. The cause, explained Philby, was a drunken fall on New Year's Eve, against the radiator in the bathroom. He had been celebrating his birthday. Since then he had not drunk any alcohol.

Elliott's explanation for his unexpected presence in Lebanon was precise. 'We have new information that you were indeed working with the Soviet intelligence service.'

Philby exploded: 'Do you want me to go into all this again?

How much more often do we have to go over that rubbish?'

Elliott remained impassive. 'But, Kim, the game's up. we know what you did.' Elliott hinted that there were new sources of information. 'We've penetrated the KGB, Kim,' said Elliott. 'There's no doubt in my mind any more that you were a KGB agent.'

Given the conviction of George Blake and the well-publicised defection of Golitsin, Philby suspected that his erstwhile stoutest defender within SIS could be telling the truth.[14]

'You had to choose between Marxism and your family,' continued Elliott, 'and you chose Marxism. I once looked up to you. My God, how I despise you now. I hope you've got enough decency left to understand why.'[15] Philby remained impassive. Elliott restored the equilibrium. 'I'm sure that we can now work something out.'

Elliott then delivered a threat. Philby's continued happy existence in Lebanon or anywhere in the West would be destroyed by SIS and its allies if he did not confess. Not renewing his passport would be just the tip of the iceberg. Residence permits would be denied, banks would refuse his account and his employment by London newspapers would be terminated. Without any source of income and no hope of residence anywhere in the West, his life would be rendered intolerable.

Philby rose and made his way to the door. In the hallway, Elliott spoke. 'I'm offering you a lifeline, Kim.' Philby's hand was on the door-handle. 'If you co-operate, we will give you immunity from prosecution. Nothing will be published.' By now the exchange was beyond the microphone's range and the door was open, flooding the flat with street noise. 'You've been a lucky chap so far, Kim. You have exactly twenty-four hours. Be back here at precisely 4 p.m. tomorrow. If you're as intelligent as I think you are, you'll accept.' Philby, continued Elliott, should return to London for debriefing and there would be no consequences. Alternatively, they could conduct the debriefing in Beirut. But immunity depended upon MI5's satisfaction that Philby had co-operated fully and revealed everything. The traitor walked out. Their meeting had lasted just five minutes.

After Philby's departure, Lunn emerged. 'Kim's broken,' said

Elliott. 'Everything's okay.' Privately, neither man was convinced. 'The next twenty-four hours were a testing time,' admitted Elliott.

At 4 p.m. the following day, Philby reappeared at the flat. Little emotion accompanied his deadpan greeting: 'Okay, here's the scoop, as it were, but first you owe me a drink. I haven't had one for ages.' Elliott opened the secretary's cupboard and poured a large brandy. 'I was recruited by Litzi,' Philby began, referring to his first Austrian-born wife, and then boasted, 'I recruited Maclean and Burgess.' Philby handed over two typewritten pages describing his early contacts with the NKVD.

'Is Nedosekin your contact?' asked Elliott, referring to the local KGB station chief.

'I've got no bloody contact,' blazed Philby. 'I broke contact with the KGB in 1949 when the Attlee government made their majority reforms and disproved Marxism.'

Elliott listened to Philby for two hours. He believed that his old friend was uttering 'a limited confession' to mitigate his sins. For his part, Philby did not ask about Elliott's new evidence because it was obvious that there would be no reply. Similarly, he volunteered no names of those whom he had recruited. Elliott, proffered a list of about twelve names, but Philby's replies were either denials or inconclusive. At 6 p.m. they agreed that the debriefing would be a long affair and that Philby would produce more written material. Before parting, Philby invited Elliott for dinner that night. His failure to come, urged Philby, would alarm Eleanor. Elliott agreed: 'I'll come after I've sent my report to Dick from the embassy.'

Understandably, Elliott's elation was shared by White. Philby's confession, albeit limited, confirmed that he had been taken by surprise and suggested that he was no longer in contact with the KGB. After all, if he had consulted the Soviets in the intervening twenty-four hours, the KGB would have ordered him to break all contact with Elliott and certainly would have forestalled a confession. Philby, White believed, had abandoned his long-rehearsed denials of treachery and was finally broken. Elliott was told to continue the debriefing.

That same evening, Elliott arrived at the Philbys' to discover his host lying comatose on the floor. In the intervening three hours, he had consumed more than a bottle of whisky. Together with Eleanor, Elliott carried the body to the bedroom and spent the remainder of the night talking with his unsuspecting wife. The following morning, the two men agreed to meet at a restaurant managed by the Belgian mistress of the British consul. There was no reason why the two old friends should not meet openly. Philby arrived with Eleanor and another woman. The conversation was warm and general, reflecting 'a social not a clandestine relationship'. When the men retired to the lavatory, Philby handed over another two typewritten pages. No names were mentioned. There was a fourth meeting the following day, during which Philby did mention names, including Tim Milne, a schoolfriend and best man at his wedding to Aileen. Milne was at that moment an SIS officer in the Far East.[16]

The stream of telegrams between Elliott and White had not mentioned any instruction to bring Philby back to London. Instead, further contact, cabled White, would be through Peter Lunn. The following day Elliott returned to London. White was effusive in his gratitude. There was no sense of urgency. White's reaction to negotiating with Philby in Beirut seemed to him at the time logical: 'He could have rejected the offer of immunity. Then I would imagine he would skip the country. But since he has accepted, he'll stay and co-operate.'

Instead of asking Elliott to remain in Beirut, reinforced by other SIS officers to cosset Philby as the debriefing progressed, White listened to Elliott's speculation in his Broadway office that Philby would never leave Beirut. Elliott added that, although Philby was attached to his wife, 'he might I suppose commit suicide'. At that moment of success, White's assessment was based upon one fundamental misconception about the KGB to which he continued to hold for the remainder of his life. In 1951, White believed, Soviet intelligence wielded only 'a limited measure of control [over Philby et al.] which left them watching helplessly while all the golden rules were broken'. He had persuaded himself that the Ring of Five were 'a bunch of interconnected amateurs' who presented the NKVD with 'a kind of intelligence nightmare'.[17]

Eleven years later, White accepted Philby's assurance that

he was not in contact with the KGB and therefore ignored the possibility that Philby might flee from the Lebanon after his confrontation with Elliott. 'White didn't even think about that,' said Lunn. 'It didn't dawn on us,' confirms Elliott. White admitted his mistake: 'It didn't arise. I thought Philby would come back for a final session.'[18] But just as he had not recognised Blunt's homosexuality during the war and had not anticipated that Donald Maclean might flee Britain in 1951, White once again did not anticipate Philby's reaction after digesting the consequences of his confession.

Having agreed that Lunn would continue the debriefing on the basis of questions sent from London, Elliott flew to the Congo. White showed no sense of urgency or alarm. No instructions were dispatched to Lunn to maintain any surveillance. In Beirut, Philby considered his plight. White's threat to destroy his life in the West could be easily implemented. He would lose his income not only from newspapers but from SIS. Destitution would be inevitable. He did not relish the prospect of working with Lunn, an unsympathetic man in his opinion.[19] Moreover, if he returned to Britain, there was no guarantee that he would not be treated like Blake, who after all had also confessed, perhaps after an offer of immunity from White. Even if White were honourable, his co-operation would eventually leak out and he would be condemned by history as a defector rather than a master spy.*

It was at that point, after Elliott's departure, that Philby contacted Petukov, his KGB control. He did not reveal his confession but did report that he was to be re-examined. The flash message to Moscow was passed to Vassili Dozhdalev, the KGB's British expert who had handled Lonsdale in London. Dozhdalev's only question to Philby was whether he could again resist an interrogation. The following day's reply from Beirut was negative: 'Philby does not think he can escape

---

* Philby, in Borovik's account (p. 342ff.) naturally conceals his confession and suggests that Elliott's arrival alone terrified him and the KGB into abandoning his success in concealing his crimes over the previous twelve years.

again.'[20] Moscow Centre's criterion was damage limitation. Extracting Philby from the Lebanon would snatch victory from defeat.

The KGB's arrangements for Philby's flight had been prepared by Dozhdalev long before Elliott arrived in Beirut. False papers, describing Philby as a seaman, were drawn from a safe. Philby was given a set of seaman's clothes and the captain of the *Dolmatova*, a Russian freighter moored in Beirut harbour, was ordered to prepare for a speedy departure. In London, Lecky was still preparing the questions which Lunn would ask Philby. Among the handicaps was a disappointing transcript of Elliott's conversation in the flat. The microphone had recorded excessive noise from the road outside, drowning some of Philby's comments. At the last moment, Hollis summoned Charles Bates, the FBI liaison officer in London. After revealing the confession and the proposed procedure, Hollis asked: 'Are there any questions the FBI would like Philby to answer?' Working through the night, Bates produced a list.

On the afternoon of Wednesday, 23 January, Philby told his wife that he was meeting a contact. He would return at 6 p.m. to change for a dinner party with Glen Balfour-Paul, a first secretary at the British embassy, itself an indication of the Foreign Office's attitude towards the traitor. Instead of returning at that time, Philby telephoned, saying that he was delayed and would meet Eleanor at Balfour-Paul's home. Coincidentally, forty minutes later, Lunn telephoned Philby. The questions had finally arrived in the regular weekly pouch from London. 'Kim's on his way to a dinner,' said Eleanor.

'Could you ask him to meet me tomorrow at the embassy?' Unsuspecting, Lunn kept a rendezvous with an agent but left a contact telephone number at home. At about midnight, Lunn's wife telephoned. 'I'm busy,' said Lunn.

'Not half as busy as you're going to be now. Eleanor has just telephoned. Kim is missing.' Lunn sped to Philby's home.

Eleanor Philby asked the SIS officer for help to find her husband. 'Call the consul in the morning,' replied Lunn, whose next call, at 2 a.m., was to the British ambassador.

During the night, Lunn wrote a long message describing all

the circumstances. At 7 a.m. he roused the female cipher clerk. 'I haven't got any make-up on,' she protested.

'Where you're going, no one will see you,' laughed Lunn.

The twenty-six-paragraph cable arrived in London as White crossed the bridge into Broadway Buildings. His reaction that morning was 'horror'. Once again he feared that he had miscalculated. In a succession of 'Decipher Yourself' 'Most Important' messages, Lunn was ordered to dispatch a search party to the home of a known mistress and to ask the Lebanese security service to check the lists of departures from the country. By lunchtime, Lunn reported that the Lebanese had found no record of Philby's departure. The unexpected sailing of the *Dolmatova* had not yet been noticed.

The overriding conviction at SIS headquarters was that Philby was hiding with a known mistress. Lunn was directed to return to the woman and search her bedroom. After his search proved unproductive, he returned to Eleanor to be shown a small safe belonging to Philby. Later that day, a British expert surreptitiously opened the lock. Among the contents were some dollar notes. Their serial numbers matched those issued recently to a Russian diplomat at a local Beirut bank. No sooner had Philby's connection to the KGB at last been established than Lunn reported the suspicious movements of the *Dolmatova*.

White dispatched a message to Elliott. The coded summons was delivered as Elliott was about to cross the Congo river. He was to fly to Beirut immediately to counsel Eleanor, by then 'hysterical'. Flying via Lagos and Rome, Elliott finally reached Philby's home. A reassuring telegram, signed by Philby, had arrived from Cairo, but an investigation revealed that there was no record of Philby's presence in Egypt.[21] Ominously, Elliott had been preceded by a KGB officer, who had sought to persuade the hapless wife to fly immediately to Moscow. 'At least I won that battle,' Elliott told White. Eleanor was escorted on to a BOAC flight to London.

Elliott was greeted at Heathrow by banner headlines reporting Philby's disappearance and an alleged hunt for Eleanor. White was infuriated by his sheer inability to do anything. Elliott sought to persuade Eleanor, upset and disoriented by unfamiliar surroundings, to remain in the West: 'They probably won't let you out, if you go to Moscow.' Sensing that he had failed to persuade his guest of her husband's duplicity, Elliott telephoned White for assistance. Within an hour White was courteously but insistently telling the incredulous woman, 'We have definitely known for the last seven years that Kim has been working for the Russians without pay.'[22] Later in Broadway, White confessed to Elliott, 'What a shame we reopened it all. Just trouble.'[23]

'I never thought he would accept the offer of immunity and then skip the country,' White shortly afterwards told Lunn. By then, he was furious about the mistake he had made. The slump in morale, although loyally disguised from outsiders, was palpable. Conspiracy theories abounded that White had deliberately intended that Philby should flee to Moscow rather than be brought to London for an embarrassing trial. Few wanted to believe that it was not a conspiracy but a cock-up. The few disenchanted with his management spoke of 'deteriorating morale'. Fergie Dempster would tell colleagues that he had actually accused White of 'demoralisation'. But, as a consummate Whitehall politician, White was displaying professional non-chalance in order to protect himself from criticism. Lunn emerged from White's office to report that the chief did not seem to be 'disappointed' by Philby's departure.

That was not the impression which White gave when, once again, he undertook the pilgrimage across the Atlantic to deliver a damage report. Pre-warned by Maurice Oldfield, the SIS liaison officer, of the fury among both CIA and FBI officers, especially Hoover, White resolved to adopt a bland but deliberate pose. Once again, McCone was polite, but Dick Helms dropped his customary restraint. Referring to Blake and Vassall, Helms snapped, 'You've mishandled the operation and allowed Philby to fly the coop.'[24] White remained silent. He knew that in the previous three years Carlton Swift, the CIA's deputy liaison officer in London, had twice delivered a formal complaint from Washington to Hollis demanding that Philby be subjected to a polygraph test. Each time, Hollis had replied, 'We don't do that sort of thing.'

'Why', Helms asked White, 'was the Agency not told about the proposed confrontation in Beirut?' Momentarily, White sensed that his prized relationship with the CIA was endangered. But on reflection Helms reasoned that espionage was a high-risk business and the fundamentals could not be allowed to suffer because of one mistake. It was another 'blip and squeeze'. The relationship, bolstered by the high reputation of British politicians and diplomats in Washington, would not be jeopardised. Philby's disappearance was of small importance compared to the agency's difficulties in Germany, Israel, Vietnam, Cuba and elsewhere.

By then, the British government's ability to resist making a public statement was crumbling in the face of feverish newspaper speculation. On his return to London, White met Edward Heath and accepted that there was no alternative: Philby's disappearance had to be acknowledged in parliament. His only consolation was that the admission would be limited. Heath's statement on 29 March confirmed only that Philby was missing. But, in Washington, Angleton, outraged that he had not been told about Flora Solomon's information or consulted about the Beirut confrontation, and embarrassed by his own unsuspecting relationship with Philby, joined with others to leak the truth. 'I tried to repair the damage caused by Dick's mistake,' recounted Elliott, 'by telephoning Jim Angleton, but it was too late.'[25] In truth, Elliott knew that he was more to blame than White. The chief had properly relied upon his judgment about Philby's intentions, but it was White who bore the criticism.

On 1 July, Heath was forced by disclosures in the American press to concede that Philby was the Third Man but added a disclaimer: 'Since Mr Philby resigned from the Foreign Service in 1951, twelve years ago, he has had no access of any kind to any official information.'[26] On 30 July, the Supreme Soviet granted Philby political asylum and citizenship. 'Ted Heath was very helpful,' White told an aide. 'It could have been worse.'

White's embarrassment was limited. Despite the headlines, few people, even in Whitehall and Westminster, still understood how senior Philby had been. SIS's existence was still denied and its activities barely understood beyond a small handful of loyal Britons. Harold Wilson's threat to embarrass the government over the affair was defused when Macmillan invited the Leader of the

Opposition to Downing Street and introduced White, who offered a full briefing. Wilson arrived convinced of a 'manifest failure of the Secret Service to keep Philby under control'.[27] He emerged confident that there had been no such failure and ordered his supporters to 'let it go'. In the Cabinet Room, White had given Wilson 'one simple fact [which] made sense of the story'. Although not revealed at the time, he had disclosed the confession and had claimed that obtaining it had been a great success considering there was no *prima facie* evidence against Philby.

Wilson was not, however, told that among the legacies of Philby's recent employment by SIS was the possible blackmail of those Arabs recruited by Philby as sources for SIS, who had become vulnerable to KGB threats of exposure. Nor was Wilson told the historical background about Soviet penetration. White hoped that he had drawn a line beneath the saga.

As a final act of house-cleaning, a security check was conducted on those staff mentioned by Philby, particularly the Milne brothers, Tony and Tim. Tony Milne, the station chief in Argentina, was asked to explain his affair with Philby's first wife, Litzi Friedmann, the communist agent, in Vienna before the war. Subsequently, he would resign for failing to disclose the relationship. Tim Milne, Philby's old schoolfriend, was questioned but cleared.

Soon afterwards, Elliott brought White a letter from Philby suggesting a meeting in either Berlin or Helsinki 'to clear matters'. The chief's order was abrupt: 'Don't even answer it.' White wanted no more explanations or embarrassments. At the end, in an unusual move, White summoned senior staff to the fourth-floor conference room and gave a short background briefing. For some, the end was 'a relief'. Others were 'livid'.

Vassall, Lonsdale, Blake, Philby and several other minor espionage cases more than irritated Macmillan and neutralised any glory earned from Penkovsky. At that moment, a tribunal was investigating the Vassall case and, to Fleet Street's outrage, two journalists had been imprisoned for refusing to name their sources for a story about the spy's relationship with Thomas Galbraith, a junior Admiralty minister.

For White, as for Macmillan, it was a moment of crisis.

White's daily routine was probably more oppressive than that of his predecessors during the Second World War. Unlike in wartime, his enemies were insidious and unseen traitors. The intelligence services were the front-line soldiers in the Cold War but there was no discernible enemy bridgehead. 'All our sources of information', reflected White, 'depicted the KGB in vast and threatening terms but were difficult to assess and only rarely provided sure and certain guidance.'[28] Recalled White: 'We had lost our balance. The sixties we knew were a time of maximum alert to the possibility of penetration. We knew we were a key target.'[29]

The prime minister was beginning to harbour a sense of foreboding about the government's vulnerability on security. On 7 May, White visited him with Hollis and Burke Trend, the new cabinet secretary and loyal supporter of the intelligence services. Their first topic was easily disposed of. When the trial of Penkovsky and Wynne started in Moscow, the government would steadfastly claim that Wynne was an innocent businessman and the victim of Soviet injustice.[30] The second topic was more complicated. It concerned sensational newspaper stories about John Profumo, the forty-eight-year-old secretary of state for war, a former brigadier in the Household Cavalry who was married to Valerie Hobson, a well-known actress.

The rumours which had reached Macmillan in early February 1963 suggested that Profumo, at a weekend party on the Cliveden estate in July 1961, had become infatuated with another guest, Christine Keeler, a nineteen-year-old prostitute.[31] Their host was Stephen Ward, a society osteopath. Profumo's affair with Keeler had eventually become known to journalists and was passed to George Wigg, the Labour Party's security specialist. When finally challenged in the House of Commons on 21 March 1963, Profumo lied: 'There was no impropriety whatsoever in my acquaintanceship with Miss Keeler.' Publicly, Macmillan accepted Profumo's denial.

But, when Macmillan met Hollis on 7 May, he was astonished to hear his Security Service chief admit that he had known about Profumo's sexual relationship with Keeler five months earlier, following a personal interview with the minister on 28 January.

At the time Hollis had decided that the affair was not a threat to security, although seventeen months earlier, in August 1961, Profumo had been warned by MI5, through an intermediary, to be cautious about his presence at Cliveden and his friendship with Stephen Ward, a 'self-confessed intermediary with the Russians'.[32] Keeler had not been mentioned. In February 1963, after Profumo's conversation with Hollis, MI5 had told Macmillan's Private Office some details about the minister's admission of an 'innocent friendship' with Keeler. Although Hollis knew that there was more to it, he believed those details to be sufficient. On 7 May, he therefore repeated that MI5 had known of Profumo's indiscretion, but he added nothing more.

On 23 May, Hollis returned to Downing Street to reveal some unpleasant complications. Keeler, Macmillan was told, had admitted to an affair with Captain Yevgeny Ivanov, the former Soviet naval attaché in London and an intelligence officer. Hollis added that Keeler had been introduced to Ivanov by Stephen Ward. There was now a direct link between Profumo and a Soviet intelligence officer. But the MI5 director general assured Macmillan that Ward was not a Soviet agent. However, he did not reveal that MI5 had been using Ward to ensnare Ivanov in a honeytrap for future blackmail. To the prime minister, MI5's lapses seemed incredible.

Over the following days, Macmillan was struck by a premonition that the newspapers, already hinting at a sex scandal, might renew their attack on his government's failure to safeguard the nation's security. Since he regarded Hollis as mediocre, the politician summoned White. Like many Whitehall insiders, White knew that Macmillan had suffered years of anguish as his wife Dorothy enjoyed a long affair with Robert Boothby, a political colleague. Macmillan had even confided his anguish to White and now speculated whether those personal difficulties had caused him to ignore the consequences of Profumo's affair.

After complaining that he was ill-served by Hollis, who had failed to warn him of Profumo's infidelity and of the Soviet connection with Keeler, Macmillan pronounced his conviction that there was a Soviet plot against him. 'I am sure', the prime minister told White, 'that there is a conspiracy directed from

Moscow to drive me from office.'[33] Macmillan's anxieties had been strengthened by a staggering revelation from Hollis. The MI5 director had returned to Downing Street to state that Philby's flight to Moscow had coincided with growing suspicions within MI5 that the Security Service itself was penetrated by another Soviet spy at the highest level. An investigation, reported Hollis, had been started. For Macmillan, ever sceptical about the value of intelligence services and disenchanted with Hollis, this was the final straw. The premier asked White to search for the evidence of a conspiracy. Although White doubted the existence of a plot, he agreed that the large number of spy cases over the previous two years suggested that Soviet penetration of Britain was serious and not easily explicable. He did not reveal his suspicions that Dorothy had influenced her husband to consider the possibility of a Soviet plot.[34] He simply agreed to review the evidence.

On 4 June, Profumo confessed that he had lied to parliament and resigned. In the midst of an emotional and hysterical newspaper campaign damning the government's immorality and incompetence, Profumo's link with Ivanov emerged. Keeler alleged she had been asked by Ward to question Profumo – while they were in bed – about NATO's contingency plans for the use of nuclear weapons and about German rearmament. Clearly there was an unexplained relationship between Ward and Ivanov, especially since MI5 was using Ward to recruit Ivanov as a spy.

The extraordinary mess was complicated by Keeler's simultaneous relationship with Ivanov, the Soviet diplomat. The security implications could not be ignored. To Macmillan's fury, Hollis had not passed on that salient fact. He had proved to be incompetent. Summoned to Downing Street, White agreed that his colleague's omissions were 'surprising'.[35]

In that tense era, only shortly after the superpower confrontations over Berlin and Cuba, the possibility of nuclear war was a source of daily concern. More than others, White was aware that if, during a nuclear alert, a key British government minister or official was compromised by the Soviets, or was actually a Soviet spy, Britain's capability or response could be fatally crippled. The intelligence services' priority, in the midst of the war of ideologies, was to protect the nation from that insidious weakness; in Macmillan's opinion, the services were failing.

On 17 June in the House of Commons, Macmillan was ferociously attacked from his own back benches for his mismanagement of the Profumo affair. Unusually, the prime minister publicly blamed Hollis for failing to inform him of the security aspects of the Keeler–Profumo relationship. At 10 p.m., the government's vote fell substantially. Sitting afterwards in the members' smoking room, Macmillan was boycotted by his colleagues.[36]

Summoning White again, Macmillan urged his faithful servant to find evidence of Moscow's involvement. White resisted, believing that the premier was seeking a scapegoat for his decline: 'I told him plainly that the Russians had no assets to organise a plot involving Profumo.'[37] Assiduously, he applied balm: 'I spent most of my time calming politicians down, soothing them, telling them not to worry unduly.'[38]

White was nonetheless sensitive to his own responsibility for Macmillan's belief in serious, undetected communist penetration in Britain. Naturally, knowledge of these suspicions was restricted to a handful of insiders. After all, Whitehall's control over MI6 had barely increased since White became chief. Neither ministers nor the Foreign Office's permanent under secretary visited Broadway or Century House and, despite gossip in clubland and Westminster, few knew the details of White's management of the service. Because 'no one outside realised how great the problems were',[39] there was no overt pressure upon White for explanations or reform.

Wholehearted confidence in both MI5 and SIS depended, White knew, upon both services proving their purity beyond doubt. That certainty no longer existed. In February 1963, at the outset of the Profumo saga White had confided to Macmillan that he had sanctioned an investigation into Graham Mitchell, the deputy director general of MI5, as a suspected communist agent. If true, the plot was more serious than even Macmillan suspected.

CHAPTER TWELVE

Molehunt

White's inspiration in the hunt for more traitors inside British intelligence was James 'Jesus' Angleton, the Godfather of the Spycatchers. Since the war, Angleton had become a legendary head of counter-intelligence in the CIA. Renowned as a keen fisherman who crafted his own flies, an expert cultivator of orchids, a chain-smoker, a heavy drinker and an indefatigable intelligence officer, he provoked divided emotions within the CIA. For some he was intellectually brilliant, generous, humorous, dedicated and outstanding. Others considered him obsessed, paranoid and dangerous.

During the 1950s, Angleton had enjoyed Allen Dulles's patronage and, when the director died, his protégé had carried the urn from the chapel. In 1963, Angleton's diligence had been rewarded with awesome powers over a near unsupervised empire and unhindered access to Dick Helms and John McCone, the CIA's director. That authority attracted special respect, especially from British intelligence officers. For, unlike so many of his subordinates, whose admiration for SIS was strained by Britain's espionage scandals, Angleton remained an Anglophile. Around him in the counter-intelligence division he had gathered a group of loyalists, lauded as 'Intelligence Fundamentalists', who understood Angleton's sensitivity to his betrayal by Philby.

Until Philby's escape, Angleton would confidently brief selected CIA officers about his doubts whether the British officer was really a traitor, but would also whisper the opposite to others.[1] Shattered by Philby's flight, Angleton scrutinised the poor transcript of the incomplete confession like a rejected suitor searching for clues to explain his partner's adultery. In due course, he seized upon Philby's claim to have recruited Burgess and Maclean: since

Philby was styled the Third Man, he asserted that there were two more undiscovered British traitors.

There could be few men apparently less similar than White and Angleton. Unlike Angleton, White was not racked by ulcers, did not torment his wife or suffer nerves. Yet both men shared a common history in counter-intelligence: the wartime double-cross operations and Philby; and both were intrigued by the complexity of their art. White had long been seduced by the notion of a Ring of Five and, considering the rash of exposed Soviet spies in the previous two years, it would have been imprudent of SIS's chief not to have taken Angleton's analysis very seriously. Although in later years White suggested that he had disagreed with Angleton's belief in KGB omnipotence and had urged, 'Keep calm, we can beat the Russians,' the contemporary evidence went the other way.[2] In 1963, White succumbed to Angleton's certainty that British intelligence was penetrated and partially endorsed the American's vision of a deception conspiracy directed from Moscow.

During 1962, Angleton had been persuaded by Anatoli Golitsin, the Soviet defector, of the existence of a KGB disinformation operation launched in the West called the 'Strategic Deception Plot'. The Soviets, explained Golitsin, were dispatching 'defectors' who appeared to betray the KGB's secrets to Western intelligence services but in fact were phoney. The 'defectors' were loyal KGB agents casting a blanket of misinformation over the CIA, Washington's politicians and other Western intelligence services. To Angleton, mesmerised by recollections of the Bolshevik 'Trust' deception of SIS and other European intelligence agencies in 1920s and the Second World War's double-cross operations, the notion was not incredible.

Soviet intelligence did seem outstanding, superior and impenetrably omnipotent. Over the previous decade, the CIA had digested the awful truth about its operations in the Soviet Union. Dozens of CIA agents, lured by elaborate KGB double-crosses into the Ukraine, Georgia and the Baltic States, had disappeared and were probably dead. The natural progression from that deception was the KGB's 'master plan', which even embraced Penkovsky. The Russian's revelations were denounced by Angleton as either untrue or chicken-feed designed to disguise reality. He would go on to describe that injection of extraordinary confusion – a nightmare for counter-intelligence officers – as the 'wilderness of mirrors', because lies could be the truth and the truth could be lies.

Although White's acceptance of the Strategic Deception Plot was less animated than Angleton's, his conviction was fed by his own wartime success against the Germans. The deception could easily be replicated by the Soviets against himself. 'White was mesmerised by the double-cross,' attested William Colby, subsequently the CIA's director. 'Like Angleton, it dominated his thinking about the Russians.'[3]

Blake, Vassall, Philby, Houghton and even Profumo helped to develop an element of Angleton's paranoia inside White. In each case British counter-intelligence, both in MI5 and SIS, had conspicuously failed to detect any traces until tipped off by Soviet defectors. Indeed, if British intelligence had relied only upon its own resources, without the CIA's assistance, neither MI5 nor SIS would ever have discovered a single Soviet spy in Britain. White was torn between two alternatives. Either MI5, the agency directly responsible for counter-intelligence, was lamentably incompetent, or the service itself was penetrated by the KGB. Adding support to the suspicion of penetration was White's own impression of the Kremlin's politics.

Unlike the CIA, both SIS and MI5 worked within a self-imposed vacuum. While the CIA invited academics and researchers from the nation's well-funded think-tanks to engage in intellectually exhausting conferences, SIS officers were bereft of exposure to open and informed debate. One reason was their service's official non-existence. Another was the quality and nature of those recruited to the service. SIS existed to spy not to analyse.

White's political assessment of Russia suggested the professional prejudice of a counter-intelligence officer. 'Nuances', observed Chester Cooper, the CIA liaison officer, 'were not White's line of country. There was no subtle understanding of foreign affairs.'[4] Seven years earlier, in his discussions with the CIA liaison officers in London, White had suggested that

Khrushchev's revelations at the Twentieth Party Conference could be 'a hoax'.[5] Unlike specialists, he had not yet appreciated that behind the public monolith of the Soviet Communist Party raged ferocious political and personal conflicts similar to the publicised power struggles in the West. To correct those mistakes, Leonard Schapiro, the Russian-speaking Soviet expert, had been introduced to SIS as an adviser. By virtue of his exclusivity, he enjoyed unusual influence upon White.

Blessed with an encyclopedic memory and a superb command of Soviet and communist history, Schapiro's dire predictions of an unprovoked Soviet attack on the West were convincingly articulated in a credible scenario about events inside the impenetrable Kremlin. Singlehandedly, he inspired White's scepticism of Soviet omnipotence while feeding his fear of the KGB's proficiency. He agreed with Angleton that the antagonism between Moscow and Peking was deliberate disinformation to destabilise the West's war against communism. In consequence, White directed that a priority target in the Red Book distributed to SIS stations throughout the world was a requirement to verify that allegation.[6] Schapiro also supported Angleton's view that Soviet agents were still buried within British intelligence.

White was therefore susceptible when Arthur Martin, the MI5 officer married to Joan Russell-King, his wartime secretary, reported a startling conclusion about Philby's escape. Martin had reopened all the files of the unresolved investigations into Soviet penetration of British intelligence since 1951. With the help of Evelyn McBarnett, he had scoured the old information and studied the new offerings from American cryptanalysts using computers to analyse the Venona messages. The results, Martin told White, showed that MI5 and the FBI had grossly underestimated Soviet intelligence activities in the West.

In particular, Martin concentrated on the allegation by Igor Gouzenko in 1945 of a Soviet source inside MI5. The defector had named the spy in British counter-intelligence as 'Elli', but at the time few British officers gave that allegation any credence. Elliott's encounter in Beirut with Philby aroused Martin's suspicions. Philby's opening remark, 'I rather thought it would be you,' and his apparent failure to ask for the new evidence proving his guilt indicated advance warning of Elliott's arrival. 'The Philby transcript and Elliott's own account suggest that he was tipped off from London before Elliott arrived,' Martin told White. The source, he concluded, was probably someone in MI5 aware of the confrontation. 'After listening to me, Dick immediately accepted that Philby was tipped off,' Martin told a colleague.

On White's advice, but without revealing his suspects, Martin approached Hollis. Explaining his suspicions, he asked permission to pursue his investigation. Hollis's response was direct: 'If Dick agrees, then go ahead.' After some weeks, Martin returned to White. He now explained the direction in which his inquiries had taken him. His two suspects for tipping off Philby were Roger Hollis and Graham Mitchell: 'I need authorisation for a full investigation.'

This request was a watershed in the history of Britain's intelligence services. White, its most respected servant since the war, was having to consider whether MI5's director general or his deputy could be a KGB agent. Pertinently, the cause of that suspicion was the misconceived confrontation with Philby organised by White himself. It was symptomatic of those confused moments that White did not pose the most salient conundrum of Martin's case: why, if Philby had expected Elliott, had he not also rehearsed his denial of being a traitor? Instead, White asked Martin to return the following day, allowing him time for reflection.

Unlike regular intelligence officers, those employed in counter-intelligence are born with their peculiar talent rather than trained in their craft. White recognised that Martin epitomised the fingertip sensitivity of the archetype who endlessly anguished over files to discover hidden answers and unanswered questions. 'Martin is the PhD in counter-intelligence,' attested Cleveland Cram, the CIA officer, 'while the rest are mere Bachelors.' To reject Martin's proposition would leave not only White but both intelligence services defenceless in the face of criticism from outside and internal strife. If proved true, the consequences would be devastating, not least the termination of Britain's relationship with the CIA and FBI.

Instinctively, White did not believe that either Hollis or
Mitchell was a traitor. Neither man had an apparent motive.
Unlike the Cambridge Ring and the atomic spies, whose youthful
path towards communism could be traced, there was no evidence
that either Hollis or Mitchell had been intellectually attracted
to the ideology or were vulnerable to blackmail, or possessed
inexplicable wealth. But White knew that he had been party to
other errors of judgment and it would be imprudent to ignore
the possibility of another.

Hollis, a dull, golfing enthusiast, was ruled out immediately.
White had known him since Oxford and for the past twenty-five
years in MI5. Yet to outsiders he would profess neutrality.
'I couldn't exclude anything,' he later told Bronson Tweedy.[7]
Although he did not particularly warm towards Mitchell, White
did regard the Wykehamist as an intellectual. He would restrict
his praise to Mitchell's introduction of positive vetting during
the 1950s as 'instrumental in ensuring that Britain's Cold
War security purge avoided the excesses of McCarthyism' –
although Blake, Vassall and other spies had revealed Mitchell's
consummate failure.[8] Wilfully, White disregarded the merits
evident in Mitchell's record: 'The problem was that we all
believed in penetration at the time.'[9]

That evening, White telephoned Hollis. Without revealing that
there were two suspects, White persuaded his protégé that in the
current atmosphere of treachery it was a sensible precaution to
permit Martin's investigation into Mitchell. Hollis's acquiescence
was inevitable given White's stature. On such matters, the SIS
chief's judgment was irreproachable. Similarly, White's trust in
Arthur Martin bestowed impeccable credentials upon the investigator.

The following day, Martin returned. White dismissed the
suspicions against Hollis but conceded that Mitchell deserved
investigation. 'We can't ignore the possibility,' he said, 'however
remote.' Hollis nominated Martin Furnival Jones, a forty-nine-
year-old shy, inarticulate but competent intelligence officer as
the MI5 supervisor. The curtain was raised on the 'Molehunt'.
Further progress, White knew, depended upon the CIA.

SIS's liaison officer in Washington was Maurice Oldfield,

who had arrived in the city in October 1962 with a reputation as a good intelligence officer – which he was – and as a man trusted by White – which was essential. Yet Oldfield was an active homosexual and vulnerable to blackmail. Although Rolfe Kingsley and other CIA officers would claim that they had suspected his sexuality within weeks of his introduction to Washington in 1960, they assumed he had been vetted and cleared in London. Oldfield knew better.

On three occasions, he had successfully lied about his sexuality in the course of security checks, making nonsense of positive vetting. In Washington, he would even be summoned by Denis Greenhill, the minister in the embassy, and cautioned about the presence of young male lodgers in his apartment. One was an American marine, the son of a CIA officer; another was an Iranian lecturer. Oldfield – 'the chief pontiff of positive vetting' according to some – laughed off any suggestion of impropriety.

Though noticing his effeminate mannerisms, White was unaware that Oldfield combined regular attendance at church with a secret quest for 'rough trade'. Once, he had asked Oldfield about allegations that he was homosexual and had accepted his denial. But his judgment was protective and flawed: 'Maurice was over-involved in his work and obsessive. He needed a good wife like Kate to get a complete change of subject in the evening.'[10]

Through no fault of his own, Oldfield operated under a handicap in Washington. SIS was a valuable partner for the CIA but nevertheless a comparatively small player. For all the easy access afforded in London to the CIA liaison officers, Oldfield rarely met Helms – busy fighting wars in Vietnam, the Middle East and Central America – and saw the CIA's director even less frequently. The second obstacle was the permanent legacy of Philby. SIS's earlier, unrestricted access to CIA officers had been sharply curtailed. On Helms's orders there was no *carte blanche*. Instead, every CIA officer's conversation with Oldfield needed prior approval, the content to be reported in writing afterwards.

To compensate for that exclusion, Oldfield assiduously courted his friends in the Agency. Working out of an office in the embassy with one-way window glass, his personal diary and contacts' list was organised to prompt regular entertainment with Washington's power-brokers. 'This is the only country in the world', he told Sam Halpern, '[whose activities] can get us into serious trouble, so we need a little advance warning.' The senior CIA officer who was most accessible, even welcoming, was Jim Angleton, not by coincidence the most interested in White's molehunt.

Regularly, Oldfield met Angleton, either at his Langley office or at the American's favourite Washington restaurant, La Niçoise. Ever since his arrival, Oldfield, in his avuncular Charles Laughton style, had sought to humour Angleton, honouring his reputation as the centre of power, aware that to offend him would undermine SIS's relationship with the CIA. 'He's found a wedge into Langley,' smiled Cleveland Cram. After innumerable Martinis, Oldfield would return to his office in the British embassy and report to White in terms which confirmed that he was SIS's most ardent convert to Angleton's theories. CIA officers noted that Oldfield 'played Angleton like a harp'.[11]

The reverse was also true. Angleton sought influence over British intelligence and therefore encouraged Oldfield and Martin to invite Anatoli Golitsin to London. In March 1963, the diminutive Ukrainian arrived in Britain. All those who suffered his unpleasant, arrogant manner in London were unaware that the staff of the CIA's Soviet Division were now minded to discard their defector as unreliable.

With White's knowledge, Golitsin undertook two separate exercises. First, he was given about one thousand files from MI5's registry to examine. In an unprecedented breach of security, the former Soviet intelligence officer was allowed to read not only MI5's operational files but also the personal files of the service's own officers. The Ukrainian's task, for which he would be paid about £10,000 a month, was to identify a background which might indicate a traitor.[12] During what Wright would later call 'the tense and almost hysterical months of 1963'[13] Golitsin fed the molehunters' assumption that 'treachery lingered in every corridor'.

The most important evidence was Peter Wright's discovery that the KGB's radio traffic from the Russian embassy to Moscow had inexplicably increased just before the arrests of Lonsdale and the Krogers. This was proof, he told Martin, that the KGB had been forewarned about the arrests by a Soviet spy inside MI5. The two officers deduced that the KGB had allowed Lonsdale's arrest to protect an important traitor, not least because the KGB would not have invested so much money in three illegals in London just to service one source, Harry Houghton. The same MI5 traitor, they conjectured, had warned Philby of Elliott's mission to Beirut.

Golitsin's arrival turned the molehunters' hypothesis into an article of faith and he fed their quest to identify the Fourth and Fifth Men of the Ring of Five by revealing that Soviet intelligence officers intending to defect avoided Britain because it was widely rumoured in Moscow that there was a high-level KGB source within MI5. As a finale, Golitsin confirmed that Mitchell possessed the qualities to rank as a suspect.[14]

Having completed his task with MI5, Golitsin was handed over to John Quine, the SIS officer, and a researcher. Ensconced for a week in a Canterbury hotel, Golitsin was shown hundreds of photographs of Russian diplomats to identify possible intelligence officers as well as a number of SIS documents as part of a limited molehunt. Nearly thirty years later, White would suggest that he was unaware of Golitsin's activities,[15] but the Ukrainian's access to SIS files could only have occurred with his approval. 'Dick wanted finally to get to the bottom of the problem,' attests a senior SIS officer close to the chief. 'He was an enthusiastic supporter of Angleton's investigation.'

By the summer, when Golitsin returned to Washington, Angleton had established a godfather influence over British counter-intelligence. The most senior officers in MI5 and SIS had been pitched into the 'wilderness of mirrors', but the Mitchell investigation had already stumbled. Without full surveillance and telephone taps, Arthur Martin complained to Hollis, he was thwarted. But the director general refused permission. First, it was too distasteful against his deputy; and, second, he was sensitive that a prospective Labour government, on hearing about the investigation, would become more sceptical about MI5. Martin exploded. Storming from Hollis's office and threatening resignation, he appealed to White for mediation and advice.

On a Sunday afternoon, three MI5 officers – Martin, Furnival Jones and Wright – were welcomed by White at Queen Anne's Gate.[16] The SIS chief poured tea and settled down to listen to the officers' catalogue of suspicions. After recounting the original reasons for suspecting a traitor in MI5 – the succession of apparent MI5 failures against the KGB and the dramatic changes in the KGB's radio traffic in London – the MI5 officers added new supporting evidence. The CIA had reported that Yuri Modin, the KGB officer who had controlled Guy Burgess in London, had arrived in Beirut just before Elliott. It was, according to the CIA's records, the first time Modin had left the Soviet Union 'since the early 1950s'.[17] That evidence, Wright and Martin told White, proved that Modin had conveyed the KGB's alert to Philby. White was impressed.

Modin had indeed travelled to Beirut, but he did not meet Philby nor was his journey related to the Briton. Their first meeting would be in Moscow. Moreover, both Modin and Vassili Dozhdalev, the KGB's British specialist, would deny that Philby was ever alerted to Elliott's arrival. Dozhdalev, who had controlled Lonsdale in London, insists that he learnt of Lonsdale's arrest only when he read the newspaper headlines. If there was increased KGB radio traffic the night before the arrest, it did not concern Lonsdale.[18]

Naturally, White was unaware of those insights in 1963. KGB officers like Modin and Dozhdalev were unknown individuals, beyond questioning, and at best recognisable in snatched, black and white photographs in MI5's files. White's only sources of information were Martin, Wright, Golitsin and Angleton. Unaware of their flaws, he was understandably impressed by their arguments. Furnival Jones added his support. Without technical surveillance of Mitchell, 'there really is little chance of finding an answer to this case'.[19] Hollis, he agreed, was being unreasonable. Once again, the fate of the molehunt depended upon White.

As an experienced counter-intelligence officer, White recognised the value of a fresh eye over old cases. He knew the limitations of his own investigation after 1951 and, more importantly, recalled the incredulity of SIS officers that Philby, their friend and associate, could be a traitor. He could not ignore a similar sentiment influencing himself. If the KGB had controlled an agent in SIS, there was good reason to suspect their success in MI5. Martin, Wright and the other molehunters, he believed, 'were the new post-war professionals. They wanted so strongly not to be taken in as we had been by Philby etc. They felt they were not going to make the same mistakes we had, and were going to clean up the service.'[20]

White's decision at the end of that Sunday's discussion was decisive: 'We have to do this investigation and we have to be seen to do this investigation, and that's almost as important.' Not only could the evidence not be ignored, but White believed the pursuit should be intensified.[21] White's decision was made without emotion. 'It just had to happen,' he told Bronson Tweedy.[22]

Once again White called Hollis. The following day, Furnival Jones was given approval to place MI5's deputy director general under constant surveillance. A camera would be placed behind a two-way mirror in his office. The headquarters of the operation was in a SIS safe house in Chelsea. SIS would supply the watchers, led by Stephen de Mowbray, an impressionable young officer with no experience in surveillance.

The investigation proved completely unproductive. The surveillance of Mitchell elicited evidence only that the deputy director general had strange personal habits. 'A calamitous investigation,' Martin told Wright. 'So hamfisted.' Nevertheless, both insisted that it should continue. Inexplicably, Mitchell, who had noticed the surveillance, never asked for an explanation. Once again, everything depended upon White's attitude.

White's integrity was not balanced by cynicism. Unusually for an intelligence officer, he trusted people until his suspicions were aroused. His tolerance of Martin, given some similarities in their backgrounds, was not surprising, although his sympathies were blinding him to his colleague's prejudice against Oxbridge types. 'Arthur has a chip on his shoulder,' he was told, but the observation was ignored.

That White extended his trust to Wright too was less easily explained. Wright was neither a trained intelligence officer nor a skilled interrogator. He was a radio expert, admired because

'he could use a slide rule'.[23] Although hard working, he had no
special understanding or knowledge of the history of espionage.
Yet such was the quality of MI5 officers that he had become,
with White's and Hollis's blessing, prominent within the service.
In 1963, White saw no reason to question his judgment or resist
the momentum of the investigation. He had fallen victim to what
Neville Robinson, a former colleague of Wright, called 'a great
gift of the gab'.[24] Robinson was not alone in judging Wright to
be 'frankly ignorant'.

After deciding that he could control the two disciples of
Angleton's creed, White suggested that MI5 share their concerns
with the CIA. At another uncomfortable meeting in Hollis's
house the following Sunday, the MI5 director general reluctantly
agreed that he would fly to Washington to brief the FBI and
CIA directors that his deputy, on the eve of retirement, was
under investigation. The report, outlining the case, was signed
in September 1963 by both White and Hollis.

Considering the circumstances, Hollis's reception would inevitably have been frosty, but that was exacerbated by Angleton's
general dislike of him. Hollis's occasional veto over the location of
CIA stations in the British Empire countries of Africa confirmed
his image as a Second World War relic, though he was merely
acceding to the Colonial Office's request to exclude the Yankee
cowboys; and his refusal after 1956 to provide information about
Hungarian refugees living in Britain for analysis by a CIA
computer outraged Angleton. Hollis was refusing to submit to
the American's patronage.

Unforgiving, Angleton's anger was passed on to Helms. Helms
recalled that in early November 1956, just after Suez, he was
driving Hollis through Washington. Despite Suez, the CIA was
lavishing upon the new MI5 director general the full treatment
of briefings and official dinners. Helms asked Hollis, 'Who's this
writer Ian Fleming?' The book, *Live and Let Die* had just been
published in the United States, and the novelist had attracted
Helms's admiration. 'Don't know,' replied Hollis, a self-regarding
intellectual. Days later, Eden had flown to Jamaica to stay with
Fleming. 'Hell,' thought Helms, 'The man lied. Hollis must have
cleared the prime minister to stay with Fleming.'[25]

That aversion greeted Hollis when he arrived to deliver his report on the Mitchell investigation. The meeting was short. The evidence, exclaimed Hoover and Bill Sullivan, the FBI's astute deputy director, was derisory.

Arthur Martin heard about Hollis's humiliation from Angleton. At the same time, Angleton invited Martin to consult him in Washington. The MI5 officer arrived in January 1964 unaware that Philby's flight had provoked a remarkable confession to the FBI.

Michael Straight, an accomplished American whose family boasted East Coast wealth and influence, had known Anthony Blunt in 1934 while studying at Trinity. Already inclined towards socialism, Straight had become immersed in Cambridge's communist movement. Before returning to America in 1937, he had been invited to join Blunt's and Burgess's conspiracy but had refused. Even thirteen years later when he met Burgess again in Washington, he volunteered that he had never betrayed his friends. But in 1963 Straight was offered a government post and, apparently fearful of exposure, he had spent June closeted with FBI officers including Bill Sullivan, detailing Blunt's futile attempt at recruitment.[26] In January 1964, Straight repeated his story to Arthur Martin. By any measure, the confession was a major breakthrough. Not surprisingly, the MI5 officer returned to Britain excited by the disclosure. The molehunt had been legitimised.

Martin gave his report to Roger Hollis and shortly afterwards the two officers conferred with their former chief in Century House. White was truly 'shaken' by the revelation. Blunt was not only director of the Courtauld Institute and a renowned art expert, but since 1945 he had also been employed at Buckingham Palace as surveyor of the king's and later the queen's pictures, regularly meeting the monarch. In 1956, he had been knighted, nearly contemporaneously with White. Blunt's honour and his career, White acknowledged, confirmed not only MI5's but his own failures.

So much had eluded his own investigations. Accusations about Blunt had become common even in Leconfield House canteen in recent years, but White, while suspecting that Blunt had known

of Burgess's treachery, was ignorant of his wartime friend's role
in the conspiracy. 'I had no idea at the time about the gay scene
and its incredible promiscuity,' he explained, nor why Blunt was
'so besotted by Burgess'.[27] White had been totally deceived. He
had been blind to Blunt's sheer totalitarianism. Although thirteen
years had passed since the saga began, his misjudgments rankled.
In self-protection, he reversed his assessment. 'I always hated
Blunt,' he would tell Trevor-Roper soon after Blunt's public
exposure. 'His hauteur was so irritating.'[28] Nevertheless, he was
still confused about the motives of the conspirators and about the
relationships between them.

White misunderstood zealots like Blunt, who rarely admitted
mistakes and offered only self-justification. He had convinced
himself that the Cambridge group was not the product of skilful
Soviet recruitment and nurturing but 'very largely self-inspired'.[29]
The genesis of the Ring of Five, he still believed, was a Comintern
plan which only later had come into 'the hands of the NKVD'. By
then, the links among all the conspirators offended the golden rule
of isolation and, he reasoned, 'must have been dreadful for them'.
Hence his continuing bewilderment that the traitors' faith had not
been shaken by the Nazi–Soviet Pact: 'What puzzles me is why
they did not come to their senses.'[30] As a non-believer, free of
the intellectual grip of religion, he conceded that he never quite
understood the Cambridge traitors. Blunt, he now hoped, would
explain everything.

Over the previous decade, Blunt had met Courtney Young, Jim
Skardon and Arthur Martin on eleven occasions, but his denials
of treachery had been unshakable. Now Straight's confession
would surely undermine his arrogance. For his next step, White
faced a difficult choice. On the one hand, the Establishment –
Whitehall, the universities and the Palace – expected protection
from embarrassment. But simply to ignore the evidence was not
a feasible option, even if some might have preferred that course.
It was professionally unacceptable and shortsighted. Any British
concealment would eventually leak in Washington. On the other
hand, a prosecution, though it would tarnish White himself and
the intelligence services, might satisfy the public interest in justice.

But in the end, after consulting Burke Trend, the cabinet

secretary, White understood how comprehensively political realities ruled out retribution. The collapse of Macmillan's government in the wake of the Profumo scandal suggested that Sir Alec Douglas-Home, the new prime minister, would do all he could to avoid gratuitous publicity about Britain's security. Even the truth about Philby's flight would be kept secret to avoid embarrassment. White therefore told Hollis that sufficient evidence could never be found to prosecute any of the Cambridge traitors. The government, he proposed, should be asked to grant Blunt immunity from prosecution, as had been offered to Philby. If accepted, the Security Service would debrief Blunt in secrecy in a bid to understand how the Soviet intelligence services had operated and to quantify the damage they had caused. The omens seemed favourable. Blunt, unlike Philby, appeared anxious to remain in Britain and therefore would welcome avoiding public exposure.

White suffered no moral qualms in recommending that Blunt retain his comfortable status. The justification was professional. In Graham Greene's dictum: 'Since espionage is basically the psychological warfare of sowing mistrust, then the most dangerous spy is the spy who is caught and publicly exposed.' Recalling his words just one year earlier to Elliott – 'What a shame we reopened it all. Just trouble' – White understood the turmoil which might befall Britain.

The consultations within Whitehall lasted until 23 April 1964. Sir Alec Douglas-Home, the head of the nation's security services, was deliberately excluded from the process. Hollis persuaded Henry Brooke, the home secretary, and Sir John Hobson, the attorney general, that the prime minister might refuse to compromise the Queen and that any successful debriefing depended upon Blunt retaining his status in the Palace.[31] On the basis of that unusual agreement, which was approved by the Queen's advisers, Arthur Martin was authorised to make the offer.

It was a dramatic moment in early April, when the diffident grammar schoolboy who had failed to enter university challenged the renowned aesthete in his untidy Portman Square office to confess in exchange for his freedom. Having poured a drink and paused for reflection, Blunt turned and spoke into an active tape recorder: 'It's true.'[32] White declared himself 'satisfied'. But Blunt's confession, instead of ending the saga, caused the molehunt to rage out of control.

Blunt severely limited his confession. To Martin's frustration, he mostly confirmed details already known, although he did offer embarrassment for White. Among the few men named as his recruits were Peter Ashbury, Brian Symon and Leo Long, a wartime MI5 officer, working in 1945 as an intelligence officer in the British Control Commission. To Long's disappointment, White had rejected his application to remain in MI5 after the war, saying that he was too well qualified – although White admitted, 'I don't think I had any suspicions of Long at that stage.'[33] Blunt also confirmed that John Cairncross, the wartime GCHQ officer who 'retired' from the Treasury in 1951, was a spy.

But he offered no answer to one critical question: whether his departure from MI5 in 1945 was unopposed by the KGB because there was another Soviet source operating within the service. For eighteen years, Martin, reflecting on Britain's beleaguered and blinded intelligence service, had been clutching at straws to construct an image of Soviet operations in Britain. The many clues, suppositions and allegations could prove either a conspiracy or simply muddle. Martin tended to believe the former and suspected that Mitchell, MI5's deputy director general, was Blunt's replacement. But Blunt said nothing to substantiate the suspicion.

Martin's conspiracy theories had become, in Hollis's opinion, a dangerous, damaging and uncontrolled obsession. That opinion was shared by Martin's superior, Malcolm Cumming, the D Branch director who had recruited White nearly thirty years earlier. In the wake of a succession of arguments, just two weeks after Blunt's confession, Hollis ordered Martin's temporary suspension. Simultaneously, to bring the matter to an end, he commissioned Ronald Symonds to trawl through all the evidence against Mitchell and produce an assessment. In October 1964, Hollis summoned a meeting to discuss Symonds's analysis. The junior officer had concluded that the case was unproven and not worth pursuing. Hollis agreed and moved to close the investigation completely. Mitchell, he declared, would not be questioned. Among those Hollis addressed were Martin and Wright.

Martin exploded. Symonds, he insisted, had not considered the powerful evidence presented by Golitsin. No director general, he continued, could terminate the hunt for the mole and ignore the inevitable wrath of Angleton. 'Mitchell', said Martin, looking intently at Hollis, 'is being run as someone's stalking horse.' Hollis understood the implication. To Martin's relief, Furnival Jones agreed that there were outstanding and unanswered issues. Too weak to resist the onslaught, Hollis procrastinated and agreed upon a further review by Patrick Stewart, a capable officer paralysed during the war.

The dissatisfaction of the two would-be slayers festered. Once again, they appealed to White for adjudication and help. In the circumstances, they explained, they had shifted their suspicions from Mitchell to Hollis himself. Unexpectedly, White showed more sympathy towards Martin and Wright than towards Hollis. The chief had not changed his 'neutrality' but Hollis's decision to forbid Mitchell's interrogation seemed 'too autocratic': 'The problem was that we all believed in penetration at the time and I personally came to believe the case against Mitchell. I got that epiphany. We thought we had our man.'[34]

Resolute in his suspicions of Mitchell, White confirmed his opinion in a personal briefing to Christopher Phillpotts, the new SIS liaison officer in Washington. Phillpotts's charm, good looks, dazzling wife and professional success as the SIS officer in Athens and Paris had won friends and admirers. For White, he was a perfect ambassador. In their conversations, the SIS chief emphasised the importance of maintaining the close relationship with Angleton and repeated Angleton's worries about Soviet penetration.

Before his departure, Phillpotts had spent days in a special room reading voluminous files recording the history of the molehunt since 1951 and beyond that to Krivitsky's evidence in 1940. He arrived in Washington as a convert, endearing himself to Angleton all the more. Like Maurice Oldfield, his predecessor, and reflecting the chief's instructions, Phillpotts willingly digested

Angleton's sermons. In turn, he reported to White the importance of the molehunt for Angleton and hence for SIS's relationship with the CIA. To satisfy Angleton, there was no alternative but to support Martin and Wright.

White's solution to the deadlock about Mitchell was hard-nosed. After consulting Burke Trend once more, he decreed that the inquiry would not be terminated, indeed quite the opposite: he would commission the most comprehensive internal review ever undertaken. A joint MI5–SIS committee codenamed Fluency was methodically to re-examine literally every suspected discrepancy in the history of Soviet espionage in Britain. If Mitchell was not MI5's mole, reasoned White, then all the 'serials' or suspicious incidents needed reinvestigation to identify the traitor. The can of worms could not be resealed. The committee, said White, would operate in the most watertight compartment. A minimum number of officers would know of its existence. Not even the politicians, not even the prime minister, would be aware of its work, unless and until it produced a critical conclusion.

Chaired by Wright, the MI5 members would be Patrick Stewart, Arthur Martin, Anne Orr-Ewing and Evelyn McBarnett, the queen of the registry. SIS would be represented by Terence Lecky and Geoffrey Hinton from R5. Other officers joined later. Although Fluency was reluctantly accepted by Hollis, the MI5 director general demoted and sidelined Martin, his protagonist, from his own investigation. He then threatened him with dismissal. Martin appealed to White for salvation, not least to save his pension. For both personal and professional reasons, White obliged. Martin was recruited to SIS and was available as a consultant to the Fluency Committee. Effectively, White signalled that he had not totally dismissed the notion that even Hollis could be a traitor.

Fluency's work was thorough. Every discrepancy was investigated and every unresolved suggestion of a Soviet spy in MI5 reported. Essentially, there were three sources. Volkov, the KGB officer in Turkey whom Philby had betrayed in 1945; Igor Gouzenko, the GRU officer who had defected in 1945; and, most important of all, Golitsin. The puzzle was the identity of a Soviet source called 'Elli', allegedly the chief of a counter-intelligence section. The issue was whether 'Elli' was Philby in SIS or someone else in MI5. By then, Wright and Martin were convinced that 'Elli' was Hollis.

Regularly a report of Fluency's findings passed through Alec MacDonald in MI5 and Maurice Oldfield, the new head of SIS's counter-intelligence branch, to Hollis and White. Invariably, each report described the good reasons for suspecting Soviet penetration of British intelligence but never delivered conclusive proof. White's official 'neutrality' was soon criticised by Oldfield. Freed from the requirements of diplomacy in Washington, he urged White to reconsider Angleton's sermon. 'He's a disaster,' he observed. White would not be deflected.

There was, however, increasing reason to fear Angleton. In September 1963, Yuri Krotkov, a KGB co-opted agent, defected to the British. His information about unhappiness among Soviet intellectuals was new and hailed as a coup. For the first time the West had more than a glimpse of the opposition to the Soviet regime and SIS proudly offered to share the windfall with the CIA's Soviet Division. The offer was eagerly accepted. Angleton adopted a contrary opinion. In a flying visit to London the following year, he told Oldfield: 'The man's a phoney. Lock him up for six months in a Scottish castle until he confesses, and in any case just push him back to the KGB at Checkpoint Charlie.'

Angleton's remedy was already being applied to Yuri Nosenko, another KGB defector, suspected as a Soviet decoy. For nearly three years, Nosenko would be incarcerated and intensely inter-rogated by CIA officers in a windowless cell outside Washington in an attempt to extract a confession.[35] Oldfield relayed Angleton's message to White. 'I've never heard such a ridiculous suggestion in my life,' gasped White. 'We'd never get another defector. It's absolutely impossible and illegal.'

In an unusual transfer of the CIA's feud to London, two Agency Soviet experts flew to Britain to test Krotkov. After two days, Dr William West and Sally Downey were introduced to Oldfield and Martin. Oldfield accepted their view of the Russian's bona fides, but Martin adopted Angleton's scepticism. White was becoming alarmed. Arthur Martin and Peter Wright had become Angleton's disciples. Both believed that the KGB had murdered

Hugh Gaitskell, the Labour Party leader; that Penkovsky had been a KGB plant; and that Harold Wilson, the new prime minister, was a KGB agent. Their extremism could not be ignored.

James Robertson, a long-serving MI5 officer, was among those outraged, especially by the suspicions against Mitchell, his brother-in-law. Robertson's fury was fuelled not least against social upstarts who doubted a Wykehamist. Arthur Martin had been transformed into an unremitting blister on the intelligence establishment. White's own attempt to find a solution had bred problems. Poison had been injected into the atmosphere at Leconfield House. Some blamed the molehunt, others blamed Hollis. The depressing succession of spy cases, Profumo and the collapse of the Conservative cause were also contributory factors. Others blamed the prospect of socialism as an unenticing honeypot for would-be defectors. The performance of the two intelligence services appeared to be depressingly mediocre.

No one openly blamed White, but, for the few activists, the heart of the problem was the poor quality of individual intelligence officers and the conservatism of both British intelligence services. The dissatisfaction had erupted when White and SIS were still bathed in the glory of Penkovsky. 'We lost our balance,' admitted White. 'Nothing like as badly as the Americans but we did lose our balance.'[36] One remedy, offered by the CIA, promised to be a lifeboat.

In November 1963, David Murphy, the new chief of the CIA's Soviet Division, had arrived in London on the last stage of a world tour. He was calling at CIA stations to galvanise agency officers to 'take on the Russians'. Based in Bavaria in the late 1940s, he had trained and dispatched agents into Russia. The human losses of his volatile anti-Soviet activities had not lessened his enthusiasm, but detractors had labelled him 'accident prone' and 'a mobile disaster area'.[37] After his disastrous support for the Ukrainian NTS in the early 1950s, he was dubbed 'always handsome, always articulate and always wrong'.[38] Undaunted and always cold-blooded, he continued waging war and attempting to recruit KGB officers. By the 1960s, his reputation, despite his temper, had improved. Fluent in Russian and German, his intellect, honesty and devotion had won the respect of many officers.

Gradually, 200 Soviet Division officers were being placed around the world to monitor Soviet diplomats and intelligence officers, and to identify potential defectors. Murphy hoped to mirror the successes of the East European Division, which under William Donnelly had spotted the weakness in Soviet security and was recruiting communist officials in Poland, Czechoslovakia, Rumania and Hungary.

Welcomed in London by Cleveland Cram, Murphy complained to the CIA's liaison officer that the British intelligence services were 'no help. They're just competing with us and not very well. Worse still, all our secrets pass through here and the security is bad. It's dangerous. It's a mess.' Cram, a Harvard-educated Anglophile, agreed. At least 250 communist intelligence officers had congregated in London under diplomatic cover – the third largest Soviet presence abroad – and yet MI5 had no plan of aggressive recruitment or penetration. 'Under Hollis, MI5 seems paralysed,' Cram grumbled. 'I blame the Foreign Office for allowing London to balloon into a spy centre for the KGB's ideological drive into the West'.

In Leconfield House, not more than twenty-five officers were targeting communist intelligence officers. Few of MI5's officers could speak Russian or any East European language. Shackled, they were dependent for translations and approaches upon freelance exiles living in Britain. In his daily conversations with MI5 officers, Cram detected their frustrated desire for a more aggressive approach. 'They're all depressed by Hollis's failure to attack the Russians,' he explained. 'They lack resources and support.' SIS, he added, 'doesn't seem much better.'

Although White had encouraged Shergold, by then chief of operations for the Soviet bloc, to approach identified KGB and GRU officers working under diplomatic cover throughout the world, Shergold never commanded more than twelve officers in London and, at most, there were thirty officers he could call upon worldwide. Even those, Murphy observed, were neither adequately trained nor properly briefed to undertake the task.

That judgment was not quite fair. Although Penkovsky had volunteered rather than been seduced, his offer had proven White's original arguments in 1956 about the foolhardiness of dispatching agents 'blind' into the Soviet bloc. The ideal, White had reasoned, was to find Soviet officials who were prepared to spy for SIS and could be encouraged to trust SIS while continuing to work for the communists, with the promise of money and future resettlement in the West. And yet, despite the investment, his theories had not become practice. Contrary to the heroic image of SIS sweeping the world in the popular James Bond films, White was not leading a service bathed in success. With the exception of the continuing success of Noddy in Poland, SIS, like MI5, had failed to recruit any significant sources, especially within the KGB – the bedrock of White's philosophy for intelligence collection.

In David Murphy's opinion, the reason was the quality of British officers, their resources and leadership. Too often their approach was unprepared. Their Russian target had become suspicious that he was the victim of an elaborate KGB loyalty test. Cram added another handicap: the prevailing fear, especially in MI5, that any Soviet recruited as a spy would be endangered by the unknown traitor within the British service. The molehunt had become a crippling cancer at the very moment the KGB was suffering a crisis of confidence. Cram urged Murphy to meet the Young Turks of MI5.

The venue was a lunch hosted at Cram's home in Chester Square. The guests were Patrick Stewart, Arthur Martin, Peter Wright, George Leggett and several other Soviet Branch officers. After strong Martinis and a good meal, Murphy delivered a rousing speech declaring war on the KGB, emphasising that assistance would be provided by the CIA. Prompted by the Penkovsky, Popov, Abel and Lonsdale cases, the CIA had established a ten man Illegals Section in Langley under Joe Evans, devoted to unearthing Soviet illegals implanted into the West. The technology supporting the section was formidable.

Experts at the National Security Agency in Washington had identified the Soviet transmitters responsible for dispatching messages to KGB and GRU illegals. Through intercepts of KGB messages across the globe, the CIA was attempting to monitor the international movements of illegals and Soviet intelligence officers. At chosen periods, every passenger's name for every aircraft at a targeted airport was entered into a CIA computer. The object was to pinpoint meetings of known Soviet intelligence officers and illegals.

The fruit of that exercise was the arrival in London in 1963 of Ed Juchniewicz, a Soviet Division officer, to recruit 'Donald Rollins', a Soviet illegal travelling as a Canadian citizen. Rollins had been spotted at the end of an expensive hunt by the Langley team. The best clue was provided by a Swiss bank official, a CIA source, monitoring the transfer of funds from Moscow to Geneva and Basle. The banker had noted that the money was later retransferred to Rollins in Tokyo.

Malcolm Cumming had only cautiously agreed to the CIA's operation, proof of Murphy's complaint. Approaching the 'Canadian' in his London apartment, Juchniewicz invited Rollins to defect. 'There are', urged the CIA officer, 'compelling reasons for you to consider our offer.' Juchniewicz sensed success but at daybreak the illegal fled. The financial cost incurred by the CIA had been enormous for no reward, an imbalance which characterised most of the Soviet Division's efforts during Murphy's tenure. But the waste of millions of dollars was apparently inconsequential. Compared to SIS's puny budget, the CIA's funds appeared unlimited.

Murphy's sermon to his MI5 luncheon guests about the CIA's efforts and dedication – 'inspiring' said some – moved on to the malaise infecting the British intelligence service. Unlike the CIA, which was even dispatching its own illegals – Poles, Czechs and Hungarians – into the Soviet bloc, Murphy said, MI5 and SIS were moribund. British intelligence officers, he exclaimed, were proficient but their techniques and scope were insular. Unlike American embassies in the Soviet bloc, the British did not embrace large numbers of local personalities as new intelligence sources. 'They're lacking a psychological stimulus, reducing their chance of recruits' was the opinion of another CIA branch chief.[39]

One ideal field for recruitment, the agency had discovered, was at international conferences in the West. Communist officials were vulnerable to approach by fellow countrymen employed by the CIA on grounds of patriotism and financial reward. Those recruited were encouraged to return home and supply information about the Soviet bloc through an increasingly elaborate but safe method of delivery. British intelligence officers seemed reluctant to be bold, partly because, unlike the CIA, the British had recruited neither ethnic Russians nor officers fluent in Slav languages. Accordingly, although Soviet activities were a major target, many SIS officers found it easier to report on local conditions.

Murphy now came to the heart of his sermon. British intelligence was becoming increasingly dependent upon the CIA. Repeatedly, MI5 and SIS requested information and assistance from the agency's registry or division chiefs. 'Don't worry,' he urged, 'if you fear a "Soviet dangle". Let's keep recruiting until we find the genuine defector. We've got the resources to provide the collateral.' To overcome British sensitivities about their superiority and sovereignty, he offered his audience an open cheque for a wartime alliance: 'I'll give you fellows all our help and all the information you need.' Murphy's speech was heard in silence; when he had finished, he was gratefully cheered. The MI5 officers clearly wanted to draw closer to the CIA. Murphy departed in a glow.

In discussions afterwards, Cram urged that the CIA send a Soviet expert to London. He would be attached to the British intelligence services: 'It will save all the requests for information passing lugubriously through the liaison office back to Langley.' Murphy agreed. A Soviet Division officer in London, he hoped, would increase British aggressive operations against the Russians. More importantly, he could pry into British secrecy and report on the molehunt.

White soon became aware of Murphy's lunch with the MI5 officers. He was not pleased, but was resigned to such a development. It was one he had anticipated. To shield SIS from weakness, he had espoused the cause of closer co-operation. One year earlier, allowing the CIA to intrude into Britain's most secret citadels would have been inconceivable. But the access to British secret files granted to Golitsin, co-operation with Angleton on the molehunt, and the general Cold War atmosphere had shattered the inviolate sovereignty of both intelligence services. White

POCKET CARTOON
by OSBERT LANCASTER

"*I must say this is a fine time for 'C' to go racing!*"

[17] Harold Macmillan's demise in 1963 was hastened by the affair between John Profumo (above, left), the Secretary of State for War, and Christine Keeler (above), a call girl. In Ascot week, the anonymous intelligence chiefs were blamed by Macmillan for failing to provide any warning of the affair (left).

[18] James 'Jesus' Angleton (right) and Cleveland Cram (above), both Anglophile CIA officers, attempted to influence White in opposite directions. For a time, White was persuaded by Angleton, photographed carrying the urn of Allen Dulles in 1969 (right), that British intelligence continued to be penetrated by a Soviet 'mole' at the highest level. Cram urged MI5 and SIS officers to ignore Angleton's paranoia.

[19] To White's dismay, the ultimate target of the 'molehunt' by MI5 which he instigated, was Roger Hollis (left), his successor as director general of the security service. Among MI5's hunters was Peter Wright (below), appointed an officer when White was the security services director general.

[20] SIS liaison officers in Washington, like Maurice Oldfield (above, left), were directed by White to support Angleton's molehunt. Oldfield's disillusionment coincided with the appointment in 1965 of Martin Furnival Jones (above), another sceptic, as MI5's director general. Harold Shergold (left) had always voiced his doubts about the 'molehunt' to White.

[21] Anthony Blunt's (above, photographed in 1979) confession in 1964 of his activities as a Soviet spy was an embarrassment to White, his wartime friend. Blunt's revelation that John Cairncross (right) was also involved added to White's discomfort since MI5 had failed to win Cairncross's confession in 1951.

[22] The public exposure of Blunt in 1979 by
Andrew Boyle opened a public 'molehunt' and
caused White's self-appointment as 'Guardian of
the Skeletons'.

[23] Among the last victims of the 'molehunt' was Victor Rothschild (left), the brilliant scientist and wartime MI5 officer. White was unable to protect his friend. Suspicions about Rothschild emerged in the wake of Peter Wright's 'Spycatcher' trial in Australia (below) – a débâcle which White had urged the government to avoid.

[24] Until his death in 1993, Dick White met
wartime MI5 colleagues involved in the Double
Cross operation for an annual lunch. Pictured
from left to right are: Cyril Mills, 'Tar' Robertson,
White, Christopher Harmer and Hugh Trevor-
Roper

bowed to Angleton's argument that the liaison relationship endangered the CIA's security, and that the Americans required reassurance.

William Allister,* the CIA officer approved by Murphy, arrived in London in June 1964. His presence was based on an informal agreement between Cram and Arthur Martin, approved by Hollis and White. Allister's selection indicated sensitivity. His family roots were on the isle of Lewis in the Outer Hebrides and his father had volunteered in both 1917 and 1941 to serve in the US Air Force in Europe. As an Anglophile with considerable experience in both the Soviet Division and counter-intelligence, he could assuage doubts about his competence and loyalty. Before leaving Washington, Murphy urged Allister, 'We must get on with operations, and the Brits are our best hope.' Murphy added one caution: 'Take care of your shoelaces because otherwise they'll steal your socks.'

Allister arrived in the midst of a bitter dispute within SIS, which his presence was intended to cure. Oldfield, the head of counter-intelligence, had for years encouraged aggressive, direct approaches to Soviet intelligence officers. Unexpectedly, his robust tone had sharply altered. He now felt ambiguous about such recruitment methods. Oldfield's change of heart was born of a recognition that Whitehall's mood was to avoid scandal; he was no less aware that madness had engulfed the CIA following rumours that Murphy himself had fallen under Angleton's suspicion as a Soviet agent; he also knew that the behaviour of Soviet intelligence officers had suddenly changed. Hitherto it had been almost impossible to approach a communist official and establish a relationship; now the communists were more forthcoming. So many Soviets were giving signs of dissatisfaction that Oldfield, and White, feared that the KGB was scattering phoney defectors to disorientate and penetrate SIS.

Oldfield's argument was focused against John Quine, recently appointed as a Soviet Orbit officer and housed in an anonymous office on Vauxhall Bridge Road. With two others, Quine was authorised to fly anywhere in the world to approach and recruit

* Allister is a pseydonym.

communist diplomats and intelligence officers. Unexpectedly, Oldfield opposed Quine's worldwide hunt for defectors. In a formal paper submitted to White, he argued that the service should wait for Soviet officers to come into SIS's net. Encouraging active recruitment, he continued, would expose SIS officers in foreign countries to expulsion and would mean that SIS was more vulnerable to a rigorous value-for-money analysis. It might, he urged, be hard to prove that SIS provided better intelligence than GCHQ.

SIS activists were puzzled by Oldfield's argument for a 'dead hand'. Allister ascribed it to the truism that 'You can't fight a war if you're paralysed by the fear of penetration.' Others suspected Oldfield's new conservatism was motivated by his concealed homosexuality. For his part, Oldfield hid behind White's ambivalent caution. 'I thought it was better', explained White, 'to resist pressure of doing something for the sake of it and exploit proper opportunities.[40]

White's nervousness was reflected in a snap decision to halt a CIA operation in London. The target was a Cuban diplomat, an intelligence officer, who was to be approached in the street and shown a dossier of blackmail photographs. 'This operation has low blow-back' was the Agency phrase. At the last moment, White's office ordered that the operation be aborted. The risk of embarrassment, he decided, was too great. At the internal inquiry, he admitted that he had faced 'a supremely difficult moment', but the threat of a diplomatic protest could not be risked.

The ripples of the argument between Oldfield and Quine reached Allister at the CIA's new headquarters in the embassy. Within a short period, the CIA officer had attracted whispered confidences and complaints from dedicated but disgruntled officers. His seduction of personnel in Leconfield House and Century House had been accomplished by means of generous hospitality in his home and even on a barge party plying through Regent's Park. His proven worldwide experience offered techniques and resources unavailable to British officers. He explained how in Moscow and other East European capitals the CIA recruited barmen, hotel managers and others to report on weaknesses for potential blackmail of communist officials. 'We've taken the war into their territory,' he quietly boasted. 'Telling a Russian diplomat that we possess a small bit of dirt will cause alarm. They won't report our approach because they'd never be allowed out of Russia again.'

To both MI5 and SIS, Allister could offer a rapid check in the CIA's vast registry on the background of any communist intelligence officer who presented himself as 'dissatisfied' and a potential recruit. On Murphy's orders, CIA registry officers were promised transfers to Mogadishu if they failed to respond to Allister's inquiries within one day. As Allister won the trust of British intelligence officers, his agenda became more evident. The CIA was not purely altruistic. The overriding fear of an undetected mole inside British intelligence endangered the CIA. One method of discovering the traitor, White had agreed with Angleton, was the recruitment of a KGB officer in London or anywhere in the world who could identify the Soviet source.

Allister was allowed access to MI5's information and techniques. To a more limited extent, he won access to SIS officers and operations. One block on his access to Century House was Nicholas Elliott, by then director of the Soviet Section. Although priding himself as an aggressive operator, Elliott was deemed 'too conservative and political' by the CIA, which ranked his methods as 'old-fashioned'. Elliott's response was similarly unmeasured: 'The CIA were dangerous cowboys.' His resistance provoked criticism.

Using the code 'ZR TAFFY', Angleton's private channel, Allister reported in late spring 1965 that security in both British services was weak and morale was low. Those at the top of both services, contemporaries of Philby and Blunt, did not enjoy the confidence of their subordinates. That report encouraged Angleton, without formal notice, to pay the occasional visit to London. Entertaining Oldfield, Martin, Wright and Allister in a private house or at Wheeler's in Old Compton Street, a favourite wartime haunt, he would listen to the complaints and orchestrate a uniform remedy. All defectors, he asserted, should be handled as suspected KGB plants. He repeatedly emphasised his conviction that a high-ranking traitor lurked within British intelligence.

Angleton also met White. Their formal conversations were never minuted and the arrangements to pursue their quest within British intelligence were concluded directly between the two men.[41] Both understood that, to complete the molehunt, White had agreed to sacrifice British sovereignty. Among the reasons for White's amenability was his hope that one Russian might be found who could provide an assessment of the damage which Philby had caused.[42] In confessing that hope to Angleton, White assumed that their partnership was solid. He was, however, being deceived.

Angleton did not mention that an investigation was under way to establish the ability of all Western security agencies to contain Soviet intelligence activities. In May 1965, Gordon Gray, a banker and a former secretary of defense under Eisenhower, and Gerald Coyne, a former FBI officer, arrived in London and were briefed by Archie Roosevelt, Cram and Allister for the CIA, and by Charles Bates for the FBI. In unison, the liaison officers criticised MI5, condemned Special Branch and queried SIS's performance.* Their report, delivered in late summer 1965, was highly critical. MI5, the investigators declared, suffered poor management, poor organisation and poor leadership, even though it employed many talented officers. Hollis, unaware that an American investigation had been undertaken, was singled out for particular criticism.

Two British intelligence officers were told about that report and also about Angleton's increasing determination to exercise more direct control over British intelligence. One was Christopher Phillpotts, the SIS liaison officer in Washington. Phillpotts reported Angleton's opinions to White, including the details of the completed Gray report. For White, it was the first inkling of Angleton's conspiracy against Hollis and of Angleton's intention to alter the relationship of equal partners to one of master and supplicant. The second British officer to become aware of Gray's report was Peter Wright. Visiting Washington, the MI5 officer dined with Angleton and, before they parted at 2 a.m., heard

---

* Contrary to Wright, *Spycatcher*, p. 274, they never entered Leconfield House or Century House.

that the CIA desired Hollis's dismissal. For Wright, convinced that Hollis was a traitor, this was a welcome development. He cabled the news to colleagues in London.

By then, the plot was already under way. Angleton, with Helms's support, suggested a direct approach to either George Brown, the deputy prime minister, or George Wigg, a confidant of Harold Wilson and designated as responsible for national security, suggesting Hollis's dismissal. The approach was to be made by David Bruce, the ambassador. In London, the proposal outraged Cram and Bruce. Helms was quickly persuaded that such direct interference in British affairs would be drastically counterproductive, especially since Hollis was retiring at the end of the year. But by now Wright's cable had been circulated in Leconfield House and the news had reached Hollis. For two days, Hollis rejected Bruce's telephone calls. The ambassador wanted to apologise and explain that Angleton's conspiracy had been unauthorised. Eventually Cram, with Furnival Jones's help, placated MI5's director general over lunch.

In 1965, Hollis retired and was replaced by Martin Furnival Jones. On the eve of his retirement, Hollis summoned Wright to his office. 'Why do you think I'm a spy?' Wright outlined the evidence. Hollis replied, according to Wright's colourful version, 'Peter, you have got the manacles on me. I can only tell you that I am not a spy.'[43]

Driven by zeal, prejudice and Angleton, Wright continued with others in the Fluency Committee to scrutinise the archives of the past twenty-five years. Repeatedly he unearthed evidence of seemingly sloppy investigations. So many leads, he complained, had been abandoned and so many tainted individuals, allegedly recruited by Burgess and Blunt, had been allowed to rise through Whitehall's ranks regardless of suspicions.

The names of forty 'guilty' men had all passed across White's desk: Alister Watson, still involved in secret Admiralty research; Dennis Proctor, a retired senior civil servant; Bernard Floud, a Labour politician; and Stuart Hampshire, a wartime cryptologist who at that moment, on White's recommendation, was investigating the efficacy of the UKUSA agreement to share intercepts. All, according to Wright and Arthur Martin, were suspected of having been recruited as Soviet spies in the 1930s.[44]

White, according to Wright, was 'desperately embarrassed at the revelation' about Hampshire.[45] As old friends, the two had lunched together often after the 1951 defections. But Hampshire had never revealed that Burgess had invited him in the 1930s to work for Soviet intelligence. On the contrary, when White had asked his friend whether Burgess could have been a spy, Hampshire had denied the possibility. White had not pursued the matter. For a brief moment, White's relationship with Hampshire sparked Wright's fevered suspicions. The files of the 1951 investigation, he complained, were so sparse and the investigation had been so poor that even the SIS chief became a suspect. After a discreet but limited investigation, Wright declared himself satisfied that White was not a spy.

Knowing that his mistakes had hampered the 1951 investigation, White's vulnerability intensified. He could no longer restrain the molehunt or the molehunters' conviction that Hollis was a traitor. Others were sceptical. Oldfield in particular loudly denounced Angleton's theories, castigating them as unsubstantiated and dangerous. His opinions were supported by a growing number of CIA officers opposed to their colleague's paranoia. White could ignore Oldfield but not Cram whom he sought to caution. John Bruce Lockhart was asked by White to approach the American. Meeting the CIA officer at the bar of the Ritz Hotel in Piccadilly, Bruce Lockhart was unsparing: 'Dick wants you to lay off, Cleve. Stop sticking pins into Angleton. You're rocking the boat. It'll get back to Angleton and we'll have difficulties.'

Both knew that their political masters, Harold Wilson and Lyndon Johnson, had privately agreed that Britain would give non-military, indirect assistance to America's war effort in Vietnam in return for Washington's support for sterling. It was a fragile agreement, which included an undertaking to provide SIS help for the CIA in south-east Asia. Nothing could be permitted to irritate that relationship. Accordingly, Angleton's quest was not to be frustrated in London. The molehunt, searching through files, radio intercepts and old interviews, was to continue uninterrupted. Hollis remained the prime suspect; Mitchell had not yet been excluded; and other candidates were under investigation.

CHAPTER THIRTEEN

Finale

White had welcomed the election in 1964 of a Labour government; some even suggested that he had himself voted Labour to win relief from tottering Conservative administrations. But, within a year of Labour's victory, SIS was responsible for a succession of intelligence failures that were to tarnish Harold Wilson's administration for years.

White's introduction to Wilson and Michael Stewart, the new foreign secretary, had passed uneventfully. By then, he had achieved a quiet celebrity among the cognoscenti who ruled Britain. He never pushed for fame in Whitehall but was rewarded with respect by the power-brokers, enjoying, unlike other directors of intelligence, easy access to everyone. He was never lost for opinions, but his utterances always seemed sensible if unmemorable. He argued for the principles of democracy and anti-communism, but not for details of policy. As a public servant, he obeyed the government's orders, retaining the discretion to decide when illegalities were appropriate. Above all, he was content to inhabit the shadows. Of those who knew him, few would claim to know him well. But his honesty was indisputable and that won favour among new ministers who feared a Conservative backlash. 'He's killing them with kindness,' observed Rolfe Kingsley, a CIA friend.

Michael Stewart, mischievously suspected of being a CIA source, had every reason to trust White as, at their initial meetings, they went through a checklist of SIS's 'hot spots'. Besides the communist bloc, where SIS's failure to predict the explosion of China's first atomic bomb on Britain's election day had exposed the perennial difficulties of penetrating the Iron Curtain, their discussion was dominated by what was left of the Empire.

In the Yemen, the war against Nasser had intensified. Terrorists had transformed Aden into an unstable battlefield beyond the British army's control; in the Far East, SIS was supporting 10,000 British troops engaged in Operation Confrontation – fighting a guerrilla war in the Borneo jungle against Sukarno's invading Indonesian army; and, in East Africa, British soldiers had just suppressed army revolts in the newly independent states of Kenya, Uganda and Tanzania.

The East African revolts in January 1964 had sparked a crisis within Whitehall, and between British intelligence and the CIA. No intelligence reports had so much as hinted at dissatisfaction among the black army officers. Not only Whitehall but Washington required explanations and remedies for the intelligence failure. White's excuse was the Attlee Doctrine. MI5 had used the Doctrine as a reason for doing nothing. The local intelligence services in each of the countries, unchanged from the Empire era of British-led officers in Special Branch, lacked sources inside the national armies and their ignorance was in turn reflected by the MI5 liaison officers. 'They suddenly woke up to the fact that friendly governments could be overthrown without HMG knowing,' said John Taylor, a senior SIS officer.[1] 'The Attlee Doctrine', White was told by Bronson Tweedy, the CIA's director for Africa, 'has gone on long enough.' An outdated bureaucratic edict was risking Western investments and allowing KGB exploitation of unrest.

Tweedy's obstacle was naturally Hollis. The American had already complained about MI5's disclosure in 1963 to the new Tanzanian government that a US diplomat was in truth a CIA officer, a disclosure that caused his expulsion. Tweedy's return to the fray after the East African revolts was irresistible. Hollis bowed and agreed to the CIA opening stations in the affected countries. SIS followed soon after. White's lack of interest in Africa was not altered by those events. SIS's responsibility, he argued, was muddled by the Doctrine and by Whitehall's confusion. It was an intelligence lacuna which Harold Wilson did not appreciate as he tottered towards the next Empire crisis.

On the eve of Britain's general election of October 1964,

Ian Smith, the prime minister of Rhodesia, had announced the first steps towards his country's independence based upon white minority rule. For Wilson, an overt sympathiser of the anticolonialist struggle and a committed Commonwealth supporter, Smith's proposition was anathema.[2] Weeks after taking office, optimistic that he could negotiate a long-term solution, Wilson encouraged Smith to desist. Supported by MI5 and SIS intelligence reports, he believed that diplomacy was succeeding despite Smith's oblique suggestions that he would declare independence unilaterally. He warned the Rhodesian that a rebel regime would be isolated and suffer 'disastrous economic damage'.[3]

As relations deteriorated during 1965, Wilson, supported by SIS reports, persuaded himself that more discussions would eventually produce an agreement protecting Rhodesia's black majority. Even after a meeting with Smith in London on 7 October confirmed the Rhodesian's determination, Wilson flew to Salisbury to warn the white settlers that economic sanctions would defeat their rebellion and destroy their country. Derided by his audience, Wilson returned to Britain still convinced that Smith's desire to avoid a breach was inhibited by hardline racists.

On 11 November, Armistice Day, Smith announced Rhodesia's 'independence'. Bewildered by his apparent irrationality, Wilson deluded himself that the Rhodesian would still seek an escape. His misjudgment was compounded in the following weeks when he publicly asserted that 'sanctions are beginning to bite'.[4] White was responsible for some of the intelligence Wilson was relying upon.

Paul Paulson, the jovial SIS controller for the Middle East and Africa, had in 1962 sub-divided his responsibilities. Alan Rowley was in charge of Africa and, in turn, John Main was assigned to the Rhodesia desk. Rowley, a competent intelligence officer, had in 1962 dispatched Jack Beauman to Salisbury under cover as a High Commission diplomat. Three years later, Beauman, advised to avoid any risks, had not penetrated Smith's Rhodesian Front party. That political objective had not been cleared by the Commonwealth Relations Office and was not entered in SIS's Red Book of targets.

White blamed the Doctrine. If the proper questions were

not passed to the intelligence service to answer, said White, SIS was not to blame. He would not take the initiative in examining government policies nor would he condemn the Joint Intelligence Committee for failing to pose the correct questions. There was no hunger to anticipate developments or to influence British foreign policy. 'Dick was not interested in Rhodesia,' observed an SIS officer directly involved, 'and Michael Stewart was not the leader to inspire change. He just reflected the Foreign Office ethos that intelligence was unnecessary.'

Accordingly, at his personal meetings in the course of 1965, White had no information enabling him to warn Wilson that Smith was deliberately misleading the British government because he intended to declare UDI. Nor was there intelligence from Beauman that the Rhodesian government's declaration of independence was delayed only by a fear that British troops might be dispatched to quash the revolt. Indeed, the rebels were comforted by Wilson's unsolicited assurance that British troops would not be dispatched to fight 'kith and kin'.)[5] Above all, the intelligence emanating from Salisbury, both from the High Commission and from SIS, did not report that white Rhodesians supported the rebellion. Instead, SIS reports written by Main in 1965 had unequivocally predicted that Smith did not intend to declare independence. In the first weeks after UDI, SIS reports emphasised that stringent petrol rationing and the sombre atmosphere on Salisbury's silent roads proved that the Rhodesians anticipated hardship as sanctions took effect.

Those reports were in Wilson's top-secret briefing when, on 10 January 1966, he arrived in Lagos, Nigeria for the Commonwealth Conference, a major event at the time. The only topic for the twenty-one heads of government and other representatives was Rhodesia. Under pressure from the black leaders to repress the rebellion, and unrestrained by any Foreign Office or intelligence service caution, Wilson uttered an immortal and self-destructive prediction: 'Sanctions might well bring the rebellion to an end within a matter of weeks rather than months.' By then oil was already flowing into Rhodesia from neighbouring South Africa and Mozambique, a Portuguese colony.

Britain's intelligence-gatherers had been deceived. Unaware

of African realities, White had not pressed Paulson or Rowley to probe and unearth the secret pledges of support to the Rhodesian rebels by the neighbouring white governments and by the British oil companies. Petrol rationing had been imposed merely to conserve stocks until the railway supply line had been established. 'We never thought that British companies would break sanctions,' observed Denis Greenhill, then the deputy under secretary of state at the Foreign Office, who advised that Rhodesia, starved of oil, would soon succumb. Greenhill, a 'very plain cook' in the opinion of Denis Healey, did not press White to explain why SIS lacked any good sources in Lisbon, Mozambique and South Africa. Nor did Bernard Burrows, the chairman of the Joint Intelligence Committee. Among those officials, SIS's limitations were accepted with resignation.

Wilson blamed SIS for his mistakes. White disagreed. The fault, he now believed, lay with the Joint Intelligence Committee, suffocating under Foreign Office control. Bernard Burrows, following Burke Trend's dictum, 'The careful way is the right way,'[6] never challenged the Attlee Doctrine or complained that the intelligence from Salisbury was inadequate. Instead, he approved the collation of information from MI5, SIS, GCHQ and the Foreign Office by the Assessment Staff and authorised the circulation of bland, misleading commentaries posing as top-secret intelligence. In Burrows's defence, White criticised the government for not producing an understandable policy. The intelligence services, he explained, could provide information only if the government explained its objectives. Wilson's policy was contradictory. The prime minister ordered Rhodesian civil servants to remain in their jobs while, at the same time, he urged the same officials not to serve an illegal regime.

On Wilson's part, he could criticise White's failure to produce a plan, as he had requested, for the overthrow of Smith. In fact, White had directed Paulson to implement the order but the planning had been delegated to John da Silva who sympathised with Rhodesia's whites and Britain's imperial role. After three weeks, Paulson reported that his officers could find no anti-Smith group in Salisbury to stage a counter-coup. Temporarily, SIS could conceal the confusion, but other events undermined their defence.

Four days after Wilson bid farewell at Lagos airport to Sir Abubakar Balewa, the country's prime minister and chairman of the conference, the Nigerian's corpse was found in a ditch. As the country tottered towards civil war, another intelligence fiasco was revealed. Neither the Foreign Office nor Downing Street had received any warning of the unrest. The MI5 liaison officer in Lagos shared their ignorance. Among the bitter complainants in London was the CIA, again denied any representative in the country by an MI5 still chanting about post-war agreements and the Doctrine. Again White failed to protest that SIS was not allowed a station in Lagos and was agreeably protected by Burke Trend's calm smothering of Wilson's complaints. SIS was never answerable in the real world for anything.

In that same month, another embarrassment in West Africa was unfolding. John Thompson, the MI5 officer in Accra, Ghana, signalled London that John Harley, the commissioner of police, had asked for assistance to overthrow Kwame Nkrumah. The Marxist's policies had plunged the country into dictatorship and financial disaster. The ideal date, Thompson reported, was during Nkrumah's visit to China in February. Martin Furnival Jones, Hollis's successor, echoing the Commonwealth Relations Office, vetoed any involvement. Harley was told by Thompson to consult Howard Bane, the CIA station chief. On 26 February, Nkrumah, with the CIA's help, was deposed.

The Wilson government's renewed complaint of poor intelligence in Africa was echoed by Bronson Tweedy, citing a wave of unrest across Africa: 'We warned you about the menace of Soviet subversion. We need change.' While he would not willingly engage in a fight for turf, White finally understood how the Doctrine had damaged the intelligence service. In those former colonies where he had fought MI5 or the Commonwealth Relations Office to establish an SIS station, it had proved beneficial, first in Malaya and Singapore and more recently in Zambia.

In October 1964, just before independence, Daphne Park had arrived as SIS officer in Lusaka. Besides organising Zambia's own intelligence services and arranging penetration of black anti-Smith groups, she had surreptitiously financed Kenneth Kaunda's successful election campaign. Since then, her personal relationship had secured the president as a source of information about the developing KGB presence, earning her the sobriquet 'the president's right-hand man', an invaluable position in the Rhodesian crisis.

On reflection, White understood his folly. He had mistakenly not challenged the Attlee Doctrine, he had tolerated the Foreign Office's leaden domination of the JIC, which distorted the intelligence services' performance; and, worst of all, he had tolerated the robber barons' rule for a decade.

Over Christmas, after consulting Burke Trend, White decided that the reform of SIS was long overdue. In early January 1966, rumours percolated through Century House that unprecedented changes were imminent. The robber barons were to be invited to retire. The bureaucratic excuse was the lowering of the retirement age to fifty-five years. Among the immediate departures were John Collins and Paul Paulson, the latter's departure cushioned by his appointment as consul general in Nice. Fulton was sidelined as head of special projects and would leave shortly afterwards. Bruce Lockhart had retired the previous year. Only Elliott remained for two more years, his mishandling of Crabb, dubbed 'a one-man Bay of Pigs', balanced by White's misjudgment of the Philby confrontation.

The new controllers were Elliott for Western Europe and later director of requirements; Harold Shergold for the Soviet Union and Eastern Europe; Tim Milne for Middle East; Stewart MacKenzie for Western Hemisphere; Ellis Morgan for Far East; and John Taylor, SIS's first controller for Africa. In their social background, the new regime differed marginally from their predecessors. But all understood that the days of fiefdoms and freebooting were history. They were to be more realistic about SIS's intentions and limitations. Some entering Century House during those days sensed a 'terrible atmosphere'.[7] In the corridors, officers talked about 'The night of the long knives'. The new breed were relieved that the robber barons had finally departed. 'Thank God, it's all over,' murmured John Briance, the architect of the changes, as the blood-letting ceased.

To consolidate his new order, White summoned a week-end conference in March 1966 at the Fort in Gosport, still a complex of Nissan huts surrounded by high walls and staffed by ex-servicemen. Mixing with his new controllers, White sensed that he had disposed of those who tucked handkerchiefs up their jacket sleeves. Their replacements were more attuned to the times. Each director was asked to deliver a résumé of his problems, successes and impressions in his area. Inevitably, each speech contained an element of self-congratulation, but there was a hint of new realism. Ellis Morgan of the Far East could claim success in Borneo, where Sukarno had been defeated, but otherwise spoke of consolidation, which contrasted with the explosion of CIA activities in support of the Vietnam war.

Tim Milne's speech suggested robust operations of a type not always disclosed to White by SIS officers in the field. Money, weapons, telephone intercepts and even the provision of pencil bombs for 'training' had been used to win influence in Lebanon, Jordan and Syria. In the Gulf states and Jordan, SIS was training local intelligence services and detecting threats to friendly regimes, arranging 'neutralisation' by surrogates where required. In the Yemen, SIS's activities had contributed to Nasser's defeat and his agreement in August 1965 to withdraw. That victory had then been forsaken by the Labour government's announcement in February 1966 of a British withdrawal from Aden by 1968, despite all previous assurances to the contrary. That was politics, not intelligence.

White was not displeased by the withdrawal. Despite John da Silva's intervention, and his complaints of a 'vacuum' in the region, White had always denounced the worthlessness of that particular fight. Terrorism had increased and the area was drifting towards murderous anarchy. In tandem with Dick Helms he had successfully urged the Saudis to forge an alliance with Israel. The Arabs' sworn enemy was now supplying Soviet arms to the Yemeni Royalists through Saudi Arabia.

Among the Middle East sections other recent successes had been the recruitment of Abdul Rahman Zaigloul, a former Syrian intelligence chief, based in Paris and funded through Switzerland; the installation in Libya by John Wyke of an intercept on the microwave transmissions of all the telephone conversations by the monarch, King Idris; Alexander 'Sandy'

Goschen's success in Somalia in directing SIS technicians to insert microphones in the new Chinese embassy; and a tap installed in the Soviet embassy in Khartoum, Sudan. The lesson was that where local security services were less inclined to protect Soviet diplomats, their buildings and personnel were vulnerable.

Finally, Milne indicated the product of good relations with Mossad, symbolised by a regular Christmas gift to White of a crate of Jaffa grapefruits. Unmentioned was GCHQ's coverage from Cyprus. The following year, GCHQ would provide the raw material which anticipated Israeli's attack on its neighbours and its victory after six days.

Stewart MacKenzie of Western Hemisphere described the close attention the SIS stations in France, Germany and Italy were paying to those governments' relations with the communist countries. Telephone intercepts and bugs placed in government buildings and private homes were showing how allied politicians were 'playing footsie with the Russians'.[8] Among the targets was Willy Brandt, the German chancellor, suspected of treachery for the Soviets. A bug, bearing a Japanese manufacturer's label to disguise its provenance, had been installed in his office. It would reveal that his special assistant was an East German intelligence officer. Other surreptitious activities had provided information on those countries' attitudes towards Britain's application to join the Common Market and their plans to challenge Britain's worldwide commercial interests. Intercepts placed in the French embassy in London would provide a daily appreciation of France's negotiating tactics. Liaison with Reinhard Gehlen had proved worthless despite a lunch hosted by White at St Ermine's Hotel. The German spy-master's material was delivered without provenance or collateral. The German service, like the French, was assumed to be penetrated by the communists.

The presentation by John Taylor, the first controller for Africa, described a rush to establish a presence. Jim Parker had been dispatched to Lagos; in Kenya, Bruce McKenzie, the Minister of Agriculture, a white settler and the confidant of President Kenyatta, had asked SIS to establish a Kenyan foreign intelligence service, a request which was accepted with alacrity;

the Rhodesian crisis was receiving priority – Anthony Freemantle had been inserted into Salisbury; Kennedy Sloane would soon arrive in Pretoria; Paul Homberger and John Pilkington would be sent to Mozambique. Privately, Taylor would issue a word of caution: 'Everyone is trying to find a solution but doesn't know where to begin.' There were no orders from the government to infiltrate the oil companies or to stop sanctions-busting. SIS, on government instructions, would remain a passive collector of information.

Harold 'Shergie' Shergold, a shy but forceful character, dubbed by admirers 'an SIS hero', presented his plans for renewed aggression against the Soviet Union. A new section under Michael Stokes would combine with MI5 to target Russians in London; Myles Ponsonby, a Russian expert, would be sent to Africa to recruit Russians with John Quine; more adventurous attempts would be made to contact Russian diplomats and KGB officers in South America, either to lure them into agreeing to co-operate or, with the help of local security agencies, to blackmail them with compromising evidence.

There was no reference by Shergold to an unfortunate embarrassment the previous year. In April 1965, Gerald Brooke, a British teacher, had been arrested in Moscow for spying. Naturally, compliant British newspapers had regurgitated SIS's line that Brooke was an innocent but misguided zealot distributing Bibles. In fact, he had been a postman for the old NTS Ukrainian crowd operating from Frankfurt, and under SIS control. On arrest, Brooke had admitted that his contact in Moscow was Anthony Bishop, the SIS officer, who was subsequently expelled. It had been a harmless but worthless expedition which had irritated Harold Wilson, keen to develop his relations with the Kremlin, and had caused SIS grief in Whitehall. White had not been amused that relations with the Ukrainians had once again proved embarrassing.

Nicholas Elliott's presentation boasted the continuing services of Noddy in Poland, now handled by Michael Pakenham in Warsaw and Robert Snelling in London. Poles had been recruited by SIS in London to find similar sources across Eastern Europe but, wisely, Elliott did not boast of any successes.

White's concluding speech was neither rousing nor revelatory. In his sincere, quiet tone, he gave encouragement and cautioned against unnecessary risks. His directors, aware of his past distaste for 'political action', sensed a change of heart. Those operating in the Middle East and Africa had urged him in the course of that weekend that their best sources of information were activists who offered intelligence only in return for support for their political objectives. 'Unless we show we're prepared to help influence events,' said Taylor, 'we won't get intelligence and it's questionable if it's worth even operating.' White, some sensed, accepted the proposition.

The weekend ended optimistically. Of all the officers returning to London, none was happier than Maurice Oldfield. In his concluding comments, White had announced, 'I can assure you that my successor will come from within the service.' Since Oldfield, the former head of counter-intelligence, was SIS's deputy chief, his inheritance seemed secure. Oldfield's successor as head of counter-intelligence, Christopher Phillpotts, had recently returned from Washington, also aspiring to inherit White's position. He persuaded himself that the chief was encouraging that ambition. Their common interest was to discover the 'mole' within British intelligence, a topic which White still regarded as paramount – as important as SIS's operational activities. That opinion was passed by White to SIS's new liaison in Washington, John da Silva: 'Penetration is the most important part of your job. Represent, report and warn but do not initiate policies.' Relations with Angleton, said White, would be 'the focal point, because only Angleton possessed an overview of penetration'.

Before his departure, da Silva spent one month reading the counter-intelligence files, to emerge amazed by the history of betrayal. I came away, he told a friend, with a complete disillusionment about Tory and Labour politicians and officials because of their involvement with the KGB. An astonishing number of people had decided, on their own initiative, to side with the Russians. His deputy would be Stephen de Mowbray, a passionate molehunter who had led the watchers during the unproductive investigation of Graham Mitchell.

Da Silva's appointment had been unsuccessfully opposed by Oldfield, now an apostate from Angleton's theories. After da Silva's departure, Oldfield repeatedly clashed with Phillpotts, who had returned 'deeply attached to Angleton' and anxious to intensify the hunt.[9] Phillpotts's charm was still evident but his lack of intellect was exposed by his unsubtle campaign to dismiss any SIS officer with a doubtful past. In meetings with White, he voiced his suspicions against several colleagues, supported by Wright and Arthur Martin. 'At the end,' recalled Wright, 'Dick would sigh and say, "I suppose he'd better go. I'll see him tomorrow."'[10] The dismissals were effected on grounds of suspicions, not proof. 'You had to give the service the benefit of the doubt,' reflected White. 'The sackings were undoubtedly the hardest thing I ever had to do as C.'[11]

Oldfield opposed this draconian cleansing and his disagreements with Phillpotts culminated in appeals to White for arbitration. Both emerged only partially satisfied. Imbued with caution, White urged Phillpotts to continue supporting Angleton, while agreeing with Oldfield that news of an investigation, inevitable once outsiders were questioned, would leak and cause a scandal, an unwelcome occurrence in Whitehall.[12]

Oldfield's prejudice against Angleton erupted in April 1966. The American arrived in London from Norway. It was the end of his world tour undertaken to launch his dream, CAZAB. By uniting all the English-speaking intelligence agencies (of Canada, Australia, New Zealand, America and Britain) in a counter-intelligence organisation based upon total disclosure, he hoped to institutionalise in regular meetings his dominance of anti-Soviet activities in the West. He now sought British membership.

To combat the unseen reality of Soviet penetration, Angleton was proposing that his own department control a communications network, divorced from the remainder of the CIA. He also intended, he told White, to create a double-cross committee embracing the CAZAB members. Mention of his wartime success would previously have flattered White but, while agreeing to join CAZAB, he remained noncommittal about closer co-operation. His opinion of the American's scenario of communist penetration was becoming jaundiced. 'It was highly complex. You had to be a pretty advanced counter-espionage professor to follow it.'[13]

For the first time, Shergold sensed that his chief was no longer hypnotised by Angleton. In odd moments, Shergold had been urging White 'to cut ourselves off from Angleton', deprecating SIS's pliant response to the American, whom he had disliked ever since a clash in wartime Italy. By summer 1966, he noticed signs that White was harbouring serious doubts. By then, Angleton was well informed about MI5's activities by Wright and Allister. Despite the confusion prevailing in Leconfield House, many files were within Allister's grasp and few secrets were withheld during his late-night sessions with Peter Wright and the other molehunters. But SIS's specialists – Lecky, Hinton and Shergold – had resisted Angleton's whims and avoided Allister's feelers.

The news had reached London that the CIA's molehunt was infecting David Murphy's Soviet Division with paranoia, reducing its effectiveness by instilling the fear that every Soviet defector was a KGB plant. Murphy would not speak in his own office without turning on the radio. Unbeknown to him, Angleton was ridiculously beginning to suspect that Murphy himself might be a Soviet mole. The paranoia was contaminating even the best achievements. Penkovsky had been declared by Angleton to be a KGB plant. 'Ridiculous,' gasped White. 'There are too many Ks dependent on this one.' Although his personal enthusiasm for Angleton was waning, he outwardly reassured SIS's ally that the molehunt in Britain would continue.

More than ever, White believed that SIS's survival depended upon its relationship with Washington, especially since the British contribution to the partnership was becoming confined to operations in specified areas such as Hanoi and Havana, from which the Agency was barred. His view was echoed by Helms: 'Britain's decline was saved by its legacy of diplomats and intelligence officers giving good advice to the United States.'[14] Since Helms 'backed both sides of the argument' on Angleton, White followed suit, encouraging Phillpotts's energetic vetting of all SIS's staff and his constant travels across the Atlantic to consult Angleton.

In 1966, the Fluency investigation had reached a new crisis.

Peter Wright, working with Patrick Stewart and Alec MacDonald, had concluded that Michael Hanley, MI5's new deputy director general, was a suspect and that the earlier suspicions about Roger Hollis were vindicated. As before, there was no direct proof but, on the assumption that there was a traitor, the circumstantial evidence pointed to one of those two men. After interrogation, Hanley was acquitted, leaving Hollis the prime suspect.

Veering towards a precipice, the Fluency Committee had entered Angleton's nether world, casting doubt on every officer and every defector – the wilderness of mirrors, where lies are the truth and the truth is lies and the reflections leave one dazzled and confused. Despite his reservations, White maintained his neutrality about Hollis. 'It's an open question,' he told one colleague, hinting that he had been offered unusual promotion by 'the highest figure' if he dropped the investigation but had refused. 'The investigation must be completed.' In fact the recent conviction as a Soviet agent of Frank Bossard, a civil servant in the British military establishment, left White with no alternative. In the face of the enormous KGB presence in Britain, he felt impelled to prove the purity of the British intelligence service.

In 1966, in Washington for his annual consultation with Helms, White called on Hoover. 'Director,' said White, preserving the courtesy which Hoover required, 'various allegations have been made against Roger Hollis and an investigation is under way.' During their fifteen-minute meeting, White gave no indication whether he believed the allegation. Nor did Hoover display any emotion. Since Philby and so much more, nothing surprised the FBI director, who reminded White that the FBI had never been penetrated. Lie detectors, positive vetting and the recruitment of all-American police types had protected the service from infiltration by political activists. White's only consolation was the American's appreciation that 'he's levelling with us'.[15]

In London, White saw every reason to restrict knowledge of the molehunt. Although the officers involved 'felt disquiet that Whitehall did not take penetration as seriously as it should have been', they did not appreciate that White deliberately cultivated the silence. Officially, he could do no more than politicians allowed, but he could capitalise on the Cold War habit of not asking questions. The only exception was Burke Trend, the cabinet secretary, a similar personality, who sympathised with White's ambition to save the beleaguered services. Together they walked into the ultimate tragi-comedy.

On 22 October 1966, George Blake escaped from Wormwood Scrubs prison. The former SIS officer had almost effortlessly climbed over the wall using a rope thrown from outside. 'I'm livid,' exploded White to anyone listening. SIS had long warned the Home Office that Blake would attempt an escape but, instead of taking increased precautions, Wormwood Scrubs had granted extra privileges to the model prisoner. Now it seemed that the KGB had lived up to their reputation for protecting their servants. A telephone call from Helms confirmed that the Agency's opinion of the British could hardly fall lower. 'It was a disaster,' admitted White, perplexed by the KGB's audacity and shamed by British incompetence.*

The escape symbolised a continuing farce. Two months earlier, George Brown had been appointed foreign secretary. Few other British politicians had been judged better drunk than sober, and none of the ministers White served had proved more emotional or more exasperating. His appointment confirmed White's opinion that Wilson was a 'poor judge' of his colleagues and that the prime minister's style was 'hardly the way to run anything'.[16] In his normal courteous way, White had submitted a request to dispatch SIS technicians to place microphones inside the Indonesian embassy in Grosvenor Square. On all previous occasions, earlier foreign secretaries had listened to a short explanation of the requirement and the risk and then either approved or denied the request. Brown's approach was unique. 'How will you actually enter the building?' he inquired with relish.

'In our normal way', replied White.

'Well, how's that?'

'Do you really want the details?'

---

* Even years later, when the story emerged that Blake had been assisted by Sean Bourke, a disgruntled Irishman, White was not convinced that the Russians had played no part.

'Yes,' boomed Brown. 'And I want to know where you're going to place these things.'

Images of Brown standing on a wet, windy night under the cover of a tree watching the buggers performing their task flashed through White's mind. With Brown's passion for alcohol, the SIS chief feared that the illegality would spill out in one of the politician's bursts of aggressive indiscretion. As he hesitated, Greenhill interjected: 'I think we can rely upon the service to carry out their task with due care, Secretary of State'. Smoothly, the mandarin passed to another item on the agenda.

In the anteroom after the meeting, White grimaced: 'If we're not careful, the foreign secretary will be outside the embassy directing the operation.'

Greenhill shrugged. 'Don't worry. I'll look after everything.'

The solution on sensitive issues was to bypass Brown whenever possible and address the prime minister directly, not least because Brown was a certain CIA source. The key issue again was Africa and in 1967 another intelligence muddle. Jim Parker in Lagos had failed to anticipate the outbreak of civil war, which imperilled BP's massive investment in Nigeria's oil industry. Sandy Goschen, his replacement, had compensated for this to some extent by recruiting a network of Nigerians, thereby obtaining secret government documents from ministries and the presidential office. But SIS had failed to secure sources inside the Biafran rebel regime.

The flaw lay in John Taylor's inheritance: too few SIS officers were in Africa and too few possessed African experience. White had agreed to increase manpower, but it took at least one year for an SIS officer to become productive. In the meantime, Wilson had convinced himself that a speedy settlement in Rhodesia was vital, and SIS were still providing little information about breaches of sanctions.

In London, black and white Rhodesians were being recruited by SIS for use either in Britain or in Rhodesia, but their deployment was still delayed; in Pretoria, Kennedy Sloane had proved to be an archetypal club man and golfer rather than a spy; in Mozambique, there had been one chance report of sanctions-busting but little more; while in Rhodesia itself, Anthony Freemantle, SIS's officer, had failed to recruit any sources in the Smith government or the civil service and, after being arrested for counting Mozambican railway trucks, had been expelled. Even GCHQ was unproductive, because the Rhodesian telephone network used landlines.

To make up for that unfortunate catalogue, White visited Wilson in Downing Street to offer an apparently secure, direct channel to Ian Smith. The messenger was Ken Flower, the head of Rhodesia's intelligence service. After the breakdown of Wilson's talks with Smith on HMS *Tiger* in December 1966, Flower had complained to SIS: 'Had I been consulted I could have helped.' He offered his services, 'although I won't be an SIS spy'. Over the following months, White communicated with Flower either through the CIA or in letters written in secret ink by an SIS officer and posted from South Africa, and was able to report to Wilson that Smith was amenable to further discussions.

In February 1968, Flower confirmed that Smith was ready for talks to settle the rebellion. The news justified a personal briefing in Downing Street by White. By then, Wilson knew that oil sanctions had failed. George Thomson, the minister for Commonwealth relations, had reported to Wilson the admission by Shell and BP executives that they were deliberately avoiding sanctions.[17] Although Wilson would claim not to have read Thomson's report, he was told the same by White. 'The government's denials that it had received information about sanctions-breaking were phoney' was the united cry of all SIS officers involved. If Wilson was ignorant, the fault lay with Bernard Burrows, the JIC chairman.

Eager for a settlement, Wilson seized upon White's news and, to ensure its reliability, in June, dispatched Arnold Goodman, his friend and solicitor, to Salisbury. Goodman's report was optimistic. By October, when Wilson met Smith on HMS *Fearless*, his hopes, reinforced by more reports from Flower via SIS, were high. But the *Fearless* talks, off Gibraltar, collapsed. Wilson was blamed for a diplomatic blunder and accused of naivety and even of a willingness to sell out. In part, however, it could be blamed on Flower's deception, which White suspected was deliberate.

Flower could no longer be trusted. On that inauspicious note, White began to plan his departure from SIS.

Ever since the wholesale removal of the barons, White's retirement had been anticipated without apprehension. Maurice Oldfield seemed his likeliest successor, although White himself had become uncomfortable with his deputy. The SIS chief was also dubious about the alternative, Christopher Phillpotts. The head of counter-intelligence had a glittering record, but he was mistrusted. As a matter of procedure, both officers were formally proposed as candidates to Greenhill, although White might have admitted that the absence of a clear-cut successor, just as there had been in 1956 when he left MI5, was an unfortunate epitaph upon his twelve-year stewardship.

Greenhill dismissed Phillpotts out of hand, a snub for which the latter never forgave White. Oldfield's candidature took slightly longer to consider. Greenhill had known Oldfield in Singapore and Washington and, while appreciating his skills, doubted whether his fussy personality made him either a leader of men or acceptable within Whitehall. 'He's an enigma to me,' said Greenhill, who had once questioned the officer in Washington about the wisdom of having young male lodgers in his house. Neither then nor in 1968 was he aware of Oldfield's homosexuality. Greenhill's negative conclusions were presented to George Brown to make the final decision. 'Why don't you take the job?' asked Brown, expressing the government's disenchantment with SIS. After some reflection, Greenhill decided that he would be ill-suited as a spymaster.

Seeking a candidate, Greenhill unsuccessfully canvassed colleagues and Ministry of Defence officials including Denis Healey. Finally, he spotted John Rennie, a comparatively lowly deputy under secretary of state in the Foreign Office who had served in Washington, Warsaw and Buenos Aires. Rennie's only connection with intelligence had been in 1953 as head of the Information Research Department, the mavericks who waged a war of propaganda and dirty tricks against the communists. To Greenhill, his colleague's lack of success in the foreign service was outweighed by his 'ingenious mind' and his unusual background as a painter and pre-war advertising executive. Rennie was noted as a generous host who offered champagne and caviar to his guests while playing recordings of W.C. Fields. Above all, Jack and his wife Jennifer were 'a nice couple who would be attractive to people in the Office'. Rennie's disabilities went unnoticed. Although a man of many parts, Intelligence was not one of them; and as an administrator he was inefficient, even incapable.

When Rennie's candidature was proposed, White passed no adverse comment. 'George Brown did not allow me to recommend my successor. He told me it would be Rennie, "and don't bother to argue with me."'[18] White was not prepared to protest or fight. SIS was still mistrusted in Whitehall. But Peter Wright's observations were shared by many: White 'knew what was best for the Service, but he seemed unable to grasp the nettle and act . . . Dick was always diffident when it came to staff matters and had not been able to summon up the gumption to bang the table.'[19]

Even Greenhill would eventually concede that Rennie's appointment was unfortunate. At lunch with Allen Dulles in Washington, Rennie would not open his mouth throughout the meal; and Rennie's son, a drug addict, would be arrested in particularly sordid circumstances. White's disclosure of Rennie's appointment to his senior officers provoked horror. Not only was the new chief a shy, inhibited nonentity, but it signalled a return to amateurism and bureaucratisation and, worse, it was a victory for the Foreign Office against an internal appointment. The only consolation was the appointment of Oldfield as Rennie's deputy, suggesting that from behind the throne a professional would continue to manage the service.

As a loyal servant, White introduced Rennie to his senior staff with a display of enthusiasm at a succession of parties in Carlton Gardens. Many by then had been told by him that Rennie's salary would be higher than his own. White's own farewell, amid personal trepidation, was protracted. Since his use of a direct lift to his tenth-floor office at Century House had made him relatively unknown, there was surprise when the remote chief suddenly appeared on other floors to bid farewell. A series of receptions for officers and their wives was followed by a dinner hosted by twenty senior colleagues at the Garrick, where each presented him with a book. In addition, there was the traditional worldwide farewell tour.

After dinner in Ottawa given by Norman Robertson, Canada's permanent secretary for external affairs, White flew to Washington for a black-tie dinner at the Chevy Chase club hosted by Helms. Sitting with Angleton, Bill Sullivan, Tracy Barnes and Rolfe Kingsley, Helms presented White with the CIA's retirement medal. Uncertain about the intended symbolism, White replied: 'I don't suppose you can buy anything with it, you can't eat it, but it's awfully nice to have it.' There was no lunch with Hoover, just a curt farewell reflecting the director's abiding distrust of British intelligence.

After passing through Australia, New Zealand and the Far East, White returned to Britain in March 1968 to erect a barrier between himself and SIS. He would never be seen at the subsequent annual reunion of officers at the Wellington Barracks where, after wine and sandwiches, his successors addressed hundreds of guests with glowing accounts of the previous year's successes. To most it suggested an unease he had not felt with MI5 officers, especially those wartime colleagues involved in the double-cross. A few murmured that White's deferment of his retirement and his new appointment suggested discontent with the service he had directed.

On 1 April White arrived in the Cabinet Office in Whitehall. As the first chairman of the new cabinet co-ordinating committee he hoped to cure the cardinal flaw marring British intelligence: its lack of credibility. Long discussions with his friend Burke Trend had drawn the two proselytisers of intelligence to acknowledge SIS's poor status in Whitehall. SIS needed to come of age. Mature intelligence services, reasoned White, were not simply spies. The vast costs could be justified only if the intelligence saved the government from expensive embarrassments.

Throughout his previous thirty years, White had witnessed the internecine warfare between the military, the Foreign Office and intelligence agencies. SIS reports, filtered and rewritten by the JIC staff, which was in turn dominated by the Foreign Office, compared unfavourably with the transcripts of conversations produced by GCHQ's intercepts. The disdain felt within the armed services and the Ministry of Defence for SIS intelligence compared to their own was undiminished. No one was comparing the covert intelligence with the mass of information publicly available through newspapers and television.

Only an independent group in Whitehall, White and Trend agreed, could co-ordinate all that information and deliver an authoritative intelligence assessment unclouded by departmental prejudices. Posing as a neutral in the Cabinet Office, White could demolish the resistance to sharing intelligence and improve written assessments based upon an impartial judgment of all the available intelligence, covert and overt. Creating such a group, cutting through the inbred contortions of the intelligence-gatherers, would be the culmination of White's experience and prevent repetition of the intelligence fiasco of Rhodesia's UDI.

Although at sixty-one White would have preferred to break from Whitehall to spend more time with his wife and his hobbies, the co-ordinator's task seemed interesting and his finances were precarious. The building of his new house at Burpham, near Arundel, had been more costly than anticipated and a share tip from Gerald Glover, a solicitor friend, had proved disastrous. So, with the encouragement of Denis Greenhill, he undertook what appeared to be his last service for the reform of Britain's intelligence community.

Unfortunately, his well-earned plaudits on retirement were soon buffeted by another intelligence embarrassment. And soon the skeletons of the past begged to be released.

CHAPTER FOURTEEN

Guardian of the Skeletons

Harold Shergold's holidays were disturbed during August 1968. Instead of enjoying the sun, SIS's Sovbloc controller was cajoling every source behind the Iron Curtain to answer one question: would the Warsaw Pact armies invade Czechoslovakia to suppress the Prague Spring? His results were not commensurate with his efforts. Using traditional and modern tradecraft – radio bursts, dead-letter drops, brush contacts and letters written in invisible ink – SIS's sources behind the Iron Curtain were reporting countless sightings of frenzied troop movements, but nothing more. SIS's handful of agents were too low-grade to discover the soldiers' orders.

All SIS's expensive and exhausting worldwide escapades to recruit Soviet 'defectors' had not produced any informant with access to the politburos in Warsaw, East Berlin or the Kremlin. Penkovsky was proved to have been a wonderful success but an aberration. Ever since, Shergold had not secured a similar high-grade source who could offer an eyewitness report about Leonid Brezhnev's actual intentions. Accordingly, he had little more to offer than his customers could read in the *Daily Telegraph*: namely, unusual troop movements around Czechoslovakia's borders.

In the Co-ordinating Office, the new centre of Britain's intelligence-gathering machine, Dick White observed the fruits of twelve years as chief of SIS. A wave of information from satellites and spy planes, vast computerised archives and a worldwide network of computer-driven eavesdropping dishes intercepting and decoding radio messages confirmed unusual military activities, detailing the position of each unit of each army. 'We even know', White confided to a CIA officer, 'how many bullets every soldier is carrying and what he's eating, but we don't know what orders he'll be given.' But the customers wanted an answer, so a guess was made. The authoritative assessments presented to the cabinet by the JIC and the new co-ordinator before 20 August discounted the possibility of an invasion of Czechoslovakia. The Warsaw Pact armies, the experts judged, would not risk the world's opprobrium by removing the Czech government.

In mitigation, White's embarrassment on the morning of 21 August, as reports of Soviet tanks crashing through Prague were broadcast on BBC Radio, was shared by every other Western intelligence agency, including the CIA. That did not lessen White's discomfort. SIS's predictions for Whitehall had been judged once again as poor. Millions were spent annually, yet the intelligence was wrong – proof to cynics of the parasitism and play-acting of espionage. Whitehall's indictment reflected a general attitude towards SIS's offerings: 'very patchy, not always acceptable and not reliable'.[1] To Greenhill and Trend, White lamented the sorry state of affairs, although among friends no criticism was passed upon SIS. Instead, the trio uttered mutual consolation that White's direction of the Co-ordinating Office offered the best hope for improvement.

Unspoken was the absurdity of that state of affairs. Neither Trend nor Greenhill understood SIS's fundamental weaknesses. Although Trend, as a supporter of SIS, ensured that the service survived its Whitehall budgetary battles with the Treasury, he lacked any sense of the internal flaws which White had not removed. Greenhill was little better. Surprised to be appointed the Foreign Office's senior official by George Brown, shortly before the politician's drunken resignation in March 1968, his imposition of the hapless Rennie on SIS confirmed his innocence.

White withheld any criticism. Trend was a supporter, while Greenhill had proved a kind and valuable friend. White's son Johnny, unable to undertake strenuous work, had become fascinated by railway timetables. Before the war, Greenhill had been an apprentice with North-East Railways, and White inquired whether his school contemporary might have any contacts who might help to secure a position for his son. Through an old acquaintance who had become head of the Southern Region, Greenhill was delighted to oblige. That kindness silenced any criticism White might harbour about his colleague. Instead, all three hoped that White's status and style might bring respectability to their new enterprise. Britain's most senior intelligence officer, privy to the personal secrets of most politicians and officials, toured Whitehall to defuse the traditional suspicions. Tense meetings, not least a particularly unpleasant confrontation with Air Chief Marshal Sir Alfred 'Tubby' Earle, director general of intelligence at the Ministry of Defence, appeared to neutralise the antagonism.

As the intelligence flowed into the Cabinet Office, and the co-ordinator's staff expanded from 'one man and his dog' to a handful, White valued his assessments and believed that that opinion was shared. He would be disappointed. After the first year, ministers and officials 'dismissed the reports as wishy-washy, speculating probabilities, and therefore unreliable.'[2] White's patience and his interest in the Co-ordinating Office began to diminish. A weariness with placating Whitehall's turf battles crept into his soul. Senior staff noticed that he preferred discussing foreign policy to intelligence. His motive for remaining was his desire to improve his pension, which, (following the abandonment of the pre-war system of payment in cash and no formal career) because his official employment began only in 1945 was not large.

There were compensations. The new prime minister Edward Heath was persuaded in 1971 to expel 105 Soviet 'diplomats', all identified as KGB officers. This draconian act followed the recruitment by MI5 officers of Oleg Lyalin, a KGB officer serving in London. For those preoccupied by the nation's security, the swift decimation of their enemy changed London's atmosphere noticeably for the better. For White, a landmark had passed: 'The 1971 expulsions levelled the field; 1951 had been the highpoint of Soviet espionage in Britain. They never had it so easy again [after 1971]. After that, it was downwards for them and upwards for us.'[3] The government's decision also reasserted MI5's sovereignty against Angleton. Both the CIA and Henry Kissinger, President Nixon's national security advisor, were furious about the absence of consultation. 'We didn't want any interference,' Furnival Jones told Cleveland Cram. Rationality was finally dispersing the fog of hysteria.

Cold War fevers were cooling. The wartime generation was handing over just as the balance was finally tilting in their favour. In his final year before retirement, White anticipated that the skeletons of his turbulent years would remain entombed and that he would stay in the shadows. Perhaps it was not coincidental that as the fear of a nuclear holocaust and the tensions of spy wars began to evaporate, an inquest into the past was ushered in. Too much had passed for lips to be for ever sealed. Unsurprisingly, as the dominant personality of that extraordinary era, White became the bodyguard, the vigilante of history. But the circumstances of his custodianship were unexpectedly unpleasant and some of the damage was self-inflicted.

The conundrum was the molehunt and White's own complicity in it. Gradually unfolding towards exposure of the bitter strife among intelligence officers, it began innocently enough in October 1967 with a succession of ground-breaking articles in the *Sunday Times* headed 'Philby: the spy who betrayed a generation'. The articles contained the first public mention of White's name, breaking taboos and causing him 'great upset'. The publicity, he told staff the following day agitatedly, 'endangers Kate and the boys'.

More pertinent was the articles' content. For the first time, the real story of Philby, the spy and not the unimportant Foreign Office official, was told. The articles washed away the protective anonymity of the intelligence services and highlighted their failures. The shroud was raised on all the riddles and intrigues which had consumed the molehunters for twenty years. Fingers were pointed, but gently. White's fears mellowed. The articles' glowing description of his pursuit of Philby cast him as the hero – 'the dynamo' of MI5[4] – against SIS's diehards, a role he would comfortably retain, but only beyond the citadel, among the unknowing.

A hint of insider's criticism came in the introduction to the new book about Philby in 1968 by John le Carré, the former MI5 and SIS officer. Pouring vitriol over the 'hocus-pocus of the spy world' and in particular over their officers, alias the 'clowns', for succumbing to Philby's duplicity, le

Carré scorned the Establishment's 'grotesque ineptitude': 'The posturing chauvinism of [Philby's] superiors would long have passed for idiotic in the outside world; in the secret world it passed for real . . . to the very end he remained dependent on the people he deceived.'[5]

An equally serious challenge to White was issued in 1968 by Kim Philby's own memoirs. *My Silent War* was the brainchild of Agajans Ivanovich, the KGB's deputy chief of intelligence, in retaliation for the CIA's earlier production of *The Penkovsky Papers*, the phoney diaries of Russia's traitor. Over eighteen months, sitting initially with Yuri Modin, Philby was asked 'to make trouble for the British and demonstrate the skills of Soviet intelligence'.[6] Written in an engaging style, the book was published, despite British government pressure, with a foreword by Graham Greene. The novelist, wartime SIS officer, and post-war freelance agent impishly perverse in his relations with official institutions and his country, disarmingly proclaimed the contents to be the 'honest' testament of a man who 'after thirty years in the underground [has] surely earned his right to a rest'.[7]

'A hornets' nest' was White's reaction to the KGB's propaganda coup. SIS was derided as 'a racket' and 'Big Dick' White was falsely credited with Philby's recruitment to SIS.[8] The book, boasting juicy revelations, though these were cocooned in self-serving distortions and false leads, was Philby's revenge. 'Philby didn't like White because he behaved rudely in the interrogations,' remembers Modin, who witnessed the author's relish. 'Philby was expressing the thoughts of MI6 friends about White. He wrote it knowing that it would meet with their pleasure.'[9] Nicholas Elliott was among those who agreed with Philby's most famous stab against White: 'He was a nice and modest character, who would have been the first to admit that he lacked outstanding qualities. His most obvious fault was a tendency to agree with the last person he spoke to.'[10]

'In fact I was a "no" person' was White's riposte.[11] 'Philby was particularly vicious about me but we should have suspected him sooner.'[12] Philby sustained his attack on White. 'I described him as ineffective etc.,' he wrote to High Trevor-Roper shortly after his book's publication, 'because I really thought he was. My judgment may have been wrong, but it was not insincere. Surely you would agree that White was pretty nondescript beside such colleagues as Liddell, Hart, Blunt, Rothschild, Masterman and others? Or perhaps not?'[13]

Philby's book cast a spell. In an era when the fictional James Bond films and le Carré's novels incarnated spies as potent images, Philby lampooned the reality: a gullible intelligence service which first employed a traitor and then allowed his escape. The more pertinent reality was unmentioned: that Philby's exposure and his uncomfortable exile in Moscow was entirely due to White.

Initially White was tempted to rebut Philby's sarcastic disclosures about British intelligence's defects, but he refrained: 'I would have had to indulge in half-truths or untruths in order not to reveal too much.'[14] There were also the advantages in burying mistakes and refusing public explanations by pleading the Official Secrets Act. But, irresistibly tempted to answer his protagonist, White wilfully launched a counter-offensive that became a self-destructive 'battle of books'. White, the student historian and aspiring author, had already conceived two books: Hugh Trevor-Roper's proving Hitler's death and Alan Moorehead's flawed portrayal of the atomic spies. In the wake of two more books about Philby, including *The Spy I Loved* by Eleanor Philby, White 'encouraged' Trevor-Roper to publish an 'accurate' version, *The Philby Affair*.

White soon regretted his complicity. Roper's elegant essay fuelled rather than stilled the debate. By admitting his own wartime membership of SIS and castigating his superiors as mindlessly basking in fictitious glories who regarded 'ideas as subversive', Roper trampled over the taboo against SIS self-publicity. Among those who saw an opportunity to profit from indiscretion was John Masterman, White's Oxford tutor. Masterman had sought since 1947 to publish his own account of the double-cross success. Britain's contribution towards Hitler's defeat, he argued, was distorted without the public's knowledge of the Twenty Committee. His proposal to break with precedent was vetoed outright, not least because Ultra was still a closely guarded secret.

Masterman's continued lobbying in the mid-1950s was robustly rebutted by White. Throughout the 1960s, that denial was echoed by Hollis, although by then Masterman had shifted his argument. Publication of the wartime success, he persisted, would balance the 'serious damage to the image of the services which came to be regarded as expensive, inefficient and unnecessary' after the Blake, Lonsdale and Philby cases.[15] In October 1967, Masterman again approached White, whose objection to publication cited 'grave difficulties' and concealed his irritation with Masterman's innate vanity. After all, Masterman had merely been the chairman of the Twenty Committee, without any responsibility for the grind involved, or indeed for the ingenuity. To the officials, procrastination appeared to be the best solution.

But in 1970 Masterman thwarted his former pupil by unveiling a 'diabolic plan' to publish his account in America and face prosecution in Britain. Outraged by Masterman's venal motives, White and Greenhill approached Sir Alec Douglas-Home, then foreign secretary, urging that the retired don be prevented from establishing a dangerous precedent. Their meeting at the Foreign Office was unusual. All three had been tutored by Masterman at Oxford. Douglas-Home sat in daunted silence, contemplating a request for punitive threats. 'But it's JC's book,' he spluttered eventually. 'To stop what he wants to do is unthinkable.'[16] To White's surprise, the minister ignored the flagrant breach of the Official Secrets Act and, negotiating a way through the Whitehall labyrinth, won permission for publication of *The Double-Cross System* in February 1972. 'Dick was furious,' said Christopher Harmer, a wartime MI5 officer, who acted as Masterman's solicitor albeit in retrospect, with regret.

Of the two principle consequences that flowed from the statutory breach, one was engineered by White, the second was unforeseen. On the eve of his final retirement, White reconsidered his 'most emphatic' veto in 1969 of an official history of British intelligence in the Second World War proposed by the Labour government. Masterman's self-glorification would be neutralised if the whole truth were told. Overcoming opposition from the intelligence services and the Cabinet Office, he persuaded Edward

Heath to endorse the project. 'Intelligence was a success story, probably our greatest victory in the war, and history is incomplete without an account,' he insisted. Heath approved and a team of writers and researchers was gathered under Professor Francis Hinsley.[17]

The second, unexpected consequence was another book by a former intelligence officer. But, instead of publishing praise, he intended to denigrate the intelligence service by rattling the skeletons. The first steps had been taken in summer 1969 when John Day, an MI5 officer, visited White at the Cabinet Office. At Furnival Jones's request, Day had spent the previous year undertaking another review of the evidence against Graham Mitchell and Roger Hollis. He had found nothing against Mitchell, but the case against MI5's former director general appeared convincing.

Hollis had retired in 1965. After a divorce, he had married his secretary and passed his days playing golf. Since then, Peter Wright's investigations had unearthed suspicious coincidences, particularly the proximity, in China in the 1930s, of Hollis and Ursula Kuczynski, Klaus Fuchs's GRU contact, who had been codenamed Sonia. Although Furnival Jones condemned the reopened investigation against Hollis as 'grotesque',[18] he accepted White's advice that, if the process was to be completed without subsequent allegations of a cover-up, there was no alternative but to go along with the Fluency inquiries. The molehunters had expanded their search, suspecting even Nicholas Elliott of treachery because of his mishandling of the Beirut confrontation with Philby, the start of their investigation in 1963. 'Elliott', said Wright, 'didn't admit to anything – he was far too clever to do that.'[19]

Accordingly, Day visited White to discuss Hollis. 'Stiff and not very welcoming', White showed some disdain for the consequences of a process which he had inaugurated. The madness, he thought, had gone too far. Wright was well intentioned but 'warped'. Everyone was infected by 'the echoes of Burgess and Maclean'. But, to clear the decks at last, White agreed that the investigation against Hollis was necessary, although his own contribution would be limited. 'What a waste of time,' thought

Day after the meeting.

In mid-1969, Hollis was summoned to London. Briefed by Day and Wright, Furnival Jones interrogated his former superior, an unprecedented occurrence. At the end of the day, Hollis was declared innocent. White welcomed that conclusion. After a decade of unsavoury, exhaustive investigations his former service had proved itself to be clean. The good news was passed to Angleton. 'They failed to bring home the bacon,' White said of the molehunters.[20]

But the skeletons were still moving. For smouldering within MI5 was the self-investigation that White had inaugurated, unaffected by the formal abandonment of the investigation of Hollis. In 1972, just after Sir Anthony Blunt's appointment as adviser for the Queen's pictures and drawings (he ceased being surveyor of her pictures that same year), there were rumours of his imminent death. The prospect loomed that his treachery, still secret, might be exposed either in his will or by a leak following his death when the threat of the libel laws was lifted. Among the few briefed about the potential time-bomb was Reginald Maudling, the relaxed home secretary. After reading a memorandum listing twenty-one unprosecuted suspected Soviet spies in Britain and a submission that Blunt had never been truthful, Maudling summoned White.

'Can you explain and justify', he asked, 'the continuing investigation into old history when there are current problems like the agitation of the hard left throughout Britain?'

'One day it will be necessary', replied White, 'to have a balance sheet on this subject. It ought not to take precedence over contemporary inquiries, yet we must know how at a particular moment in our history we were messed about and bewildered by all this.'[21] Unspoken was White's own desire to understand how he and others had been deceived. The politician had shown no interest in history, but White had nevertheless protected his own creation.

'The molehunt continued to tear MI5 apart but Furnival Jones refused to stop it,' Rolfe Kingsley, the new CIA liaison officer in London, reported.[22] Two of the best molehunters in MI5, Alec MacDonald and Patrick Stewart, had rejected advice from CIA officers sceptical of Angleton's scenarios about Soviet penetration.

'They both refused to listen.' Even Furnival Jones, Kingsley said, refused to intervene. That persistent obsession influenced Philip Allen, the permanent secretary at the Home Office, to propose James Waddell, a senior Home Office official, as successor to Furnival Jones. 'I don't trust the insiders,' complained Allen. 'They lack imagination, they have no political antennae and they're splendid at telling us what happened after the event but never give us any warning. We need to let in some fresh air.'[23]

The conspiracy against Waddell was hatched between Peter Wright and Victor Rothschild, the complicated third baron who had been appointed director of Edward Heath's Central Policy Review Staff. Back inside Whitehall, Rothschild, who had never lost his interest in intelligence, had reinvolved himself in MI5's internal politics, and Peter Wright was more than a good source of gossip, regaling White's wartime friend with his discontent about Hollis's 'acquittal'. The interrogation, Wright told Rothschild, had been inconclusive. Hollis had been evasive on the critical issue of his friendships in China. Rothschild was persuaded that the hunt should continue and that MI5's morale would suffer if an unsympathetic outsider like Waddell were imposed.

Rothschild recruited White to stop the appointment. White was supportive. Fearing repetition of the problems caused by Rennie in SIS, White persuaded Heath to veto Waddell and appoint Michael Hanley, MI5's deputy director general, as the new chief. White would soon realise his mistake, for Hanley suffered from the very faults which Allen had sought to eradicate. But White was more concerned to protect the service and its self-purification, which an outsider was unlikely to understand; and he still trusted Wright's intentions.

But Hanley, to the surprise of White and Wright, halted the molehunt. The new director general, unimpressed by Angleton, wanted his service to address the real problems. Alec MacDonald retired, dejected by the saga; Peter Wright was sidelined, the 'serials' or evidence indicating a traitor within MI5 stored in his safe; and then, at last, the British patron of the hunt departed.

In 1972, White quietly slipped out of Whitehall, seemingly for ever. Traditional patriotism rather than idealism had motivated him throughout his career, but it was his tolerant pragmatism, expelling the delusions about the sunshine past, which, he believed, had laid the foundations for a modern intelligence service. He made few claims for his achievements. 'I was there from 1936 to 1972, a remarkable period and saw everything. I lasted well and shopped nobody.'[24]

In Burpham, reading books, writing the occasional poem, tending his new garden, helping to build the local village hall, paying visits to the Swiss Alps and enjoying country walks, White gratefully bade farewell to Whitehall. Occasionally his neighbour, the Duke of Norfolk, asked whether he might arrange a favour or introduction; sometimes he visited Klop Ustinov's widow. Increasingly, he met MI5 colleagues, especially those from wartime, but there were few contacts with SIS officers. Most of all, he enjoyed his happy marriage. Regularly, he travelled to London to lunch with a widening range of friends at the Garrick, which would vote him life membership and save him the annual fees. To everyone he seemed the epitome of discretion. He was the guardian of the secrets, the keeper of the skeletons. The protectorship seemed secure. As president of the Old Stortfordians, he agreed to be guest of honour on Speech Day but to his host's disappointment 'produced no rattling yarns'.[25] Even for schoolboys, he was the man who kept the secrets.

But the past would not disappear. Two years into retirement, White was summoned by Sir John Hunt, the new cabinet secretary. The new generation required guidance. Despite Hanley's best intentions, Angleton's spell was still potent – both in MI5, where some new officers had 'bought the whole story',[26] and in SIS. Hunt disclosed that Stephen de Mowbray, SIS's former deputy liaison officer in Washington, had, in June 1974, unexpectedly called at 10 Downing Street. In a display of reckless bravado, he repeated the allegations against Hollis and protested about the failure to resolve the suspicions of Soviet penetration. 'As de Mowbray's eyes glazed over,' Hunt told a colleague, 'I had the feeling of dangerous obsession. I had confidence in Hanley's honesty but not his judgment or intellectual ability. I therefore consulted White.'

'Is de Mowbray a screwball?' asked the cabinet secretary.

'No, he's not mad,' replied White. 'He's patriotic, hard-working but obsessed.'

Four years earlier, White had hinted to Oldfield that some of de Mowbray's opinions were unreliable, because his conversion to Angleton's theories had proved irreversible. Instead, de Mowbray was retained in Century House as a production officer for Iberia, sinking into gloom as Angleton's warnings appeared to be increasingly ignored. Finally, he had burst into Hunt's office with his astonishing tale.

'Was Hollis a spy?' asked Hunt.

'I'd be surprised,' replied White unemotionally, leaving Hunt with the impression that it was nonetheless conceivable.

'But how did it get to this?' asked the senior mandarin, genuinely shocked that, unknown to senior Whitehall officials, the intelligence services had been plagued by internecine warfare.

White searched back in his mind. Where did it begin? With Philby, with Krivitsky or even before with unknown Soviet illegals in Cambridge? For White, it was so difficult to explain to a new generation his foreboding fifteen years earlier of the vast and threatening KGB which had seemingly penetrated every institution and every secret establishment in Britain. Even the name Angleton meant nothing to the sophisticated cabinet secretary. By the end of their meeting, Hunt understood the wisdom of preparing an answer for those who, in the future, would hint of cover-ups. This, after all, was the era of Watergate.

Although Hollis had died in October 1973, Hunt recommended the appointment of Burke Trend, his predecessor, to investigate the whole molehunt. One year later, Trend reported that both Mitchell and Hollis had been loyal servants who had performed their duties properly. Hollis, Trend concluded, was not a spy. But Trend, in his civil servant's manner, had craftily written his conclusions so that he could 'have it both ways': he would be covered 'if a spy was found the next day'.[27]

Trend's report coincided with the final dismemberment of the Old Guard. Helms had retired in 1973. Stripped of his protector, Angleton had been fired at the end of the following year by Helms's successor, William Colby. The CIA's assessment of Angleton's tenure was sensational: he had become a dangerous liability and even a disaster for the agency and for all the Western intelligence services.

Wright retired in 1976 to Australia, acknowledging that, although his American mentor had probably gone too far, Soviet penetration in Britain had never been resolved. He also departed grumbling about his inadequate pension, a fuse of resentment. Coincidentally, White was complaining about the inadequacy of his own pension and sought help from, among others, Victor Rothschild, who lobbied on his behalf. His subsequent plea to Margaret Thatcher was rejected.

In his living room overlooking the garden he had created, White contemplated his old enemy – the communists. Occasionally he would re-read Arthur Koestler's *Darkness at Noon*, fascinated by Gletkin, the chilling NKVD interrogator, an ambitious cog in Stalin's machinery of tyranny. For White, intrigued by the battle of the dogmas, Gletkin was 'the biggest argument possible against the ruthless Soviet system'. But he was still unsure whether communism would soon be defeated. Unlike Malcolm Muggeridge, whom he occasionally visited, White did not interpret the brave protests by isolated dissidents in the Soviet Union as proof of communism's inevitable decline. Nor did he accept arguments that the Soviets' public deification of Philby and Lonsdale proved their weakness. The Cold War had not yet been won.

More extreme sentiments were harboured by Angleton in Washington. The CIA's new director, William Colby, was publicly confessing in senate hearings to a catalogue of sins committed by his predecessors. Gradually stripped of its secrecy, the Agency's reputation was irretrievably sliding into a quagmire. Aggrieved by his dismissal and rendered distraught by the malign interpretations placed on his activities, Angleton began welcoming selected journalists who sought his advice and showed themselves willing to record his version of the battle against KGB penetration. Among the visitors was Andrew Boyle, a British author and a senior BBC Radio producer. Boyle had embarked on a general study of Cambridge in the 1930s entitled *The Climate of Treason*. The timing was opportune. Emotions had relaxed and eyewitnesses were less reluctant to speak. The writer cast his net wide and arrived in Washington to obtain confirmation of a sensational allegation.

One of the first men Boyle had approached was Goronwy Rees, by then widely discredited and disliked for his own articles and books about the Cambridge Ring. To Boyle's astonishment, at their initial meeting in March 1977 in a Chiswick pub, Rees volunteered the information that Blunt, recruited by Burgess, was the Fourth Man. It was a turning point in the molehunt. Boyle had neither suspected Blunt nor expected the revelation. But, soon afterwards, Rees's allegation was confirmed by Tom Howarth, a don at Magdalene, Cambridge and a friend of several SIS officers.

On 25 August 1977, Boyle travelled to Burpham. By then, White was writing a private history of British intelligence from 1930 to 1970. Speculation about the Fourth Man was already rife, even feverish. *The Times* had recently bungled by naming Donald Beves, an innocuous academic, as a Soviet spy, and then had to publish an apology. 'Anyone who knows the toughness of the Soviet Secret Service', commented White forgetfully, 'will dismiss the thought of a remote but busy Cambridge don doing the kind of work Soviet intelligence would expect.'[28]

Boyle found White 'cagey' about the British traitors. Although he listened patiently for six hours to Boyle's account of his research, White did not reveal his suspicion that Rees was himself a traitor. But at the last moment he dropped his guard. As Boyle was leaving, the author mentioned his suspicions about Blunt. White replied, 'There we are on difficult and embarrassing ground. Watch how you go with that one.'[29] Just before Christmas, Boyle wrote asking White outright if Blunt was a traitor. Testily White replied, 'I know nothing about that subject whatsoever.' The professional brush-off appeared irrevocable.

White's mood changed in January 1978. His pretext was the publication of *The Pencourt File*, an account of the investigation by Barrie Penrose and Roger Courtiour of Harold Wilson's suspicions of a plot by right-wing MI5 officers, in conjunction with the CIA and South African intelligence, to undermine his premiership. Wilson's allegations against those whom White had dubbed the 'Young Turks' had propelled his beloved service into unexpected controversy. White of course knew that, ever since Golitsin's visit to Britain in 1963, Wright and other molehunters had placed a sinister interpretation on Harold Wilson's frequent post-war visits to the Soviet Union. Golitsin's more sensational allegations that Hugh Gaitskell, the former Labour Party leader, might have been murdered in January 1963 to allow Harold Wilson, a KGB agent, to become the party leader had even been investigated by Arthur Martin.

All that arrant nonsense, White feared, would seep into the public domain. His life's work to prove the reliability of the intelligence services could be destroyed by ignorant speculation. In self-interest but quoting his conviction that better public understanding would improve the status of Britain's intelligence services and suffocate the sensationalism, he decided that, if Blunt was to be exposed, MI5's reputation should not be damaged. Regardless of the draconian strictures imposed upon him by the Official Secrets Act, he judged that he knew best how to protect MI5 and himself: namely, by guiding Boyle away from damaging errors.

On White's initiative, Boyle returned to Burpham on 27 April 1978. Over tea, White heard a further account of Boyle's research, including his interview with James Klugman, a Marxist ideologue and intellectual long suspected by MI5 of talent-spotting for Soviet intelligence in the 1930s. In 1951, Klugman had resisted MI5's requests for interviews. But the communist had agreed to meet Boyle shortly before his death in September 1977. White was impressed: 'We could never have done that, or begun to get anywhere close.' The former MI5 and SIS chief had been converted to the notion that some journalists were better investigators than his own officers. With the relaxation of security signalled by the imminent publication of the official series on wartime intelligence, he persuaded himself that it was in the public interest to release accurate facts to protect himself and his service.

So when Boyle voiced his conviction that Blunt was the Fourth Man White did not repeat his earlier denial. Instead, he restricted himself to two comments. 'Blunt did not confess while I was in MI5,' implying that he had done so after 1956; and 'We found less than expected on searching Burgess's flat,' implying that there was no evidence to link Burgess with espionage, and leaving open the possibility that Blunt had pocketed incriminating material before the official search. Effectively, White had confirmed Blunt's treachery. By then, many knew of Blunt's confession and Boyle easily obtained further confirmation: from Sir Robert Mackenzie and George Carey Foster, the Foreign Office security officers who had been told by White; and Nicholas Elliott. In May 1978, Boyle flew to Washington and met Angleton at the Army and Navy Club. Over several hours, the American whispered secrets, mixing fact and fiction, and reconfirmed Blunt's treachery. Overwhelmed by Angleton's wave of disclosures and swallowing his fabrications as true, Boyle's letter of thanks praised the CIA officer's 'single-handed achievement in "rumbling" Donald Maclean', an absurd suggestion.[30]

In early April 1979, Boyle sent White the manuscript of his book. Ignoring the errors, not least those wilder and unsubstantiated tales spawned by Angleton, White made only a limited number of comments. But his mere imprimatur bestowed credibility. By any measure, his breach of the rules of silence was to affect the status of the intelligence services for ever. His motives were in part straightforward. The first volume of the official history of *British Intelligence in the Second World War* had been published to mixed reactions. Critics lamented the absence of named personalities, their arguments and the conflicts of interest in handling the intelligence. But the book fulfilled White's criterion of 'No monsters, no heroes', and, to his delight, broke the taboo by describing the role of intelligence in the conduct of the war. 'No harm, only good was achieved by its publication,' he said. 'Secrecy for its own sake is damaging.'[31]

Less manifest was White's fear that his investigation of treachery and the consequent molehunt would be misunderstood. Still pained by Philby's book and conscious that those writing the history of his period were not eyewitnesses to the turmoil of the times, he wanted to bequeath an understanding of how he had blown the past asunder. However messy, Philby's flight in 1963 had terminated the era.

That autumn, as Boyle's manuscript was transformed into a book, Britain became mesmerised by espionage. On BBC

Television, Alec Guinness portrayed George Smiley in a seven-part dramatisation of John le Carré's *Tinker, Tailor, Soldier, Spy*, while le Carré's next offering, *Smiley's People*, was fervently discussed. Transfixed by the hunt for a fictional mole in the 'Circus', the nation was suddenly presented with a real, living corpse.

On 4 November 1979, *The Climate of Treason* was published. Four days later, Boyle's disguise of Blunt as 'Maurice' was exposed by *Private Eye*. Sir Robert Armstrong, the new cabinet secretary, was handed a bulky file labelled 'Blunt' from the Cabinet Office archives. Inside was a statement, carefully prepared a decade earlier for just such a moment. Margaret Thatcher knew of its existence before her election as prime minister from Victor Rothschild, her unofficial adviser on security. Although Blunt still hoped that the immunity deal struck with MI5 would protect him from official confirmation, Thatcher saw no advantage in joining the conspiracy of silence. On 15 November, she announced Blunt's guilt to the House of Commons.

The revelation provoked a wave of anger against those who had protected a traitor suspected of causing the deaths of anti-communists. 'The stench of hypocrisy and Establishment cover-up is overwhelming', commented the *Daily Mail*. 'A totally abject recital of official self-protection and dishonesty,' carped the *Guardian*. A favoured comparison in newspapers and television was between the condoning of Blunt's treason and the punishment of Fuchs and Nunn May. The nation was not united in its condemnation. Blunt, the arrogant, aesthetic homosexual, was protected by his own. Some praised Blunt's services to art, defending his right to act according to his conscience and denouncing the government for betraying an understanding not to disclose the immunity agreement. Theirs was a sense of history which White had sought to understand nearly thirty years before.

Three days after that debate, Boyle sat at the bedside of Goronwy Rees, dying in Charing Cross Hospital. In his last testament, the stricken outcast bequeathed a poisoned chalice that was to destroy White's strategy. 'Guy Liddell', he gasped, 'was a traitor.' Like Blunt, he continued, Liddell had had a homosexual relationship with Burgess; and Blunt had confessed in 1964 only because Liddell had died and 'there were no more conspirators to protect'.

The accusation against Liddell stung White. Not only was Liddell a friend and his mentor, but he had been cleared by the investigation. 'Grotesque and preposterous,' White told the *Sunday Times*.[32] 'Guy had married a Baring,' he told friends, still believing that a marriage, albeit broken, precluded a homosexual relationship. Regardless of the incredibility of Rees's venomous testament, the bitter history of the molehunt began to leak into the public domain.

White's confirmation of Blunt's treachery unleashed a journalistic molehunt. Boyle claimed there were 'at least another twenty-five unnamed spies', and the skeletons began to move. The first was John Cairncross, who admitted to the *Sunday Times* that he was part of the same conspiracy. Effectively in 1979, a Fifth Man was named and had confessed.[33] Then others – Sir Dennis Proctor, Alister Watson and Leo Long – came under the spotlight as suspected spies. Those skeletons were moved by disgruntled but anonymous MI5 molehunters, interested witnesses of White's participation in the unfolding drama.

Among the casualties was the prime minister's order to delay indefinitely publication of White's treasured volume four of the series *British Intelligence in the Second World War*. The volume described MI5's activities. 'Furious' about her veto,[34] White encouraged a new writer, Rupert Allason, alias Nigel West, to write the history of MI5 up to 1945. With his assistance, Allason would be introduced to Tar Robertson and the MI5 officers who had run the double-cross operation. Masterman's vainglory, White ensured, would be undermined and the true heroes would be recognised.

In Downing Street, the gradual discernment of White's activities puzzled the new generation of senior officials. Absolute discretion appeared to have been forsaken. 'Out of character,' Hunt observed of a man who had become a source for those publicising the molehunt. White was impervious to their criticism. More than ever, he despaired of unnecessary secrecy and feared that, if his achievement in purifying MI5 and SIS was not properly explained, Britain's intelligence services would suffer vilification and misunderstanding as the CIA had done. But his vision – fuelling the battle of the books – was limited. The mole-hunters' discontent had been reignited and their prey was White's friend, Victor Rothschild. The former MI5 officer was among the names stealthily put forward as a suspected Soviet spy. Rothschild recoiled in terror.

As a student at Cambridge, Rothschild had known all the traitors and had not only worked with them during the war, but was the owner of the house in Bentinck Street rented in wartime to Burgess and Blunt. Those visiting the house would always recall the close friendship between Tessa Mayor, later Lady Rothschild, and Anthony Blunt.[35] They would also recall that Rothschild had introduced Blunt to Liddell, securing the traitor's entry into MI5. Rothschild's friendship with Blunt had continued uninterrupted, even after 1964 when Peter Wright, following the confession, formally questioned both Rothschilds. His sensitivity about his wife's friendship with Blunt emerged in the aftermath of the art historian's exposure in 1979. Anxiously, Rothschild turned to White for help.

During the 1970s, White had resumed a closer relationship with Rothschild. Their regular encounters in the Cabinet Office continued during his retirement when he and Kate had stayed at the Rothschilds' Cambridge home. 'You woke up in the morning,' observed another former SIS officer and guest, 'and saw what looked like a Picasso on the wall. On closer inspection, you realised "It is a Picasso!"' During those weekends, White and Rothschild discussed and dissected MI5 'endlessly' – a source of fascination for the host which his guest tolerated out of affection for a friend whose company he enjoyed and whom he trusted. White did not believe his friend was a traitor. But the speculation and analysis were unhelpful to Rothschild in his new predicament. Receiving no direct assistance, he embarked on what White categorised as 'a terrible mistake'. He turned to Peter Wright for help.

During his period in the Cabinet Office, Rothschild had become intrigued by Wright's account of MI5's frustrated investigations. He had also heard about a more sinister aspect of Wright's career: that after Heath's election defeat in February 1974, Wright had masterminded a maverick plot to smear Harold Wilson, his 'kitchen cabinet' friends and some Labour ministers as communist agents. Rothschild was untroubled by those activities. Telephoning Wright in Australia, he persuaded the retired MI5 officer to accept a prepaid airline ticket to London. Wright, he hoped, would produce an affidavit testifying to his innocence.

On his return to London, Wright revealed that there was an incomplete manuscript, based on copies of MI5 files, of his hunt for another Fifth Man, alias Roger Hollis. To Rothschild, publication of Wright's suspicions seemed an ideal distraction from the suspicions directed against himself. He telephoned Chapman Pincher, a journalist then famed for his scoops about the intelligence services and spies, and invited him to meet a unique source. After discussions, Pincher agreed to write an account of Wright's frustrated investigation and divide the profits. The book, completed in early 1981, ostensibly disguised Wright's participation.

Six weeks before publication, the manuscript of *Their Trade Is Treachery* was read by Sir Robert Armstrong and senior officers in MI5 and SIS. Inactivity seemed the best course. A public application for an injunction, it was agreed, would cause a rumpus, and publication, albeit unfortunate, would release the skeletons in a managed fashion. Armstrong's reasoning proved to be flawed. The book, identifying Mitchell as a suspect and Hollis as the unprosecuted Fifth Man, detonated a new frenzy of public speculation, parliamentary activity and sensational headlines.

On 26 March 1981, Margaret Thatcher, denouncing the book as 'inaccurate and distorted', admitted for the first time that Hollis had been investigated as a Soviet spy. The ambivalence of the molehunt, and by implication White's management of the skeletons, was laid bare. The Hollis investigation, she admitted, 'did not conclusively prove his innocence ... But no evidence was found that incriminated him.' The conclusion, she added, 'was that he had not been an agent of the Russian intelligence service'. The aftertaste irritated White. Without difficulty, he had identified Pincher's undisclosed source: 'Pincher didn't do his homework since nearly all his material has come from Wright and they have got it wrong.' Thatcher's statement was correct, but it fed the cynics.

White was summoned to London to explain his history once more to a new generation. For days, he read the Hollis files in Leconfield House. Personnel files, the Fluency files and operational files were all provided for White to compile another account of his protégé's life. In a show of measured self-congratulation, he emerged to declare that Hollis was 'no slouch, the leading sleuth in MI5 and a reasonably good spycatcher'. But the files also revealed that Hollis 'had no real interest in Soviet operations, was regarded as ignorant; and had no true taste for the job'.[36] Most importantly, they confirmed for White that the molehunt was truly over. The hunt for the Fifth Man had been a canard, a damaging mistake born of the distant, tense epoch when Britain had appeared under threat. There were so many Cambridge 'spies' – discovered and undiscovered – that no single one could be called the Fifth Man. As he stood in Whitehall, the realisation was sobering. What seemed a lifetime spent pursuing a cancer had proved to be a hunt for a shadow. Yet in failure there was success. He had proved the service to be clean.

The new generation of Cabinet Office mandarins were unimpressed. Detached from the investigation and the era, they blamed White for a mess: 'He had failed to handle the 1951 issues. There was no courageous intellectual investigation on the body politic by White.' The blame was, however, shared: 'There had been no pressure on him from ministers or Westminster.'[37] Whitehall's stinging criticism was repeated to White. Few, it seemed to him, understood the turmoil which his officers had endured and overcome. He felt the need to explain the background. When Paul Greengrass, a television producer, telephoned and suggested that, in anticipation of a visit to Wright in Australia, he would like to be briefed, White was amenable.

At the end of the first of three meetings White handed Greengrass a copy of *Wilderness of Mirrors*, a recent book by David Martin, an American journalist who, for the first time, exposed what White called 'Angleton, a corrupted intellectual'. This, White told Greengrass, 'explains the problem perfectly'.[38] Books seemed an appropriate medium for managing the skeletons.

Expressly, White asserted that he had never trusted Angleton. 'From the beginning,' he told Cleveland Cram in 1981, 'I always had grave reservations about Angleton.'[39] Later, he would explain the nature of Angleton and Wright: 'You know what it's like – whether in the BBC or MI5 – employees of inward-looking organisations are very narrow-minded characters. Counter-intelligence people thrive on conspiracies. Working in a very constricted and secret world, without any windows, they can't tell the difference between the substance and the shadows.'[40]

Wright's agreement with Greengrass in 1984 to appear on television, in breach of the law, surprised White. For the first time he understood the threat of the corrupted molehunt. If it gained credibility, the British intelligence services might fall victim to the opprobrium which had befallen the CIA. White asked Downing Street for permission to counter on television Wright's allegations that the molehunt was incomplete. His request was rejected and the management of the skeletons fell slowly beyond his control. Television turned Wright's particular allegation against Hollis into widespread revelations about MI5's failed hunt for Soviet spies in Britain.

In June 1986, the news leaked that Wright had co-operated with Greengrass to write *Spycatcher*.[41] Simultaneously, the *Observer* revealed that White's recent discussions with journalists about Blunt had 'blown a large hole in the security service's claim that they have all taken a vow of silence'. As the government prepared to appeal to the Australian courts to prevent publication of *Spycatcher*, White urged officials calling from Whitehall 'not to touch the law'. Instead of leaving it to outsiders, he advised, 'we should publish an insider's book and avoid judicial inquiries'. His advice was ignored, especially by Thatcher. 'We are too cautious for anyone's good,' warned White, but his words fell on deaf ears in London. 'It was left to MI5's so-called legal experts,' he lamented, 'and they've all had a field day at the expense of the taxpayer. All for the sake of a third-rate book.'

The courtroom débâcle in Sydney, as the government haplessly sought to prevent publication of *Spycatcher*, had many victims. The first was Victor Rothschild, openly suspected of treachery after the revelation that he had organised Wright's initial disclosures. His public demand in a letter to the *Daily Telegraph* for public exculpation was not satisfied. 'It was very sad for Victor,' conceded White, suspected by some of having encouraged Rothschild's original ploy of introducing Wright to a journalist. The source of suspicion was Rothschild himself, alleging that his ruse had been undertaken with 'higher authority'. In 1990, Rothschild suddenly died – killed, some would say, by the stress.

The second victim was MI5 itself. More leaks from disgruntled former officers after the 1984 conviction for espionage of Michael Bettaney, an MI5 officer, suggested an ill-managed and notably unsuccessful security service. The third victim was SIS, now seen as an expensive and equally unsuccessful intelligence service.

White was unmoved. The intelligence services, he believed, would prosper if slightly exposed to daylight. He had exposed the skeletons, but the war had been won. The vanquished lived in Moscow. From that city came reports of the traitors suffering discomfort and bickering. Burgess had died miserably of alcoholism, while Philby, Maclean and Blake survived to argue among themselves.

Angry that Philby had seduced his wife Melinda, Maclean had broken with his co-conspirator. Initially Blake and Philby met weekly with their Russian wives. But Philby regarded Blake as 'a young upstart' less important than himself;[42] after he had double-crossed Blake over the use of a family photograph, and had bickered over their status when Blake received the Order of Lenin before he did, they never met again. Philby's later comment – to Phillip Knightly – that Blake's escape might have been organised by SIS was, Blake said, 'pure spite'. Blake and Maclean remained close friends, working together in an institute for international affairs, until the older man's death in March 1983. Blake, his executor, inherited his library. Two weeks later, Blunt died.

In Burpham, as *glasnost* allowed visitors to Moscow the chance to meet Philby, Blake and their KGB controllers, White enjoyed hearing reports about how his faceless enemies and the traitors were having to witness the progressive collapse of communism. Their ultimate failure was greeted with chill satisfaction. Few would not relish the satisfaction of participating in triumphs over two deadly opponents – Nazism and communism – but until the end White's pleasure was modestly expressed. His victory, over two tyrannical ideologies and the most deceitful of men, had never corrupted his own decency. Occasionally he had been overwhelmed, but he never drowned. Unlike others, he had survived, his honour intact. To the end he remained a good man, enjoying conversation and friendships, quietly convinced that eventually history would acknowledge the value of an honest intelligence service to the nation's government.

'I've got cancer,' he told me when we last met in the autumn of 1992. 'My good neighbour, a doctor, has written me off. But I'll show him. I'll beat this.' Until the last days, he read voraciously, anxious to understand why men deceive their families, deny history and give their lives for dogmas. Perhaps also regretting that he had never completed a volume of reminiscences; he had never fulfilled his true ambition as a writer. And then, on 22 February, holding his beloved wife's hand, he slipped away. He had lost his life but won the final battle.

Two months later, the public servant was given an unusual memorial service. Three hundred gathered at the Guards' Chapel in Wellington Barracks. The son of a modest family from Kent was honoured by former prime ministers, peers and the best of the British intelligence services. Entering from the shadows behind the altar to read two lessons were Stella Rimington, the director general of MI5, and Colin McColl, the chief of SIS. Their public presence showed that Dick White's legacy was acknowledged. Thanks to his efforts, Britain, for all its weaknesses, could boast, more than before, competent, loyal and productive intelligence services, respected throughout the world – by both friends and enemies. Those intelligence services were mirrors of White himself, the perfect English spy.

Appendix: Into Retirement

During his life, White wrote a collection of verses. Many of
his colleagues were surprised by this unknown aspect of the chief.
'Into Retirement' was read at White's memorial service.

Now that I lead a quiet life,
And babble of green fields around my home,
I've time enough to learn from natural things
Not to desire a wisdom of my own;
Content to learn those lessons that derive
From nothing more than knowing I'm alive.

Here in our house are self-imaged things,
My friend and architect has realised,
Simple, and sane, and manageable things
Whose self-attendance makes them double prized:
Walls of plain wood and floors of warm green stone,
Windows that make the world outside our own.

And on our hillside I have planted trees,
And colonised shrubs amid the downland grass,
A kind of English 'maquis' growing free
To mirror English seasons as they pass.
Perhaps it's less a garden than a ground
In living things to share the peace we've found.

And from this plot are paths that point the way
Through fields and farms, and woods, and over downs,
From whose green summits we can see the sea
And the dark outlines of tormented towns.
To walk these paths is nothing less for me
Than a last lesson in the ways to see.

'Where's the ambition in it?' some will say,
'He used to share the lives of men of power,
Here's one grey eminence has gone to ground,
Escaping the crises of the hour.'
That's true, of course, there's no more drama here,
But then again there's nothing left to fear.

And all the long days given me to live,
The life I've sensed behind the need to act,
I've played the part my karma has decreed,
Some would say 'well', some 'ill'. I say: 'accept
Success and failure for the things they are,
Neither a blessing nor a fallen star.'

So some will say: 'here is his Sabine farm,
And here his crystal spring that never fails;
No need to envy, and no need to praise;
To each the destiny that most avails.
At least he's shed the power that must hide
Self from the self that may not be denied.'

Finding that dearer self has been a task
That's more akin to waiting than to will.
I've studied hard, but nowhere from my books has
Come the message that understanding is:
To move, to breathe, to listen and to see,
To wait without impatience, and to be.

Who knows these things can count his blessings free
A house, a plot of ground, a home indeed,
shelter for those he loves and leaves behind,
A place in which a man can meet a friend
And slowly and decently await his end.

D.G. White

Sources

The most important source of this book was Dick White [DW] himself. My interviews with White are marked TB/DW. Andrew Boyle's [AB] interview notes with White and the material from his incomplete manuscript are marked accordingly. Other interviews I have used were those recorded separately by Barrie Penrose, Paul Greengrass and Alan Moorehead [AM] and there are letters between White and all the above named and others.

Over the past fifteen years, I conducted interviews with many retired MI5 and SIS officers. I have only sourced by name those who, since the interviews, have died. Most of the CIA, FBI and all the KGB officers were prepared to be named. A few former CIA officers requested that the interviews be unsourced.

In some cases, former MI5, SIS and CIA officers asked that their names should not be mentioned in the text. If their names have never been published, I have usually agreed to that request. In a few exceptional instances, I did not feel under an obligation and did not believe that the request was justified.

For the Public Records Office references:

CAB are Cabinet papers;

FO are Foreign Office papers;

PREM are the prime minister's papers.

Preface
1   Powers, *The Man Who Kept the Secrets*, p. 297.

Chapter One: A True Englishman
1   AB/DW.
2   Ibid.
3   Ibid.
4   AB notes, p. 13.
5   TB/Walter Strawn.
6   AB notes, p. 11.

7 AB/DW; AB notes, p. 14.
8 Commonwealth Fund Fellowship Archives, New York [CF].
9 Masterman, *On the Chariot Wheel*, p. 137.
10 Ibid., p. 125.
11 AB/DW.
12 TB/Bulmer-Thomas.
13 TB/Elvin.
14 AB manuscript, ch. 2/3.
15 CF.
16 AB/DW.
17 Masterman, *On the Chariot Wheel*, pp. 125–6.
18 AB/DW.
19 Masterman, *On the Chariot Wheel*, pp. 183–4.
20 Christ Church Archives.
21 Ibid.
22 CF.
23 AB/DW.
24 TB/Bock.
25 AB/DW.
26 CF.
27 Linklater, *Juan in America*, p. 120.
28 CF.
29 TB/Forbes.
30 CF General review, p. 2.
31 Penrose/DW, 15 July 1985.
32 Ibid.
33 AB/Adam Smith.
34 AB/DW.
35 Whitgift School records.
36 Letters, F.H.G. Percy and John Cummings to Andrew Boyle 1989; Boyle notes.
37 AB/Adam Smith.
38 AB/private information.
39 AB/Hugh Kingsmill.
40 AB/DW.

Chapter Two: A Reluctant Spy

1 TB/Greenhill.
2 Hinsley, *British Intelligence*, iv, p. 7.
3 West, MI5, p. 36.
4 Ibid., p. 78ff.
5 AB/DW.
6 Ibid.

7   AB/private information.
8   Letter, Dick White to Chapman Pincher, 10 March 1982.
9   Masterman, *On the Chariot Wheel*, p. 218ff.
10   AB/DW.
11   Hinsley, *British Intelligence*, i, p. 12ff.
12   Boyle, *Climate of Treason*, p. 137.
13   Letter, Dick White to Chapman Pincher, 10 March 1982.
14   Andrew, *Secret Service*, p. 334.
15   AB/DW.
16   Penrose/DW, 15 July 1985.
17   Penrose and Freeman, *Conspiracy of Silence*, p. 264.
18   Andrew, *Secret Service*, p. 384.
19   Hinsley, *British Intelligence*, iv, p. 9.
20   Ibid., p. 11.
21   Ibid.
22   AB/DW.
23   TB/Peter Ustinov.
24   Andrew, *Secret Service*, pp. 397–8.
25   AB/F. Winterbotham.
26   AB/DW.
27   Ibid.
28   Ibid.
29   TB/DW.
30   Boyle, *Climate of Treason*, p. 199.
31   TB/'Tar' Robertson; West, MI5 p. 73.
32   Boyle, *Climate of Treason*, p. 200.
33   AB/DW.
34   TB/DW.

Chapter Three: The Jigsaw
1   Hinsley, *British Intelligence*, iv, pp. 30–2.
2   Ibid., p. 39.
3   Ibid., p. 69.
4   Informationsheft Grossbritannien; West, MI5, p. 104.
5   Hinsley, *British Intelligence*, iv, p. 69.
6   Penrose/DW, 15 July 1985.
7   Masterman, *On the Chariot Wheel*, p. 219.
8   TB/DW.
9   Hinsley, *British Intelligence*, iv, p. 66.
10   Andrew, *Secret Service*, p. 456.
11   Hinsley, *British Intelligence*, iv, p. 65.
12   Andrew, *Secret Service*, p. 479.
13   TB/DW.

14 West, *Faber Book of Espionage*, p. 199.
15 Hinsley, *British Intelligence*, iv, p. 68.
16 Ibid., p. 178.
17 TB/DW.
18 Hinsley, *British Intelligence*, iv, p. 68.
19 Masterman, *On the Chariot Wheel*, p. 218.
20 Hinsley, *British Intelligence*, iv, p. 91.
21 TB/P. McCullum.
22 Hinsley, *British Intelligence*, iv, p. 97.
23 Ibid., v, p. 13.
24 Ibid., iv, p. 98.
25 Ibid., p. 99.
26 Ibid., v, p. 7.
27 Ibid.
28 TB/Robertson.
29 TB/DW.
30 Ibid.
31 Ibid.
32 Ibid.
33 AB/Robertson.
34 AB/DW.
35 TB/DW. Cf. Modin, *My Five Cambridge Friends*, p. 80.
36 Ibid.
37 AB/DW, manuscript ch. 8/2/1.
38 Boyle, *Climate of Treason*, revised ed., pbk, p. 195.
39 Penrose and Freeman, *Conspiracy of Silence*, p. 265.
40 Penrose/DW, 15 July 1985.
41 Boyle, *Climate of Treason*, p. 215.
42 Penrose and Freeman, *Conspiracy of Silence*, p. 268.
43 Hinsley, *British Intelligence*, iv, p. 179.
44 AB/DW.
45 Hinsley, *British Intelligence*, iv, p. 175.
46 Ibid.
47 Winks, *Cloak and Gown*, p. 260.
48 Hinsley, *British Intelligence*, iv, p. 175.
49 Ibid., p. 134.
50 TB/Lord Dacre.
51 Hinsley, *British Intelligence*, iv, pp. 126, 135.
52 Philby, *My Silent War*, p. 55.
53 Hinsley, *British Intelligence*, iv, p. 137.
54 Leigh, *Wilson Plot*, p. 74.
55 Borovik, *Philby Files*, pp. 157, 160; contra Modin, *My Five Cambridge Friends*, p. 58.

56 AB/DW; Boyle, *Climate of Treason*, p. 220.
57 Borovik, *Philby Files*, p. 52.
58 Trevor-Roper, *Philby Affair*, p. 29.
59 TB/DW; cf. Knightley, *Philby*, p. 84.
60 Philby, *My Silent War*, p. 74.
61 Hinsley, *British Intelligence*, iv, pp. 127–8.
62 TB/confidential MI5 source.
63 Hinsley, *British Intelligence*, iv, pp. 129–30.
64 Ibid., v, p. 25; letter, Wavell to Churchill, 25 May 1942.
65 AB/DW.
66 Hinsley, *British Intelligence*, i, p. 199.
67 Ibid., iv, p. 283.
68 TB/DW.
69 Hinsley, *British Intelligence*, iv, p. 284.
70 Ibid., p. 20.
71 Ibid., p. 56.
72 Ibid., p. 288.
73 Richelson and Ball, *Ties that Bind*, p. 140.
74 AB/DW.
75 Ibid.
76 TB/Pforzheimer.
77 AB/DW.
78 AB/Major General Kenneth Strong; 6 March 1978.
79 Bower, *Blind Eye to Murder*, p. 137.
80 Trevor-Roper, *Philby Affair*, p. 7; Glees, *Secrets of the Service*, p. 206.
81 TB/DW.
82 Hinsley, *British Intelligence*, iv, p. 237ff.
83 Ibid., iii/2, p. 893.
84 JIC File 091.41, NA Washington.
85 TB/DW.
86 AB/DW.
87 TB/D. Bristow.
88 TB/R. Ingram.
89 Boyle, *Climate of Treason*, pbk revised edition, pp. 282ff.
90 AB manuscript, 10/3/8–9.
91 Hinsley, *British Intelligence*, iii/2, p. 438.
92 Wilmot, *The Struggle for Europe*, p. 690.
93 AB/DW, AB manuscript 12/2/2.
94 AB/Reed.
95 Gilbert, *Churchill*, vii, p. 1289.
96 Churchill, *Second World War*, v, p. 542; Boyle, *Climate of Treason*, p. 244.

97 AB/Cowley; Pearson Holmes's diary, Beinecke Library, Yale Library.
98 Hinsley, *British Intelligence*, iv, p. 188.
99 TB/DW.
100 Ibid.
101 AB/DW, AB manuscript 12/2/2.
102 Bradley, *Soldier's Story*, p. 536.
103 RG 331 SHAEF AG Decimal File 1945 200. 63–2.
104 AB manuscript, 12/3/6.
105 TB/DW.
106 Penrose/DW, 15 July 1985.
107 TB/DW.
108 Ibid.
109 AB manuscript, 12/2/91.
110 Padfield, *Himmler*, p. 611.
111 TB/Lord Dacre.
112 TB/DW.
113 TB/confidential SIS source.

Chapter Four: Dangerous Innocence
1 TB/DW.
2 Ibid.
3 Sillitoe, *Cloak Without Dagger*, p. 158.
4 TB/DW.
5 Leigh, *Wilson Plot*, p. 23.
6 Penrose/DW, 15 July 1985.
7 Boyle, *Climate of Treason*, p. 277.
8 TB/DW.
9 Ibid.
10 Ibid.
11 TB/confidential MI5 source.
12 Knightley, *Philby*, p. 133.
13 Borovik, *Philby Files*, p. 239.
14 Moorehead, *Traitors*, p. 23.
15 TB/confidential SIS source.
16 West, *Matter of Trust*, p. 28.
17 Harris, *Attlee*, p. 394.
18 *Daily Telegraph*, 28 October 1946.
19 TB/DW.
20 Borovik, *Philby Files*, p. 212.
21 Ibid., pp. 196–201.
22 TB/Modin.
23 Ibid.

24   TB/Dozhdalev.
25   TB/Carey Foster.
26   Andrew, *Secret Service*, pp. 406–7.
27   TB/Carey Foster.
28   TB/DW.
29   Greengrass/DW, 6 March 1984.
30   Leigh, *Wilson Plot*, p. 41.
31   Smith, *Papers of General Clay*, v. 2, p. 568.
32   Penrose/DW, 15 July 1985.
33   TB/confidential MI5 source.
34   TB/Carey Foster.
35   Ibid.
36   TB/confidential MI5 source; TB/McCullum.
37   Lamphere, *FBI–KGB War*, p. 138.
38   Moorehead Papers, University of Canberra.
39   AB/Peierls; Boyle, *Climate of Treason*, pbk, p. 268.
40   Moss, *Klaus Fuchs*, p. 31.
41   Moorehead, *Traitors*, p. 76.
42   AM/DW, Moorehead Papers, 21 September 1951.
43   Ibid.
44   Ibid., 24 September 1951.
45   Moss, *Klaus Fuchs*, p. 52.
46   AM/DW, Moorehead Papers, 24 September 1951.
47   Ibid., 21 September 1951.
48   Ibid.
49   West, *Matter of Trust*, p. 106, confirmed by MI5 sources.
50   AM/DW, Moorehead Papers, 21 September 1951.
51   Moss, *Klaus Fuchs*, p. 133.
52   TB/DW.
53   Ibid.
54   Wright, *Spycatcher*, p. 301 is wrong.
55   TB/DW.
56   Moorehead, *Traitors*, p. 215.
57   AB/DW, 25 August 1977.
58   AM/DW, Moorehead Papers.
59   Ibid.
60   Moss, *Klaus Fuchs*, p. 166.
61   Richelson and Ball, *Ties that Bind*, p. 137.
62   Lamphere, *FBI–KGB War*, p. 151.
63   TB/DW.
64   AM/DW, Moorehead Papers.
65   TB/DW.
66   Boyle, *Climate of Treason*, pbk, p. 326.

67   TB/AM.
68   Moorehead, *Traitors*, p. 205.
69   TB/DW.
70   Moorehead, *Traitors*, p. 207.
71   AM/DW, Moorehead Papers.
72   TB/Reilly.
73   TB/Carey Foster.
74   Ibid.; Cecil, *A Divided Life*, p. 110.
75   TB/Modin.
76   TB/Carey Foster.
77   Ibid.
78   TB/DW.
79   TB/Modin.
80   Ibid.
81   Borovik, *Philby Files*, p. 292.
82   TB/Modin.
83   Ibid.
84   Carey Foster notes.
85   TB/Carey Foster.
86   Boyle, *Climate of Treason*, p. 407; TB/DW.
87   AB/Mackenzie, October 1988.
88   TB/Modin. Modin now suggests that Blunt was also responsible. Modin, op. cit. p. 205.
89   White Paper Misc. No. 17 (1955), *Report Concerning the Disappearance of Two Former Foreign Office Officials*, Cmd 9577.
90   TB/DW.

Chapter Five: The Unthinkable
1   TB/Carey Foster.
2   Penrose/DW, 15 July 1985.
3   Penrose and Freeman, *Conspiracy of Silence*, p. 56.
4   TB/DW.
5   TB/confidential MI5 source.
6   Ibid.
7   AB/DW.
8   TB/Modin.
9   TB/Carey Foster.
10   TB/DW.
11   Boyle, *Climate of Treason*, p. 215.
12   Ibid., pbk, p. 161.
13   TB/Modin.
14   Boyle, *Climate of Treason*, p. 412.
15   Penrose and Freeman, *Conspiracy of Silence*, p. 382.

16   TB/confidential MI5 source.
17   AB/DW.
18   Cecil, *A Divided Life*, p. 149.
19   AB/DW.
20   TB/Sir Jack Easton.
21   Philby, *My Silent War*, p. 163ff.
22   Seale and McConville, *Philby*, p. 222.
23   AB/John Reed.
24   TB/Sir Jack Easton.
25   Philby, *My Silent War*, p. 165.
26   Letter, Dick White to Phillip Knightley, 11 July 1985.
27   TB/Modin.
28   Boyle, *Climate of Treason*, p. 185.
29   Letter, Dick White to Phillip Knightley, 11 July 1985.
30   Ibid.
31   Wright, *Spycatcher*, p. 300.
32   TB/confidential MI5 source.
33   TB/Carey Foster.
34   TB/DW.
35   Penrose and Freeman, *Conspiracy of Silence*, p. 395.
36   Letter, Kim Philby to Hugh Trevor-Roper, 30 April 1968.
37   TB/DW.
38   Ibid.
39   TB/confidential MI5 source.
40   TB/DW.
41   Ibid.
42   Ibid.
43   AB/DW.
44   TB/DW.
45   TB/Carey Foster.
46   Costello and Tsarev, *Deadly Illusions* p. 139; Borovik, *Philby Files*, p. 302.
47   Penrose and Freeman, *Conspiracy of Silence*, p. 391.
48   Boyle, *Climate of Treason*, p. 413.
49   Penrose and Freeman, *Conspiracy of Silence*, p. 382.
50   TB/Carey Foster.
51   Boyle, *Climate of Treason*, p. 377.
52   TB/Reed.
53   TB/Modin.
54   TB/DW.
55   TB/Lord Dacre.
56   TB/DW; Boyle, *Climate of Treason*, p. 428.
57   TB/DW.

58   TB/confidential SIS source.
59   Leigh, *Wilson Plot*, p. 35.
60   AB/DW.
61   TB/DW.
62   AB/M. Muggeridge.

Chapter Six: Frustrations
 1   TB/DW.
 2   Ibid.
 3   Ibid.
 4   TB/Cram.
 5   TB/DW.
 6   Wright, *Spycatcher*, p. 54.
 7   AB/DW.
 8   TB/Hunt.
 9   TB/Allen.
10   Ibid.
11   Wright, *Spycatcher*, p. 120.
12   TB/Bates.
13   Wright, *Spycatcher*, p. 29.
14   Ibid., p. 24.
15   Ibid., p. 54.
16   Ibid., p. 79.
17   Ibid., p. 82.
18   Penrose/DW, 15 July 1985.
19   Letter, Dick White to Phillip Knightley, 11 July 1985.
20   Andrew and Gordievsky, *KGB*, p. 152.
21   TB/Blake.
22   TB/DW; TB/Carey Foster.
23   AB/DW.
24   TB/Easton.
25   TB/Allen.
26   AB/DW.
27   Ibid.
28   Knightley, *Philby*, p. 194.
29   TB/DW.
30   Ibid.
31   CAB 129/78.
32   TB/Stark.
33   TB/DW.
34   Knightley, *Philby*, p. 196.
35   Philby, *My Silent War*, p. 74.
36   TB/Helms.

37 TB/confidential SIS source.
38 TB/Dean.
39 Rhodes James, *Eden*, p. 436.
40 TB/confidential SIS source.
41 TB/N. Elliott.
42 Wright, *Spycatcher*, p. 74.
43 TB/DW.
44 Ibid.
45 Ibid.

Chapter Seven: The Office
 1 TB/J. Easton.
 2 TB/DW.
 3 TB/confidential SIS source.
 4 TB/DW.
 5 TB/confidential SIS source.
 6 Blake, *No Other Choice*, p. 168.
 7 TB/confidential SIS source.
 8 Ibid.
 9 Ibid.
10 TB/DW.
11 TB/Wyke.
12 TB/Cram.
13 TB/Hilton.
14 TB/confidential SIS source.
15 Ibid.
16 TB/Easton.
17 TB/Elliott.
18 TB/Hunt.
19 TB/Easton.
20 TB/DW.
21 TB/Easton.
22 Ibid.
23 Ibid.
24 TB/Halpern.
25 TB/confidential SIS source.
26 TB/Hilton.
27 TB/confidential SIS source.
28 TB/Cooper.
29 Ibid.

Chapter Eight: The Inheritance
 1 Kyle, *Suez*, p. 136.

2   Nutting, quoted in Mosley, *Dulles*, p. 408.
3   Kyle, *Suez*, pp. 84, 99, 125, 155, 257.
4   TB/Easton.
5   TB/DW.
6   Ibid.
7   Kyle, *Suez*, p. 43.
8   Ibid., p. 84.
9   Ibid., p. 102, quoting Eveland.
10 Ibid., p. 64.
11 TB/confidential SIS source.
12 Eveland, *Ropes of Sand*, pp. 169–70; Kyle, *Suez*, p. 102.
13 Eveland, *Ropes of Sand*, pp. 181–2.
14 *New York Times*, 18 October 1956.
15 TB/DW.
16 Kyle, *Suez*, p. 148.
17 TB/Reilly.
18 Young speech, date unknown.
19 TB/Cooper.
20 Ibid.; Kyle, *Suez*, p. 150.
21 Wright, *Spycatcher*, pp. 84, 160–1.
22 Cooper, *The Lion's Last Roar*, p. 117.
23 Mosley, *Dulles*, p. 410ff.
24 Cooper, *The Lion's Last Roar* p. 128.
25 Kyle, *Suez*, p. 211.
26 Ibid., pp. 210, 226.
27 TB/Dean.
28 TB/Hunt.
29 TB/Tweedy.
30 Kyle, *Suez*, p. 254.
31 Ibid., pp. 275, 278.
32 Ibid., p. 67.
33 TB/DW.
34 Ibid.
35 Ibid., TB/Sir Patrick Dean.
36 TB/DW.
37 Ibid.
38 TB/Helms.
39 Ibid.
40 Kyle, *Suez*, p. 341.
41 Wright, *Spycatcher*, p. 84.
42 Kyle, *Suez*, p. 386.
43 Cooper, *The Lion's Last Roar*, p. 158.
44 TB/Cooper.

45　Cooper, *The Lion's Last Roar*, p. 181.
46　FO 800/721, 5 November 1956.
47　Cooper, *The Lion's Last Roar*, p. 204.
48　Kyle, *Suez*, p. 148; West, *The Friends*, p. 115.
49　TB/Dean.
50　TB/DW.
51　Ibid.
52　TB/John Bross.
53　TB/DW.
54　Bower, *Red Web*, p. 121.
55　TB/Al Ulmer.
56　Ibid.
57　Powers, *Man Who Kept the Secrets*, p. 46.
58　TB/DW.
59　Ibid.
60　TB/Dunderdale.
61　TB/Easton.
62　TB/DW.
63　TB/confidential SIS source.
64　TB/Cram.
65　AB/DW.
66　TB/Deneufville.
67　TB/confidential SIS source.
68　Bower, *Klaus Barbie*, p. 168.
69　TB/confidential SIS source.
70　TB/Easton.
71　West, *The Friends*, p. 26.
72　TB/Leslie Mitchell.
73　KGB source.
74　TB/DW.
75　TB/Cooper.
76　TB/Dean.

Chapter Nine: Empire Wars

1　TB/DW.
2　TB/Easton.
3　TB/Elliott.
4　TB/DW.
5　Horne, *Macmillan*, ii, p. 207.
6　TB/Devlin.
7　Horne, *Macmillan*, ii, p. 195.
8　TB/Richard Bissell.
9　TB/DW.

10   TB/Halpern.
11   Ibid.
12   Powers, *Man Who Kept the Secrets*, p. 89.
13   Mosley, *Dulles*, p. 436.
14   TB/confidential SIS source.
15   TB/Tweedy.
16   TB/DW.
17   TB/Amery.
18   George Young speech, date unknown.
19   FO 371/162812.
20   PREM 11/3430, 4 September 1961.
21   TB/DW.
22   TB/Harel.
23   Harel, *House on Garibaldi Street*, p. 131; TB/Harel.
24   Ledger, *Shifting Sands*, p. 12.
25   FO 371/168810.
26   Confidential source.
27   TB/Amery.
28   PREM 11/4356, 28 December 1962.
29   TB/Amery.
30   Gandy speech, 1984.
31   PREM 11/4356, 28 January 1963.
32   Ibid., 8 February 1963.
33   PREM 11/4357, 25 February 1963.
34   TB/Amery.
35   PREM 11/4356.
36   Ibid.
37   CAB 129/112, 10 January 1963.
38   PREM 11/4357, 28 February 1963.
39   Gandy speech, 1984.
40   PREM 11/4357, 4 March 1963.
41   TB/confidential SIS source.
42   TB/confidential SIS source.
43   TB/Amery.
44   FO 371/168809, 16 October 1963.
45   TB/Critchfield.
46   TB/confidential SIS source.
47   TB/Smiley.
48   TB/Confidential SIS source.
49   TB/Fees.

Chapter Ten: Traitors, Heroes and Noddy

1   TB/Elliott.

2   TB/confidential CIA source.
3   Ibid.
4   TB/confidential SIS source.
5   Wright, *Spycatcher*, p. 294.
6   TB/DW.
7   TB/Blake.
8   TB/confidential SIS source
9   TB/Blake.
10 TB/DW.
11 TB/Wyke.
12 TB/Easton.
13 TB/DW.
14 TB/Carlton Swift.
15 TB/Blake.
16 Blake, *No Other Choice*, p. 198.
17 Ibid.
18 TB/DW.
19 Ibid.
20 Ibid.
21 Ibid.
22 TB/Cram.
23 TB/Caswell.
24 TB/DW.
25 TB/Helms.
26 Ibid.
27 Cf. Blake, *No Other Choice*, p. 7.
28 TB/DW.
29 TB/Joe Bulik.
30 Ibid.
31 TB/DW.
32 TB/Bulik.
33 Ibid.
34 TB/DW.
35 TB/Modin.
36 Transcript of Penkovsky debriefing supplied by CIA under the Freedom of Information Act.
37 Letter, Dick White to author, 11 May 1991.
38 TB/Bulik.
39 Letter, Dick White to author, 11 May 1991.
40 TB/Hunt.
41 TB/DW.
42 Ibid.
43 Beschloss, *Kennedy v. Khrushchev*, p. 223.

44 Ibid., p. 306.
45 Ibid., p. 328.
46 TB/DW.
47 TB/Helms.
48 TB/Bulik.
49 Schechter, *The Spy Who Saved the World*, p. 292.
50 TB/Bulik.
51 Letter, Dick White to author, 20 May 1991.
52 TB/DW.
53 TB/Chistyakov.
54 TB/DW.
55 TB/Bulik.
56 TB/DW.
57 TB/Semichastney.
58 TB/DW.
59 TB/Chistyakov.
60 TB/Semichastney.
61 TB/Chistyakov.
62 TB/Helms.
63 *The Times*, 20 November 1962.
64 TB/Chistyakov.
65 Ibid.
66 TB/Peyton.
67 TB/Chistyakov.
68 TB/DW.

Chapter Eleven: Scandal

1 TB/Elliott.
2 Ibid.
3 TB/DW; TB/Elliott; contra Knightley, *Philby*, p. 206.
4 TB/Elliott.
5 TB/Dozhdalev.
6 Knightley, *Philby*, p. 211.
7 Horne, *Macmillan*, ii, p. 461.
8 TB/DW.
9 Ibid.
10 Ibid.
11 TB/Elliott.
12 TB/DW.
13 Knightley, *Philby*, p. 217.
14 TB/Elliott; TB/confidential SIS source.
15 Boyle, *Climate of Treason*, pp. 436–7.
16 TB/Elliott; confidential SIS sources.

17 Letter, Dick White to Phillip Knightley, 11 July 1985.
18 TB/DW.
19 AB/Elliott, 23 October 1978.
20 TB/Dozhdalev.
21 FO 953/2165.
22 Eleanor Philby, *Kim Philby*, p. 56.
23 TB/Elliott.
24 TB/Helms.
25 TB/Elliott.
26 Hansard, 1 July 1963.
27 Wilson, *The Labour Government*, p. 239.
28 Roger Hollis entry written by Dick White, *Dictionary of National Biography* 1971–1980, p. 423.
29 Greengrass/DW, 6 March 1984.
30 Horne, *Macmillan*, ii, p. 477.
31 Ibid., p. 474.
32 CAB 128/37.
33 TB/DW.
34 Ibid.
35 Ibid.
36 Horne, *Macmillan*, ii, p. 481ff.
37 TB/DW.
38 Greengrass/DW.
39 TB/Hunt.

Chapter Twelve: Molehunt
 1 TB/Critchfield.
 2 TB/DW.
 3 TB/Colby.
 4 TB/Cooper.
 5 Ibid.
 6 TB/confidential SIS source.
 7 TB/Tweedy; TB/confidential SIS source.
 8 *The Times*, 3 January 1985.
 9 Greengrass/DW, 6 March 1984.
10 TB/DW.
11 TB/Cram.
12 Mangold, *Cold Warrior*, p. 72, quoting Wright.
13 Wright, *Spycatcher*, p. 315.
14 Ibid., p. 176.
15 Mangold, *Cold Warrior*, p. 76.
16 Wright, *Spycatcher*, p. 191.
17 Ibid., p. 193.

18 TB/Modin; TB/Dozhdalev.
19 Wright, *Spycatcher*, p. 192.
20 Greengrass/DW.
21 Wright, *Spycatcher*, p. 193.
22 TB/Tweedy.
23 TB/Lee.
24 Leigh, *Wilson Plot*, p. 32.
25 TB/Helms.
26 Penrose and Freeman, *Conspiracy of Silence*, p. 430; Straight, *After Long Silence* p. 319.
27 Penrose and Freeman, *Conspiracy of Silence*, p. 439.
28 TB/Lord Dacre.
29 Letter, Dick White to Phillip Knightley, 11 July 1985.
30 Penrose/DW, 15 July 1985.
31 Boyle, *Climate of Treason*, p. 477.
32 Penrose and Freeman, *Conspiracy of Silence*, p. 448.
33 Ibid., p. 321.
34 Greengrass/DW, 6 March 1984.
35 Mangold, *Cold Warrior*, pp. 70, 153, 161.
36 Greengrass/DW, 6 March 1984.
37 TB/McCoy.
38 TB/Polgar.
39 TB/confidential CIA source.
40 TB/DW.
41 Ibid.
42 TB/Allister.
43 Wright, *Spycatcher*, p. 290.
44 Ibid., p. 266.
45 Ibid., p. 249.

Chapter Thirteen: Finale

1   TB/confidential SIS source.
2   Ziegler, *Wilson*, p. 232.
3   Pimlott, *Harold Wilson*, p. 368.
4   Ibid., p. 376.
5   Ibid., p. 373; Wilson, *The Labour Government*, p. 179.
6   TB/Greenhill.
7   TB/confidential SIS source.
8   TB/Halpern.
9   TB/Tweedy.
10 Greengrass/Wright.
11 TB/confidential SIS source; Greengrass/DW.
12 TB/confidential SIS source.

13 Letter, Dick White to Andrew Boyle, June 1978.
14 TB/Helms.
15 TB/Moore.
16 AB/DW.
17 Bailey, *Oilgate*, pp. 194, 199.
18 TB/DW.
19 Wright, *Spycatcher*, pp. 350–1.

Chapter Fourteen: Guardian of the Skeletons
1 Confidential MI5 and SIS sources.
2 TB/confidential Cabinet Office source.
3 TB/DW.
4 Philby, *My Silent War*, foreword, p. 137.
5 Ibid., pp. 12, 13.
6 TB/Modin.
7 Philby, *My Silent War*, p. 9.
8 Ibid., p. 48.
9 TB/Modin.
10 Philby, *My Silent War*, p. 74.
11 TB/DW.
12 AB/DW.
13 Letter, Kim Philby to Hugh Trevor-Roper, 30 April 1968.
14 AB/DW.
15 Masterman, *On the Chariot Wheel*, pp. 350–1.
16 TB/Greenhill.
17 Letter, Colonel Bevan to Colonel Wild regarding Peter ⁻
   Fleming's book about deception, 7 December 1969 in AB notes;
   TB/Michael Howard.
18 Wright, *Spycatcher*, p. 295.
19 Greengrass/Wright.
20 Greengrass/DW, 10 November 1984.
21 Penrose and Freeman, *Conspiracy of Silence*, p. 511.
22 TB/Kingsley.
23 TB/Allen.
24 TB/DW.
25 *Old Stortfordian Newsletter*, May 1993.
26 TB/Kingsley.
27 Greengrass/DW, 13 June 1984.
28 AB notes.
29 Ibid.
30 Letter, Andrew Boyle to James Angleton, 5 June 1978.
31 TB/DW.
32 *Sunday Times*, 20 January 1980.

33   Ibid., 23 December 1979.
34   TB/Howard.
35   Wright, *Spycatcher*, p. 214ff.
36   TB/DW.
37   TB/Hunt.
38   TB/Greengrass.
39   TB/Cram.
40   AB/DW.
41   *Observer*, 26 June 1986.
42   TB/Blake.

Bibliography

The bibliography of books about espionage is enormous. I have listed only those which I found immediately relevant to the current undertaking. Omission does not imply that those not mentioned have not been immensely valuable over the years to my understanding of intelligence matters.

Andrew, Christopher, *Secret Service*, Heinemann, 1985.
Andrew, C. & Gordievsky O., *KGB, The Inside Story*, Hodder & Stoughton, 1990.
Bailey, Martin, *Oilgate*, Coronet, 1979.
Beschloss, Michael, *Kennedy v. Khrushchev*, Faber and Faber, 1991.
Blake, George, *No Other Choice*, Cape, 1990.
Borovik, Genrikh, *The Philby Files*, Little Brown, 1994.
Bower Tom, *Blind Eye to Murder*, André Deutsch, 1981.
—*Klaus Barbie, Butcher of Lyons*, Corgi, 1985.
—*The Red Web*, Aurum Press, 1989.
Boyle, Andrew, *The Climate of Treason*, Hutchinson, 1979 & revised edition, Coronet, 1980.
Bradley, Omar, *A Soldier's Story*, London 1952.
Cecil, Robert, *A Divided Life*, The Bodley Head, 1988.
Churchill, Winston, *Second World War*, vol. 5, Cassell, 1952.
Cooper, Chester, *The Lion's Last Roar*, Harper & Row, 1978.
Costello, John, and Tsarev, Oleg, *Deadly Illusions*, Crown, New York, 1993.
Eveland, Wilbur, *Ropes of Sand*, Norton, 1980.
Fielding Xan, *One Man in His Time*, Macmillan, 1990.
Gilbert, Martin, *Churchill*, vol. 7, Heinemann, 1986.
Glees, Anthony, *The Secrets of the Service*, Cape, 1987.
Harel, Isser, *The House on Garibaldi Street*, Corgi, 1976.
Harris, Kenneth, *Attlee*, Weidenfeld & Nicholson, 1982.
Hinsley F. et al., *British Intelligence in the Second World War*,

vols 1 to 5, HMSO, 1979—90.

Horne, Alistair, *Macmillan*, 2 vols, Macmillan, 1989.

Knightley, Phillip, *Philby, KGB Masterspy*, André Deutsch, 1988.

—*An Affair of State, The Profumo Case*, Cape, 1987.

Kyle, Keith, *Suez*, Weidenfeld & Nicholson, 1991.

Lamphere, Robert, *The FBI–KGB War*, Berkeley Books, 1987.

Ledger, David *Shifting Sands*, Peninsular Publishing, 1983.

Leigh, David, *The Wilson Plot*, Heinemann, 1988.

Linklater, Eric, *Juan in America*, London, 1931.

Mangold, Tom, *Cold Warrior*, Simon & Schuster, 1991.

Masterman, J.C., *On the Chariot Wheel*, OUP, 1975.

Modin, Yuri, *My Five Cambridge Friends*, Headline, 1994.

Moorehead, Alan, *The Traitors*, Hamish Hamilton, 1952.

Mosley, Leonard, *Dulles*, Dial Press, 1978.

Moss, Norman, *Klaus Fuchs, The Man Who Stole the Atom Bomb*, Grafton, 1987.

Padfield, Peter, *Himmler*, Macmillan, 1990.

Page, B., Leitch, D., Knightley, P., *Philby, The Spy who Betrayed a Generation*, André Deutsch, 1968.

Penrose, Barrie, and Freeman, Simon, *Conspiracy of Silence*, Grafton, 1987.

Philby, Eleanor, *Kim Philby, The Spy I Loved*, Pan, 1968.

Philby, Kim, *My Silent War*, Panther Books, 1969.

Pimlott, Ben, *Harold Wilson*, HarperCollins, 1992.

Pincher, Chapman, *Their Trade is Treachery*, Sidgwick & Jackson, 1981.

Powers, Thomas, *The Man Who Kept the Secrets, Richard Helms and the CIA*, Alfred Knopf, 1979.

Ranelagh, John, *The Agency, The Rise and Decline of the CIA*, Simon and Schuster, 1986.

Rhodes James, Robert, *Anthony Eden*, Papermac, 1987.

Richelson, Jeffrey & Ball, Desmond, *The Ties that Bind*, Allen & Unwin, 1985.

Schecter, J. & Deriabin, P. *The Spy Who Saved the World*, Scribners, 1992.

Seale P. & McConville M., *Philby, The Long Road to Moscow*, Penguin, 1978.

Sillitoe, Sir Percy, *Cloak Without Dagger*, Cassell, 1955.

Smiley, David, *Arabian Assignment*, Leo Cooper, 1975.

Smith, Jean, *The Papers of General Lucius Clay*, Indiana University Press, 1974.

Straight, Michael, *After Long Silence*, Collins, 1983.

Trevor-Roper, Hugh, *The Philby Affair*, Kimber, 1968.

West, Nigel, *A Matter of Trust, MI5 1945–72*, London, Weidenfeld
    & Nicholson, 1982.
—*MI5, British Security Service Operations 1909–45*, Stein & Day, 1982.
—*The Friends, Britain's Post-War Secret Intelligence Operations*,
    Weidenfeld & Nicholson, 1988.
—*Faber Book of Espionage*, Faber & Faber, 1993.
Wilmot, C. *The Struggle for Europe*, Collins, London, 1952.
Wilson, Harold, *The Labour Government 1964–1970*, Weidenfeld
    & Nicholson, 1971.
Winks, Robin, *Cloak and Gown*, Morrow, 1987.
Wright, Peter, *Spycatcher: The Candid Autobiography of a Senior
    Intelligence Officer*, New York, Viking Press, 1987.
Ziegler, Philip, *Wilson*, Weidenfeld & Nicholson, 1993.

Index

Index